A Beginner's Guide to

Structural
Equation
Modeling

Third Edition

A Beginner's Guide to

Structural Equation Modeling

Third Edition

Randall E. Schumacker
The University of Alabama

Richard G. Lomax
The Ohio State University

Routledge
Taylor & Francis Group
New York   London

Routledge
Taylor & Francis Group
270 Madison Avenue
New York, NY 10016

Routledge
Taylor & Francis Group
27 Church Road
Hove, East Sussex BN3 2FA

Printed in the United States of America on acid-free paper
10 9 8 7 6 5 4 3 2 1

International Standard Book Number: 978-1-84169-890-8 (Hardback) 978-1-84169-891-5 (Paperback)

Library of Congress Cataloging-in-Publication Data

Schumacker, Randall E.
 A beginner's guide to structural equation modeling / authors, Randall E. Schumacker, Richard G. Lomax.-- 3rd ed.
  p. cm.
 Includes bibliographical references and index.
 ISBN 978-1-84169-890-8 (hardcover : alk. paper) -- ISBN 978-1-84169-891-5 (pbk. : alk. paper)
 1. Structural equation modeling. 2. Social sciences--Statistical methods. I. Lomax, Richard G. II. Title.

 QA278.S36 2010
 519.5'3--dc22
                                                                    2010009456

Visit the Taylor & Francis Web site at
http://www.taylorandfrancis.com

and the Psychology Press Web site at
http://www.psypress.com

To Our Colleagues and SEM Researchers Worldwide

Contents

About the Authors

RANDALL E. SCHUMACKER received his Ph.D. in educational psychology from Southern Illinois University. He is currently professor of educational research at the University of Alabama, where he teaches courses in structural equation modeling, multivariate statistics, multiple regression, and program evaluation. His research interests are varied, including modeling interaction in SEM, robust statistics (normal scores, centering, and variance inflation factor issues), and SEM specification search issues as well as measurement model issues related to estimation, mixed-item formats, and reliability.

He has published in several journals including *Academic Medicine, Educational and Psychological Measurement, Journal of Applied Measurement, Journal of Educational and Behavioral Statistics, Journal of Research Methodology, Multiple Linear Regression Viewpoints*, and *Structural Equation Modeling*. He has served on the editorial boards of numerous journals and is a member of the American Educational Research Association, American Psychological Association—Division 5, as well as past-president of the Southwest Educational Research Association, and emeritus editor of *Structural Equation Modeling* journal. He can be contacted at the University of Alabama College of Education.

RICHARD G. LOMAX received his Ph.D. in educational research methodology from the University of Pittsburgh. He is currently a professor in the School of Educational Policy and Leadership, Ohio State University, where he teaches courses in structural equation modeling, statistics, and quantitative research methodology.

His research primarily focuses on models of literacy acquisition, multivariate statistics, and assessment. He has published in such diverse journals as *Parenting: Science and Practice, Understanding Statistics: Statistical Issues in Psychology, Education, and the Social Sciences, Violence Against Women, Journal of Early Adolescence, and Journal of Negro Education*. He has served on the editorial boards of numerous journals, and is a member of the American Educational Research Association, the American Statistical Association, and the National Reading Conference. He can be contacted at Ohio State University College of Education and Human Ecology.

Preface

Approach

This book presents a basic introduction to structural equation modeling (SEM). Readers will find that we have kept to our tradition of keeping examples rudimentary and easy to follow. The reader is provided with a review of correlation and covariance, followed by multiple regression, path, and factor analyses in order to better understand the building blocks of SEM. The book describes a basic structural equation model followed by the presentation of several different types of structural equation models. Our approach in the text is both conceptual and application oriented.

Each chapter covers basic concepts, principles, and practice and then utilizes SEM software to provide meaningful examples. Each chapter also features an outline, key concepts, a summary, numerous examples from a variety of disciplines, tables, and figures, including path diagrams, to assist with conceptual understanding. Chapters with examples follow the conceptual sequence of SEM steps known as model specification, identification, estimation, testing, and modification.

The book now uses LISREL 8.8 student version to make the software and examples readily available to readers. Please be aware that the student version, although free, does not contain all of the functional features as a full licensed version. Given the advances in SEM software over the past decade, you should expect updates and patches of this software package and therefore become familiar with any new features as well as explore the excellent library of examples and help materials. The LISREL 8.8 student version is an easy-to-use Windows PC based program with pull-down menus, dialog boxes, and drawing tools. To access the program, and/or if you're a Mac user and are interested in learning about Mac availability, please check with Scientific Software (http://www.ssicentral.com). There is also a hotlink to the Scientific Software site from the book page for *A Beginner's Guide to Structural Equation Modeling, 3rd edition* on the Textbook Resources tab at www.psypress.com.

The SEM model examples in the book do not require complicated programming skills nor does the reader need an advanced understanding of statistics and matrix algebra to understand the model applications. We have provided a chapter on the matrix approach to SEM as well as an appendix on matrix operations for the interested reader. We encourage the understanding of the matrices used in SEM models, especially for some of the more advanced SEM models you will encounter in the research literature.

Goals and Content Coverage

Our main goal in this third edition is for students and researchers to be able to conduct their own SEM model analyses, as well as be able to understand and critique published SEM research. These goals are supported by the conceptual and applied examples contained in the book and several journal article references for each advanced SEM model type. We have also included a SEM checklist to guide your model analysis according to the basic steps a researcher takes.

As for content coverage, the book begins with an introduction to SEM (what it is, some history, why conduct it, and what software is available), followed by chapters on data entry and editing issues, and correlation. These early chapters are critical to understanding how missing data, non-normality, scale of measurement, non-linearity, outliers, and restriction of range in scores affects SEM analysis. Chapter 4 lays out the basic steps of model specification, identification, estimation, testing, and modification, followed by Chapter 5, which covers issues related to model fit indices, power and sample size. Chapters 6 through 10 follow the basic SEM steps of modeling, with actual examples from different disciplines, using regression, path, confirmatory factor and structural equation models. Logically the next chapter presents information about reporting SEM research and includes a SEM checklist to guide decision-making. Chapter 12 presents different approaches to model validation, an important final step after obtaining an acceptable theoretical model. Chapters 13 through 16 provide SEM examples that introduce many of the different types of SEM model applications. The final chapter describes the matrix approach to structural equation modeling by using examples from the previous chapters.

Theoretical models are present in every discipline, and therefore can be formulated and tested. This third edition expands SEM models and applications to provide the students and researchers in medicine, political science, sociology, education, psychology, business, and the biological sciences the basic concepts, principles, and practice necessary to test their theoretical models. We hope you become more familiar with structural equation modeling after reading the book, and use SEM in your own research.

New to the Third Edition

The first edition of this book was one of the first books published on SEM, while the second edition greatly expanded knowledge of advanced SEM models. Since that time, we have had considerable experience utilizing the book in class with our students. As a result of those experiences, the third edition represents a more useable book for teaching SEM. As such it is an ideal text for introductory graduate level courses in structural equation modeling or factor analysis taught in departments of psychology, education, business, and other social and healthcare sciences. An understanding of correlation is assumed.

The third edition offers several new surprises, namely:

1. Our instruction and examples are now based on freely available software: LISREL 8.8 student version.

2. More examples presented from more disciplines, including input, output, and screenshots.

3. Every chapter has been updated and enhanced with additional material.

4. A website with raw data sets for the book's examples and exercises so they can be used with any SEM program, all of the book's exercises, hotlinks to related websites, and answers to all of the exercises for instructors only. To access the website visit the book page or the Textbook Resource page at www.psypress.com.

5. Expanded coverage of advanced models with more on multiple-group, multi-level, and mixture modeling (Chs. 13 and 15), second-order and dynamic factor models (Ch. 14), and Monte Carlo methods (Ch. 16).

6. Increased coverage of sample size and power (Ch. 5), including software programs, and reporting research (Ch. 11).

7. New journal article references help readers better understand published research (Chs. 13–17).

8. Troubleshooting tips on how to address the most frequently encountered problems are found in Chapters 3 and 11.

9. Chapters 13 to 16 now include additional SEM model examples.

10. 25% new exercises with answers to half in the back of the book for student review (and answers to all for instructors only on the book and/or Textbook Resource page at www.psypress.com).

11. Added Matrix examples for several models in Chapter 17.

12. Updated references in all chapters on all key topics.

Overall, we believe this third edition is a more complete book that can be used to teach a full course in SEM. The past several years have seen an explosion in SEM coursework, books, websites, and training courses. We are proud to have been considered a starting point for many beginner's to SEM. We hope you find that this third edition expands on many of the programming tools, trends and topics in SEM today.

Acknowledgments

The third edition of this book represents more than thirty years of interacting with our colleagues and students who use structural equation modeling. As before, we are most grateful to the pioneers in the field of structural equation modeling, particularly to Karl Jöreskog, Dag Sörbom, Peter Bentler, James Arbuckle, and Linda and Bengt Muthèn. These individuals have developed and shaped the new advances in the SEM field as well as the content of this book, plus provided SEM researchers with software programs. We are also grateful to Gerhard Mels who answered our questions and inquiries about SEM programming problems in the chapters. We also wish to thank the reviewers: James Leeper, The University of Alabama, Philip Smith, Augusta State University, Phil Wood, the University of Missouri–Columbia, and Ke-Haie Yuan, the University of Notre Dame.

This book was made possible through the encouragement of Debra Riegert at Routledge/Taylor & Francis who insisted it was time for a third edition. We wish to thank her and her editorial assistant, Erin M. Flaherty, for coordinating all of the activity required to get a book into print. We also want to thank Suzanne Lassandro at Taylor & Francis Group, LLC for helping us through the difficult process of revisions, galleys, and final book copy.

Randall E. Schumacker
The University of Alabama

Richard G. Lomax
The Ohio State University

1

Introduction

Key Concepts

Latent and observed variables

Independent and dependent variables

Types of models

    Regression

    Path

    Confirmatory factor

    Structural equation

History of structural equation modeling

Structural equation modeling software programs

Structural equation modeling can be easily understood if the researcher has a grounding in basic statistics, correlation, and regression analysis. The first three chapters provide a brief introduction to structural equation modeling (SEM), basic data entry, and editing issues in statistics, and concepts related to the use of correlation coefficients in structural equation modeling. Chapter 4 covers the essential concepts of SEM: model specification, identification, estimation, testing, and modification. This basic understanding provides the framework for understanding the material presented in chapters 5 through 8 on model-fit indices, regression analysis, path analysis, and confirmatory factor analysis models (measurement models), which form the basis for understanding the structural equation models (latent variable models) presented in chapters 9 and 10. Chapter 11 provides guidance on reporting structural equation modeling research. Chapter 12 addresses techniques used to establish model validity and generalization of findings. Chapters 13 to 16 present many of the advanced SEM models currently appearing in journal articles: multiple group, multiple indicators–multiple causes, mixture, multilevel, structured means, multitrait–multimethod, second-order factor, dynamic factor, interaction models, latent growth curve models, and Monte Carlo studies. Chapter 17 presents matrix notation for one of our SEM applications, covers the different matrices used in structural equation modeling, and presents multiple regression and path analysis solutions using matrix algebra. We include an introduction to matrix operations in the Appendix for readers who want a more mathematical understanding of matrix operations. To start our journey of understanding, we first ask, What is structural equation modeling? Then, we give a brief history of SEM, discuss the importance of SEM, and note the availability of SEM software programs.

1.1 What Is Structural Equation Modeling?

Structural equation modeling (SEM) uses various types of models to depict relationships among observed variables, with the same basic goal of providing a quantitative test of a theoretical model hypothesized by the researcher. More specifically, various theoretical models can be tested in SEM that hypothesize how sets of variables define constructs and how these constructs are related to each other. For example, an educational researcher might hypothesize that a student's home environment influences her later achievement in school. A marketing researcher may hypothesize that consumer trust in a corporation leads to increased product sales for that corporation. A health care professional might believe that a good diet and regular exercise reduce the risk of a heart attack.

In each example, the researcher believes, based on theory and empirical research, sets of variables define the constructs that are hypothesized to be related in a certain way. The goal of SEM analysis is to determine the extent to which the theoretical model is supported by sample data. If the sample data support the theoretical model, then more complex theoretical models can be hypothesized. If the sample data do not support the theoretical model, then either the original model can be modified and tested, or other theoretical models need to be developed and tested. Consequently, SEM tests theoretical models using the scientific method of hypothesis testing to advance our understanding of the complex relationships among constructs.

SEM can test various types of theoretical models. Basic models include regression (chapter 6), path (chapter 7), and confirmatory factor (chapter 8) models. Our reason for covering these basic models is that they provide a basis for understanding structural equation models (chapters 9 and 10). To better understand these basic models, we need to define a few terms. First, there are two major types of variables: *latent variables* and *observed variables*. Latent variables (constructs or factors) are variables that are not directly observable or measured. Latent variables are indirectly observed or measured, and hence are inferred from a set of observed variables that we actually measure using tests, surveys, and so on. For example, intelligence is a latent variable that represents a psychological construct. The confidence of consumers in American business is another latent variable, one representing an economic construct. The physical condition of adults is a third latent variable, one representing a health-related construct.

The observed, measured, or indicator variables are a set of variables that we use to define or infer the latent variable or construct. For example, the Wechsler Intelligence Scale for Children—Revised (WISC-R) is an instrument that produces a measured variable (scores), which one uses to infer the construct of a child's intelligence. Additional indicator variables, that is, intelligence tests, could be used to indicate or define the construct of intelligence (latent variable). The Dow-Jones index is a standard measure of the American corporate economy construct. Other measured variables might include gross national product, retail sales, or export sales. Blood pressure is one of many health-related variables that could indicate a latent variable defined as "fitness." Each of these observed or indicator variables represent one definition of the latent variable. Researchers use sets of indicator variables to define a latent variable; thus, other measurement instruments are used to obtain indicator variables, for example, the Stanford–Binet Intelligence Scale, the NASDAQ index, and an individual's cholesterol level, respectively.

Variables, whether they are observed or latent, can also be defined as either *independent variables* or *dependent variables*. An independent variable is a variable that is not influenced by any other variable in the model. A dependent variable is a variable that is influenced by another variable in the model. Let us return to the previous examples and specify the independent and dependent variables. The educational researcher hypothesizes that a student's home environment (independent latent variable) influences school achievement (dependent latent variable). The marketing researcher believes that consumer trust in a corporation (independent latent variable) leads to increased product sales (dependent latent variable). The health care professional wants to determine whether a good diet and regular exercise (two independent latent variables) influence the frequency of heart attacks (dependent latent variable).

The basic SEM models in chapters 6 through 8 illustrate the use of observed variables and latent variables when defined as independent or dependent. A regression model consists solely of observed variables where a single dependent observed variable is predicted or explained by one or more independent observed variables; for example, a parent's education level (independent observed variable) is used to predict his or her child's achievement score (dependent observed variable). A path model is also specified entirely with observed variables, but the flexibility allows for multiple independent observed variables and multiple dependent observed variables—for example, export sales, gross national product, and NASDAQ index influence consumer trust and consumer spending (dependent observed variables). Path models, therefore, test more complex models than regression models. Confirmatory factor models consist of observed variables that are hypothesized to measure one or more latent variables (independent or dependent); for example, diet, exercise, and physiology are observed measures of the independent latent variable "fitness." An understanding of these basic models will help in understanding structural equation modeling, which combines path and factor analytic models. Structural equation models consist of observed variables and latent variables, whether independent or dependent; for example, an independent latent variable (home environment) influences a dependent latent variable (achievement), where both types of latent variables are measured, defined, or inferred by multiple observed or measured indicator variables.

1.2 History of Structural Equation Modeling

To discuss the history of structural equation modeling, we explain the following four types of related models and their chronological order of development: regression, path, confirmatory factor, and structural equation models.

The first model involves linear regression models that use a correlation coefficient and the least squares criterion to compute regression weights. Regression models were made possible because Karl Pearson created a formula for the correlation coefficient in 1896 that provides an index for the relationship between two variables (Pearson, 1938). The regression model permits the prediction of dependent observed variable scores (*Y scores*), given a linear weighting of a set of independent observed scores (*X scores*) that minimizes the sum of squared residual error values. The mathematical basis for the linear regression model is found in basic algebra. Regression analysis provides a test of a theoretical model that may be useful for prediction (e.g., admission to graduate school or budget projections). In an example study, regression analysis was used to predict student exam scores in statistics (dependent variable) from a series of collaborative learning group assignments (independent variables; Delucchi, 2006). The results provided some support for collaborative learning groups improving statistics exam performance, although not for all tasks.

Some years later, Charles Spearman (1904, 1927) used the correlation coefficient to determine which items correlated or went together to create the factor model. His basic idea was that if a set of items correlated or went together, individual responses to the set of items could be summed to yield a score that would measure, define, or infer a construct. Spearman was the first to use the term *factor analysis* in defining a two-factor construct for a theory of intelligence. D.N. Lawley and L.L. Thurstone in 1940 further developed applications of factor models, and proposed instruments (sets of items) that yielded observed scores from which constructs could be inferred. Most of the aptitude, achievement, and diagnostic tests, surveys, and inventories in use today were created using factor analytic techniques. The term *confirmatory factor analysis* (CFA) is used today based in part on earlier work by Howe (1955), Anderson and Rubin (1956), and Lawley (1958). The CFA method was more fully developed by Karl Jöreskog in the 1960s to test whether a set of items defined a construct. Jöreskog completed his dissertation in 1963, published the first article on CFA in 1969, and subsequently helped develop the first CFA software program. Factor analysis has been used for over 100 years to create measurement instruments in many academic disciplines, while today CFA is used to test the existence of these theoretical constructs. In an example study, CFA was used to confirm the "Big Five" model of personality by Goldberg (1990). The five-factor model of extraversion, agreeableness, conscientiousness, neuroticism, and intellect was confirmed through the use of multiple indicator variables for each of the five hypothesized factors.

Sewell Wright (1918, 1921, 1934), a biologist, developed the third type of model, a path model. Path models use correlation coefficients and regression analysis to model more complex relationships among observed variables. The first applications of path analysis dealt with models of animal behavior. Unfortunately, path analysis was largely overlooked until econometricians reconsidered it in the 1950s as a form of simultaneous equation modeling (e.g., H. Wold) and sociologists rediscovered it in the 1960s (e.g., O. D. Duncan and H. M. Blalock). In many respects, path analysis involves solving a set of simultaneous regression equations that theoretically establish the relationship among the observed variables in the path model. In an example path analysis study, Walberg's theoretical model of educational productivity was tested for fifth- through eighth-grade students (Parkerson et al., 1984). The relations among the following variables were analyzed in a single model: home environment, peer group, media, ability, social environment, time on task, motivation, and instructional strategies. All of the hypothesized paths among those variables were shown to be statistically significant, providing support for the educational productivity model.

The final model type is structural equation modeling (SEM). SEM models essentially combine path models and confirmatory factor models;

that is, SEM models incorporate both latent and observed variables. The early development of SEM models was due to Karl Jöreskog (1969, 1973), Ward Keesling (1972), and David Wiley (1973); this approach was initially known as the JKW model, but became known as the *linear* structural *rela-*tions model (LISREL) with the development of the first software program, LISREL, in 1973. Since then, many SEM articles have been published; for example, Shumow and Lomax (2002) tested a theoretical model of parental efficacy for adolescent students. For the overall sample, neighborhood quality predicted parental efficacy, which predicted parental involvement and monitoring, both of which predicted academic and social-emotional adjustment.

Jöreskog and van Thillo originally developed the LISREL software program at the Educational Testing Service (ETS) using a matrix command language (i.e., involving Greek and matrix notation), which is described in chapter 17. The first publicly available version, LISREL III, was released in 1976. Later in 1993, LISREL8 was released; it introduced the SIMPLIS (SIMPle LISrel) command language in which equations are written using variable names. In 1999, the first interactive version of LISREL was released. LISREL8 introduced the dialog box interface using pull-down menus and point-and-click features to develop models, and the path diagram mode, a drawing program to develop models. Karl Jöreskog was recognized by Cudeck, DuToit, and Sörbom (2001) who edited a Festschrift in honor of his contributions to the field of structural equation modeling. Their volume contains chapters by scholars who address the many topics, concerns, and applications in the field of structural equation modeling today, including milestones in factor analysis; measurement models; robustness, reliability, and fit assessment; repeated measurement designs; ordinal data; and interaction models. We cover many of these topics in this book, although not in as great a depth. The field of structural equation modeling across all disciplines has expanded since 1994. Hershberger (2003) found that between 1994 and 2001 the number of journal articles concerned with SEM increased, the number of journals publishing SEM research increased, SEM became a popular choice amongst multivariate methods, and the journal *Structural Equation Modeling* became the primary source for technical developments in structural equation modeling.

1.3 Why Conduct Structural Equation Modeling?

Why is structural equation modeling popular? There are at least four major reasons for the popularity of SEM. The first reason suggests that researchers are becoming more aware of the need to use multiple observed variables to better understand their area of scientific inquiry. Basic statistical methods only utilize a limited number of variables, which are not capable of dealing with the sophisticated theories being developed. The use of a small number of variables to understand complex phenomena is limiting. For instance, the use of simple bivariate correlations is not sufficient for examining a sophisticated theoretical model. In contrast, structural equation modeling permits complex phenomena to be statistically modeled and tested. SEM techniques are therefore becoming the preferred method for confirming (or disconfirming) theoretical models in a quantitative fashion.

A second reason involves the greater recognition given to the validity and reliability of observed scores from measurement instruments. Specifically, measurement error has become a major issue in many disciplines, but measurement error and statistical analysis of data have been treated separately. Structural equation modeling techniques explicitly take measurement error into account when statistically analyzing data. As noted in subsequent chapters, SEM analysis includes latent and observed variables as well as measurement error terms in certain SEM models.

A third reason pertains to how structural equation modeling has matured over the past 30 years, especially the ability to analyze more advanced theoretical SEM models. For example, group differences in theoretical models can be assessed through multiple-group SEM models. In addition, analyzing educational data collected at more than one level—for example, school districts, schools, and teachers with student data—is now possible using multilevel SEM modeling. As a final example, interaction terms can now be included in an SEM model so that main effects and interaction effects can be tested. These advanced SEM models and techniques have provided many researchers with an increased capability to analyze sophisticated theoretical models of complex phenomena, thus requiring less reliance on basic statistical methods.

Finally, SEM software programs have become increasingly user-friendly. For example, until 1993 LISREL users had to input the program syntax for their models using Greek and matrix notation. At that time, many researchers sought help because of the complex programming requirement and knowledge of the SEM syntax that was required. Today, most SEM software programs are Windows-based and use pull-down menus or drawing programs to generate the program syntax internally. Therefore, the SEM software programs are now easier to use and contain features similar to other Windows-based software packages. However, such ease of use necessitates statistical training in SEM modeling and software via courses, workshops, or textbooks to avoid mistakes and errors in analyzing sophisticated theoretical models.

1.4 Structural Equation Modeling Software Programs

Although the LISREL program was the first SEM software program, other software programs have subsequently been developed since the mid-1980s. Some of the other programs include AMOS, EQS, Mx, Mplus, Ramona, and Sepath, to name a few. These software programs are each unique in their own way, with some offering specialized features for conducting different SEM applications. Many of these SEM software programs provide statistical analysis of raw data (e.g., means, correlations, missing data conventions), provide routines for handling missing data and detecting outliers, generate the program's syntax, diagram the model, and provide for import and export of data and figures of a theoretical model. Also, many of the programs come with sets of data and program examples that are clearly explained in their user guides. Many of these software programs have been reviewed in the journal *Structural Equation Modeling.*

The pricing information for SEM software varies depending on individual, group, or site license arrangements; corporate versus educational settings; and even whether one is a student or faculty member. Furthermore, newer versions and updates necessitate changes in pricing. Most programs will run in the Windows environment; some run on MacIntosh personal computers. We are often asked to recommend a software package to a beginning SEM researcher; however, given the different individual needs of researchers and the multitude of different features available in these programs, we are not able to make such a recommendation. Ultimately the decision depends upon the researcher's needs and preferences. Consequently, with so many software packages, we felt it important to narrow our examples in the book to LISREL–SIMPLIS programs.

We will therefore be using the LISREL 8.8 student version in the book to demonstrate the many different SEM applications, including regression models, path models, confirmatory factor models, and the various SEM models in chapters 13 through 16. The free student version of the LISREL software program (Windows, Mac, and Linux editions) can be downloaded from the website: http://www.ssicentral.com/lisrel/student. html. (*Note:* The LISREL 8.8 Student Examples folder is placed in the main directory C:/ of your computer, not the LISREL folder under C:/Program Files when installing the software.)

Once the LISREL software is downloaded, place an icon on your desktop by creating a shortcut to the LISREL icon. The LISREL icon should look something like this:

LISREL 8.80 Student.lnk

When you click on the icon, an empty dialog box will appear that should look like this:

NOTE: Nothing appears until you open a program file or data set using the *File* or open folder icon; more about this in the next chapter.

We do want to mention the very useful HELP menu. Click on the question mark (?), a HELP menu will appear, then enter *Output Questions* in the search window to find answers to key questions you may have when going over examples in the Third Edition.

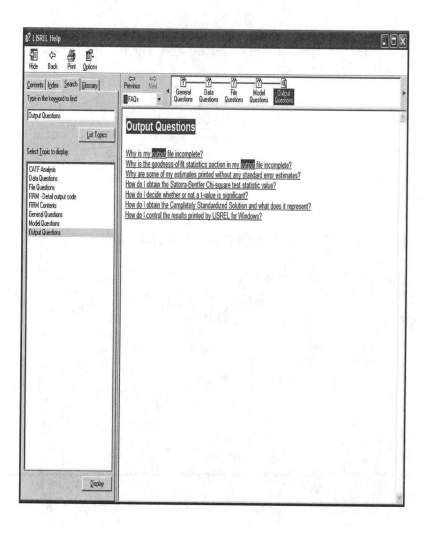

1.5 Summary

In this chapter we introduced structural equation modeling by describing basic types of variables—that is, latent, observed, independent, and dependent—and basic types of SEM models—that is, regression, path, confirmatory factor, and structural equation models. In addition, a brief history of structural equation modeling was provided, followed by a discussion of the importance of SEM. This chapter concluded with a brief listing of the different structural equation modeling software programs and where to obtain the LISREL 8.8 student version for use with examples in the book, including what the dialog box will first appear like and a very useful HELP menu.

In chapter 2 we consider the importance of examining data for issues related to measurement level (nominal, ordinal, interval, or ratio), restriction of range (fewer than 15 categories), missing data, outliers (extreme values), linearity or nonlinearity, and normality or nonnormality, all of which can affect statistical methods, and especially SEM applications.

Exercises

1. Define the following terms:
   a. Latent variable
   b. Observed variable
   c. Dependent variable
   d. Independent variable
2. Explain the difference between a dependent latent variable and a dependent observed variable.
3. Explain the difference between an independent latent variable and an independent observed variable.
4. List the reasons why a researcher would conduct structural equation modeling.
5. Download and activate the student version of LISREL: http://www.ssicentral.com
6. Open and import SPSS or data file.

References

Anderson, T. W., & Rubin, H. (1956). Statistical inference in factor analysis. In J. Neyman (Ed.), *Proceedings of the third Berkeley symposium on mathematical statistics and probability, Vol. V* (pp. 111–150). Berkeley: University of California Press.

Cudeck, R., Du Toit, S., & Sörbom, D. (2001) (Eds). *Structural equation modeling: Present and future. A Festschrift in honor of Karl Jöreskog.* Lincolnwood, IL: Scientific Software International.

Delucchi, M. (2006). The efficacy of collaborative learning groups in an undergraduate statistics course. *College Teaching, 54,* 244–248.

Goldberg, L. (1990). An alternative "description of personality": Big Five factor structure. *Journal of Personality and Social Psychology, 59,* 1216–1229.

Hershberger, S. L. (2003). The growth of structural equation modeling: 1994–2001. *Structural Equation Modeling, 10*(1), 35–46.

Howe, W. G. (1955). *Some contributions to factor analysis* (Report No. ORNL-1919). Oak Ridge National Laboratory, Oak Ridge, Tennessee.

Jöreskog, K. G. (1963). *Statistical estimation in factor analysis: A new technique and its foundation.* Stockholm: Almqvist & Wiksell.

Jöreskog, K. G. (1969). A general approach to confirmatory maximum likelihood factor analysis. *Psychometrika, 34,* 183–202.

Jöreskog, K. G. (1973). A general method for estimating a linear structural equation system. In A. S. Goldberger & O. D. Duncan (Eds.), *Structural equation models in the social sciences* (pp. 85–112). New York: Seminar.

Keesling, J. W. (1972). *Maximum likelihood approaches to causal flow analysis.* Unpublished doctoral dissertation. Chicago: University of Chicago.

Lawley, D. N. (1958). Estimation in factor analysis under various initial assumptions. *British Journal of Statistical Psychology, 11,* 1–12.

Parkerson, J. A., Lomax, R. G., Schiller, D. P., & Walberg, H. J. (1984). Exploring causal models of educational achievement. *Journal of Educational Psychology, 76,* 638–646.

Pearson, E. S. (1938). *Karl Pearson. An appreciation of some aspects of his life and work.* Cambridge: Cambridge University Press.

Shumow, L., & Lomax, R. G. (2002). Parental efficacy: Predictor of parenting behavior and adolescent outcomes. *Parenting: Science and Practice, 2,* 127–150.

Spearman, C. (1904). The proof and measurement of association between two things. *American Journal of Psychology, 15,* 72–101.

Spearman, C. (1927). *The abilities of man.* New York: Macmillan.

Wiley, D. E. (1973). The identification problem for structural equation models with unmeasured variables. In A. S. Goldberger & O. D. Duncan (Eds.), *Structural equation models in the social sciences* (pp. 69–83). New York: Seminar.

Wright, S. (1918). On the nature of size factors. *Genetics, 3,* 367–374.

Wright, S. (1921). Correlation and causation. *Journal of Agricultural Research, 20,* 557–585.

Wright, S. (1934). The method of path coefficients. *Annals of Mathematical Statistics, 5,* 161–215.

2

Data Entry and Data Editing Issues

Key Concepts

Importing data file

System file

Measurement scale

Restriction of range

Missing data

Outliers

Linearity

Nonnormality

An important first step in using LISREL is to be able to enter raw data and/or import data, such as files from other programs (SPSS, SAS, EXCEL, etc.). Other important steps involve being able to use LISREL–PRELIS to save a system file, as well as output and save files that contain the variance–covariance matrix, the correlation matrix, means, and standard deviations of variables so they can be input into command syntax programs. The LISREL–PRELIS program will be briefly explained in this chapter to demonstrate how it handles raw data entry, importing of data, and the output of saved files.

There are several key issues in the field of statistics that impact our analyses once data have been imported into a software program. These data issues are commonly referred to as the measurement scale of variables, restriction in the range of data, missing data values, outliers, linearity, and nonnormality. Each of these data issues will be discussed because they not only affect traditional statistics, but present additional problems and concerns in structural equation modeling.

We use LISREL software throughout the book, so you will need to use that software and become familiar with their Web site. You should have downloaded by now the free student version of the LISREL software.

We use some of the data and model examples available in the free student version to illustrate SEM applications. (*Note:* The *LISREL 8.8 Student Examples* folder is placed in the main directory C:/ of your computer.) The free student version of the software has a user guide, help functions, and tutorials. The Web site also contains important research, documentation, and information about structural equation modeling. However, be aware that the free student version of the software does not contain the full capabilities available in their full licensed version (e.g., restricted to 15 observed variables in SEM analyses). These limitations are spelled out on their Web site.

2.1 Data Entry

The LISREL software program interfaces with PRELIS, a preprocessor of data prior to running LISREL (matrix command language) or SIMPLIS (easier-to-use variable name syntax) programs. The newer Interactive LISREL uses a spreadsheet format for data with pull-down menu options. LISREL offers several different options for inputting data and importing files from numerous other programs. The **New, Open**, and **Import Data** functions provide maximum flexibility for inputting data.

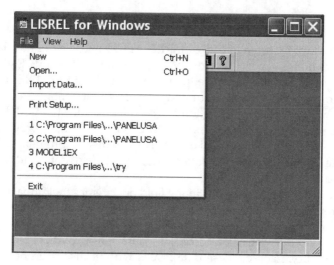

The **New** option permits the creation of a command syntax language program (PRELIS, LISREL, or SIMPLIS) to read in a PRELIS data file, or to open SIMPLIS and LISREL saved projects as well as a previously saved Path Diagram.

The **Open** option permits you to browse and locate previously saved PRELIS (.pr2), LISREL (.ls8), or SIMPLIS (.spl) programs; each with their unique file extension. The student version has distinct folders containing several program examples, for example LISREL (LS8EX folder), PRELIS (PR2EX folder), and SIMPLIS (SPLEX folder).

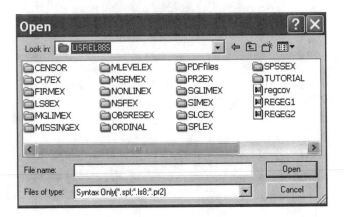

The **Import Data** option permits inputting raw data files or SPSS saved files. The raw data file, *lsat6.dat*, is in the PRELIS folder (PR2EX). When selecting this file, you will need to know the number of variables in the file.

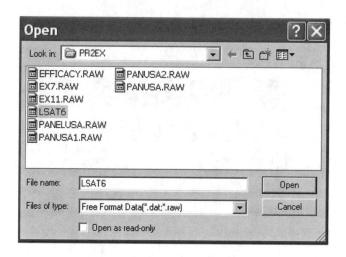

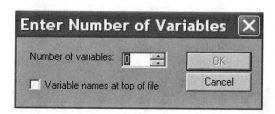

An SPSS saved file, *data100.sav*, is in the SPSS folder (SPSSEX). Once you open this file, a PRELIS system file is created.

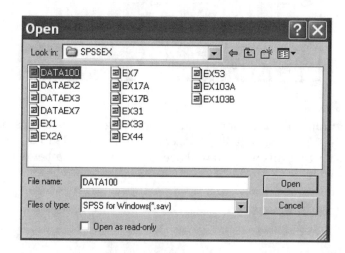

Once the PRELIS system file becomes active, then it needs to be saved for future use. (*Note:* # symbol may appear if columns are to narrow; simply use your mouse to expand the columns so that the missing values—999999.00 will appear. Also, if you right-mouse click on the variable names, a menu appears to define missing values, etc.). The PRELIS system file (.psf) activates a pull-down menu that permits data editing features, data transformations, statistical analysis of data, graphical display of data, multilevel modeling, and many other related features.

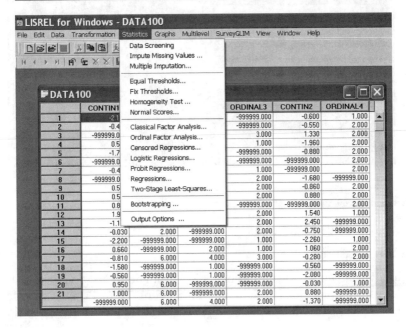

The statistical analysis of data includes factor analysis, probit regression, least squares regression, and two-stage least squares methods. Other important data editing features include imputing missing values, a homogeneity test, creation of normal scores, bootstrapping, and data output options. The data output options permit saving different types of variance–covariance matrices and descriptive statistics in files for use in LISREL and SIMPLIS command syntax programs. This capability is very important, especially when advanced SEM models are analyzed in chapters 13 to 16. We will demonstrate the use of this Output Options dialog box in this chapter and in some of our other chapter examples.

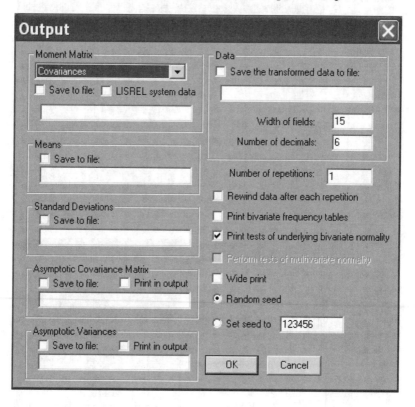

2.2 Data Editing Issues

2.2.1 Measurement Scale

How variables are measured or scaled influences the type of statistical analyses we perform (Anderson, 1961; Stevens, 1946). Properties of scale also guide our understanding of permissible mathematical operations.

For example, a nominal variable implies mutually exclusive groups; a biological gender has two mutually exclusive groups, male and female. An individual can only be in one of the groups that define the levels of the variable. In addition, it would not be meaningful to calculate a mean and a standard deviation on the variable gender. Consequently, the number or percentage of individuals at each level of the gender variable is the only mathematical property of scale that makes sense. An ordinal variable, for example, attitude toward school, that is scaled *strongly agree, agree, neutral, disagree,* and *strongly disagree,* implies mutually exclusive categories that are ordered or ranked. When levels of a variable have properties of scale that involve mutually exclusive groups that are ordered, only certain mathematical operations are meaningful, for example, a comparison of ranks between groups. SEM final exam scores, an example of an interval variable, possesses the property of scale, implying equal intervals between the data points, but no true zero point. This property of scale permits the mathematical operation of computing a mean and a standard deviation. Similarly, a ratio variable, for example, weight, has the property of scale that implies equal intervals and a true zero point (weightlessness). Therefore, ratio variables also permit mathematical operations of computing a mean and a standard deviation. Our use of different variables requires us to be aware of their properties of scale and what mathematical operations are possible and meaningful, especially in SEM, where variance–covariance (correlation) matrices are used with means and standard deviations of variables. Different correlations among variables are therefore possible depending upon the level of measurement, but they create unique problems in SEM (see chapter 3). PRELIS designates continuous variables (CO), ordinal variables (OR), and categorical variables (CL) to make these distinctions.

2.2.2 Restriction of Range

Data values at the interval or ratio level of measurement can be further defined as being discrete or continuous. For example, SEM final exam scores could be reported in whole numbers (discrete). Similarly, the number of children in a family would be considered a discrete level of measurement—or example, 5 children. In contrast, a continuous variable is reported using decimal values; for example, a student's grade point average would be reported as 3.75 on a 5-point scale.

Karl Jöreskog (1996) provided a criterion in the PRELIS program based on his research that defines whether a variable is ordinal or interval, based on the presence of 15 distinct scale points. If a variable has fewer than 15 categories or scale points, it is referenced in PRELIS as ordinal (OR), whereas a variable with 15 or more categories is referenced as continuous (CO). This 15-point criterion allows Pearson correlation coefficient values to vary between +/–1.0. Variables with fewer distinct scale points restrict the value of the Pearson correlation coefficient such that it may only vary between +/–0.5. Other factors that affect the Pearson correlation coefficient are presented in this chapter and discussed further in chapter 3.

2.2.3 Missing Data

The statistical analysis of data is affected by missing data values in variables. That is, not every subject has an actual value for every variable in the dataset, as some values are missing. It is common practice in statistical packages to have default values for handling missing values. The researcher has the options of deleting subjects who have missing values, replacing the missing data values, or using robust statistical procedures that accommodate for the presence of missing data.

The various SEM software handle missing data differently and have different options for replacing missing data values. Table 2.1 lists many of the various options for dealing with missing data. These options can dramatically affect the number of subjects available for analysis, the magnitude and direction of the correlation coefficient, or create problems if means, standard deviations, and correlations are computed based on different sample sizes. The *Listwise* deletion of cases and *Pairwise* deletion of cases are not always recommended options due to the possibility of losing a large number of subjects, thus dramatically reducing the sample size. Mean substitution works best when only a small number of missing values is present in the data, whereas regression imputation provides a useful approach with a moderate amount of missing data. In LISREL–PRELIS the expectation maximization (EM), Monte Carlo Markov Chain (MCMC), and matching response pattern approaches are recommended when larger amounts of data are missing at random.

TABLE 2.1

Options for Dealing with Missing Data

Listwise	Delete subjects with missing data on any variable
Pairwise	Delete subjects with missing data on each pair of variables used
Mean substitution	Substitute the mean for missing values of a variable
Regression imputation	Substitute a predicted value for the missing value of a variable
Expectation maximization (EM)	Find expected value based on expectation maximization algorithm
Matching response pattern	Match cases with incomplete data to cases with complete data to determine a missing value

More information about missing data is available in resources such as Enders (2006), McKnight, McKnight, Sidani and Aurelio (2007), and Peng, Harwell, Liou, and Ehman (2007). Davey and Savla (2010) have more recently published an excellent book with SAS, SPSS, STATA, and Mplus source programs to handle missing data in SEM in the context of power analysis.

2.2.4 LISREL–PRELIS Missing Data Example

Imputation of missing values is possible for a single variable (Impute Missing Values) or several variables simultaneously (Multiple Imputation) by selecting Statistics from the tool bar menu. The Impute Missing Values option uses the matching response pattern approach. The value to be substituted for the missing value of a single case is obtained from another case (or cases) having a similar response pattern over a set of matching variables. In data sets where missing values occur on more than one variable, you can use multiple imputation of missing values with mean substitution, delete cases, or leave the variables with defined missing values as options in the dialog box. In addition, the Multiple Imputation option uses either the expectation maximization algorithm (EM) or Monte Carlo Markov Chain (MCMC, generating random draws from probability distributions via Markov chains) approaches to replacing missing values across multiple variables.

We present an example from LISREL–PRELIS involving the cholesterol levels for 28 patients treated for heart attacks. We assume the data to be missing at random (MAR) with an underlying multivariate normal distribution. Cholesterol levels were measured after 2 days (VAR1), after 4 days (VAR2), and after 14 days (VAR3), but were only complete for 19 of the 28 patients. The data are shown from the PRELIS System File, *chollev.psf.* The PRELIS system file was created by selecting **File, Import Data**, and selecting the raw data file *chollev.raw* located in the **Tutorial** folder [C:\LISREL 8.8 Student Examples\Tutorial]. *We must know the number of variables in the raw data file.* We must also select **Data**, then **Define Variables**, and then select **–9.00** as the missing value for the **VAR3** variable [Optionally, right mouse click on VAR1 in the PRELIS *chollev* file].

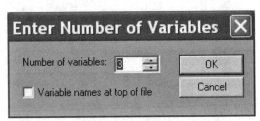

cholev	VAR1	VAR2	VAR3
1	270.000	218.000	156.000
2	236.000	234.000	-9.000
3	210.000	214.000	242.000
4	142.000	116.000	-9.000
5	280.000	200.000	-9.000
6	272.000	276.000	256.000
7	160.000	146.000	142.000
8	220.000	182.000	216.000
9	226.000	238.000	248.000
10	242.000	288.000	-9.000
11	186.000	190.000	168.000
12	266.000	236.000	236.000
13	206.000	244.000	-9.000
14	318.000	258.000	200.000
15	294.000	240.000	264.000
16	282.000	294.000	-9.000
17	234.000	220.000	264.000
18	224.000	200.000	-9.000
19	276.000	220.000	188.000
20	282.000	186.000	182.000
21	360.000	352.000	294.000
22	310.000	202.000	214.000
23	280.000	218.000	-9.000
24	278.000	248.000	198.000
25	288.000	278.000	-9.000
26	288.000	248.000	256.000
27	244.000	270.000	280.000
28	236.000	242.000	204.000

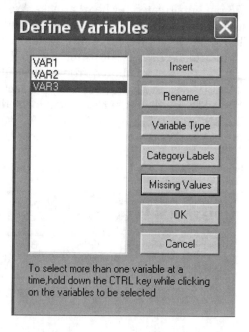

Define Variables

VAR1
VAR2
VAR3

Insert

Rename

Variable Type

Category Labels

Missing Values

OK

Cancel

To select more than one variable at a
time, hold down the CTRL key while clicking
on the variables to be selected

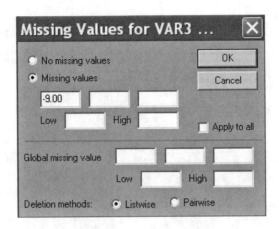

We now click on **Statistics** on the tool bar menu and select **Impute Missing Values** from the pull-down menu.

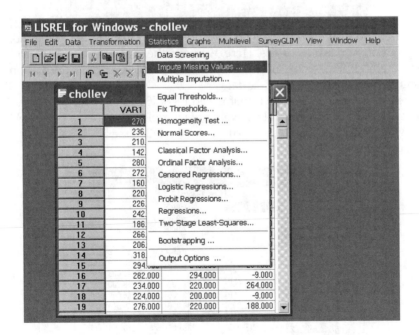

We next select **Output Options** and save the transformed data in a new PRELIS system file *cholnew.psf*, and output the new correlation matrix, mean, and standard deviation files.

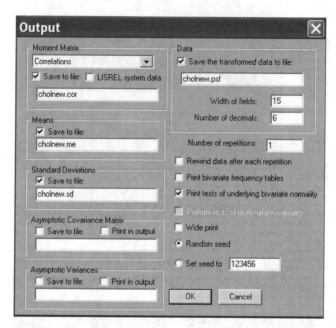

We should examine our data both before (Table 2.2) and after (Table 2.3) imputation of missing values. Here, we used the matching response pattern method. This comparison provides us with valuable information about the nature of the missing data.

We can also view our new transformed PRELIS System File, *cholnew.psf*, to verify that the missing values were in fact replaced; for example, VAR3 has values replaced for Case 2 = 204, Case 4 = 142, Case 5 = 182, Case 10 = 280, and so on.

cholnew	VAR1	VAR2	VAR3
1	270.000	218.000	156.000
2	236.000	234.000	204.000
3	210.000	214.000	242.000
4	142.000	116.000	142.000
5	280.000	200.000	182.000
6	272.000	276.000	256.000
7	160.000	146.000	142.000
8	220.000	182.000	216.000
9	226.000	238.000	248.000
10	242.000	288.000	280.000
11	186.000	190.000	168.000
12	266.000	236.000	236.000
13	206.000	244.000	248.000
14	318.000	258.000	200.000
15	294.000	240.000	264.000
16	282.000	294.000	256.000
17	234.000	220.000	264.000
18	224.000	200.000	216.000
19	276.000	220.000	188.000

TABLE 2.2

Data Before Imputation of Missing Values

Number of Missing Values per Variable

	VAR1	VAR2	VAR3
	0	0	9

Distribution of Missing Values

Total Sample Size =	28		
Number of Missing Values		0	1
Number of Cases		19	9

Effective Sample Sizes
Univariate (in Diagonal) and Pairwise Bivariate (off
 Diagonal)

	VAR1	VAR2	VAR3
VAR1	28		
VAR2	28	28	
VAR3	19	19	19

Percentage of Missing Values
Univariate (in Diagonal) and Pairwise Bivariate (off
 Diagonal)

	VAR1	VAR2	VAR3
VAR1	0.00		
VAR2	0.00	0.00	
VAR3	32.14	32.14	32.14

Correlation Matrix

	VAR1	VAR2	VAR3
VAR1	1.000		
VAR2	0.673	1.000	
VAR3	0.395	0.665	1.000

Means

VAR1	VAR2	VAR3
253.929	230.643	221.474

Standard Deviations

VAR1	VAR2	VAR3
47.710	46.967	43.184

TABLE 2.3

Data After Imputation of Missing Values

```
Number of Missing Values per Variable
                    VAR1              VAR2              VAR3
          ------------------  ----------------  ----------------
                     0                 0                 9

Imputations for      VAR3
Case  2 imputed with value 204 (Variance Ratio = 0.000), NM=  1
Case  4 imputed with value 142 (Variance Ratio = 0.000), NM=  1
Case  5 imputed with value 182 (Variance Ratio = 0.000), NM=  1
Case 10 imputed with value 280 (Variance Ratio = 0.000), NM=  1
Case 13 imputed with value 248 (Variance Ratio = 0.000), NM=  1
Case 16 imputed with value 256 (Variance Ratio = 0.000), NM=  1
Case 18 imputed with value 216 (Variance Ratio = 0.000), NM=  1
Case 23 imputed with value 188 (Variance Ratio = 0.000), NM=  1
Case 25 imputed with value 256 (Variance Ratio = 0.000), NM=  1

Number of Missing Values per Variable After Imputation
                    VAR1              VAR2              VAR3
          ------------------  ----------------  ----------------
                     0                 0                 0

Total Sample Size = 28

Correlation Matrix
                    VAR1              VAR2              VAR3
          ------------------  ----------------  ----------------
VAR1               1.000
VAR2               0.673             1.000
VAR3               0.404             0.787             1.000

Means
                    VAR1              VAR2              VAR3
          ------------------  ----------------  ----------------
                  253.929           230.643           220.714

Standard Deviations
                    VAR1              VAR2              VAR3
          ------------------  ----------------  ----------------
                   47.710            46.967            42.771
```

We have noticed that selecting matching variables with a higher correlation to the variable with missing values provides better imputed
values for the missing data. We highly recommend comparing any analyses before and after the replacement of missing data values to fully
understand the impact missing data values have on the parameter estimates and standard errors. LISREL–PRELIS also permits replacement

of missing values using the EM and MCMC approaches, which may be practical when matching sets of variables are not possible. A comparison of EM and MCMC is also warranted in multiple imputations to determine the effect of using a different algorithm on the replacement of missing values.

2.2.5 Outliers

Outliers or influential data points can be defined as data values that are extreme or atypical on either the independent (X variables) or dependent (Y variables) variables or both. Outliers can occur as a result of observation errors, data entry errors, instrument errors based on layout or instructions, or actual extreme values from self-report data. Because outliers affect the mean, the standard deviation, and correlation coefficient values, they must be explained, deleted, or accommodated by using robust statistics. Sometimes, additional data will need to be collected to fill in the gap along either the Y or X axes. LISREL–PRELIS has outlier detection methods available that include the following: box plot display, scatterplot, histogram, and frequency distributions.

2.2.6 Linearity

Some statistical techniques, such as SEM, assume that the variables are linearly related to one another. Thus, a standard practice is to visualize the coordinate pairs of data points of two continuous variables by plotting the data in a scatterplot. These bivariate plots depict whether the data are linearly increasing or decreasing. The presence of curvilinear data reduces the magnitude of the Pearson correlation coefficient, even resulting in the presence of a zero correlation. Recall that the Pearson correlation value indicates the magnitude and direction of the *linear* relationships between two variables. Figure 2.1 shows the importance of visually displaying the bivariate data scatterplot.

FIGURE 2.1
Left: correlation is linear. Right: correlation is nonlinear.

TABLE 2.4

Data Transformation Types

$y = \ln(x)$ or $y = \log10(x)$ or $y = \ln(x+0.5)$	Useful with clustered data or cases where the standard deviation increases with the mean
$y = \text{sqrt}(x)$	Useful with Poisson counts
$y = \arcsin((x + 0.375)/(n + 0.75))$	Useful with binomial proportions $[0.2 < p = x/n < 0.8]$
$y = 1/x$	Useful with gamma-distributed x variable
$y = \text{logit}(x) = \ln(x/(1 - x))$	Useful with binomial proportions $x = p$
$y = \text{normit}(x)$	Quantile of normal distribution for standardized x
$y = \text{probit}(x) = 5 + \text{normit}(x)$	Most useful to resolve nonnormality of data

Note: probit(x) is same as normit(x) plus 5 to avoid negative values.

2.2.7 Nonnormality

In basic statistics, several transformations are given to handle issues with nonnormal data. Some of these common transformations are in Table 2.4.

Inferential statistics often rely on the assumption that the data are normally distributed. Data that are *skewed* (lack of symmetry) or more frequently occurring along one part of the measurement scale will affect the variance–covariance among variables. In addition, *kurtosis* (peakedness) in data will impact statistics. *Leptokurtic* data values are more peaked than the normal distribution, whereas *platykurtic* data values are flatter and more dispersed along the X axis, but have a consistent low frequency on the Y axis—that is, the frequency distribution of the data appears more rectangular in shape.

Nonnormal data can occur because of the scaling of variables (e.g., ordinal rather than interval) or the limited sampling of subjects. Possible solutions for skewness are to resample more participants or to perform a linear transformation as outlined above. Our experience is that a probit data transformation works best in correcting skewness. Kurtosis in data is more difficult to resolve; some possible solutions in LISREL–PRELIS include additional sampling of subjects, or the use of bootstrap methods, normalizing scores, or alternative methods of estimation (e.g., WLS or ADF).

The presence of skewness and kurtosis can be detected in LISREL–PRELIS using univariate tests, multivariate tests, and measures of skewness and kurtosis that are available in the pull-down menus or output. One recommended method of handling nonnormal data is to use an asymptotic covariance matrix as input along with the sample covariance matrix in the LISREL–PRELIS program, as follows:

```
LISREL
  CM = boy.cov
  AC = boy.acm
SIMPLIS
  Covariance matrix from file boy.cov
  Asymptotic covariance matrix from file boy.acm
```

We can use the asymptotic covariance matrix in two different ways: (a) as a weight matrix when specifying the method of estimation as weighted least squares (WLS), and (b) as a weight matrix that adjusts the normal-theory weight matrix to correct for bias in standard errors and fit statistics. The appropriate moment matrix in PRELIS, using OUTPUT OPTIONS, must be selected before requesting the calculation of the asymptotic covariance matrix.

PRELIS recognizes data as being continuous (CO), ordinal (OR), or classes (CL), that is gender (boy, girl). Different correlations are possible depending upon the level of measurement. A variance–covariance matrix with continuous variables would use Pearson correlations, while ordinal variables would use Tetrachoric correlations. If skewed nonnormal data is present, then consider a linear transformation using **Probit**. In SEM, researchers typically output and use an **asymptotic variance–covariance matrix**. When using a PRELIS data set, consider the **normal score** option in the menu to correct for nonnormal variables.

2.3 Summary

Structural equation modeling is a correlation research method; therefore, the measurement scale, restriction of range in the data values, missing data, outliers, nonlinearity, and nonnormality of data affect the variance–covariance among variables and thus can impact the SEM analysis. Researchers should use the built-in menu options to examine, graph, and test for any of these problems in the data prior to conducting any SEM model analysis. Basically, researchers should know their data characteristics. Data screening is a very important first step in structural equation modeling. The next chapter illustrates in more detail issues related to the use of correlation and variance–covariance in SEM models. There, we provide specific examples to illustrate the importance of topics covered in this chapter. A troubleshooting box summarizing these issues is provided in Box 2.1.

BOX 2.1   TROUBLESHOOTING TIPS

Issue	Suggestions
Measurement scale	Need to take the measurement scale of the variables into account when computing statistics such as means, standard deviations, and correlations.
Restriction of range	Need to consider range of values obtained for variables, as restricted range of one or more variables can reduce the magnitude of correlations.
Missing data	Need to consider missing data on one or more subjects for one or more variables as this can affect SEM results. Cases are lost with listwise deletion, pairwise deletion is often problematic (e.g., different sample sizes), and thus modern imputation methods are recommended.
Outliers	Need to consider outliers as they can affect statistics such as means, standard deviations, and correlations. They can either be explained, deleted, or accommodated (using either robust statistics or obtaining additional data to fill-in). Can be detected by methods such as box plots, scatterplots, histograms or frequency distributions.
Linearity	Need to consider whether variables are linearly related, as nonlinearity can reduce the magnitude of correlations. Can be detected by scatterplots. Can be dealt with by transformations or deleting outliers.
Nonnormality	Need to consider whether the variables are normally distributed, as nonnormality can affect resulting SEM statistics. Can be detected by univariate tests, multivariate tests, and skewness and kurtosis statistics. Can be dealt with by transformations, additional sampling, bootstrapping, normalizing scores, or alternative methods of estimation.

Exercises

1. LISREL uses which command to import data sets?
   a. **File**, then **Export Data**
   b. **File**, then **Open**
   c. **File**, then **Import Data**
   d. **File**, then **New**

2. Define the following levels of measurement.
   a. Nominal
   b. Ordinal
   c. Interval
   d. Ratio

3. Mark each of the following statements true (T) or false (F).
   a. LISREL can deal with missing data.
   b. PRELIS can deal with missing data.

    c. LISREL can compute descriptive statistics.
    d. PRELIS can compute descriptive statistics.

  4. Explain how each of the following affects statistics:
    a. Restriction of range
    b. Missing data
    c. Outliers
    d. Nonlinearity
    e. Nonnormality

References

Anderson, N. H. (1961). Scales and statistics: Parametric and non-parametric. *Psychological Bulletin, 58*, 305–316.

Davey, A., & Savla, J. (2009). *Statistical power analysis with missing data: A structural equation modeling approach.* Routledge, Taylor & Francis Group: New York.

Enders, C. K. (2006). Analyzing structural equation models with missing data. In G.R. Hancock & R.O. Mueller (Eds.), *Structural equation modeling: A second course* (pp. 313–342). Greenwich, CT: Information Age.

Jöreskog, K. G., & Sörbom, D. (1996). *PRELIS2: User's reference guide.* Lincolnwood, IL: Scientific Software International.

McKnight, P. E., McKnight, K. M., Sidani, S., & Aurelio, J. F. (2007). *Missing data: A gentle introduction.* New York: Guilford.

Peng, C.-Y. J., Harwell, M., Liou, S.-M., & Ehman, L. H. (2007). Advances in missing data methods and implications for educational research. In S.S. Sawilowsky (Ed.), *Real data analysis.* Charlotte: Information Age.

Stevens, S. S. (1946). On the theory of scales of measurement. *Science, 103*, 677–680.

3

Correlation

Key Concepts

    Types of correlation coefficients

    Factors affecting correlation

    Correction for attenuation

    Nonpositive definite matrices

    Bivariate, part, and partial correlation

    Suppressor variable

    Covariance and causation

In chapter 2 we considered a number of data preparation issues in structural equation modeling. In this chapter, we move beyond data preparation in describing the important role that correlation (covariance) plays in SEM. We also include a discussion of a number of factors that affect correlation coefficients as well as the assumptions and limitations of correlation methods in structural equation modeling.

3.1 Types of Correlation Coefficients

Sir Francis Galton conceptualized the correlation and regression procedure for examining covariance in two or more traits, and Karl Pearson (1896) developed the statistical formula for the correlation coefficient and regression based on his suggestion (Crocker & Algina, 1986; Ferguson & Takane, 1989; Tankard, 1984). Shortly thereafter, Charles Spearman (1904) used the correlation procedure to develop a factor analysis technique. The correlation, regression, and factor analysis techniques have for many decades formed the basis for generating tests and defining constructs. Today, researchers are expanding their understanding of the roles that correlation, regression, and factor analysis play in theory and construct definition to include latent variable, covariance structure, and confirmatory factor measurement models.

The relationships and contributions of Galton, Pearson, and Spearman to the field of statistics, especially correlation, regression, and factor analysis, are quite interesting (Tankard, 1984). In fact, the basis of association between two variables—that is, correlation or covariance—has played a major role in statistics. The Pearson correlation coefficient provides the basis for point estimation (test of significance), explanation (variance accounted for in a dependent variable by an independent variable), prediction (of a dependent variable from an independent variable through linear regression), reliability estimates (test–retest, equivalence), and validity (factorial, predictive, concurrent).

The Pearson correlation coefficient also provides the basis for establishing and testing models among measured and/or latent variables. The partial and part correlations further permit the identification of specific bivariate relationships between variables that allow for the specification of unique variance shared between two variables while controlling for the influence of other variables. Partial and part correlations can be tested for significance, similar to the Pearson correlation coefficient, by simply using the degrees of freedom, $n - 2$, in the standard correlation table of significance values (Table A.3) or an F test in multiple regression which tests the difference in R^2 values between full and restricted models (Table A.5).

Although the Pearson correlation coefficient has had a major impact in the field of statistics, other correlation coefficients have emerged depending upon the level of variable measurement. Stevens (1968) provided the properties of scales of measurement that have become known as nominal, ordinal, interval, and ratio. The types of correlation coefficients developed for these various levels of measurement are categorized in Table 3.1.

TABLE 3.1

Types of Correlation Coefficients

Correlation Coefficient	Level of Measurement
Pearson product-moment	Both variables interval
Spearman rank, Kendall's tau	Both variables ordinal
Phi, contingency	Both variables nominal
Point biserial	One variable interval, one variable dichotomous
Gamma, rank biserial	One variable ordinal, one variable nominal
Biserial	One variable interval, one variable artificial[a]
Polyserial	One variable interval, one variable ordinal with underlying continuity
Tetrachoric	Both variables dichotomous (nominal artificial[a])
Polychoric	Both variables ordinal with underlying continuities

[a] *Artificial* refers to recoding variable values into a dichotomy.

Many popular computer programs, for example, SAS and SPSS, typically do not compute all of these correlation types. Therefore, you may need to check a popular statistics book or look around for a computer program that will compute the type of correlation coefficient you need—for example, the phi and point-biserial coefficient are not readily available. In SEM analyses, the Pearson coefficient, tetrachoric or polychoric (for several ordinal variable pairs) coefficient, and biserial or polyserial (for several continuous and ordinal variable pairs) coefficient are typically used (see PRELIS for the use of Kendall's tau-c or tau-b, and canonical correlation). LISREL permits *mixture models*, which use variables with both ordinal and interval-ratio levels of measurement (chapter 15). Although SEM software programs are now demonstrating how mixture models can be analyzed, the use of variables with different levels of measurement has traditionally been a problem in the field of statistics—for example, multiple regression and multivariate statistics.

3.2 Factors Affecting Correlation Coefficients

Given the important role that correlation plays in structural equation modeling, we need to understand the factors that affect establishing relationships among multivariable data points. The key factors are the level of measurement, restriction of range in data values (variability, skewness, kurtosis), missing data, nonlinearity, outliers, correction for attenuation, and issues related to sampling variation, confidence intervals, effect size, significance, sample size, and power.

3.2.1 Level of Measurement and Range of Values

Four types or levels of measurement typically define whether the characteristic or scale interpretation of a variable is nominal, ordinal, interval, or ratio (Stevens, 1968). In structural equation modeling, each of these types of scaled variables can be used. However, it is not recommended that they be included together or mixed in a correlation (covariance) matrix. Instead, the PRELIS data output option should be used to save an asymptotic covariance matrix for input along with the sample variance-covariance matrix into a LISREL or SIMPLIS program.

Initially, SEM required variables measured at the interval or ratio level of measurement, so the Pearson product-moment correlation coefficient was used in regression, path, factor, and structural equation modeling. The interval or ratio scaled variable values should also have a sufficient range of score values to introduce variance (15 or more scale points). If the range of scores is restricted, the magnitude of the correlation value is decreased. Basically, as a group of subjects become more homogeneous, score variance decreases, reducing the correlation value between the variables. So, there must be enough variation in scores to allow a correlation relationship to manifest itself between variables. Variables with fewer than 15 categories are treated as ordinal variables in LISREL–PRELIS, so if you are assuming continuous interval-level data, you will need to check whether the variables meet this condition. Also, the use of the same scale values for variables can help in the interpretation of results and/or relative comparison among variables. The meaningfulness of a correlation relationship will depend on the variables employed; hence, your theoretical perspective is very important. You may recall from your basic statistics course that a spurious correlation is possible when two sets of scores correlate significantly, but their relationship is not meaningful or substantive in nature.

If the distributions of variables are widely divergent, correlation can also be affected, and so several data transformations are suggested by Ferguson and Takane (1989) to provide a closer approximation to a normal, homogeneous variance for skewed or kurtotic data. Some possible transformations are the square root transformation (sqrt X), the logarithmic transformation (log X), the reciprocal transformation ($1/X$), and the arcsine transformation (arcsin X). The probit transformation appears to be most effective in handling univariate skewed data.

Consequently, the type of scale used and the range of values for the measured variables can have profound effects on your statistical analysis (in particular, on the mean, variance, and correlation). The scale and range of a variable's numerical values affects statistical methods, and this is no different in structural equation modeling. The PRELIS program is available to provide tests of normality, skewness, and kurtosis on variables and to compute an asymptotic covariance matrix for input into LISREL if required. The use of normal scores is also an option in PRELIS.

3.2.2 Nonlinearity

The Pearson correlation coefficient indicates the degree of linear relationship between two variables. It is possible that two variables can indicate no correlation if they have a curvilinear relationship. Thus, the extent to which the variables deviate from the assumption of a linear relationship will affect the size of the correlation coefficient. It is therefore important to check for linearity of the scores; the common method is to graph the coordinate data points in a scatterplot. The linearity assumption should not be confused with recent advances in testing interaction in structural equation models discussed in chapter 16. You should also be familiar with the *eta* coefficient as an index of nonlinear relationship between two variables and with the testing of linear, quadratic, or cubic effects. Consult an intermediate statistics text, for example, Lomax (2007) to review these basic concepts.

The heuristic data sets in Table 3.2 will demonstrate the dramatic effect a lack of linearity has on the Pearson correlation coefficient value. In the first data set, the Y values increase from 1 to 10, and the X values increase from 1 to 5, then decrease from 5 to 1 (nonlinear). The result is a Pearson correlation coefficient of $r = 0$; although a nonlinear relationship does exist in the data, it is not indicated by the Pearson correlation coefficient. The restriction of range in values can be demonstrated using the fourth heuristic data set in Table 3.2. The Y values only range between 3 and 7, and the X values only range from 1 to 4. The Pearson correlation coefficient is also $r = 0$ for these data. The fifth data set indicates how limited sampling can affect the Pearson coefficient. In these sample data, only three pairs of scores are sampled, and the Pearson correlation is $r = -1.0$, or perfectly negatively correlated.

TABLE 3.2

Heuristic Data Sets

Nonlinear Data		Complete Data		Missing Data	
Y	X	Y	X	Y	X
1.00	1.00	8.00	6.00	8.00	—
2.00	2.00	7.00	5.00	7.00	5.00
3.00	3.00	8.00	4.00	8.00	—
4.00	4.00	5.00	2.00	5.00	2.00
5.00	5.00	4.00	3.00	4.00	3.00
6.00	5.00	5.00	2.00	5.00	2.00
7.00	4.00	3.00	3.00	3.00	3.00
8.00	3.00	5.00	4.00	5.00	—
9.00	2.00	3.00	1.00	3.00	1.00
10.00	1.00	2.00	2.00	2.00	2.00
Range of Data		Sampling Effect			
Y	X	Y	X		
3.00	1.00	8.00	3.00		
3.00	2.00	9.00	2.00		
4.00	3.00	10.00	1.00		
4.00	4.00				
5.00	1.00				
5.00	2.00				
6.00	3.00				
6.00	4.00				
7.00	1.00				
7.00	2.00				

3.2.3 Missing Data

A complete data set is also given in Table 3.2 where the Pearson correlation coefficient is $r = .782$, $p = .007$, for $n = 10$ pairs of scores. If missing data were present, the Pearson correlation coefficient would drop to $r = .659$, $p = .108$, for $n = 7$ pairs of scores. The Pearson correlation coefficient changes from statistically significant to not statistically significant. More importantly, in a correlation matrix with several variables, the various correlation coefficients could be computed on different sample sizes. If we used *listwise deletion* of cases, then any variable in the data set with a missing value would cause a subject to be deleted, possibly causing a substantial reduction in our sample size, whereas *pairwise deletion* of cases would result in different sample sizes for our correlation coefficients in the correlation matrix.

Researchers have examined various aspects of how to handle or treat missing data beyond our introductory example using a small heuristic data set. One basic approach is to eliminate any observations where some of the data are missing, *listwise deletion*. Listwise deletion is not recommended because of the loss of information on other variables, and statistical estimates are based on reduced sample size. *Pairwise deletion* excludes data only when they are missing on the pairs of variables selected for analysis. However, this could lead to different sample sizes for the different correlations and related statistical estimates. A third approach, *data imputation*, replaces missing values with an estimate, for example, the mean value on a variable for all subjects who did not report any data for that variable (Beale & Little, 1975; also see chapter 2).

Missing data can arise in different ways (Little & Rubin, 1987, 1990). *Missing completely at random* (MCAR) implies that data on variable X are missing unrelated statistically to the values that have been observed for other variables as well as X. *Missing at random* (MAR) implies that data values on variable X are missing conditional on other variables, but are unrelated to the values of X. A third situation, *nonignorable* data, implies probabilistic information about the values that would have been observed. For MCAR data, mean substitution yields biased variance and covariance estimates, whereas listwise and pairwise deletion methods yield consistent solutions. For MAR data, mean substitution, listwise, and pairwise deletion methods produce biased results. When missing data are nonignorable, all approaches yield biased results. It would be prudent for the researcher to investigate how parameter estimates are affected by the use or nonuse of a data imputation method. A few references are provided to give a more detailed understanding of missing data (Arbuckle, 1996; Enders, 2006; McKnight, McKnight, Sidani & Aurelio, 2007; Peng, Harwell, Liou & Ehman, 2007; Wothke, 2000; Davey & Savla, 2009).

3.2.4 Outliers

The Pearson correlation coefficient can be drastically affected by a single outlier on X or Y. For example, the two data sets in Table 3.3 indicate a $Y = 27$ value (Set A) versus a $Y = 2$ value (Set B) for the last subject. In the first set of data, $r = .524$, $p = .37$, whereas in the second set of data, $r = -.994$, $p = .001$. Is the $Y = 27$ data value an outlier based on limited sampling or is it a data entry error? A large body of research has been undertaken to examine how different outliers on X, Y, or both X, and Y affect correlation relationships, and how to better analyze the data using robust statistics (Anderson & Schumacker, 2003; Ho & Naugher, 2000; Huber, 1981; Rousseeuw & Leroy, 1987; Staudte & Sheather, 1990).

TABLE 3.3

Outlier Data Sets

Set A		Set B	
X	Y	X	Y
1	9	1	9
2	7	2	7
3	5	3	5
4	3	4	3
5	27	5	2

3.2.5 Correction for Attenuation

A basic assumption in psychometric theory is that observed data contain measurement error. A test score (observed data) is a function of a true score and measurement error. A Pearson correlation coefficient will have different values, depending on whether it was computed with observed scores or the true scores where measurement error has been removed. The Pearson correlation coefficient can be corrected for attenuation or unreliable measurement error in scores, thus yielding a true score correlation; however, the corrected correlation coefficient can become greater than 1.0! Low reliability in the independent and/or dependent variables, coupled with a high correlation between the independent and dependent variable, can result in correlations greater than 1.0. For example, given a correlation of $r = .90$ between the observed scores on X and Y, the Cronbach alpha reliability coefficient of .60 for X scores, and the Cronbach alpha reliability coefficient of .70 for Y scores, the Pearson correlation coefficient, corrected for attenuation (r^*) , is greater than 1.0:

$$r^*_{xy} = \frac{r_{xy}}{\sqrt{r_{xx}r_{yy}}} = \frac{.90}{\sqrt{.60(.70)}} = \frac{.90}{.648} = 1.389$$

When this happens, a nonpositive definite error message occurs stopping the SEM program.

3.2.6 Nonpositive Definite Matrices

Correlation coefficients greater than 1.0 in a correlation matrix cause the correlation matrix to be *nonpositive definite*. In other words, the solution is not admissible, indicating that parameter estimates cannot be computed. Correction for attenuation is not the only situation that causes nonpositive matrices to occur (Wothke, 1993). Sometimes the ratio of covariance to the product of variable variances yields correlations greater than 1.0. The following variance–covariance matrix is nonpositive definite because it contains a correlation coefficient greater than 1.0 between the Relations and Attribute latent variables (denoted by an asterisk):

Variance–Covariance Matrix

Task	1.043			
Relations	.994	1.079		
Management	.892	.905	.924	
Attribute	1.065	1.111	.969	1.12

Correlation Matrix

Task	1.000			
Relations	.937	1.000		
Management	.908	.906	1.000	
Attribute	.985	1.010*	.951	1.000

Nonpositive definite covariance matrices occur when the determinant of the matrix is zero or the inverse of the matrix is not possible. This can be caused by correlations greater than 1.0, linear dependency among the observed variables, multicollinearity among the observed variables, a variable that is a linear combination of other variables, a sample size less than the number of variables, the presence of a negative or zero variance (Heywood Case), variance–covariance (correlation) values outside the permissible range, for example, correlation beyond +/–1.0, and bad *start values* in the user-specified model. A Heywood case also occurs when the communality estimate is greater than 1.0. Possible solutions to resolve this error are to reduce communality or fix communality to less than 1.0, extract a different number of factors (possibly by dropping paths), rescale observed variables to create a more linear relationship, or eliminate a *bad* observed variable that indicates linear dependency or multicollinearity.

Regression, path, factor, and structural equation models mathematically solve a set of simultaneous equations typically using ordinary least squares

(OLS) estimates as initial estimates of coefficients in the model. However, these initial estimates or coefficients are sometimes distorted or too different from the final admissible solution. When this happens, more reasonable *start values* need to be chosen. It is easy to see from the basic regression coefficient formula that the correlation coefficient value and the standard deviation values of the two variables affect the initial OLS estimates:

$$b = r_{xy} \left(\frac{s_y}{s_x} \right).$$

3.2.7 Sample Size

A common formula used to determine sample size when estimating means of variables was given by McCall (1982): $n = (Z \, \sigma/\varepsilon)^2$, where n is the sample size needed for the desired level of precision, ε is the effect size, Z is the confidence level, and σ is the population standard deviation of scores (σ can be estimated from prior research studies, test norms, or the range of scores divided by 6). For example, given a random sample of ACT scores from a defined population with a standard deviation of 100, a desired confidence level of 1.96 (which corresponds to a .05 level of significance), and an effect size of 20 (difference between sampled ACT mean and population ACT mean), the sample size needed would be $[1.96 \, (100)/20]^2 = 96$.

In structural equation modeling, however, the researcher often requires a much larger sample size to maintain power and obtain stable parameter estimates and standard errors. The need for larger sample sizes is also due in part to the program requirements and the multiple observed variables used to define latent variables. Hoelter (1983) proposed the *critical N* statistic, which indicates the sample size needed to obtain a chi-square value that would reject the null hypothesis in a structural equation model. The required sample size and power estimates that provide a reasonable indication of whether a researcher's data fits their theoretical model or to estimate parameters is discussed in more detail in chapter 5.

SEM software programs estimate coefficients based on the user-specified theoretical model, or *implied model*, but also must work with the saturated and independence models. A *saturated model* is the model with all parameters indicated, while the *independence model* is the null model or model with no parameters estimated. A saturated model with p observed variables has $p \, (p + 3)/2$ free parameters [*Note:* Number of independent elements in the symmetric covariance matrix $= p(p + 1)/2$. Number of means $= p$, so total number of independent elements $= p \, (p + 1)/2 + p = p$ $(p + 3)/2$]. For example, with 10 observed variables, $10(10 + 3)/2 = 65$ free parameters. If the sample size is small, then there is not enough information to estimate parameters in the saturated model for a large number of variables. Consequently, the chi-square fit statistic and derived statistics such as Akaike's Information Criterion (AIC) and the root-mean-square error of approximation (RMSEA) cannot be computed. In addition, the fit of the independence model is required to calculate other fit indices such as the Comparative Fit Index (CFI) and the Normed Fit Index (NFI).

Ding, Velicer, and Harlow (1995) located numerous studies (e.g., Anderson & Gerbing, 1988) that were in agreement that 100 to 150 subjects is the *minimum* satisfactory sample size when conducting structural equation models. Boomsma (1982, 1983) recommended 400, and Hu, Bentler, and Kano (1992) indicated that in some cases 5,000 is insufficient! Many of us may recall rules of thumb in our statistics texts, for example, 10 subjects per variable or 20 subjects per variable. Costello and Osborne (2005) demonstrated in their Monte Carlo study that 20 subjects per variable is recommended for best practices in factor analysis. In our examination of published SEM research, we have found that many articles used from 250 to 500 subjects, although the greater the sample size, the more likely it is one can validate the model using cross-validation (see chapter 12). For example, Bentler and Chou (1987) suggested that a ratio as low as five subjects per variable would be sufficient for normal and elliptical distributions when the latent variables have multiple indicators and that a ratio of at least 10 subjects per variable would be sufficient for other distributions.

Determination of sample size is now better understood in SEM modeling and further discussed in chapter 5.

3.3 Bivariate, Part, and Partial Correlations

The types of correlations indicated in Table 3.1 are considered bivariate correlations, or associations between two variables. Cohen & Cohen (1983), in describing correlation research, further presented the correlation between two variables controlling for the influence of a third variable. These correlations are referred to as *part* and *partial* correlations, depending upon how variables are controlled or partialled out. Some of the various ways in which three variables can be depicted are illustrated in Figure 3.1. The diagrams illustrate different situations among variables where (a) all the variables are uncorrelated (Case 1), (b) only one pair of variables is correlated (Cases 2 and 3), (c) two pairs of variables are correlated (Cases 4 and 5), and (d) all of the variables are correlated (Case 6). It is obvious that with more than three variables the possibilities become overwhelming. It is therefore important to have a theoretical perspective to suggest why certain variables are correlated and/or controlled in a study. A theoretical perspective is essential in specifying a model and forms the basis for testing a structural equation model.

The *partial correlation coefficient* measures the association between two variables while controlling for a third variable, for example, the association

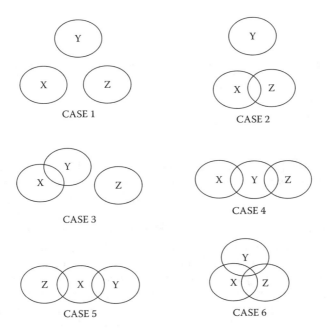

FIGURE 3.1
Possible three-variable relationships.

between age and reading comprehension, controlling for reading level. Controlling for reading level in the correlation between age and comprehension partials out the correlation of reading level with age and the correlation of reading level with comprehension. *Part correlation*, in contrast, is the correlation between age and comprehension with reading level controlled for, where only the correlation between comprehension and reading level is removed before age is correlated with comprehension.

Whether a part or partial correlation is used depends on the specific model or research question. Convenient notation helps distinguish these two types of correlations (1 = age, 2 = comprehension, 3 = reading level): partial correlation, $r_{12.3}$, part correlation, $r_{1(2.3)}$ or $r_{2(1.3)}$. Different correlation values are computed depending on which variables are controlled or partialled out. For example, using the correlations in Table 3.4, we can compute the partial correlation coefficient $r_{12.3}$ (correlation between age and comprehension, controlling for reading level) as follows:

$$r_{12.3} = \frac{r_{12} - r_{13} r_{23}}{\sqrt{(1 - r_{13}^2)(1 - r_{23}^2)}}$$

$$= \frac{.45 - (.25)\,(.80)}{\sqrt{[1 - (.25)^2]\,[1 - (.80)^2]}} = .43$$

TABLE 3.4

Correlation Matrix ($n = 100$)

Variable	Age	Comprehension	Reading Level
1. Age	1.00		
2. Comprehension	.45	1.00	
3. Reading level	.25	.80	1.00

Notice that the partial correlation coefficient should be smaller in magnitude than the Pearson product-moment correlation between age and comprehension, which is $r_{12} = .45$. If the partial correlation coefficient is not smaller than the Pearson product-moment correlation, then a *suppressor variable* may be present (Pedhazur, 1997). A suppressor variable correlates near zero with a dependent variable but correlates significantly with other predictor variables. This correlation situation serves to control for variance shared with predictor variables and not the dependent variable. The partial correlation coefficient increases in magnitude once this effect is removed from the correlation between two predictor variables with a criterion. Partial correlations will be greater in magnitude than part correlations, except when independent variables are zero correlated with the dependent variable; then, part correlations are equal to partial correlations.

The part correlation coefficient $r_{1(2.3)}$, or correlation between age and comprehension where reading level is controlled for in comprehension only, is computed as

$$r_{1(2.3)} = \frac{r_{12} - r_{13}r_{23}}{\sqrt{1 - r_{23}^2}} = \frac{.45 - (.25)(.80)}{\sqrt{1 - .80^2}} = .42,$$

or, in the case of correlating comprehension with age where reading level is controlled for age only is

$$r_{2(1.3)} = \frac{r_{12} - r_{13}r_{23}}{\sqrt{1 - r_{13}^2}} = \frac{.45 - (.25)(.80)}{\sqrt{1 - .25^2}} = .26.$$

The correlation, whether zero-order (bivariate), part, or partial can be tested for significance, interpreted as variance accounted for by squaring each coefficient, and diagrammed using Venn or Ballentine figures to conceptualize their relationships. In our example, the zero-order relationships among the three variables can be diagrammed as in Figure 3.2. However, the partial correlation of age with comprehension controlling for reading level would be $r_{12.3} = .43$, or area a divided by the combined area of a and e [$a/(a + e)$]; see Figure 3.3. A part correlation of age with comprehension

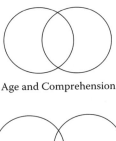

Age and Comprehension

Age and Reading

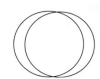

Reading and Comprehension

FIGURE 3.2
Bivariate correlations.

while controlling for the correlation between reading level and comprehension would be $r_{1(2.3)} = .42$, or just area a; see Figure 3.4.

These examples consider only controlling for one variable when correlating two other variables (partial), or controlling for the impact of one variable on another before correlating with a third variable (part). Other higher-order part correlations and partial correlations are possible (e.g., $r_{12.34}$, $r_{12(3.4)}$), but are beyond the scope of this book. Readers should refer to references for

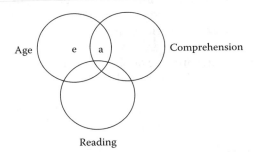

FIGURE 3.3
Partial correlation area.

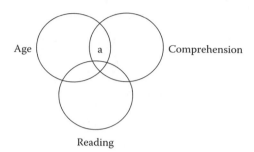

FIGURE 3.4
Part correlation area.

a more detailed discussion of part and partial correlation (Cohen & Cohen, 1983; Pedhazur, 1997; Hinkle, Wiersma & Jurs, 2003; Lomax, 2007).

3.4 Correlation versus Covariance

The type of data matrix used for computations in structural equation modeling programs is a variance–covariance matrix. A variance–covariance matrix is made up of variance terms on the diagonal and covariance terms on the off-diagonal. If a correlation matrix is used as the input data matrix, most of the computer programs by default convert it to a variance–covariance matrix using the standard deviations of the variables, unless specified otherwise. The researcher has the option to input raw data, a correlation matrix, or a variance–covariance matrix. The correlation matrix provides the option of using standardized or unstandardized variables for analysis purposes. If a correlation matrix is input with a row of variable means (although optional) and a row of standard deviations, then a variance–covariance matrix is used with unstandardized output. If only a correlation matrix is input, the means and standard deviations, by default, are set at 0 and 1, respectively, and standardized output is printed. When raw data are input, a variance–covariance matrix is computed.

The number of distinct elements in a variance–covariance matrix S is $p(p + 1)/2$, where p is the number of observed variables. For example, the variance–covariance matrix for the following three variables, X, Y, and Z, is as follows:

		X	Y	Z
	X	15.80		
$S =$	Y	10.16	11.02	
	Z	12.43	9.23	15.37

It has $3 (3 + 1)/2 = 6$ distinct values: 3 variance and 3 covariance terms.

Correlation is computed using the variances and covariance among the bivariate variables, using the following formula:

$$r = \frac{s_{XY}^2}{\sqrt{s_X^2 * s_Y^2}}$$

Dividing the covariance between two variables (covariance terms are the off-diagonal values in the matrix) by the square root of the product of the two variable variances (variances of variables are on the diagonal of the matrix) yields the following correlations among the three variables:

$$r_{xy} = 10.16/(15.80 * 11.02)^{1/2} = .77$$

$$r_{xz} = 12.43/(15.80 * 15.37)^{1/2} = .80$$

$$r_{yz} = 9.23/(11.02 * 15.37)^{1/2} = .71.$$

Structural equation software uses the variance–covariance matrix rather than the correlation matrix because Boomsma (1983) found that the analysis of correlation matrices led to imprecise parameter estimates and standard errors of the parameter estimates in a structural equation model. In SEM, incorrect estimation of the standard errors for the parameter estimates could lead to statistically significant parameter estimates and an incorrect interpretation of the model—that is, the parameter divided by the standard error indicates a ratio statistic or T-value, which can be compared to tabled critical t-values for statistical significance at different alpha levels (Table A.2). Browne (1982), Jennrich and Thayer (1973), and Lawley and Maxwell (1971) have suggested corrections for the standard errors when correlations or standardized coefficients are used in SEM. In general, a variance–covariance matrix should be used in structural equation modeling, although some SEM models require variable means, for example, structured means models (see chapter 13).

3.5 Variable Metrics (Standardized versus Unstandardized)

Researchers have debated the use of unstandardized or standardized variables (Lomax, 2007). The standardized coefficients are thought to be sample specific and not stable across different samples because of changes in the variance of the variables. The unstandardized coefficients permit an examination of change across different samples. The standardized coefficients are useful, however, in determining the relative importance of each variable to other variables for a given sample. Other reasons for using standardized variables are that variables are on the same scale of measurement, are more easily interpreted, and can easily be converted back to the raw scale metric. In a SIMPLIS program, adding the command *LISREL OUTPUT SS SC* provides a standardized solution (observed variables) and a completely standardized solution (observed variables and latent variables).

3.6 Causation Assumptions and Limitations

As previously discussed, the Pearson correlation coefficient is limited by the range of score values and the assumption of linearity, among other things. Even if the assumptions and limitations of using the Pearson correlation coefficient are met, a cause-and-effect relationship still has not been established. The following conditions are necessary for cause and effect to be inferred between variables X and Y (Tracz, 1992): (a) temporal order (X precedes Y in time), (b) existence of covariance or correlation between X and Y, and (c) control for other causes, for example, partial Z out of X and Y.

These three conditions may not be present in the research design setting, and in such a case, only association rather than causation can be inferred. However, if *manipulative* variables are used in the study, then a researcher could change or manipulate one variable in the study and examine subsequent effects on other variables, thereby determining cause-and-effect relationships (Resta & Baker, 1972). In structural equation modeling, the amount of influence rather than a cause-and-effect relationship is assumed and interpreted by direct, indirect, and total effects among variables, which are explained in chapter 7 where we discuss path models.

Philosophical differences exist between assuming causal versus inference relationships among variables, and the resolution of these issues requires a sound theoretical perspective. Bullock, Harlow, and Mulaik (1994) provided an in-depth discussion of causation issues related to structural equation modeling research. We feel that structural equation models will evolve beyond model fit into the domain of model testing as witnessed by the many new SEM model applications today. Model testing rather than model fit can involve testing significance of parameters, parameter change, or other factors that affect the model outcome values, and whose effects can be assessed. This approach, we believe, best depicts a causal assumption. In addition, structural models in longitudinal research can depict changes in latent variables over time (Collins & Horn, 1992). Pearl (2009) more recently has renewed a discussion about causality and firmly believes it is not mystical or metaphysical, but rather can be understood in terms of processes (models) that can be expressed in mathematical expressions ready for computer analysis.

3.7 Summary

In this chapter, we have described some of the basic correlation concepts underlying structural equation modeling. This discussion included various types of bivariate correlation coefficients, part and partial correlation, variable metrics, factors affecting correlation, the assumptions required in SEM, and causation versus inference debate in SEM modeling.

Most computer programs do not compute all the types of correlation coefficients used in statistics, so the reader should refer to a standard statistics textbook for computational formulas and understanding (Hinkle, Weirsma, & Jurs, 2003; Lomax, 2007). Structural equation modeling programs use a variance–covariance matrix, and include features to output the type of matrices they use. In SEM, categorical and/or ordinal variables with underlying continuous latent-variable attributes have been used with tetrachoric or polychoric correlations (Muthén, 1982, 1983, 1984; Muthén & Kaplan, 1985). PRELIS has been developed to permit a correlation matrix of various types of correlations to be conditioned or converted into an asymptotic covariance matrix for input into structural equation modeling programs (Jöreskog & Sörbom, 1993). The use of various correlation coefficients and subsequent conversion into a variance–covariance matrix will continue to play a major role in structural equation modeling, especially given *mixture models* (see chapter 15).

The chapter also presented numerous factors that affect the Pearson correlation coefficient, for example, restriction of range in the scores, outliers, skewness, and nonnormality. SEM software also converts correlation matrices with standard deviations into a variance–covariance matrix, but if attenuated correlations are greater than 1.0, a nonpositive definite error message will occur because of an inadmissible solution. Nonpositive definite error messages are all too common among beginners because they do not screen the data, thinking instead that structural equation modeling will be unaffected. Another major concern is when OLS initial estimates lead to bad start values for the coefficients in a model; however, changing the number of default iterations sometimes solves this problem. A troubleshooting box summarizes these issues (see Box 3.1). In chapter 4, we begin to deal with the basic steps a researcher takes in conducting SEM, which follows throughout the chapters in the book.

BOX-3.1   TROUBLESHOOTING TIPS

Issue	Suggestions
Measurement scale	Need to take the measurement scale of the variables into account when computing correlations.
Restriction of range	Need to consider range of values obtained for variables, as restricted range of one or more variables can reduce the magnitude of correlations. Can consider data transformations for nonnormal data.
Missing data	Need to consider missing data on one or more subjects for one or more variables as this can affect SEM results. Cases are lost with listwise deletion, pairwise deletion is often problematic (e.g., different sample sizes), and thus modern methods are recommended.
Outliers	Need to consider outliers as they can affect correlations. They can either be explained, deleted, or accommodated (using either robust statistics or obtaining additional data to fill-in). Can be detected by methods such as box plots, scatterplots, histograms or frequency distributions.
Linearity	Need to consider whether variables are linearly related, as nonlinearity can reduce the magnitude of correlations. Can be detected by scatterplots and dealt with by transformations or deleting outliers.
Correction for attenuation	Less than perfect reliability on observed measures can reduce the magnitude of correlations and lead to nonpositive definite error message. Best to use multiple, high quality measures.
Nonpositive definite matrices	Can occur in a correlation or covariance matrix due to a variable that a linear combination of other variables, collinearity, sample size less than the number of variables, negative or zero variances, correlations outside of the permissible range, or bad start values. Solutions include eliminating the bad variables, rescaling variables, and using more reasonable starting values.
Sample size	Small samples can reduce power and precision of parameter estimates. At least 100 to 150 cases is necessary for smaller models with well-behaved data.

Exercises

1. Given the Pearson correlation coefficients $r_{12} = .6$, $r_{13} = .7$, and $r_{23} = 4$, compute the part and partial correlations $r_{12.3}$ and $r_{1(2.3)}$.
2. Compare the variance explained in the bivariate, partial, and part correlations of Exercise 1.
3. Explain causation and describe when a cause-and-effect relationship might exist.

4. Given the following variance-covariance matrix, compute the Pearson correlation coefficients: r_{XY}, r_{XZ}, and r_{YZ}:

	X	*Y*	*Z*
X	15.80		
Y	10.16	11.02	
Z	12.43	9.23	15.37

References

Anderson, J. C., & Gerbing, D. W. (1988). Structural equation modeling in practice: A review and recommended two step approach. *Psychological Bulletin, 103*, 411–423.

Anderson, C., & Schumacker, R. E. (2003). A comparison of five robust regression methods with ordinary least squares regression: Relative efficiency, bias, and test of the null hypothesis. *Understanding Statistics, 2*, 77–101.

Arbuckle, J. L. (1996). Full information estimation in the presence of incomplete data. In G. A. Marcoulides and R. E. Schumacker (Eds.). *Advanced structural equation modeling* (pp. 243–277). Mahwah, NJ: Lawrence Erlbaum Associates.

Beale, E. M. L., & Little, R. J. (1975). Missing values in multivariate analysis. *Journal of the Royal Statistical Society Series B, 37*, 129–145.

Bentler, P. M., & Chou, C. (1987). Practical issues in structural equation modeling. *Sociological Methods and Research, 16*, 78–117.

Boomsma, A. (1982). The robustness of LISREL against small sample sizes in factor analysis models. In K. G. Jöreskog & H. Wold (Eds.), *Systems under indirect observation: Causality, structure, prediction (Part I)* (pp. 149–173). Amsterdam: North-Holland.

Boomsma, A. (1983). *On the robustness of LISREL against small sample size and non-normality.* Amsterdam: Sociometric Research Foundation.

Browne, M. W. (1982). *Covariance structures.* In D. M. Hawkins (Ed.), *Topics in applied multivariate analysis* (pp. 72–141). Cambridge: Cambridge University Press.

Bullock, H. E., Harlow, L. L., & Mulaik, S. A. (1994). Causation issues in structural equation modeling. *Structural Equation Modeling: A Multidisciplinary Journal, 1*, 253–267.

Cohen, J., & Cohen, P. (1983). *Applied multiple regression/correlation analysis for the behavioral sciences* (2nd ed.). Hillsdale, NJ: Lawrence Erlbaum Associates.

Collins, L. M., & Horn, J. L. (Eds.). (1992). *Best methods for the analysis of change: Recent advances, unanswered questions, future directions.* Washington, DC: American Psychological Association.

Costello, A. B., & Osborne, J. (2005). Best practices in exploratory factor analysis: four recommendations for getting the most from your analysis. *Practical Assessment Research & Evaluation, 10*(7), 1–9.

Crocker, L., & Algina, J. (1986). *Introduction to classical and modern test theory.* New York: Holt, Rinehart & Winston.

Davey, A., & Savla, J. (2009). *Statistical power analysis with missing data: A structural equation modeling approach.* Routledge, Taylor & Francis Group: New York.

Ding, L., Velicer, W. F., & Harlow, L. L. (1995). Effects of estimation methods, number of indicators per factor, and improper solutions on structural equation modeling fit indices. *Structural Equation Modeling: A Multidisciplinary Journal, 2,* 119–143.

Enders, C. K. (2006). Analyzing structural equation models with missing data. In G. R. Hancock & R. O. Mueller (Eds.), *Structural equation modeling: A second course* (pp. 313–342). Greenwich, CT: Information Age.

Ferguson, G. A., & Takane, Y. (1989). *Statistical analysis in psychology and education* (6th ed.). New York: McGraw-Hill.

Hinkle, D. E., Wiersma, W., & Jurs, S. G. (2003). *Applied statistics for the behavioral sciences* (5th ed.). Boston: Houghton Mifflin.

Ho, K., & Naugher, J. R. (2000). Outliers lie: An illustrative example of identifying outliers and applying robust methods. *Multiple Linear Regression Viewpoints, 26*(2), 2–6.

Hoelter, J. W. (1983). The analysis of covariance structures: Goodness-of-fit indices. *Sociological Methods and Research, 11,* 325–344.

Hu, L., Bentler, P. M., & Kano, Y. (1992). Can test statistics in covariance structure analysis be trusted? *Psychological Bulletin, 112,* 351–362.

Huber, P. J. (1981). *Robust statistics.* New York: Wiley.

Jennrich, R. I., & Thayer, D. T. (1973). A note on Lawley's formula for standard errors in maximum likelihood factor analysis. *Psychometrika, 38,* 571–580.

Jöreskog, K. G., & Sörbom, D. (1993). *PRELIS2 user's reference guide.* Chicago: Scientific Software International.

Lawley, D. N., & Maxwell, A. E. (1971). *Factor analysis as a statistical method.* London: Butterworth.

Little, R. J., & Rubin, D. B. (1987). *Statistical analysis with missing data.* New York: Wiley.

Little, R. J., & Rubin, D. B. (1990). The analysis of social science data with missing values. *Sociological Methods and Research, 18,* 292–326.

Lomax, R. G. (2007). *An introduction to statistical concepts* (2nd ed.). Mahwah, NJ: Lawrence Erlbaum Associates, Inc.

McCall, C. H., Jr. (1982). *Sampling statistics handbook for research.* Ames: Iowa State University Press.

McKnight, P. E., McKnight, K. M., Sidani, S., & Aurelio, J. F. (2007). *Missing data: A gentle introduction.* New York: Guilford.

Muthén, B. (1982). A structural probit model with latent variables. *Journal of the American Statistical Association, 74,* 807–811.

Muthén, B. (1983). Latent variable structural equation modeling with categorical data. *Journal of Econometrics, 22,* 43–65.

Muthén, B. (1984). A general structural equation model with dichotomous, ordered categorical, and continuous latent variable indicators. *Psychometrika, 49,* 115–132.

Muthén, B., & Kaplan, D. (1985). A comparison of some methodologies for the factor analysis of non-normal Likert variables. *British Journal of Mathematical and Statistical Psychology, 38,* 171–189.

Pearl, J. (2009). *Causality: Models, reasoning, and inference* (2nd edition). Cambridge University Press: London.

Pearson, K. (1896). Mathematical contributions to the theory of evolution. Part 3. Regression, heredity and panmixia. *Philosophical Transactions, A, 187,* 253–318.

Pedhazur, E. J. (1997). *Multiple regression in behavioral research: Explanation and prediction* (3rd ed.). Fort Worth: Harcourt Brace.

Peng, C.-Y. J., Harwell, M., Liou, S.-M., & Ehman, L. H. (2007). Advances in missing data methods and implications for educational research. In S. S. Sawilowsky (Ed.), *Real Data Analysis.* Charlotte: Information Age.

Resta, P. E., & Baker, R. L. (1972). *Selecting variables for educational research.* Inglewood, CA: Southwest Regional Laboratory for Educational Research and Development.

Rousseeuw, P. J., & Leroy, A. M. (1987). *Robust regression and outlier detection.* New York: Wiley.

Spearman, C. (1904). The proof and measurement of association between two things. *American Journal of Psychology, 15,* 72–101.

Staudte, R. G., & Sheather, S. J. (1990). *Robust estimation and testing.* New York: Wiley.

Stevens, S. S. (1968). Measurement, statistics, and the schempiric view. *Science, 161,* 849–856.

Tankard, J. W., Jr. (1984). *The statistical pioneers.* Cambridge, MA: Schenkman.

Tracz, S. M. (1992). The interpretation of beta weights in path analysis. *Multiple Linear Regression Viewpoints, 19*(1), 7–15.

Wothke, W. (1993). *Nonpositive definite matrices in structural equation modeling.* In K. A. Bollen & S. J. Long (Eds.), *Testing structural equation models* (pp. 256–293). Newbury Park, CA: Sage.

Wothke, W. (2000). Longitudinal and multi-group modeling with missing data. In T. D. Little, K. U. Schnabel, & J. Baumert (Eds.), *Modeling longitudinal and multiple group data: Practical issues, applied approaches and specific examples* (pp. 1–24). Mahwah, NJ: Lawrence Erlbaum Associates.

4

SEM Basics

Key Concepts

Model specification and specification error
Fixed, free, and constrained parameters
Under-, just-, and over-identified models
Recursive versus nonrecursive models
Indeterminancy
Different methods of estimation
Specification search

In this chapter we introduce the basic building blocks of SEM analyses, which follow a logical sequence of five steps or processes: model specification, model identification, model estimation, model testing, and model modification. In subsequent chapters, we further illustrate these five steps. These basic building blocks are absolutely essential to conducting SEM models.

4.1 Model Specification

Model specification involves using all of the available relevant theory, research, and information to develop a theoretical model. Thus, prior to any data collection or analysis, the researcher specifies a particular model that should be confirmed using variance–covariance data. In other words, available information is used to decide which variables to include in the theoretical model (which implicitly also involves which variables not to include in the model) and how these variables are related. *Model specification* involves determining every relationship and parameter in the model that is of interest to the researcher. Cooley (1978) indicated that this was the hardest part of structural equation modeling.

A given model is properly specified when the true population model is deemed consistent with the implied theoretical model being tested—that is, the sample covariance matrix S is sufficiently reproduced by the implied theoretical model. The goal of the applied researcher is, therefore, to determine the best possible model that generates the sample covariance matrix. The sample covariance matrix implies some underlying, yet unknown, theoretical model or structure (known as covariance structure), and the researcher's goal is to find the model that most closely fits that covariance structure. Take the simple example of a two-variable situation involving observed variables X and Y. We know from prior research that X and Y are highly correlated, but why? What theoretical relationship is responsible for this correlation? Does X influence Y, does Y influence X, or does a third variable Z influence both X and Y? There can be many possible reasons why X and Y are related in a particular fashion. The researcher needs prior research and theories to choose among plausible explanations and therefore provide the rationale for specifying a model—that is, testing an implied theoretical model (model specification).

Ultimately, an applied researcher wants to know the extent to which the true model that generated the data deviates from the implied theoretical model. If the true model is not consistent with the implied theoretical model, then the implied theoretical model is *misspecified*. The difference between the true model and the implied model may be due to errors of omission and/or inclusion of any variable or parameter. For example, an important parameter may have been omitted from the model tested (model did not indicate that X and Y are related), or an important variable may have been omitted (model did not include an important variable, such as amount of education or training). Likewise, an unimportant parameter and/or unimportant variable may have been included in the model, that is, there is an error of inclusion.

The exclusion or inclusion of unimportant variables will produce implied models that are misspecified. Why should we be concerned about this? The problem is that a misspecified model may result in biased parameter estimates, in other words, estimates that are systematically different from what they really are in the true model. This bias is known as *specification error*. In the presence of specification error, it is likely that one's theoretical model may not fit the data and be deemed statistically unacceptable (see *model testing* in section 4.4). There are a number of procedures available for the detection of specification error so that a more properly specified model may be evaluated. The *model modification* procedures are described in section 4.5.

4.2 Model Identification

In structural equation modeling, it is crucial that the researcher resolve the *identification problem* prior to the estimation of parameters. In the identification problem, we ask the following question: On the basis of the sample data contained in the sample covariance matrix S and the theoretical model implied by the population covariance matrix Σ, can a unique set of parameter estimates be found? For example, the theoretical model might suggest that $X + Y =$ some value, the data might indicate that $X + Y = 10$, and yet it may be that no unique solution for X and Y exists. One solution is that $X = 5$ and $Y = 5$, another is that $X = 2$ and $Y = 8$, and so on, because there are an infinite number of possible solutions for this problem, that is, there is an *indeterminacy* or the possibility that the data fits more than one implied theoretical model equally well. The problem is that there are not enough constraints on the model and the data to obtain unique estimates of X and Y. Therefore, if we wish to solve this problem, we need to impose some constraints. One such constraint might be to fix the value of X to 1; then Y would have to be 9. We have solved the identification problem in this instance by imposing one constraint. However, except for simplistic models, the solution to the identification problem in structural equation modeling is not so easy (although algebraically one can typically solve the problem).

Each potential parameter in a model must be specified to be either a free parameter, a fixed parameter, or a constrained parameter. A *free* parameter is a parameter that is unknown and therefore needs to be estimated. A *fixed* parameter is a parameter that is not free, but is fixed to a specified value, typically either 0 or 1. A *constrained* parameter is a parameter that is unknown, but is constrained to equal one or more other parameters.

Model identification depends on the designation of parameters as fixed, free, or constrained. Once the model is specified and the parameter specifications are indicated, the parameters are combined to form one and only one Σ (model implied variance–covariance matrix). The problem still exists, however, in that there may be several sets of parameter values that can form the same Σ. If two or more sets of parameter values generate the same Σ, then they are *equivalent*, that is, yield equivalent models (Lee & Hershberger, 1990; MacCallum, Wegener, Uchino, & Fabrigar, 1993; Raykov & Penev, 2001). If a parameter has the same value in all equivalent sets, then the parameter is identified. If all of the parameters of a model are identified, then the entire model is identified. If one or more of the parameters are not identified, then the entire model is not identified.

Traditionally, there have been three levels of model identification. They depend on the amount of information in the sample variance–covariance matrix S necessary for uniquely estimating the parameters of the model. The three levels of model identification are as follows:

1. A model is *under-identified* (or not identified) if one or more parameters may not be uniquely determined because there is not enough information in the matrix S.

2. A model is *just-identified* if all of the parameters are uniquely determined because there is just enough information in the matrix S.

3. A model is *over-identified* when there is more than one way of estimating a parameter (or parameters) because there is more than enough information in the matrix S.

If a model is either just- or over-identified, then the model is identified. If a model is under-identified, then the parameter estimates are not to be trusted, that is, the degrees of freedom for the model is negative. However, such a model may become identified if additional constraints are imposed, that is, the degrees of freedom equal 0 or greater than 0 (positive value).

There are several conditions for establishing the identification of a model. A necessary, but not the only sufficient condition for identification is the *order condition*, under which the number of free parameters to be estimated must be less than or equal to the number of distinct values in the matrix S, that is, only the diagonal variances and one set of off-diagonal covariance terms are counted. For example, because $s_{12} = s_{21}$ in the off-diagonal of the matrix, only one of these covariance terms is counted. The number of distinct values in the matrix S is equal to $p(p + 1)/2$, where p is the number of observed variables. The number of free parameters (saturated model—all paths) with the number of means = p is equal to $p(p + 1)/2 + p = p(p + 3)/2$ free parameters. For a sample matrix S with 3 observed variables, there are six distinct values [3(3 + 1)/2 = 6] and 9 free (independent) parameters [3(3 + 3)/2] that can be estimated. Consequently, the number of free parameters estimated in any theoretical implied model must be less than or equal to the number of distinct values in the S matrix. However, this is only one necessary condition for model identification; it does not by itself imply that the model is identified. For example, if the sample size is small (n = 10) relative to the number of variables (p = 20), then not enough information is available to estimate parameters in a saturated model. This explanation of the order condition is referred to as the "t rule" by Bollen (1989).

Whereas the *order condition* is easy to assess, other sufficient conditions are not—for example, the *rank condition*. The *rank condition* requires an algebraic determination of whether each parameter in the model can be estimated from the covariance matrix S. Unfortunately, proof of this rank condition is often problematic in practice, particularly for the applied researcher. However, there are some procedures that the applied researcher can use. For a more detailed discussion on the rank condition, we refer to Bollen (1989) or Jöreskog and Sörbom (1988). The basic concepts and a set of procedures to handle problems in model identification are discussed next and in subsequent chapters.

Three different methods for avoiding identification problems are available. The first method is in the measurement model, where we decide which observed variables measure each latent variable. Either one indicator for each latent variable must have a factor loading fixed to 1, or the variance of each latent variable must be fixed to 1. The reason for imposing these constraints is to set the measurement scale for each latent variable, primarily because of *indeterminacy* between the variance of the latent variable and the loadings of the observed variables on that latent variable. Utilizing either of these methods will eliminate the scale indeterminacy problem, but not necessarily the identification problem, and so additional constraints may be necessary.

The second method comes into play where reciprocal or nonrecursive structural models are used; such models are sometimes a source of the identification problem. A structural model is *recursive* when all of the structural relationships are unidirectional (two latent variables are not reciprocally related), that is, no feedback loops exist whereby a latent variable feeds back upon itself. *Nonrecursive* structural models include a reciprocal or bidirectional relationship, so that there is feedback—for example, models that allow product attitude and product interest to influence one another. For a nonrecursive model, ordinary least squares (OLS; see *model estimation* in section 4.3) is not an appropriate method of estimation.

The third method is to begin with a parsimonious (simple) model with a minimum number of parameters. The model should only include variables (parameters) considered to be absolutely crucial. If this model is identified, then you can consider including other parameters in subsequent models.

A second set of procedures involves methods for checking on the identification of a model. One method is Wald's (1950) rank test. A second, related method is described by Wiley (1973), Keesling (1972), and Jöreskog and Sörbom (1988). This test has to do with the inverse of the information matrix and is computed in LISREL. Unfortunately, these methods are not 100% reliable, and there is no general "necessary and sufficient" test available for the applied researcher to use. Our advice is to use whatever methods are available for identification. If you still suspect that there is an identification problem, follow the recommendation of Jöreskog and Sörbom (1988). The first step is to analyze the sample covariance matrix S and save the estimated population matrix Σ. The second step is to analyze the estimated population matrix Σ. If the model is identified, then the estimates from both analyses should be identical. Another option, often recommended, is to use different starting values in separate analyses. If the model is identified, then the estimates should be identical.

4.3 Model Estimation

In this section we examine different methods for estimating parameters in a model—that is, estimates of the population parameters in a structural equation model. We want to obtain estimates for each of the parameters specified in the model that produce the implied matrix Σ, such that the parameter values yield a matrix as close as possible to S, our sample covariance matrix of the observed or indicator variables. When elements in the matrix S minus the elements in the matrix Σ equal zero ($S - \Sigma = 0$), then $\chi^2 = 0$,—that is, one has a perfect model fit to the data.

The estimation process involves the use of a particular *fitting function* to minimize the difference between Σ and S. Several fitting functions or estimation procedures are available. Some of the earlier estimation methods included unweighted or ordinary least squares (ULS or OLS), generalized least squares (GLS), and maximum likelihood (ML).

The ULS estimates are consistent, have no distributional assumptions or associated statistical tests, and are scale dependent—that is, changes in observed variable scale yield different solutions or sets of estimates. In fact, of all the estimators described here, only the ULS estimation method is scale dependent. The GLS and ML methods are scale free, which means that if we transform the scale of one or more of our observed variables, the untransformed and transformed variables will yield estimates that are properly related—that is, that differ by the transformation. The GLS procedure involves a weight matrix W, such as S^{-1}, the inverse of the sample covariance matrix. Both GLS and ML estimation methods have desirable asymptotic properties—that is, large sample properties, such as minimum variance and unbiasedness. Also, both GLS and ML estimation methods assume multivariate normality of the observed variables (the sufficient conditions are that the observations are independent and identically distributed and that kurtosis is zero). The weighted-least squares (WLS) estimation method generally requires a large sample size and as a result is considered an asymptotically distribution-free (ADF) estimator, which does not depend on the normality assumption. Raykov and Widaman (1995) further discussed the use of ADF estimators.

If standardization of the latent variables is desired, one may obtain a standardized solution (and thereby standardized estimates), where the variances of the latent variables are fixed at 1 by adding the command line LISREL OUTPUT SS SC to the SIMPLIS program. A separate but related issue is standardization of the observed variables. When the unit of measurement for the indicator variables is of no particular interest to the researcher—that is, arbitrary or irrelevant—then only an analysis of the correlation matrix is typically of interest. The analysis of correlations usually gives correct chi-square goodness-of-fit values but estimates the standard errors incorrectly. There are ways to specify a model, analyze a correlation matrix, and obtain correct standard errors. For example, the SEPATH structural equation modeling program by Steiger (1995) does permit correlation matrix input and computes the correct standard errors. Since the correlation matrix involves a standardized scaling among the observed variables, the parameters estimated for the measurement model—for example, the factor loadings—will be of the same order of magnitude, that is, on the same scale. When the same indicator variables are measured either over time (longitudinal analysis), for multiple samples, or when equality constraints are imposed on two or more parameters, an analysis of the covariance matrix is appropriate and recommended so as to capitalize on the metric similarities of the variables (Lomax, 1982).

More recently, other estimation procedures have been developed for the analysis of covariance structure models. Beginning with LISREL, automatic starting values have been provided for all of the parameter estimates. These are referred to as *initial estimates* and involve a fast, noniterative procedure (unlike other methods such as ML, which is iterative). The initial estimates involve the instrumental variables and least-squares methods (ULS and two-stage least-squares method TSLS) developed by Hagglund (1982). Often, the user may wish to obtain only the initial estimates (for cost efficiency) or to use them as starting values in subsequent analyses. The initial estimates are consistent and rather efficient relative to the ML estimator, and have been shown, as in the case of the centroid method, to be considerably faster, especially in large-scale measurement models (Gerbing & Hamilton, 1994).

If one can assume multivariate normality of the observed variables, then moments beyond the second—that is, skewness and kurtosis—can be ignored. When the normality assumption is violated, parameter estimates and standard errors are suspect. One alternative is to use GLS, which assumes multivariate normality and stipulates that kurtosis be zero (Browne, 1974). Browne (1982, 1984) later recognized that the weight matrix of GLS may be modified to yield ADF or WLS estimates, standard errors, and test statistics. Others (Bentler, 1983; Shapiro, 1983) have developed more general classes of ADF estimators. All of these methods are based on the GLS method and specify that the weight matrix be of a certain form, although none of these methods takes multivariate kurtosis into account. Research by Browne (1984) suggests that goodness-of-fit indices and standard errors of parameter estimates derived under the assumption of multivariate normality should not be employed if the distribution of the observed variables has a nonzero value for kurtosis.

An implicit assumption of ML estimators is that information contained in the first and second order moments (mean, and variance, respectively) of the observed variables is sufficient so that information contained in higher-order moments (skewness and kurtosis) can be ignored. If the observed variables are interval scaled and multivariate normal, then the ML estimates, standard errors, and chi-square test are appropriate. However, if the observed variables are ordinal-scaled and/or extremely skewed or peaked (nonnormally distributed), then the ML estimates, standard errors, and chi-square test may not be robust.

The use of binary and ordinal response variables in structural equation modeling was pioneered by Muthén (1982, 1984). Muthén proposed a three-stage limited-information, GLS estimator that provided a large sample chi-square test of the model and large sample standard errors. The Muthén categorical variable methodology (CVM) is believed to produce more suitable coefficients of association than the ordinary Pearson product moment correlations and covariance applied to ordered categorical variables (Muthén, 1983). This is especially the case with markedly skewed categorical variables, where correlations must be adjusted to assume values throughout the −1 to +1 range, as is done in the PRELIS program.

The PRELIS computer program handles ordinal variables by computing a polychoric correlation for two ordinal variables (Olsson, 1979), and a polyserial correlation for an ordinal and an interval variable (Olsson, Drasgow, & Dorans, 1982), where the ordinal variables are assumed to have an underlying bivariate normal distribution, which is not necessary with the Muthén approach. All correlations (Pearson, polychoric, and polyserial) are then used by PRELIS to create an asymptotic covariance matrix for input into LISREL. The reader is cautioned to *not directly* use mixed types of correlation matrices or covariance matrices in a LISREL–SIMPLIS program, but instead use an asymptotic variance–covariance matrix produced by PRELIS along with the sample variance–covariance matrix as input in a LISREL–SIMPLIS or LISREL matrix program. The Satorra–Bentler scaled chi-square would then be reported for the robust model-fit measure.

During the past 15 or 20 years, we have seen considerable research on the behavior of methods of estimation under various conditions. The most crucial conditions are characterized by a lack of multivariate normality and interval level variables. When the data are generated from nonnormally distributed populations and/or represent discrete variables, the normal theory estimators of standard errors and model-fit indices discussed in chapter 5 could be suspect. However, recent simulation research by Lei and Lomax (2005) indicated that the ML and GLS estimators are quite comparable in the case of small to moderate nonnormality for interval data (bias is generally quite small and, in fact, ML tends to slightly outperform GLS). Similar results were obtained by Fan & Wang (1998). In the case of severe nonnormality for interval data, one of the distribution free or weighted procedures (ADF, WLS, or GLS) is recommended (Lomax, 1989). In dealing with noninterval variables, the research indicates that only when categorical data show small to moderate skewness and kurtosis values (range of −1 to +1, or −1.5 to +1.5) should ML be used. When these conditions are not met, several options already mentioned are recommended. These include the use of tetrachoric, polyserial, and polychoric correlations rather than Pearson product-moment correlations, or the use of distribution-free or weighted procedures available in the SEM software. Considerable research remains to be conducted to determine what the optimal estimation procedure is for a given set of conditions. In summary, we recommend the use of ML estimation for slight to moderate nonnormal interval and ordinal data, and ADF, WLS, or GLS estimation for severely nonnormal interval and ordinal data.

4.4 Model Testing

Once the parameter estimates are obtained for a specified SEM model, the researcher should determine how well the data fit the model. In other words, to what extent is the theoretical model supported by the obtained sample data? There are two ways to think about model fit. The first is to consider some global type omnibus test of the fit of the entire model. The second is to examine the fit of individual parameters in the model.

We first consider the global tests in SEM known as model-fit criteria. Unlike many statistical procedures that have a single, most powerful fit index—for example, F test in ANOVA—in SEM there are an increasingly large number of model-fit indices. Many of these measures are based on a comparison of the model implied covariance matrix Σ to the sample covariance matrix S. If Σ and S are similar in some fashion, then one may say that the data fit the theoretical model. If Σ and S are quite different, then one may say that the data do not fit the theoretical model. We explain model-fit indices in more detail in chapter 5.

Second, we consider the individual parameters of the model. Three main features of the individual parameters can be considered. One feature is whether a free parameter is significantly different from zero. Once parameter estimates are obtained, standard errors for each estimate are also computed. A ratio of the parameter estimate to the estimated standard error can be formed as a *critical value*, which is assumed to be normally distributed (unit normal distribution)—that is, the critical value equals the parameter estimate divided by the standard error of the parameter estimate. If the *critical value* exceeds the expected value at a specified α level—for example, $\alpha = .05$, two tailed test, tabled $t = 1.96$—then that parameter is significantly different from zero. The parameter estimate, standard error, and critical value are routinely provided in the computer output for a model. A second feature is whether the sign of the parameter agrees with what is expected from the theoretical model. For example, if the expectation is that more education will yield a higher income level, then an estimate with a positive sign would support that expectation. A third feature is that parameter estimates should make sense—that is, they should be within an expected range of values. For instance, variances should not have negative values and correlations should not exceed 1. Thus, all free parameters should be in the expected direction, be statistically different from zero, and be meaningfully interpreted.

4.5 Model Modification

If the fit of the implied theoretical model is not as strong as one would like (which is typically the case with an initial model), then the next step is to modify the model and subsequently evaluate the new modified model. In order to determine how to modify the model, there are a number of procedures available for the detection of specification errors so that more properly specified alternative models may be evaluated during respecification process. In general, these procedures are used for performing what is called a *specification search* (Leamer, 1978). The purpose of a specification search is to alter the original model in the search for a model that is better fitting in some sense and yields parameters having practical significance and substantive meaning. If a parameter has no substantive meaning to the applied researcher, then it should never be included in a model. Substantive interest must be the guiding force in a specification search; otherwise, the resultant model will not have practical value or importance. There are procedures designed to detect and correct for specification errors. Typically, applications of structural equation modeling include some type of specification search, informal or formal, although the search process may not always be explicitly stated in a research report.

An obvious intuitive method is to consider the statistical significance of each parameter estimated in the model. One specification strategy would be to fix parameters that are not statistically significant—that is, have small *critical values,* to 0 in a subsequent model. Care should be taken, however, because statistical significance is related to power and sample size (see chapter 5); parameters may not be significant with small samples but significant with larger samples. Also, substantive theoretical interests must be considered. If a parameter is not significant, but is of sufficient substantive interest, then the parameter should probably remain in the model. The guiding rule should be that the parameter estimates make sense to you. If an estimate makes no sense to you, how are you going to explain it, how is it going to be of substantive value or meaningful?

Another intuitive method of examining misspecification is to examine the residual matrix, that is, the differences between the observed covariance matrix S and the model-implied covariance matrix Σ; these are referred to as fitted residuals in the LISREL program output. These values should be small in magnitude and should not be larger for one variable than another. Large values overall indicate serious general model misspecification, whereas large values for a single variable indicate misspecification for that variable only, probably in the structural model (Bentler, 1989). Standardized or normalized residuals can also be examined. Theoretically, these can be treated like standardized z scores, and hence problems can be more easily detected from the standardized residual matrix than from the unstandardized residual matrix. Large standardized residuals (larger than, say, 1.96 or 2.58) indicate that a particular covariance structure is not well explained by the model. The model should be examined to determine ways in which this particular covariance structure could be explained, for example, by freeing some parameters in the model.

Sörbom (1975) considered misspecification of correlated measurement error terms in the analysis of longitudinal data. Sörbom proposed considering the first order partial derivatives, which have values of zero for free parameters and nonzero values for fixed parameters. The largest value, in absolute terms, indicates the fixed parameter most likely to improve model fit. A second model, with this parameter now free, is then estimated and goodness of fit assessed. Sörbom defines an acceptable fit as occurring when the difference between the two model chi-square values is not significant. The derivatives of the second model are examined, and the process continues until an acceptable fit is achieved. This procedure, however, is restricted to the derivatives of the observed variables and provides indications of misspecification only in terms of correlated measurement error.

More recently, other procedures have been developed to examine model specification. In the LISREL–SIMPLIS program, modification indices are reported for all nonfree parameters. These indices were developed by Sörbom (1986) and represent an improvement over the first order partial derivatives already described. A modification index for a particular nonfree parameter indicates that if this parameter were allowed to become free in a subsequent model, then the chi-square goodness-of-fit value would be predicted to decrease by at least the value of the modification index. In other words, if the value of the modification index for a nonfree parameter is 50, then when this parameter is allowed to be free in a subsequent model, the value of chi-square will decrease by at least 50. Thus, modification indices would suggest ways that the model might be altered by allowing the corresponding parameters to become free to be estimated with the researcher arriving at a better fitting model. As reported in an earlier LISREL manual (Jöreskog & Sörbom, 1988), "This procedure seems to work well in practice" (p. 44).

The LISREL program also provides squared multiple correlations for the observed variables in the measurement equations. These values indicate how well the observed variables serve as measures of the latent variables (reliability measure) and are scaled from 0 to 1. Squared multiple correlations are also given for the variables in the structural equations. These values serve as an indication of the strength of the structural relationships (prediction measure) and are also scaled from 0 to 1.

A relatively new index, the *expected parameter change*, now appears in the LISREL program computer output. The expected parameter change

(EPC) statistic in the LISREL program computer output indicates the estimated change in the magnitude and direction of each nonfree parameter if set free to be estimated (rather than the predicted change in the goodness-of-fit test as with the modification indices). This could be useful, for example, if the sign of the potential free parameter is not in the expected direction (positive instead of negative). This would suggest that such a parameter should remain fixed.

Empirical research suggests that specification searches are most successful when the model tested is very similar to the model that generated the data. More specifically, these studies begin with a known true model from which sample data are generated. The true model is then intentionally misspecified. The goal of the specification search is to begin with the misspecified model and determine whether the true model can be located as a result of the search. If the misspecified model is more than two or three parameters different from the true model, then it is difficult to locate the true model. Unfortunately, in these studies the true model was almost never located through the specification search, regardless of the search procedure or combination of procedures that were used (Gallini, 1983; Gallini & Mandeville, 1984; Saris & Stronkhorst, 1984; MacCallum, 1986; Baldwin & Lomax, 1990; Tippets, 1992).

What is clear is that there is no single existing procedure sufficient for finding a properly specified model. As a result, there has been a flurry of research in recent years to determine what combination of procedures is most likely to yield a properly specified model (Chou & Bentler, 1990; Herbing & Costner, 1985; Kaplan, 1988, 1989, 1990; MacCallum, 1986; Saris, Satorra & Sörbom, 1987; Satorra & Saris, 1985; Silvia & MacCallum, 1988). No optimal strategy has been found. A computer program known as TETRAD was developed by Glymour, Scheines, Spirtes, and Kelly (1987), and the new version, TETRAD II (Spirtes, Scheines, Meek, & Glymour, 1994), thoughtfully reviewed by Wood (1995), offers new search procedures. A newer specification search procedure, known as Tabu, recently developed by Marcoulides, Drezner, and Schumacker (1998) can today readily provide a set of optimum models. If one selected all of the paths in the model as optional, then all possible models would be listed; for example, a multiple regression equation with 17 independent variables and 1 dependent variable would yield 2^{17} or 131,072 regression models, not all of which would be theoretically meaningful. Selection of the "best" equation would require the use of some fit criteria for comparing models. Applying Tabu in SEM, for example, $\chi^2 - df$, AIC, or BIC would be used for selecting best models. Current modeling software permits the formulation of all possible models; however, the outcome of any specification search should still be guided by theory and practical considerations as well as the time and cost of acquiring the data.

Given our lengthy discussion about specification search procedures, some practical advice is warranted for the researcher. The following is our suggested eight-step procedure for a specification search:

1. Let substantive theory and prior research guide your model specification.

2. When you are satisfied that Rule 1 has been met, test your implied theoretical model and move to Rule 3.

3. Conduct a specification search, first on the measurement model, and then on the structural model.

4. For each model tested, look to see if the parameters are of the expected magnitude and direction, and examine several appropriate goodness-of-fit indices.

   Steps 5 through 7 can be followed in an iterative fashion. For example, you might go from Step 5 to Step 6, and successively on to Steps 7, 6, 5, and so on.

5. Examine the statistical significance of the nonfixed parameters. Look to see if any nonfixed parameters should be fixed in a subsequent model.

6. Examine the modification indices, expected parameter change statistics. Look to see if any fixed parameters should be freed in a subsequent model.

7. Consider examining the standardized residual matrix to see if anything suspicious is occurring (larger values for a particular observed variable).

8. Once you determine a final acceptable model, cross-validate it with a new sample, or use half of the sample to find a properly specified model and use the other half to check it (cross-validation index, or CVI), or report a single sample cross-validation index (ECVI) for alternative models (Cudeck & Browne, 1983; Kroonenberg & Lewis, 1982). Cross-validation procedures are discussed in chapter 12.

4.6 Summary

In this chapter we considered the basics of structural equation modeling. The chapter began with a look at model specification (fixed, free, and constrained parameters) and then moved on to model identification (under-, just-, and over-identified models). Next, we discussed the various types of estimation procedures. Here we considered each estimation method, its underlying assumptions, and some general guidelines as to when each is appropriate. We then moved on to a general discussion of model testing, where the fit of a given model is assessed. Finally, we described the specification search process, where information is used to arrive at a more properly specified model that is theoretically meaningful. Troubleshooting tips summarizing these key issues are provided in Box 4.1.

BOX 4.1   TROUBLESHOOTING TIPS

Issue	Suggestions
Identification problem	Solutions include fixing parameters (either latent variable variances or one factor loading for each latent variable), avoiding nonrecursive models, utilizing parsimonious models, or determining if a positive degree of freedom exists when subtracting total number of elements in matrix from number of free parameters to be estimated in the model.
Estimation method	For normal and slight to moderate nonnormal interval and ordinal data, use ML; otherwise consider WLS, ADF, GLS, or CVM methods.
Specification search	Examine the statistical significance of free parameters, standardized residuals, modification indices, goodness-of-fit indices, squared multiple correlations, as well as expected parameter change.

In chapter 5, we discuss the numerous goodness-of-fit indices in the LISREL computer output to determine whether a model is parsimonious, which alternative models are better, and to examine submodels (nested models). We classify the model-fit indices according to whether a researcher is testing model fit, seeking a more parsimonious model (complex to simple), or comparing nested models. In addition, we discuss hypothesis testing, parameter significance, power, and sample size, as these affect our interpretation of model fit and statistical significance of parameter estimates.

Exercises

1. Define model specification.
2. Define model identification.
3. Define model estimation.
4. Define model testing.

5. Define model modification.
6. Determine the number of distinct values (variances and covariances) in the following variance–covariance matrix S:

$$S = \begin{bmatrix} 1.0 & & \\ .25 & 1.0 & \\ .35 & .45 & 1.00 \end{bmatrix}$$

7. How many distinct values are in a variance–covariance matrix for the following variables {hint: $[p(p + 1)/2]$}:
   a. Five variables
   b. Ten variables

8. A saturated model with p variables has $p(p + 3)/2$ free parameters. Determine the number of free parameters for the following number of variables in a model:
   a. Three observed variables
   b. Five observed variables
   c. Ten observed variables

References

Baldwin, B., & Lomax, R. G. (1990). *Measurement model specification error in LISREL structural equation models.* Paper presented at the annual meeting of the American Educational Research Association, Boston.

Bentler, P. M. (1983). Some contributions to efficient statistics in structural models: Specification and estimation of moment structures. *Psychometrika, 48,* 493–517.

Bentler, P. M. (1989). *Theory and implementation of EQS: A structural equations program.* Los Angeles: BMDP Statistical Software.

Bollen, K. A. (1989). *Structural equations with latent variables.* New York: Wiley.

Browne, M. W. (1974). Generalized least-squares estimators in the analysis of covariance structures. *South African Statistical Journal, 8,* 1–24.

Browne, M. W. (1982). Covariance structures. In D. M. Hawkins (Ed.), *Topics in applied multivariate analysis* (pp. 72–141). Cambridge: Cambridge University Press.

Browne, M. W. (1984). Asymptotically distribution-free methods for the analysis of covariance structures. *British Journal of Mathematical and Statistical Psychology, 37,* 62–83.

Chou, C. -P., & Bentler, P. M. (1990). *Power of the likelihood ratio, Lagrange multiplier, and Wald tests for model modification in covariance structure analysis.* Paper presented at the annual meeting of the American Educational Research Association, Boston.

Cooley, W. W. (1978). Explanatory observational studies. *Educational Researcher, 7*(9), 9–15.

Cudeck, R., & Browne, M. W. (1983). Cross-validation of covariance structures. *Multivariate Behavioral Research, 18,* 147–167.

Fan, X., & Wang, L. (1998). Effects of potential confounding factors on fit indices and parameter estimates for true and misspecified models. *Structural Equation Modeling: A Multidisciplinary Journal, 5,* 701–735.

Gallini, J. K. (1983). Misspecifications that can result in path analysis structures. *Applied Psychological Measurement, 7,* 125–137.

Gallini, J. K., & Mandeville, G. K. (1984). An investigation of the effect of sample size and specification error on the fit of structural equation models. *Journal of Experimental Education, 53,* 9–19.

Gerbing, D. W., & Hamilton, J. G. (1994). The surprising viability of a simple alternate estimation procedure for construction of large-scale structural equation measurement models. *Structural Equation Modeling: A Multidisciplinary Journal, 1,* 103–115.

Glymour, C. R., Scheines, R., Spirtes, P., & Kelly, K. (1987). *Discovering causal structure.* Orlando: Academic.

Hagglund, G. (1982). Factor analysis by instrumental variable methods. *Psychometrika, 47,* 209–222.

Herbing, J. R., & Costner, H. L. (1985). Respecification in multiple indicator models. In H. M. Blalock, Jr. (Ed.), *Causal models in the social sciences* (2nd ed., pp. 321–393). New York: Aldine.

Jöreskog, K. G., & Sörbom, D. (1988). *LISREL 7: A guide to the program and applications.* Chicago: SPSS.

Kaplan, D. (1988). The impact of specification error on the estimation, testing, and improvement of structural equation models. *Multivariate Behavioral Research, 23,* 69–86.

Kaplan, D. (1989). Model modification in covariance structure analysis: Application of the parameter change statistic. *Multivariate Behavioral Research, 24,* 285–305.

Kaplan, D. (1990). Evaluating and modifying covariance structure models: A review and recommendation. *Multivariate Behavioral Research, 25,* 137–155.

Keesling, J. W. (1972). *Maximum likelihood approaches to causal flow analysis.* Unpublished dissertation. University of Chicago, Department of Education.

Kroonenberg, P. M., & Lewis, C. (1982). Methodological issues in the search for a factor model: Exploration through confirmation. *Journal of Educational Statistics, 7,* 69–89.

Leamer, E. E. (1978). *Specification searches.* New York: Wiley.

Lee, S., & Hershberger, S. (1990). A simple rule for generating equivalent models in covariance structure modeling. *Multivariate Behavioral Research, 25,* 313–334.

Lei, M., & Lomax, R. G. (2005). The effect of varying degrees of nonnormality in structural equation modeling. *Structural Equation Modeling: A Multidisciplinary Journal, 12,* 1–27.

Lomax, R. G. (1982). A guide to LISREL-type structural equation modeling. *Behavior Research Methods & Instrumentation, 14*, 1–8.

Lomax, R. G. (1989). Covariance structure analysis: Extensions and developments. In B. Thompson (Ed.), *Advances in social science methodology* (Vol. 1, pp. 171–204). Greenwich, CT: JAI.

MacCallum, R. C. (1986). Specification searches in covariance structure modeling. *Psychological Bulletin, 100*, 107–120.

MacCallum, R. C., Wegener, D. T., Uchino, B. N., & Fabrigar, L. R. (1993). The problem of equivalent models in applications of covariance structure analysis. *Psychological Bulletin, 114*, 185–199.

Marcoulides, G. A., Drezner, Z., & Schumacker, R. E. (1998). Model specification searches in structural equation modeling using Tabu search. *Structural Equation Modeling: A Multidisciplinary Journal, 5*, 365–376.

Muthén, B. (1982). Some categorical response models with continuous latent variables. In K. G. Jöreskog & H. Wold (Eds.), *Systems under indirect observation: Causality, structure, prediction, Part I* (pp. 65–79). Amsterdam: North-Holland.

Muthén, B. (1983). Latent variable structural equation modeling with categorical data. *Journal of Econometrics, 22*, 43–65.

Muthén, B. (1984). A general structural equation model with dichotomous, ordered categorical, and continuous latent variable indicators. *Psychometrika, 49*, 115–132.

Olsson, U. (1979). Maximum likelihood estimation of the polychoric correlation coefficient. *Psychometrika, 44*, 443–460.

Olsson, U., Drasgow, F., & Dorans, N. J. (1982). The polyserial correlation coefficient. *Psychometrika, 47*, 337–347.

Raykov, T., & Penev, S. (2001). The problem of equivalent structural equation models: An individual residual perspective. In G. A. Marcoulides & R. E. Schumacker (Eds.), *New developments and techniques in structural equation modeling* (pp. 297–321). Mahwah, NJ: Lawrence Erlbaum.

Raykov, T., & Widaman, K. F. (1995). Issues in applied structural equation modeling research. *Structural Equation Modeling: A Multidisciplinary Journal, 2*, 289–318.

Saris, W. E., Satorra, A., & Sörbom, D. (1987). The detection and correction of specification errors in structural equation models. In C. C. Clogg (Ed.), *Sociological methodology* (pp. 105–130). Washington, DC: American Sociological Association.

Saris, W. E., & Stronkhorst, L. H. (1984). *Causal modeling in nonexperimental research: An introduction to the LISREL approach.* Amsterdam: Sociometric Research Foundation.

Satorra, A., & Saris, W. E. (1985). Power of the likelihood ratio test in covariance structure analysis. *Psychometrika, 50*, 83–90.

Shapiro, A. (1983). Asymptotic distribution theory in the analysis of covariance structures (a unified approach). *South African Statistical Journal, 17*, 33–81.

Silvia, E. S. M., & MacCallum, R. (1988). Some factors affecting the success of specification searches in covariance structure modeling. *Multivariate Behavioral Research, 23*, 297–326.

Sörbom, D. (1975). Detection of correlated errors in longitudinal data. *British Journal of Mathematical and Statistical Psychology, 27*, 229–239.

Sörbom, D. (1986). *Model modification* (Research Report 86-3). University of Uppsala, Department of Statistics, Uppsala, Sweden.

Spirtes, P., Scheines, R., Meek, C., & Glymour, C. (1994). *TETRAD II: Tools for causal modeling.* Hillsdale, NJ: Lawrence Erlbaum.

Steiger, J. H. (1995). SEPATH. In STATISTICA 5.0. Tulsa, OK: StatSoft.

Tippets, E. (1992). *A comparison of methods for evaluating and modifying covariance structure models.* Paper presented at the annual meeting of the American Educational Research Association, San Francisco.

Wald, A. (1950). A note on the identification of economic relations. In T. C. Koopmans (Ed.), *Statistical inference in dynamic economic models* (pp. 238–244). New York: Wiley.

Wiley, D. E. (1973). The identification problem for structural equation models with unmeasured variables. In A. S. Goldberger & O. D. Duncan (Eds.), *Structural equation models in the social sciences* (pp. 69–83). New York: Seminar.

Wood, P. K. (1995). Toward a more critical examination of structural equation models. *Structural Equation Modeling: A Multidisciplinary Journal, 2,* 277–287.

5

Model Fit

Key Concepts

Confirmatory models, alternative models, model generating

Specification search

Saturated models and independence models

Model fit, model comparison, and model parsimony fit indices

Measurement model versus structural model interpretation

Model and parameter significance

Power and sample size determination

In chapter 4, we considered the basic building blocks of SEM, namely, model specification, model identification, model estimation, model testing, and model modification. These five steps fall into three main approaches for going from theory to a SEM model in which the covariance structure among variables is analyzed. In the confirmatory approach, a researcher hypothesizes a specific theoretical model, gathers data, and then tests whether the data fit the model. In this approach, the theoretical model is either confirmed or disconfirmed, based on a chi-square statistical test of significance and/or meeting acceptable model-fit criteria. In the second approach using alternative models, the researcher creates a limited number of theoretically different models to determine which model the data fit best. When these models use the same data set, they are referred to as nested models. The alternative approach conducts a chi-square difference test to compare each of the alternative models. The third approach, model generating, specifies an initial model (theoretical model), but usually the data do not fit this initial model at an acceptable model-fit criterion level, so modification indices are used to add or delete paths in the model to arrive at a final best model. The goal in model generating is to find a model that the data fit well statistically, but that also has practical and substantive theoretical meaning. The process of finding the best-fitting model is also referred to as a specification search, implying that if an initially specified model does not fit the data, then the model is modified in an effort to improve the fit (Marcoulides & Drezner, 2001; 2003). Recent advances in *Tabu search algorithms* have permitted the generation of a set of models that the data fit equally well with a final determination by the researcher of which model to accept (Marcoulides, Drezner, & Schumacker, 1998).

5.1 Types of Model-Fit Criteria

Finding a statistically significant theoretical model that also has practical and substantive meaning is the primary goal of using structural equation modeling to test theories. A researcher typically uses the following three criteria in judging the statistical significance and substantive meaning of a theoretical model:

1. The first criterion is the nonstatistical significance of the chi-square test and the root-mean-square error of approximation (RMSEA) values, which are global fit measures. A nonstatistically significant chi-square value indicates that the sample covariance matrix and the reproduced model implied covariance matrix are similar. A RMSEA value less than or equal to .05 is considered acceptable.

2. The second criterion is the statistical significance of individual parameter estimates for the paths in the model, which are values computed by dividing the parameter estimates by their respective standard errors. This is referred to as a *t* value, and is typically compared to a tabled *t* value of 1.96 at the .05 level of significance (two-tailed). [*Note*: LISREL 8.8 student version now reports the standard error, z-value, and p-value for each parameter.]

3. The third criterion is the magnitude and direction of the parameter estimates, paying particular attention to whether a positive or negative coefficient makes sense for the parameter estimate. For example, it would not be theoretically meaningful to have a negative parameter (coefficient) relating number of hours spent studying and grade point average.

We now describe the numerous criteria for assessing model fit, and offer suggestions on how and when these criteria might be used. Determining model fit is complicated because several model-fit criteria have been developed to assist in interpreting structural equation models under different model-building assumptions. In addition, the determination of model fit in structural equation modeling is not as straightforward as it is in other statistical approaches in multivariable procedures, such as the analysis of variance, multiple regression, discriminant analysis, multivariate analysis of variance, and canonical correlation analysis. These multivariable methods use observed variables that are assumed to be measured without error and have statistical tests with known distributions. Many SEM model-fit indices have no single statistical test of significance that identifies a correct model, given the sample data, especially since *equivalent models* or *alternative models* can exist that yield exactly the same data to model fit.

Chi-square (χ^2) is the only statistical test of significance for testing the theoretical model (see Table 5.1 for fit indices and their interpretation). The chi-square value ranges from zero for a saturated model with all paths included to a maximum value for the independence model with no paths included. The theoretical model chi-square value lies somewhere between these two extremes. This can be visualized as follows:

Saturated model   ⟷   Independence model
(all paths in model)   (no paths in model)
$\chi^2 = 0$ $\chi^2 = $ maximum value

A chi-square value of zero indicates a perfect fit or no difference between values in the sample covariance matrix S and the reproduced implied covariance matrix Σ that was created, based on the specified (implied) theoretical model. Obviously, a theoretical model in SEM with all paths specified is of limited interest (saturated model). The goal in structural equation modeling is to achieve a parsimonious model with a few substantive meaningful paths and a nonsignificant chi-square value close to the saturated model value of zero, thus indicating little difference between the sample covariance matrix and the reproduced implied covariance matrix. The difference between these two covariance matrices is output in a residual matrix (add command line Print Residual to SIMPLIS program). When the chi-square value is nonsignificant (close to zero), residual values in the residual matrix are close to zero, indicating that the theoretical implied model fits the sample data, hence there is little difference between the sample covariance matrix and the model implied (reproduced) covariance matrix.

Many of the model-fit criteria are computed-based on knowledge of the saturated model, independence model, sample size, degrees of freedom, and/or the chi-square values to formulate an index of model fit that ranges in value from 0 (no fit) to 1 (perfect fit). These various model-fit indices, however, are subjectively interpreted when determining an acceptable model fit. Some researchers have suggested that a structural equation model with a model-fit value of .90 or .95 or higher is acceptable (Baldwin, 1989; Bentler & Bonett, 1980), whereas more recently a noncentrality parameter close to zero [NCP = max(0, $\chi^2 - df$)] has been suggested

TABLE 5.1

Model-Fit Criteria and Acceptable Fit Interpretation

Model-Fit Criterion	Acceptable Level	Interpretation
Chi-square	Tabled χ^2 value	Compares obtained χ^2 value with tabled value for given *df*
Goodness-of-fit index (GFI)	0 (no fit) to 1 (perfect fit)	Value close to .90 or .95 reflect a good fit
Adjusted GFI (AGFI)	0 (no fit) to 1 (perfect fit)	Value adjusted for *df*, with .90 or .95 a good model fit
Root-mean square residual (RMR)	Researcher defines level	Indicates the closeness of Σ to *S* matrices
Standardized RMR (SRMR)	< .05	Value less than .05 indicates a good model fit
Root-mean-square error of approximation (RMSEA)	.05 to .08	Value of .05 to .08 indicate close fit
Tucker–Lewis Index (TLI)	0 (no fit) to 1 (perfect fit)	Value close to .90 or .95 reflects a good model fit
Normed fit index (NFI)	0 (no fit) to 1 (perfect fit)	Value close to .90 or .95 reflects a good model fit
Parsimony fit index (PNFI)	0 (no fit) to 1 (perfect fit)	Compares values in alternative models
Akaike information criterion (AIC)	0 (perfect fit) to positive value (poor fit)	Compares values in alternative models

(Browne & Cudeck, 1993; Steiger, 1990). The various structural equation modeling programs report a variety of model-fit criteria, and thus only those output by LISREL are shown in this chapter. It is recommended that various model-fit criteria be used in combination to assess *model fit, model comparison,* and *model parsimony* as global fit measures (Hair, Anderson, Tatham, & Black, 1992).

Some of the fit indices are computed given knowledge of the null model χ^2 (independence model, where the covariance terms are assumed to be zero in the model), null model *df*, hypothesized model χ^2, hypothesized model *df*, number of observed variables in the model, number of free parameters in the model, and sample size. The formula for the goodness-of-fit index (GFI), normed fit index (NFI), relative fit index (RFI), incremental fit index (IFI), Tucker-Lewis index (TLI), comparative fit index (CFI), model AIC, null AIC, and RMSEA using these values are as follows:

$$GFI = 1 - [\chi^2_{model}/\chi^2_{null}]$$
$$NFI = (\chi^2_{null} - \chi^2_{model})/\chi^2_{null}$$
$$RFI = 1 - [(\chi^2_{model}/df_{model})/(\chi^2_{null}/df_{null})]$$
$$IFI = (\chi^2_{null} - \chi^2_{model})/(\chi^2_{null} - df_{model})$$
$$TLI = [(\chi^2_{null}/df_{null}) - (\chi^2_{model}/df_{model})]/[(\chi^2_{null}/df_{null}) - 1]$$
$$CFI = 1 - [(\chi^2_{model} - df_{model})/(\chi^2_{null} - df_{null})]$$

Model AIC = χ^2_{model} + 2q (number of free parameters)

Null AIC = χ^2_{null} + 2q (number of free parameters)

$$RMSEA = \sqrt{[\chi^2_{Model} - df_{Model}]/[(N-1)df_{Model}]}$$

These model-fit statistics can also be expressed in terms of the noncentrality parameter (NCP), designated by λ. The estimate of NCP (λ) using the maximum likelihood chi-square is $\chi^2 - df$. A simple substitution reexpresses these model-fit statistics using NCP. For example, CFI, TLI, and RMSEA are as follows:

CFI = 1 – [$\lambda_{Model}/\lambda_{Null}$]

TLI = 1 – [$(\lambda_{Model}/df_{Model})/(\lambda_{Null}/df_{Null})$]

$$RMSEA = \sqrt{\lambda_{Model}/[(N-1)df_{Model}]}$$

Bollen and Long (1993), as well as Hu and Bentler (1995), have thoroughly discussed several issues related to model fit, and we recommend reading their assessments of how model-fit indices are affected by small sample bias, estimation methods, violation of normality and independence, and model complexity, and for an overall discussion of the various model-fit indices.

5.1.1 LISREL–SIMPLIS Example

Our purpose in this chapter is to better understand the model-fit criteria output by LISREL–SIMPLIS. The theoretical model in Figure 5.1a is analyzed to aid in the understanding of model-fit criteria, significance of parameter estimates, and power and sample size determination. The theoretical basis for this model is discussed in more detail in chapter 8. The two factor confirmatory model is based on data from Holzinger and Swineford (1939) using data collected on 26 psychological tests from 301 children in a suburban school district of Chicago. Over the years, different subsamples of the children and different subsets of the variables in this dataset have been analyzed and presented in various multivariate statistics textbooks (Gorsuch, 1983; Harmon, 1976), and SEM software program guide (Jöreskog & Sörbom, 1993, example 5, pp. 2–28). For our analysis, we used data on the first six psychological variables for all 301 subjects. The theoretical model is depicted in Figure 5.1a.

5.1.1.1 Data

The LISREL program can easily import many different file types. To import the SPSS data file *holz.sav*, simply click on **File**, then select **Import Data**. Next select **SPSS for Windows(*.sav)** from the pull-down menu for **Files of type:** and then select **HOLZ** data file. (*Note:* The data file may be in a different location, so you may have to search to locate it).

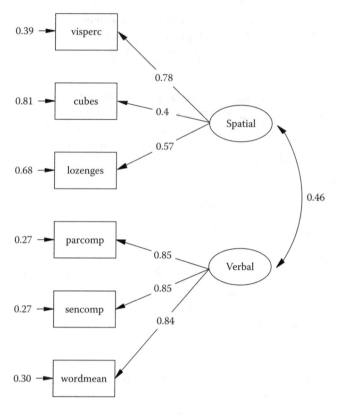

FIGURE 5.1a

Common factor model. (From Holzinger, K. J., & Swineford, F. A. [1939]. *A study in factor analysis: The stability of a bi-factor solution.* Supplementary Educational Monographs, No. 48. Chicago: University of Chicago, Dept. of Education.)

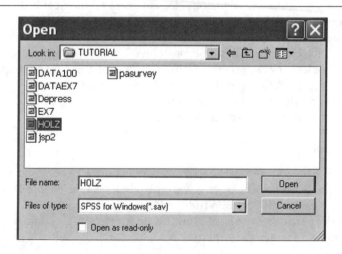

After clicking on **Open**, a *Save As* dialog box appears to save a PRELIS System File, so enter *holz.psf*.

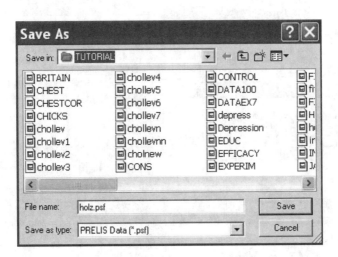

A spreadsheet should appear that contains the variable names and data. Also, an expanded tool bar menu appears that begins with File, includes Edit, Data, Transformation, Statistics, Graphs, etc., and ends with the Help command. The **File** command also permits the use of an **Export LISREL** *Data* option. The **File**, then **Import Data** option should be used to save a PRELIS System File whenever possible to take advantage of data screening, imputing missing values, computation of normal scores, output data options, and many other features in LISREL–PRELIS. For our purposes, click on **Statistics**, then select the **Output** *Options*. The *Output* dialog box will be used to save a correlation matrix file (*holz.cor*), a means file (*holz.me*), and standard deviations file (*holz.sd*) for the variables we will use to analyze our theoretical model in Figure 5.1a. The correlation, means, and standard deviation files must be saved (or moved) to the same directory as the LISREL–SIMPLIS program file. Click **OK** and descriptive statistics appear in the computer output (frequencies, means, standard deviations, skewness, kurtosis, etc.).

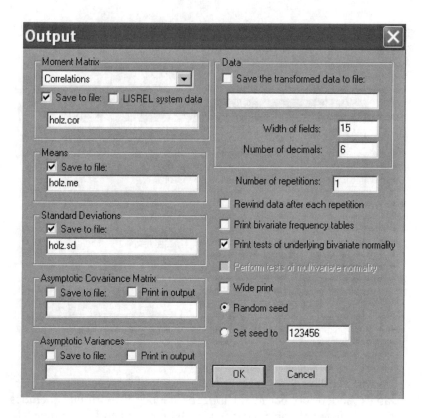

5.1.1.2 Program

The next step is to create the LISREL–SIMPLIS program syntax file that will specify the model analysis for Figure 5.1a. This is accomplished by selecting **File** on the tool bar, then clicking on **New**, select **Syntax Only**, and then enter the program syntax. If you forget the SIMPLIS program syntax, refer to the LISREL–SIMPLIS manual or modify an existing program. We created a LISREL–SIMPLIS program named *holz.spl* that contains the following program syntax. (*Note*: The first three observed variables listed— gender, ageyear, and birthmon—are contained in the raw data, but are not analyzed in the SEM model.)

```
LISREL Figure 5.1a Program
Observed Variables
 gender ageyear birthmon visperc cubes lozenges parcomp    C
sencomp wordmean
Correlation matrix from file holz.cor
Means from file holz.me
Standard deviations from file holz.sd
Sample Size 301
```

```
Latent Variables
 Spatial Verbal
Relationships
 visperc - lozenges = Spatial
 parcomp - wordmean = Verbal
Number of decimals = 5
Path Diagram
End of Problem
```

Select **File**, then **Save As**, to save the file as *holz.spl* (SIMPLIS file type).

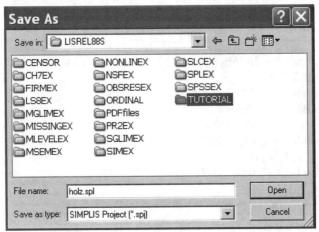

You are now ready to run the analysis using the *holz.spl* file you just cre-ated. Click on the running **L** on the tool bar menu and the ASCII text file *holz.out* will appear. The LISREL–SIMPLIS output file will contain several model-fit indices; however, a LISREL–SIMPLIS program (*holz.spl*) and a LISREL8 command program (*holz.ls8*) will report and use different chi-square fit values in the model-fit indices—that is, the minimum fit func-tion chi-square (C1), the normal theory weighted least-squares fit function (C2), the Satorra–Bentler scaled chi-square (C3), and the Browne adjusted chi-square (C4) (see chapter note in Power and Sample Size section for more detail).

5.1.1.3 Output

5.1.1.3.1 Goodness-of-Fit Statistics—Original Model

Degrees of Freedom = 8
Minimum Fit Function Chi-Square = 24.28099 (P = 0.0020559)
Normal Theory Weighted Least Squares Chi-Square = 24.40679
    (P = 0.0019581)
Estimated Noncentrality Parameter (NCP) = 16.40679
90 Percent Confidence Interval for NCP = (5.18319 ; 35.23399)

Minimum Fit Function Value = 0.080937
Population Discrepancy Function Value (F0) = 0.054689
90 Percent Confidence Interval for F0 = (0.017277 ; 0.11745)
Root Mean Square Error of Approximation (RMSEA) = 0.082681
90 Percent Confidence Interval for RMSEA = (0.046472 ; 0.12116)
P-Value for Test of Close Fit (RMSEA < 0.05) = 0.066396

Expected Cross-Validation Index (ECVI) = 0.16802
90 Percent Confidence Interval for ECVI = (0.13061 ; 0.23078)
ECVI for Saturated Model = 0.14000
ECVI for Independence Model = 2.49266

Chi-Square for Independence Model with 15 Degrees of Freedom = 735.79891
Independence AIC = 747.79891
Model AIC = 50.40679
Saturated AIC = 42.00000
Independence CAIC = 776.04157
Model CAIC = 111.59922
Saturated CAIC = 140.84932

Normed Fit Index (NFI) = 0.96700
Nonnormed Fit Index (NNFI) = 0.95765
Parsimony Normed Fit Index (PNFI) = 0.51573
Comparative Fit Index (CFI) = 0.97741
Incremental Fit Index (IFI) = 0.97763
Relative Fit Index (RFI) = 0.93813

Critical N (CN) = 249.24177

Root Mean Square Residual (RMR) = 2.01027
Standardized RMR = 0.047008
Goodness-of-Fit Index (GFI) = 0.97360
Adjusted Goodness-of-Fit Index (AGFI) = 0.93069
Parsimony Goodness-of-Fit Index (PGFI) = 0.37089

The chi-square statistic is *significant*, indicating a less-than-adequate model fit to the sample variance–covariance matrix (Minimum Fit Function Chi-Square = 24.28099, $df = 8$, $p = 0.0020559$). Several of the other model-fit indices for the theoretical model in Figure 5.1a indicated a reasonable data to model fit, for example, GFI = .97360, RMSEA = 0.082681, Standardized RMR = .047008, and NFI = 0.96700. Modification indices in the computer output, however, offer suggestions on how to further improve the model to data-fit:

The Modification Indices Suggest to Add the

Path to	from	Decrease in Chi-Square	New Estimate
visperc	Verbal	10.4	2.62
lozenges	Verbal	9.2	-2.32
sencomp	Spatial	7.9	-0.79

The Modification Indices Suggest to Add an Error Covariance

Between	and	Decrease in Chi-Square	New Estimate
cubes	visperc	9.2	-8.53
lozenges	cubes	10.4	8.59
wordmean	parcomp	7.9	-5.86

We wanted our theoretical model to keep Verbal and Spatial as separate constructs (latent variables) with three separate sets of observed variables. Therefore, we were not interested in adding any paths to either latent variable from the other latent variables observed variables. So, we choose to select the adding of an error covariance between lozenges and cubes that would decrease the model-fit chi-square value by an estimated 10.4. We, therefore, added the following command line to our LISREL–SIMPLIS program:

Let the error covariance of lozenges and cubes correlate

Our modified theoretical model is diagrammed in Figure 5.1b. The resulting computer output indicated a better model fit to the data with a *nonsignificant* Minimum Fit Function $\chi^2 = 13.92604$, $df = 7$, and $p = .052513$; RMSEA = .056209; Standardized RMR = 0.032547, and GFI = .98508 . (*Note*: We used a strict interpretation of $p = .05$ for model fit, so $p = .053$ was considered nonsignificant for model fit).

5.1.1.3.2 *Goodness-of-Fit Statistics—Modified Model*

Degrees of Freedom = 7
Minimum Fit Function Chi-Square = 13.92604 (P = 0.052513)
Normal Theory Weighted Least Squares Chi-Square = 13.63496 (P = 0.058068)
Estimated Noncentrality Parameter (NCP) = 6.63496
90 Percent Confidence Interval for NCP = (0.0 ; 21.19420)

Minimum Fit Function Value = 0.046420
Population Discrepancy Function Value (F0) = 0.022117
90 Percent Confidence Interval for F0 = (0.0 ; 0.070647)
Root Mean Square Error of Approximation (RMSEA) = 0.056209
90 Percent Confidence Interval for RMSEA = (0.0 ; 0.10046)
P-Value for Test of Close Fit (RMSEA < 0.05) = 0.35494

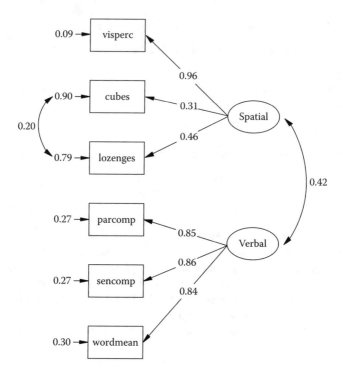

FIGURE 5.1b
Modified common factor model. (From Holzinger, K. J., & Swineford, F. A. [1939]. *A study in factor analysis: The stability of a bi-factor solution.* Supplementary Educational Monographs, No. 48. Chicago: University of Chicago, Dept. of Education.)

Expected Cross-Validation Index (ECVI) = 0.13878
90 Percent Confidence Interval for ECVI = (0.11667 ; 0.18731)
ECVI for Saturated Model = 0.14000
ECVI for Independence Model = 2.49266

Chi-Square for Independence Model with 15 Degrees of Freedom = 735.79891
Independence AIC = 747.79891
Model AIC = 41.63496
Saturated AIC = 42.00000
Independence CAIC = 776.04157
Model CAIC = 107.53450
Saturated CAIC = 140.84932

Normed Fit Index (NFI) = 0.98107
Nonnormed Fit Index (NNFI) = 0.97941
Parsimony Normed Fit Index (PNFI) = 0.45783

Comparative Fit Index (CFI) = 0.99039
Incremental Fit Index (IFI) = 0.99050
Relative Fit Index (RFI) = 0.95944

Critical N (CN) = 399.01152

Root Mean Square Residual (RMR) = 1.34928
Standardized RMR = 0.032547
Goodness-of-Fit Index (GFI) = 0.98508
Adjusted Goodness-of-Fit Index (AGFI) = 0.95523
Parsimony Goodness-of-Fit Index (PGFI) = 0.32836

Our LISREL–SIMPLIS example will further serve to help our understanding of how the various model-fit indices are computed and illustrate how power and sample size can be determined. Overall, the fit indices fall into the three main categories of *model fit, model comparison,* and *model parsimony* fit indices. Next, we discuss the fit indices in these three categories to understand their development and recommended applications. [*Note:* Extensive comparisons and discussions of many of these fit indices can be found in issues of the following journals: *Structural Equation Modeling: A Multidisciplinary Journal, Psychological Bulletin, Psychological Methods,* and *Multivariate Behavioral Research.*]

5.2 Model Fit

Model fit determines the degree to which the sample variance–covariance data fit the structural equation model. Model-fit criteria commonly used are chi-square (χ^2), the goodness-of-fit index (GFI), the adjusted goodness-of-fit index (AGFI), and the root-mean-square residual index (RMR) (Jöreskog & Sörbom, 1989). These criteria are based on differences between the observed (original, S) and model-implied (reproduced, Σ) variance–covariance matrices.

5.2.1 Chi-Square (χ^2)

A significant χ^2 value relative to the degrees of freedom indicates that the observed and implied variance–covariance matrices differ. Statistical significance indicates the probability that this difference is due to sampling variation. A nonsignificant χ^2 value indicates that the two matrices are similar, indicating that the implied theoretical model significantly reproduces the sample variance–covariance relationships in the matrix.

The researcher is interested in obtaining a nonsignificant χ^2 value with associated degrees of freedom. Thus it may be more appropriate to call the chi-square test a measure of badness-of-fit.

The chi-square test of model fit can lead to erroneous conclusions regarding analysis outcomes. The χ^2 model-fit criterion is sensitive to sample size because as sample size increases (generally above 200), the χ^2 statistic has a tendency to indicate a significant probability level. In contrast, as sample size decreases (generally below 100), the χ^2 statistic indicates nonsignificant probability levels. The chi-square statistic is therefore affected by sample size, as noted by its calculation, $\chi^2 = (n - 1) F_{ML}$, where F is the maximum likelihood (ML) fit function. The χ^2 statistic is also sensitive to departures from multivariate normality of the observed variables.

Three estimation methods are commonly used to calculate χ^2 in latent variable models (Loehlin, 1987): maximum likelihood (ML), generalized least squares (GLS), and unweighted least squares (ULS). Each approach estimates a best-fitting solution and evaluates the model fit. The ML estimates are consistent, unbiased, efficient, scale invariant, scale free, and normally distributed if the observed variables meet the multivariate normality assumption. The GLS estimates have the same properties as the ML approach under a less stringent multivariate normality assumption and provide an approximate chi-square test of model fit to the data. The ULS estimates do not depend on a normality distribution assumption; however, the estimates are not as efficient, nor are they scale invariant or scale free. The ML χ^2 statistic is $\chi^2 = (n - 1) F_{ML}$, the GLS χ^2 statistic is $\chi^2 = (n - 1) F_{GLS}$, and the ULS χ^2 statistic is $\chi^2 = (n - 1) F_{ULS}$. (*Note*: see Chapter Footnote.)

In our model analysis, we chose the maximum likelihood chi-square estimation method (default setting). The ML χ^2 statistic uses the minimum fit function value, which is reported in the computer output. The minimum fit function chi-square for our modified model is calculated as: $\chi^2 = (301 - 1) .046420 = 13.926$. (*Note*: add command line *Number of decimals* = 5 to SIMPLIS program so Minimum Fit Function Value = 0.046420 will not differ due to rounding error.)

5.2.2 Goodness-of-Fit Index (GFI) and Adjusted Goodness-of-Fit Index (AGFI)

The goodness-of-fit index (GFI) is based on the ratio of the sum of the squared differences between the observed and reproduced matrices to the observed variances, thus allowing for scale. The GFI measures the amount of variance and covariance in S that is predicted by the reproduced matrix Σ. In our original model, GFI = .97, so 97% of the S matrix is predicted by the reproduced matrix Σ, which improved in the modified model to 99% where GFI = 0.98508.

The GFI index can be computed for ML, GLS, or ULS estimates (Bollen, 1989). For our modified model the formula expression is:

$$GFI = 1 - [\chi^2_{model}/\chi^2_{null}]$$

$$GFI = 1 - [13.92604/735.79891]$$

$$GFI = 1 - .0189264$$

$$GFI = .98 \sim .99$$

(*NOTE*: The χ^2_{null} is the Chi-Square for Independence Model with 15 Degrees of Freedom.)

The adjusted goodness-of-fit index (AGFI) is adjusted for the degrees of freedom of a model relative to the number of variables. The AGFI index is computed as $1 - [(k/df) (1 - GFI)]$, where k is the number of unique distinct values in S, which is $p(p + 1)/2$, and df is the number of degrees of freedom in the model. The GFI index in our modified model analysis was .985, therefore the AGFI index is

$$1 - [(k/df)(1 - GFI)] = 1 - [(15/7)(1 - .985)]$$

$$= 1 - [2.14285(.015)]$$

$$= 1 - .03$$

$$= .97$$

The GFI and AGFI indices can be used to compare the fit of two different models with the same data or compare the fit of a single model using different data, such as separate datasets for males and females, for example, or examine measurement invariance in group models.

5.2.3 Root-Mean-Square Residual Index (RMR)

The RMR index uses the square root of the mean-squared differences between matrix elements in S and Σ. Because it has no defined acceptable level, it is best used to compare the fit of two different models with the same data. The RMR index is computed as

$$RMR = [(1/k) \Sigma_{ij} (s_{ij} - \sigma_{ij})^2]^{1/2}.$$

For our example, the original model Root Mean Square Residual (RMR) = 2.01027 compared to the modified model Root Mean Square Residual (RMR) = 1.34928. There is also a standardized RMR, known as Standardized RMR, which has an acceptable level when less than .05. For our original model, the Standardized RMR = 0.047008, compared to the modified model with a Standardized RMR = 0.032547, which is deemed a more acceptable fit. (*Note*: The residual covariance matrix can be requested in a LISREL–SIMPLIS program by adding the command line, *Print Residuals*.)

5.3 Model Comparison

Given the role chi-square has in the model fit of latent variable models, three other indices have emerged as variants for comparing alternative models: the Tucker–Lewis index (TLI) or Bentler–Bonett nonnormed fit index (NNFI), the Bentler–Bonett normed fit index (NFI) (Bentler & Bonett, 1980; Loehlin, 1987), and the comparative fit index (CFI). These criteria typically compare a proposed model with a null model (independence model). In LISREL the null model is indicated by the independence-model chi-square value. The null model could also be any model that establishes a baseline from which one could expect other alternative models to be different.

5.3.1 Tucker–Lewis Index (TLI)

Tucker and Lewis (1973) initially developed the TLI for factor analysis but later extended it to structural equation modeling. The measure can be used to compare alternative models or to compare a proposed model against a null model. The TLI is computed using the χ^2 statistic as

$$[(\chi^2_{null}/df_{null}) - (\chi^2_{proposed}/df_{proposed})]/[(\chi^2_{null}/df_{null}) - 1]$$

It is scaled from 0 (no fit) to 1 (perfect fit). For our modified model analysis, the NNFI, as it is known in LISREL, was computed as

Nonnormed Fit Index (NNFI)

$$= [(\chi^2_{null}/df_{null}) - (\chi^2_{proposed}/df_{proposed})]/[(\chi^2_{null}/df_{null}) - 1]$$

$$= [(735.79891/15) - (13.92604/7)]/[(735.7989/15) - 1]$$

$$= [(49.05326 - 1.98943)/(49.05326 - 1)]$$

$$= [47.06383/48.05326]$$

$$= 0.97941$$

5.3.2 Normed Fit Index (NFI) and Comparative Fit Index (CFI)

The NFI is a measure that rescales chi-square into a 0 (no fit) to 1.0 (perfect fit) range (Bentler & Bonett, 1980). It is used to compare a restricted model with a full model using a baseline null model as follows: $(\chi^2_{null} - \chi^2_{model})/$ χ^2_{null}. In our modified model analysis this was computed as

$$\text{Normed Fit Index (NFI)} = (\chi^2_{null} - \chi^2_{model})/\chi^2_{null}$$

$$= (735.7989 - 13.92604)/735.7989$$

$$= .98107$$

Bentler (1990) subsequently developed a coefficient of comparative fit within the context of specifying a population parameter and distribution, such as a population comparative fit index, to overcome the deficiencies in NFI for nested models. The rationale for assessment of comparative fit in the nested-model approach involves a series of models that range from least restrictive (M_i) to saturated (M_s). Corresponding to this sequence of nested models is a sequence of model-fit statistics with associated degrees of freedom. The comparative fit index (CFI) measures the improvement in noncentrality in going from model M_i to M_k (the theoretical model) and uses the noncentral χ^2 (d_k) distribution with noncentrality parameter λ_k to define comparative fit as $(\lambda_i - \lambda_k)/\lambda_i$. In our modified model output the Comparative Fit Index (CFI) = 0.99039.

McDonald and Marsh (1990) further explored the noncentrality and model-fit issue by examining nine fit indices as functions of noncentrality and sample size. They concluded that only the Tucker-Lewis Index and their relative noncentrality index (RNI) were unbiased in finite samples and recommended them for testing null or alternative models. For absolute measures of fit that do not test null or alternative models, they recommended d_k (Steiger & Lind, 1980), because it is a linear function of χ^2, or a normed measure of centrality m_k (McDonald, 1989), because neither of these varies systematically with sample size. These model fit measures of centrality are useful when selecting among a few competing models based upon theoretical considerations.

5.4 Model Parsimony

Parsimony refers to the number of estimated parameters required to achieve a specific level of model fit. Basically, an over-identified model is compared with a restricted model. The AGFI measure discussed previously also provides an index of model parsimony. Other indices that indicate model parsimony are the parsimony normed fit index (PNFI), and the Akaike information criterion (AIC). Parsimony-based fit indices for multiple indicator models were reviewed by Williams and Holahan (1994). They found that the AIC performed the best (see their article for more details on additional indices and related references). The model parsimony goodness-of-fit indices take into account the number of parameters required to achieve a given value for chi-square. Lower values for PNFI and AIC indicate a better model fit given a specified number of parameters in a model.

5.4.1 Parsimony Normed Fit Index (PNFI)

The PNFI measure is a modification of the NFI measure (James, Mulaik, & Brett, 1982). The PNFI, however, takes into account the number of degrees of freedom used to obtain a given level of fit. Parsimony is achieved with a high degree of fit for fewer degrees of freedom in specifying the coefficients to be estimated. The PNFI is used to compare models with different degrees of freedom and is calculated as PNFI $= (df_{proposed} /df_{null})$ NFI. In our modified model analysis the PNFI was:

$$\text{Parsimony Normed Fit Index (PNFI)} = (df_{proposed}/df_{null}) \text{ NFI}$$

$$= (7/15) .98107$$

$$= 0.45783$$

5.4.2 Akaike Information Criterion (AIC)

The AIC measure is used to compare models with differing numbers of latent variables, much as the PNFI is used (Akaike, 1987). The AIC can be calculated in two different ways: $\chi^2 + 2q$, where q = number of free parameters in the model, or as $\chi^2 - 2df$. The first AIC is positive (as computed in LISREL), and the second AIC is negative, but either AIC value close to zero indicates a more parsimonious model. The AIC indicates model fit (S and Σ elements similar) and model parsimony (over-identified model). In our modified model analysis, the computer output gives several AIC values for the theoretical model, saturated model, and independence model; however, we only report two AIC fit indices. (*Note*: AIC uses Normal theory weighted least squares chi-square not the minimum fit function chi-square.)

$$\text{Model AIC} = \text{Normal Theory } \chi^2 + 2q$$

$$= 13.63496 + 2 (14)$$

$$= 41.63496$$

Independence AIC = Chi-Square for Independence Model + 2(df -1)

$$= 735.79891 + 2(6)$$

$$= 747.79891$$

5.4.3 Summary

Mulaik, James, Alstine, Bennett, Lind, and Stilwell (1989) evaluated the χ^2, NFI, GFI, AGFI, and AIC goodness-of-fit indices. They concluded that these indices fail to assess parsimony and are insensitive to misspecification of structural relationships (see their definitive work for additional information). Their findings should not be surprising because it has been suggested that a *good* fit index is one that is independent of sample size, accurately reflects differences in fit, imposes a penalty for inclusion of additional parameters (Marsh, Balla, & McDonald, 1988), and supports the choice of the true model when it is known (McDonald & Marsh, 1990). *No model-fit criteria can actually meet all of these criteria.*

We have presented several model-fit indices that are used to assess model fit, model comparison, or model parsimony. In addition, we calculated many of these based on the model analyzed in this chapter. The LISREL program outputs many different model-fit criteria because more than one should be reported. The LISREL user guides also provide an excellent discussion of the model-fit indices in their program. We recommend that once you feel comfortable using these fit indices for your specific model applications, you check the references cited for additional information on their usefulness and/or limitations. Following their initial description, there has been much controversy and discussion on their subjective interpretation and appropriateness under specific modeling conditions (see Marsh, Balla, & Hau [1996] for further discussion). Further research and discussion will surely follow; for example, Kenny & McCoach (2003) indicated that RMSEA improves as more variables are added to a model, whereas TLI and CFI both decline in correctly specified models as more variables are added.

When deciding on which model-fit indices to report, first consider whether the fit indices were created for model fit, model parsimony, or model comparison. At the risk of oversimplification, we suggest that χ^2, RMSEA, and Standardized RMR be reported for all types of models with additional fit indices reported based on purpose of modeling. For example, the CFI should be reported if comparing models. Overall, more than one model-fit index should be reported. If a majority of the fit indices on your list indicate an acceptable model, then your theoretical model is supported by the data.

5.5 Parameter Fit

Individual parameter estimates in a model can be meaningless even though model-fit criteria indicate an acceptable measurement or structural model. Therefore, interpretation of parameter estimates in any model analysis is essential. The following steps are therefore recommended:

1. Examine the parameter estimates to determine whether they have the correct sign (either positive or negative).

2. Examine parameter estimates (standardized coefficients) to determine whether they are out of bounds or exceed an expected range of values.

3. Examine the parameter estimates for statistical significance (T or Z-values = parameter estimate divided by standard error of parameter estimate).

4. Test for measurement invariance by setting parameter estimates equal (constraints) in different groups, for example, girls and boys, then make relative comparisons among the parameter estimates.

An examination of initial parameter estimates can also help in identifying a faulty or misspecified model. In this instance, initial parameter estimates can serve as start values—for example, initial two-stage least-squares (TSLS) estimates in LISREL. The researcher then replaces the TSLS estimate with a user-defined start value. Sometimes parameter estimates take on impossible values, as in the case of a correlation between two variables that exceeds 1.0. Sometimes negative variance is encountered (known as a *Heywood* case). Also, if the error variance for a variable is near zero, the indicator variable implies an almost perfect measure of the latent variable, which may not be the case. Outliers can also influence parameter estimates. Use of sufficient sample size ($n > 100$ or 150) and several indicators per latent variable (four is recommended based on the TETRAD approach) has also been recommended to produce reasonable and stable parameter estimates (Anderson & Gerbing, 1984).

Once these issues have been taken into consideration, the interpretation of modification indices and expected parameter change can begin to modify the model, but there is still a need for guidance provided by the rationale for the theoretical model and the researcher's expertise. Researchers should use the model-fit indices as potential indicators of misfit when respecifying or modifying a model. Cross-validation or replication using another independent sample, once an acceptable model is achieved, is always recommended to ensure stability of parameter estimates and validity of the model (Cliff, 1983). Bootstrap procedures also afford a resampling method, given a single sample, to determine the efficiency and precision of sample estimates (Lunneborg, 1987). These model validation topics are discussed further in chapter 12.

5.6 Power and Sample Size

The determination of power and/or sample size in SEM is complicated because theoretical models can have several variables or parameter estimates and parameters are typically not independent in a model and have different standard errors. In SEM we also compare models, oftentimes nested models with the same data set. Consequently, power and sample size determination in the situation where a researcher is hypothesis testing (testing a model fit to data), comparing alternative models, or desiring to test a parameter estimate for significance will be covered with SAS, SPSS, and G*Power 3 examples using the LISREL–SIMPLIS example in the chapter. The *power* for hypothesis testing, or the probability of rejecting H_o when H_a is true, depends on the true population model, significance level, degrees of freedom, and sample size, which involves specifying an effect size, alpha, and sample size; while *sample size* determination is achieved given power, effect size, and alpha level of significance. Daniel S. Soper has a user friendly website that provides effect size, power and sample size determination in statistics (http://www.danielsoper.com/statcalc/).

Hypothesis testing involves confirming that a theoretical model fits the sample variance–covariance data, comparing fit between alternative models, or testing parameter coefficients for significance; even whether coefficients are equal between groups. These hypothesis testing methods should involve constrained models with fewer parameters than the initial model. The initial (full) model represents the null hypothesis (H_o) and the alternative (constrained) model with fewer parameters is denoted H_a. Each model generates a χ^2 goodness-of-fit measure, and the difference between the models for significance testing is computed as $D^2 = \chi^2_o - \chi^2_a$, with $df_d = df_o - df_a$. The D^2 statistic is tested for significance at a specified alpha level (probability of Type I error), where H_o is rejected if D^2 exceeds the critical tabled χ^2 value with df_d degrees of freedom (Table A.4). The chi-square difference test or likelihood ratio test is used with GLS, ML, and WLS estimation methods.

The *significance* of parameter estimates that do not require two separate models to yield separate χ^2 values includes: (a) generating a two-sided t or z value for the parameter estimate (T or Z = parameter estimate divided by standard error of the parameter estimate), and (b) interpreting the modification index directly for the parameter estimate as a χ^2 test with 1 degree of freedom. The relationship is simply $T^2 = D^2 = MI$ (modification index) for large sample sizes. Gonzalez and Griffin (2001), however, indicated that the standard errors of the parameter estimates are sensitive to how the model is identified, that is, alternative ways of identifying a model may yield different standard errors, and hence different T values for the statistical significance of a parameter estimate. This lack of invariance due to model identification could result in different conclusions about a parameter's significance level from different, yet equivalent, models on the same data. The authors recommended that parameter estimates be tested for significance using the likelihood ratio (LR) test because it is invariant to model identification, rather than the T test (or z test).

5.6.1 Model Fit

A traditional approach in SEM is to hypothesize a theoretical model, collect sample data, and test whether the model fits the data. In this chapter we have discussed various fit indices to determine if the theoretical model fits the data. When the theoretical model does not fit the data, we look to modification indices for suggestions on how to modify the model for an improved fit. The power to reject a null hypothesis and sample size impacts our decision of whether sample data fit a theoretical model. Power and sample size are therefore discussed next.

5.6.1.1 Power

Saris and Satorra (1993) provided an easy to use approach for calculating power of a theoretical model. Basically, an alternative model is estimated with sample data to indicate what percent of the time we would correctly reject the null hypothesis under the assumption that the null hypothesis (H_o) is false. The minimum fit function chi-square value obtained from fitting data to the theoretical model provides an estimate of the noncentrality parameter (NCP). NCP is calculated as Normal Theory Weighted Least Squares $\chi^2 - df_{model}$. For our modified model the NCP = 13.63496 − 7 = 6.63496, which is provided in the *Goodness-of-Fit* section of the computer output. This makes computing power using SAS 9.1, SPSS 16.0, or G*Power 3 straightforward, using their respective command functions.

(*Note:* $\chi^2 = 3.841$, $df = 1$, $p = .05$ is the critical tabled value for testing our hypothesis of model fit.) Examples for each using NCP are provided next.

SAS syntax—power

```
data chapter5;
do obs=1;
ncp = 6.63496;
power = 1 - PROBCHI(3.841, 1, ncp);
output;
end;
proc print;
var ncp power;
run;
```

SPSS syntax—power

```
DATA LIST FREE / obs.
BEGIN DATA.
1
END DATA.
compute ncp = 6.63496.
compute power = 1 - NCDF.CHISQ(3.841, 1, ncp).
formats ncp power (f8.5).
List.
```

In our modified model, NCP = 6.63496, so our power = .73; the output from the SAS or SPSS syntax was:

obs	ncp	power
1.00	6.63496	.73105

Power, given your model fit, can also be determined using G*power 3 (Faul, Erdfelder, Lang & Buchner, 2007). The free G*Power 3 software download is available from the Web site: http://www.psycho.uni-duesseldorf.de/abteilungen/aap/gpower3/, which is somewhat easier than running the SAS and SPSS programs. Power and sample size estimates for a priori and post-hoc statistical applications are available using G*power 3. (*Note:* We used G*Power 3, Windows, Release 3.1.0, 2008, but a MAC OS version is also available). After download and installation, click on the G*Power 3 desktop icon and you should see the following dialog box:

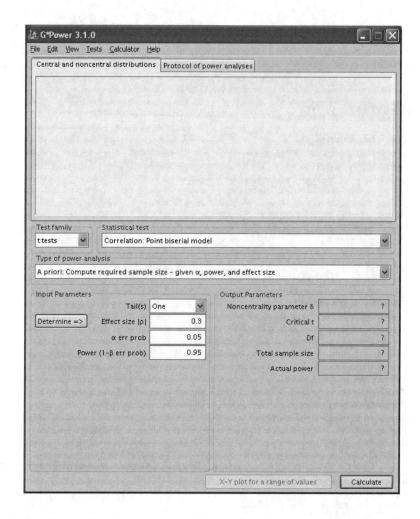

In the *Test family* window select "χ^2 tests"; in the Statistical test window select "Generic χ^2 test"; and in the *Type of power analysis* window, select *"Post-hoc: Compute power – given α, and noncentrality parameter."* Our modified model had NCP = 6.63496, so we entered this value in the *"noncentrality parameter λ"* window along with df = 1 and α = .05. The dialog box should look like:

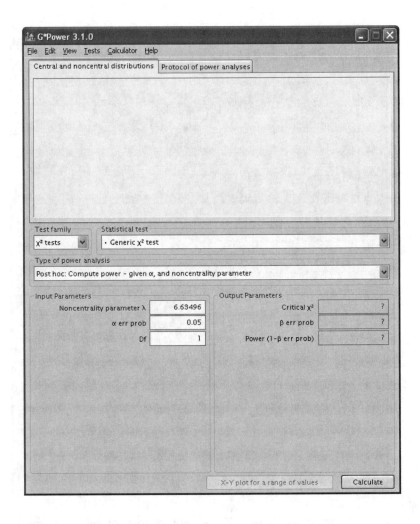

Click the *Calculate* button. The power = .731015 value matches our earlier calculations. The dialog box should now look like:

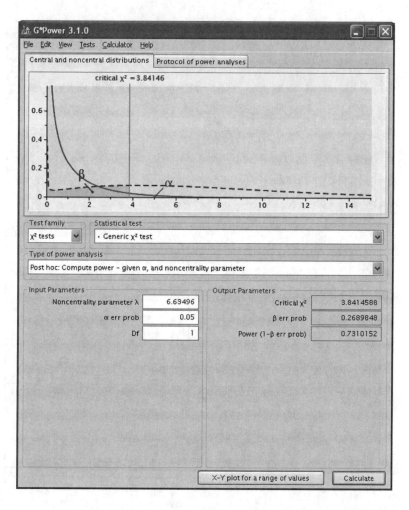

Our modified model has a 73 percent chance of rejecting the null hypothesis at the .05 level of significance, which falls short of the .80 level commonly accepted for power. If we replace the critical chi-square value in the formula, you can determine power for other alpha levels of significance. In Table 5.2, we have replaced the critical chi-square value and ran the SPSS syntax program for alpha values ranging from .10 to .001. If we test our modified model fit at the $p = .10$ level, then we achieve an acceptable level of power; other alpha levels from .05 to .001 fall below a .80 power value.

TABLE 5.2

Power for Alpha Levels Given Modified Model NCP

NCP	Critical Chi-Square	Alpha	Power
6.63496	2.706	.10	.82405
6.63496	3.841	.05	.73105
6.63496	5.412	.02	.59850
6.63496	6.635	.01	.50000
6.63496	10.827	.001	.23743

Note: Critical χ^2 values for $df = 1$ from Table A.4.

5.6.1.2 Sample Size

An earlier way to determine an appropriate sample size in SEM was given by Hoelter (1983) as the Critical N (CN) statistic, where $CN \geq 200$ was considered adequate. The Critical N is calculated as:

$$CN = (\chi^2_{\text{critical}} / F_{\text{min}}) + 1$$

The critical chi-square (χ^2_{critical}) is obtained for the model degrees of freedom at the .05 level of significance. The CN statistic is output by the LISREL–SIMPLIS program. In our final modified model of Figure 5.1b, $CN = 399$, F_{min} was determined to be .0353432 and $\chi^2_{\text{critical}} = 14.067$ for $df = 7$ at .05 level of significance (see Table A.4); so $CN = (14.067/.0353432) + 1 = 399$. (*Note:* our modified model computer output indicated $F_{\text{min}} = .04642$, $p = .0525$, but CN uses F_{min} at $p = .05$). CN gives the sample size at which the F_{min} value leads to a rejection of H_{o}. Our sample size was N = 301 with a nonsignificant chi-square (minimum fit function χ^2, $p = .052$; or normal theory weighted least squares χ^2, $p = .058$) and several good model-fit indices, so even if we used Hoelter's suggestion, we had sufficient sample size. For a further discussion about CN refer to Bollen and Liang (1988) or Bollen (1989).

Sample size influences the calculation of the minimum fit function χ^2. Recall that the Minimum Fit Function χ^2 in the modified model was computed as:

$$\text{Minimum Fit Function } \chi^2 = (N - g) \times F_{\text{min}}$$

$$= (301 - 1) \times (.046420)$$

$$= 13.92604$$

Sample size also influences the calculation of the F_{min} values as follows:

$$F_{min} = \text{Minimum Fit Function } \chi^2/(N-g)$$

$$= 13.92604/(301-1)$$

$$= .046420$$

The F_{min} is computed using the minimum fit function χ^2 in the computer output, sample size (N), and number of groups (g); while the noncentrality parameter (NCP) is computed using the Normal Theory χ^2 minus the degrees of freedom in the model. NCP is therefore computed as:

$$NCP = \text{Normal Theory Weighted Least Squares } \chi^2 - df_{model}$$

$$= 13.63496 - 7$$

$$= 6.63496$$

Estimated sample size (N) using these NCP and F_{min} values is less than our actual sample size of N = 301:

$$N = (NCP/F_{min}) + g$$

$$= (6.63496/.046420) + 1$$

$$= 143.93 \sim 144$$

You have probably noticed that F_{min} is calculated using the Minimum Fit Function χ^2, but NCP is calculated using the Normal Theory Weighted Least Squares χ^2. LISREL, unlike other SEM software calculates some measures of fit (NCP, RMSEA, and Independence model χ^2) using the normal theory weighted least squares χ^2, but uses the minimum fit function χ^2 for others. Differences between these two can be small if the multivariate normality assumption holds or very different if not (see Chapter Footnote for detailed description of standard errors and four different χ^2 values: C1 = minimum fit function χ^2; C2 = normal theory weighted least squares χ^2; C3 = Satorra–Bentler scaled χ^2; C4 = χ^2 corrected for nonnormality).

To determine sample size for given df, alpha, and power for a theoretical model, the F_{min} value would be fixed (F_{min} value from your final model; our modified model had F_{min} = .046420), but the NCP value would vary. For our modified model, the SAS program can be run for differing NCP values to obtain corresponding sample size and power estimates. (*Note*: We are changing values of power in the SAS syntax program, but you can also fix power and change alpha values to obtain different sample sizes for different alpha levels at a specified power level, for example, power = .80).

SAS syntax—sample size

```
data chapter5;
do obs = 1;
g = 1;
* change values of alpha to obtain sample size for given
power;
alpha = .05;
fmin = .046420;
df = 1;
* change values of power to obtain sample size for given
alpha;
power = .60;
chicrit = quantile('chisquare',1 - alpha, df);
ncp = CINV(power,df,chicrit);
n = (ncp/fmin) + g;
output;
end;
proc print;
 var power n alpha ncp fmin g;
run;
```

The output from this first run with power = .60 would look like this:

```
obs    power     n      alpha    ncp      fmin     g    chicrit
 1      .6    106.535    .05   4.89892  .04642    1    3.84146
```

We created Table 5.3 by changing the value of power for alpha = .05 for a critical $\chi^2 = 3.841$, $df = 1$. (*Note: fmin* is fixed at the value from our

TABLE 5.3

Sample Size for Given Power with Alpha = .05

Power	n	Alpha	ncp	fmin	g	χ^2 critical
.60	106.535	.05	4.89892	.04642	1	3.84146
.70	133.963	.05	6.17213	.04642	1	3.84146
.73	**143.594**	**.05**	**6.61923**	**.04642**	**1**	**3.84146**
.80	170.084	.05	7.84890	.04642	1	3.84146
.90	227.356	.05	10.5074	.04642	1	3.84146
.95	280.938	.05	12.9947	.04642	1	3.84146

Note: n should be rounded up, for example, 106.535 = 107.

modified model; *alpha* is fixed at .05, so *chicrit* will be fixed at 3.84146).
A sample size of N = 144 for power = .73 from our modified model was
also correctly computed and indicated in the table. We see in Table 5.3
that sample size requirements increase as power increases, which is
expected.

In our modified model we have N = 301, NCP = 6.63496, and our *post-hoc* power = .73 calculated at the .05 level of significance. A sample size of
N = 170 would have given us power = .80 at the .05 level of significance.
Are you puzzled? Well, recall that NCP = $\chi^2 - df_{model}$, so if our model had
resulted in a NCP = 7.84890 with *N* = 170 at the .05 level of significance,
then we would have achieved an acceptable level of power = .80. We find
that the noncentrality parameter (NCP) is affected by the model chi-square but also the degrees of freedom, which indicates a certain level of
model complexity.

We can also use the **SAS syntax—sample size** program to examine how
changing the level of significance affects sample size for a fixed power
value. Recall that F_{min} is fixed at .04642 from our modified model. Table 5.4
contains the output from the SAS program. We see in Table 5.4 that sample
size requirements increase as the level of significance (alpha) for testing
our model decreases, which is expected.

TABLE 5.4

Sample Size for Given Alpha with Power = .80

Power	n	Alpha	ncp	fmin	g	$\chi^2_{critical}$
.8	134.194	.10	6.18288	.04642	1	2.70554
.8	170.084	.05	7.84890	.04642	1	3.84146
.8	217.201	.02	10.0360	.04642	1	5.41189
.8	252.593	.01	11.6790	.04642	1	6.63490
.8	368.830	.001	17.0746	.04642	1	10.8276

Note: $\chi^2_{critical}$ values correspond to alpha values in Table A.4.

We used G*Power 3 to calculate various NCP values given alpha and
power because SPSS 16.0 does not have a command function at this
time to determine the noncentrality parameter (NCP) given power,
df, and critical χ^2. (*Note:* SAS, S-Plus, Stata and other statistical soft-ware have this capability) In the *Test family* drop-down menu, select
"χ^2 *test*"; in the *Statistical Test* drop-down menu select, "*Generic* χ^2 *test*";
and in the *Type of power analysis*, select "*Sensitivity: Compute noncentral-ity parameter – given* α, *and power.*" In the *Input Parameters* boxes, change

the power value to .80 and the *df* value to 1. Your dialog box should now appear as:

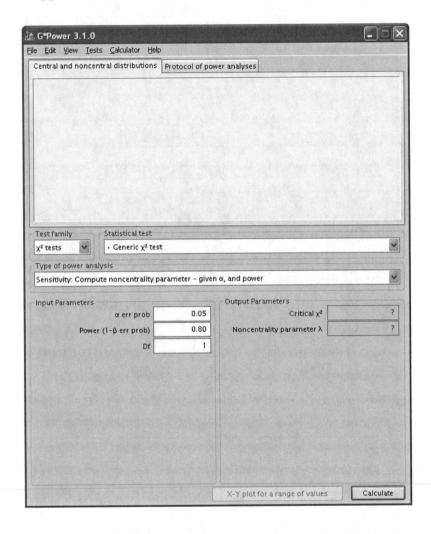

Click on the *Calculate* button; the *Output Parameters*, "*Critical* χ^2" and "*Noncentrality parameter* λ" will appear. The G*Power 3.1.0 dialog box will now display the Critical $\chi^2 = 3.84146$ (associated with alpha = .05, *df* = 1) and corresponding noncentrality parameter for power = .80. Your dialog box should now look like:

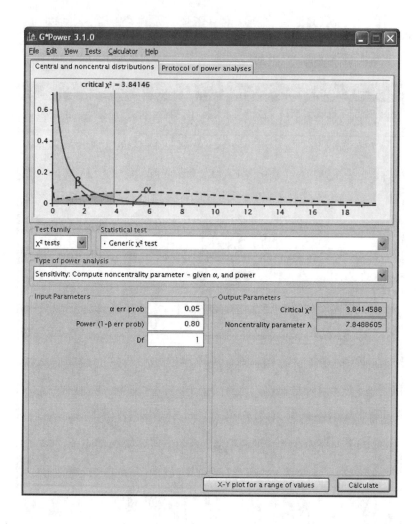

Table 5.3 reports these same values using the program **SAS syntax—sample size**.

You can click on the *X-Y plot for a range of values* button to enter a range of power values that can be plotted by corresponding noncentrality parameter values. (*Note*: Check the box for *"and displaying the values in the plot"* and change the *"in steps of"* from .01 to .10 for clarity in the output of the graph.) The dialog box should look like this:

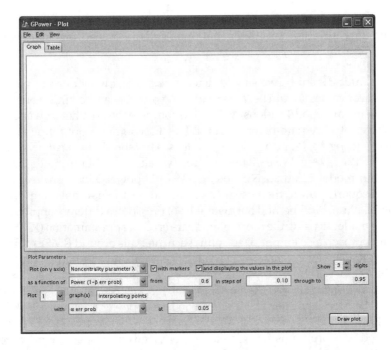

Click on *Draw plot*. Your graph will now appear and should look like the dialog box below:

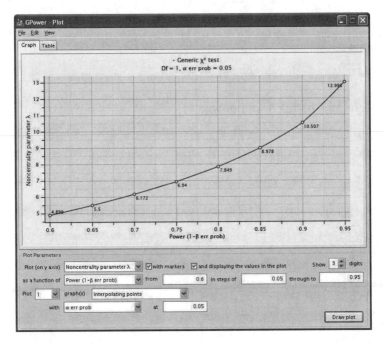

(NOTE: A range of power values entered from .6 to .95 indicates the levels of the noncentrality parameter that one needs to exceed for that level of power [see Table 5.3].)

In planning a study, we should determine a priori what our sample size and power values should be. After gathering our data and running our SEM model (and any modifications), we should compute the post-hoc power using our noncentrality parameter from the LISREL computer output or sample size (N) using NCP and model F_{min} values. This should be easy given that $N = (NCP/F_{min}) + g$. We can *a priori* specify values or obtain the F_{min} value from our model, calculate NCP using SAS or G*power 3 for a given *df*, critical chi-square, power, then use these values to calculate sample size (N).

MacCallum, Browne, and Sugawara (1996) provided a different approach to testing model-fit using the root mean square error of approximation (RMSEA). Their approach also emphasized confidence intervals around RMSEA, rather than a single point estimate, so they suggested null and alternative values for RMSEA (exact fit: *Ho* = .00 versus *Ha* = .05; Close fit: *Ho* = .05 versus *Ha* = .08; and Not close fit: *Ho* = .05 versus *Ha* = .10); researchers can also select their own. The MacCallum et al. (1996) method tests power, given exact fit (*Ho*; RMSEA = 0), close fit (*Ho*, RMSEA ≤ .05), or not close fit (*Ho*, RMSEA ≥ .05); and included SAS programs for calculating power given sample size or sample size given power using RMSEA. RMSEA is calculated as:

$$RMSEA = \sqrt{(NCP/N - 1)/df}$$

For our modified model, NCP = 6.63496; N = 301; and *df* = 7, so RMSEA = 0.056209:

$$RMSEA = \sqrt{(6.63496/300)/7} = .056209$$

SAS syntax—RMSEA and power

```
data chapter5;
do obs = 1;
n = 301;
df = 7;
alpha = .05;
* change rmseaHo and rmseaHa values to correspond to exact,
close, and not close values;
rmseaHo = .05;
rmseaHa = .08;
ncpHo = (n-1)*df*rmseaHo*rmseaHo;
ncpHa = (n-1)*df*rmseaHa*rmseaHa;
chicrit = quantile('chisquare',1-alpha,df);
if rmseaHo < rmseaHa then power = 1 -
PROBCHI(chicrit,df,ncpHa);
```

```
if rmseaHo > rmseaHa then power = PROBCHI(chicrit,df,ncpHa);
output;
end;
Proc print;
Var n df alpha rmseaHo rmseaHa ncpHo ncpHa chicrit power;
Run;
```

SPSS syntax—RMSEA and power

```
DATA LIST FREE / obs.
BEGIN DATA.
1
END DATA.
compute n = 301.
compute df = 7.
compute alpha = .05.
comment change rmseaHo and rmseaHa values to correspond with
exact, close, not close values.
compute rmseaHo = .05.
compute rmseaHa = .08.
compute ncpHo = (n-1)*df*rmseaHo*rmseaHo.
compute ncpHa = (n-1)*df*rmseaHa*rmseaHa.
compute chicrit = IDF.CHISQ(1-alpha,df).
do if (rmseaHo < rmseaHa).
compute power = 1 - NCDF.CHISQ(chicrit, df, ncpHa).
else if (rmseaHo > rmseaHa).
compute power = NCDF.CHISQ(chicrit, df, ncpHa).
end if.
formats chicrit ncpHo ncpHa power (f8.5).
List.
```

The resulting SAS or SPSS output for close fit was given as:

```
obs     n  df alpha rmseaHo rmseaHa ncpHo ncpHa chicrit  power
1.00  301   7   .05     .05     .08   5.25 13.44 14.0671 .76813
```

We ran the recommended RMSEA values given by MacCallum et al. (1996) and listed them in Table 5.5. For exact fit, power = .33, for close fit, power = .76, and for not close fit, power = .06 ~ .057. A RMSEA model-fit value between .05 and .08 is considered an acceptable model-fit index, when reported with other fit indices. Our modified model RMSEA = .056209 and for close fit had power = .76813.

TABLE 5.5

MacCallum et al. (1996) Null and Alternative Values for RMSEA Test of Fit

MacCallum Test	Ho	Ha	Power
Exact	.00	.05	.33034
Close	.05	.08	.76813
Not Close	.05	.01	.05756

Figure 5.1, Modified model ($\alpha = .05$, $df = 7$, $N = 301$).

5.6.2 Model Comparison

A likelihood ratio (LR) test is possible between alternative models to examine the difference in χ^2 values between the initial model and a modified model. The LR test with degrees of freedom equal to $df_{\text{Initial}} - df_{\text{Modified}}$ is calculated as:

$$\text{LR} = \chi^2_{\text{Initial}} - \chi^2_{\text{Modified}}$$

For our example, the initial model had $\chi^2 = 24.28099$, $df = 8$, and the modified model had $\chi^2 = 13.92604$, $df = 7$; therefore, LR = 10.35495 with $df = 1$, which is a statistically significant chi-square value at the .05 level of significance ($\chi^2 > 3.84$, $df = 1$, $\alpha = .05$), indicating the models are different.

$$\text{LR}_{df=1} = 24.28099 - 13.92604 = 10.35495$$

The LR test between models is possible when adding or dropping a single parameter (path or variable). In LISREL–SIMPLIS, a researcher will most likely be guided by the modification indices with their associated change (decrease) in chi-square when respecifying or modifying a model. On the basis of our LISREL–SIMPLIS modification indices, we chose to *add* an error covariance between *lozenges* and *cubes* by adding the following command in our subsequent model analysis because it gave us our largest *decrease* in model chi-square (see Figure 5.1b):

Let the error covariance of lozenges and cubes correlate

MacCallum, Browne, and Cai (2006) presented an approach to compare nested models when the between model degrees of freedom are ≥ 1. They showed that when testing close fit, power results may differ depending upon the degrees of freedom in each model. Basically, the power to detect differences will be greater when models being compared have more degrees of freedom. For any given sample size, power increases as the model degrees of freedom increases. They defined an effect size (δ) in terms of model RMSEA and degrees of freedom for the two models, so in our example, the effect size (δ) would be computed as:

$$\delta = (df_{Initial} * RMSEA^2_{Initial} - df_{Modified} * RMSEA^2_{Modified})$$

$$\delta = ([8 * (.080937)^2] - [7 * (.046420)^2])$$

$$\delta = (.0524056 - .0150836)$$

$$\delta = .037322$$

The noncentrality parameter is computed as:

$$NCP = (N - 1)\ \delta$$

So, for our example:

$$NCP = (301 - 1) * (\ .037322)$$

$$NCP = 11.1966$$

Using G*Power 3, we enter this NCP = 11.1966, .05 level of significance, and $df = 1$ (model degree of freedom difference) and obtained power = .917. The G*Power 3 dialog box should look like this:

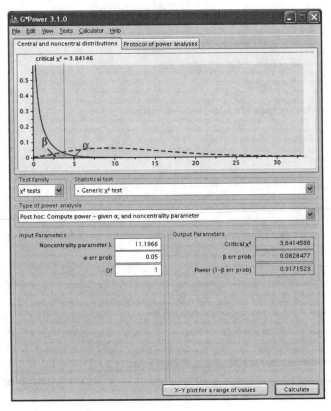

Power to detect a difference in RMSEA values is therefore possible for a given sample size with various degrees of freedom. The SAS program below will also provide an ability to make power comparisons for different model degrees of freedom using RMSEA values from two nested models.

SAS syntax—effect size, RMSEA, and power

```
data chapter5;
 do obs = 1;
 n = 301;
 alpha = .05;
 dfa = 8;
 rmseaA = .080937;
 dfb = 7;
 rmseaB = .046420;
 delta = (dfa*rmseaA*rmseaA) - (dfb*rmseaB*rmseaB);
 ncp = (n - 1)*delta;
 dfdiff = dfa - dfb;
 chicrit = quantile('chisquare',1 - alpha, dfdiff);
 power = 1 - PROBCHI(chicrit, dfdiff,ncp);
 output;
 end;
 Proc print;
 var n dfa rmseaA dfb rmseaB delta ncp dfdiff chicrit power;
 run;
```

The computer output should look like this:

Obs	n	dfa	rmseaA	dfb	rmseaB
1	301	8	0.080937	7	0.04642

delta	ncp	dfdiff	chicrit	power
.037323	11.1968	1	3.84146	.91716

The power = .91716 indicates a 91% chance of detecting a difference between the model RMSEA values.

Power is affected by the size of the model degrees of freedom (degrees of freedom implies a certain degree of model complexity). The G*Power 3 program or the SAS program can be used for models where the difference in degrees of freedom is greater than one. We therefore ran a comparison for our model with different levels of degrees of freedom to show how power is affected. In Table 5.6, power increases dramatically when the level of degrees of freedom increases from 5 to 14 while maintaining a model degrees of freedom difference at $df = 1$. You can also output program values for $df \geq 2$ to see effect on power.

TABLE 5.6

MacCallum et al. (2006) Power
at Increasing Model Degrees of
Freedom

dfa	dfb	Power
5	4	.76756
8	7	.91716*
11	10	.97337
14	13	.99206

(RMSEA approach)
Figure 5.1b Model ($\alpha = .05$, $N = 301$).

5.6.3 Parameter Significance

A single parameter can be tested for significance using nested models. *Nested models* involve an initial model being compared to a modified model in which a single parameter has been fixed to zero (dropped) or estimated (added). In structural equation modeling, the intent is to determine the significance of the decrease in the χ^2 value for the modified model from the initial model. The LR test was used before to test the difference in the models for our single parameter that we added (error covariance between *lozenges* and *cubes*).

Power can be computed for testing the significance of an individual parameter estimate. For GLS, ML, and WLS estimation methods, this involves determining the significance of χ^2 with one degree of freedom ($\chi^2 > 3.84$, $df = 1$, $\alpha = .05$) for a single parameter estimate, thus determining the significance of the reduction in χ^2 that should equal or exceed the modification index value for the parameter estimate fixed to zero. Power values for modification index values can be computed using SAS because the modification index (MI) is a noncentrality parameter (NCP). The power of a MI value (NCP) at the .05 level of significance, $df = 1$, critical chi-square value = 3.841 is computed in the following SAS syntax program for our MI = 10.4 when adding the error covariance between *lozenges* and *cubes*. Power = .89, so in testing the statistical significance of MI for our parameter (error covariance), we have an 89% chance of correctly rejecting the null hypothesis and accepting the alternative hypothesis that MI is different from zero.

SAS syntax—power for parameter MI value

```
data chapter5;
  do obs = 1;
  mi = 10.4;
  alpha = .05;
```

```
df = 1;
chicrit = quantile('chisquare',1 - alpha, df);
power = 1 - PROBCHI(chicrit, df, mi);
output;
end;
Proc print;
var mi power alpha df chicrit;
run;
```

The SAS output indicated the following:

Obs	mi	power	alpha	df	chicrit
1	10.4	.89075	.05	1	3.84146

Power values for parameter estimates can also be computed using a SAS program because a squared T or Z value for a parameter estimate is asymptotically distributed as a noncentral chi-square, that is, $NCP = T^2$. Our modified model indicated an error covariance = 8.34 (modification index indicated a *New Estimate* at 8.59), with standard error = 2.62, so $T = 8.34/2.62 = 3.19$; LISREL program output provided these values for the added parameter:

Error Covariance for lozenges and cubes = 8.34

(2.62)

3.19

(**NOTE**: LISREL 8.8 student version lists standared error, Z value, and p-value in the output)

The power of a squared T value for our parameter estimate is computed in a SAS program as follows:

SAS syntax—power for parameter T value

```
data chapter5;
 do obs = 1;
 T = 3.19;
 ncp = T*T;
 alpha = .05;
 df = 1;
 chicrit = quantile('chisquare',1 - alpha, df);
 power = 1 - PROBCHI(chicrit, df, ncp);
 output;
 end;
 Proc print;
 var ncp power alpha df chicrit;
 run;
```

The SAS output looks like this:

Obs	ncp	power	alpha	df	chicrit
1	10.1761	.89066	.05	1	3.84146

Power = .89, so in testing the statistical significance of our parameter estimate, we have an 89% chance of correctly rejecting the null hypothesis and accepting the alternative hypothesis that T is different from zero. (*Note*: The other model-fit indices [GFI, AGFI, NFI, IFI, CFI, etc.] do not have a test of statistical significance and therefore do not involve power calculations).

5.6.4 Summary

Research suggests that certain model-fit indices are more susceptible to sample size than others, hence, power. We have already learned that χ^2 is affected by sample size, that is, $\chi^2 = (N - 1) F_{ML}$, where F_{ML} is the maximum likelihood fit function for a model, and therefore χ^2 increases in direct relation to $N - 1$ (Bollen, 1989). Kaplan (1995) also pointed out that power in SEM is affected by the size of the misspecified parameter, sample size, and location of the parameter in the model. Specification errors induce bias in the standard errors and parameter estimates, and thus affect power. These factors also affect power in other parametric statistical tests (Cohen, 1988). Saris and Satorra (1993) pointed out that the larger the noncentrality parameter, the greater is the power of the test, that is, an evaluation of the power of the test is an evaluation of the noncentrality parameter.

Muthén and Muthén (2002) outlined how Monte Carlo methods can be used to decide on the power for a given specified model using the *Mplus* program. Power is indicated as the percentage of significant coefficients or the proportion of replications for which the null hypothesis that a parameter is equal to zero is rejected at the .05 level of significance, two-tailed test, with a critical value of 1.96. The authors suggested that power equal or exceed the traditional .80 level for determining the probability of rejecting the null hypothesis when it is false.

Marsh et al. (1988, 1996) also examined the influence of sample size on 30 different model-fit indices and found that the Tucker–Lewis index (Tucker & Lewis, 1973) and four new indices based on the Tucker–Lewis index were the only ones relatively independent of sample size. Bollen (1990) argued that the claims regarding which model-fit indices were affected by sample size needed further clarification. There are actually two sample size effects that are confounded: (a) whether sample size enters into the calculation of the model-fit index, and (b) whether the means of the sampling distribution of the model-fit index are related to sample size. Sample size was shown not to affect the calculation of NFI, TLI, GFI, AGFI, and CN, but the means of the sampling distribution of these model-fit indices were related to sample size. Bollen (1990) concluded that, given a lack of consensus on the best measure of fit, it is prudent to report multiple measures rather than to rely on a single choice; we concur.

Muthén and Muthén (2002) also used *Mplus* to determine appropriate sample sizes in the presence of model complexity, distribution of variables, missing data, reliability, and variance–covariance of variables. For example, given a two-factor CFA model and 10 indicator variables with normally distributed nonmissing data, a sample size of 150 is indicated with power = .81. In the presence of missing data, sample size increases to $n = 175$. Given nonnormal missing data, sample size increases to $n = 315$. Davey & Savla (2009) provide an excellent treatment of statistical power analysis with missing data via a structural equation modeling approach. Their examples cover many different types of modeling situations using SAS, STATA, SPSS, or LISREL syntax programs. This is a must-read book on the subject of power and sample size, especially in the presence of missing data.

Finally, one should beware of claims of sample size influence on fit measures that do not distinguish the type of sample size effect (Satorra & Bentler, 1994). Cudeck and Henly (1991) also argued that a uniformly negative view of the effects of sample size in model selection is unwarranted. They focused instead on the predictive validity of models in the sense of cross-validation in future samples while acknowledging that sample size issues are a problem in the field of statistics in general and unavoidable in structural equation modeling.

5.7 Two-Step Versus Four-Step Approach to Modeling

Anderson and Gerbing (1988) proposed a two-step model-building approach that emphasized the analysis of two conceptually distinct models: a measurement model followed by the structural model (Lomax, 1982). The *measurement* model, or factor model, specifies the relationships among measured (observed) variables underlying the latent variables. The *structural* model specifies relationships among the latent variables as posited by theory. The measurement model provides an assessment of convergent and discriminant validity, and the structural model provides an assessment of nomological validity.

Mulaik et al. (1989) expanded the idea of model fit by assessing the relative fit of the structural model among latent variables, independently of assessing the fit of the indicator variables in the measurement model. The relative normed fit index (RNFI) makes the following adjustment to separately estimate the effects of the structural model from the measurement model: $RNFI_j = (F_u - F_j)/[F_u - F_m - (df_j - df_m)]$, where $F_u = \chi^2$ of the full model, $F_j = \chi^2$ of the structural model, $F_m = \chi^2$ of the measurement model, df_j is the degrees of freedom for the structural model, and df_m is the degrees of freedom for the measurement model. A corresponding relative parsimony ratio (RP) is given by $RP_j = (df_j - df_m)/(df_u - df_m)$, where df_j is the degrees of freedom for the structural model, df_m is the degrees of freedom for the measurement model, and df_u is the degrees of freedom for the null model. In comparing different models for fit, Mulaik et al. multiplied RP_j by $RNFI_j$ to obtain a relative parsimony fit index appropriate for assessing how well and to what degree the models explained both relationships in the measurement of latent variables and the structural relationships among the latent variables by themselves. McDonald and Marsh (1990), however, doubted whether model parsimony and goodness of fit could be captured by this multiplicative form because it is not a monotonic increasing function of model complexity. Obviously, further research will be needed to clarify these issues.

Mulaik and Millsap (2000) also presented a four-step approach to testing a nested sequence of SEM models:

- Step 1 pertains to specifying an unrestricted measurement model, namely conducting an exploratory common factor analysis to determine the number of factors (latent variables) that fit the variance–covariance matrix of the observed variables.

- Step 2 involves a confirmatory factor analysis model that tests hypotheses about certain relations among indicator variables and latent variables. Basically, certain factor loadings are fixed to zero in an attempt to have only a single nonzero factor loading for each indicator variable of a latent variable. Sometimes this leads to a lack of measurement model fit because an indicator variable may have a relation with another latent variable.

- Step 3 involves specifying relations among the latent variables in a structural model. Certain relations among the latent variables are fixed to zero so that some latent variables are not related to one another.

- Step 4 continues if an acceptable fit of the structural model is achieved, that is, CFI > .95 and RMSEA < .05. In Step 4, a researcher tests planned hypotheses about free parameters in the model. Several approaches are possible: (a) perform simultaneous tests in which free parameters are fixed based on theory or estimates obtained from other research studies; (b) impose fixed parameter values on freed parameters in a nested sequence of models until a misspecified model is achieved (misspecified parameter); or (c) perform a sequence of confidence-interval tests around free parameters using the standard errors of the estimated parameters.

We agree with the basic Mulaik and Millsap (2000) approach and recommend that the measurement models for latent variables be established first and then structural models establishing relationships among the latent independent and dependent variables be formed. It is in the formulation of measurement models that most of the model modifications occur to obtain acceptable data to model fit. In fact, a researcher could begin model generation by using exploratory factor analysis (EFA) on a sample of data to find the number and type of latent variables in a plausible model (Costello & Osborne, 2005). Once a plausible model is determined, another sample of data could be used to confirm or test the factor model, that is, confirmatory factor analysis (CFA) (Jöreskog, 1969). Exploratory factor analysis is even recommended as a precursor to confirmatory factor analysis when the researcher does not have a substantive theoretical model (Gerbing & Hamilton, 1996).

Measurement invariance is also important to examine, which refers to considering similar measurement models across different groups; for example, does the factor (latent variable) imply the same thing to boys and girls? This usually involves adding between group constraints in the measurement model. If measurement invariance cannot be established, then the finding of a between group difference is questionable (Cheung & Rensvold, 2002). Cheung and Rensvold (2002) also recommend that the comparative fit index (CFI), gamma hat, and McDonald's noncentrality index (NCI) be used for testing between group measurement invariance of CFA models rather than the goodness-of-fit index (GFI) or the likelihood ratio test (LR), also known as the chi-square difference test. Byrne and Watkins (2003) questioned whether measurement invariance could be established given that individual items on an instrument could exhibit invariance or group differences. Later, Byrne and Sunita (2006) provided a step-by-step approach for examining measurement invariance.

5.8 Summary

In this chapter, we began by discussing three approaches a researcher could take in structural equation modeling: confirmatory models, alternative models, and model generation. We then considered categories of model-fit indices—namely, model-fit, model comparison, and model parsimony. In addition, current and new innovative approaches to specification searches were mentioned for the assessment of model fit in structural equation modeling. We examined in detail the different categories of model-fit criteria because different fit indices have been developed depending on the type of specified model tested. Generally, no single model-fit index is sufficient for testing a hypothesized structural model. An ideal fit index just does not exist. This is not surprising because it has been suggested that an ideal fit index is one that is independent of sample size, accurately reflects differences in fit, imposes a penalty for inclusion of additional parameters (Marsh et al., 1988), and supports the choice of a true model when it is known (McDonald & Marsh, 1990). The current model fitting practice in LISREL involves the use of modification indices and/or expected parameter change values, but other advances in specification search techniques have been investigated (Tabu and optimization algorithms), with a specification search approach already in AMOS (SPSS, 2009).

A two-factor confirmatory model was analyzed using the LISREL computer program with model-fit output to enhance our understanding of the many different model-fit criteria. We concluded in this chapter with a discussion of a four-step approach to SEM modeling, the significance of parameters in a model, power, and sample size. An understanding of model-fit criteria, power, and sample size will help your understanding of the examples presented in the remaining chapters of the book.

Exercises

1. Define confirmatory models, alternative models, and model-generating approaches.
2. Define model fit, model comparison, and model parsimony.
3. Calculate the following fit indices for the model output in Figure 5.1:

   $GFI = 1 - (\chi^2_{model}/\chi^2_{null})$
   $NFI = (\chi^2_{null} - \chi^2_{model})/\chi^2_{null}$
   $RFI = 1 - [(\chi^2_{model}/df_{model})/(\chi^2_{null}/df_{null})]$
   $IFI = (\chi^2_{null} - \chi^2_{model})/(\chi^2_{null} - df_{model})$
   $TLI = [(\chi^2_{null}/df_{null}) - (\chi^2_{model}/df_{model})]/[(\chi^2_{null}/df_{null}) - 1]$
   $CFI = 1 - [(\chi^2_{model} - df_{model})/(\chi^2_{null} - df_{null})]$
   Model AIC $= \chi^2_{model} + 2q$ (q is the number of free parameters)
   Null AIC $= \chi^2_{null} + 2q$ (q is the number of free parameters)

   $$RMSEA = \sqrt{[\chi^2_{Model} - df_{Model}]/[(N-1)df_{Model}]}$$
   or
   $$RMSEA = \sqrt{(NCP/N-1)/df}$$

4. How are modification indices in LISREL--SIMPLIS used?
5. What steps should a researcher take in examining parameter estimates in a model?
6. How should a researcher test for the difference between two alternative models?

7. How are structural equation models affected by sample size and power considerations?
8. Describe the four-step approach for modeling in SEM.
9. What new approaches are available to help a researcher identify the best model?
10. Use G*Power 3 to calculate power for modified model with NCP = 6.3496 at $p = .05$, $p = .01$, and $p = .001$ levels of significance. What happens to power when alpha increases?
11. Use G*Power 3 to calculate power for modified model with alpha = .05 and NCP = 6.3496 at $df = 1$, $df = 2$, and $df = 3$ levels of model complexity. What happens to power when degrees of freedom increases?

Chapter Footnote

LISREL computes two different sets of standard errors for parameter estimates and up to four different chi-squares for testing overall fit of the model. These new standard errors and chi-squares can be obtained for single-group problems as well as multiple-group problems using variance–covariance matrices with or without means.

Which standard errors and which chi-squares will be reported depends on whether an asymptotic covariance matrix is provided and which method of estimation is used to fit the model (ULS, GLS, ML, WLS, DWLS). The asymptotic covariance matrix is a consistent estimate of N times the asymptotic covariance matrix of the sample matrix being analyzed.

Standard Errors

Standard errors are estimated under nonnormality if an asymptotic covariance matrix is used. Standard errors are estimated under multivariate normality if no asymptotic covariance matrix is used.

Chi-Squares

Four different chi-squares are reported and denoted below as C1, C2, C3, and C4, where the x indicates that it is reported for any of the five estimation methods.

Asymptotic covariance matrix not provided:

	ULS	GLS	ML	WLS	DWLS
C1	—	×	×	—	—
C2	×	×	×	—	—
C3	—	—	—	—	—
C4	—	—	—	—	—

Asymptotic covariance matrix provided:

	ULS	GLS	ML	WLS	DWLS
C1	—	×	×	×	—
C2	×	×	×	—	×
C3	×	×	×	—	×
C4	×	×	×	—	×

NOTE: 1. C1 is $n - 1$ times the minimum value of the fit function; C2 is $n - 1$ times the minimum of the WLS fit function using a weight matrix estimated under multivariate normality; C3 is the Satorra–Bentler scaled chi-square statistic or its generalization to mean and covariance structures and multiple groups (Satorra & Bentler, 1994); C4 is computed from equations in Browne (1984) or Satorra (1993) using the asymptotic covariance matrix.

The corresponding chi-squares are now given in the output as follows:

C1: Minimum fit function chi-square

C2: Normal theory weighted least squares chi-square

C3: Satorra-Bentler scaled chi-square

C4: Chi-square corrected for nonnormality

NOTE 2: Under multivariate normality of the observed variables, C1 and C2 are asymptotically equivalent and have an asymptotic chi-square distribution if the model holds exactly and an asymptotic noncentral chi-square distribution if the model holds approximately. Under normality and nonnormality, C2 and C4 are correct asymptotic chi-squares, but may not be the best chi-square in small and moderate samples. Hu, Bentler, and Kano (1992) and Yuan and Bentler (1997) found that C3 performed better given different types of models, sample size, and degrees of nonnormality.

References

Akaike, H. (1987). Factor analysis and AIC. *Psychometrika, 52*, 317–332.

Anderson, J. C., & Gerbing, D. W. (1984). The effects of sampling error on convergence, improper solutions and goodness-of-fit indices for maximum likelihood confirmatory factor analysis. *Psychometrika, 49*, 155–173.

Anderson, J. C., & Gerbing, D. W. (1988). Structural equation modeling in practice: A review and recommended two-step approach. *Psychological Bulletin, 103*, 411–423.

Baldwin, B. (1989). A primer in the use and interpretation of structural equation models. *Measurement and Evaluation in Counseling and Development, 22*, 100–112.

Bentler, P. M. (1990). Comparative fit indexes in structural models. *Psychological Bulletin, 107*, 238–246.

Bentler, P. M., & Bonett, D. G. (1980). Significance tests and goodness-of-fit in the analysis of covariance structures. *Psychological Bulletin, 88*, 588–606.

Bollen, K. A. (1989). *Structural equations with latent variables.* New York: Wiley.

Bollen, K. A. (1990). Overall fit in covariance structure models: Two types of sample size effects. *Psychological Bulletin, 107*, 256–259.

Bollen, K. A., & Liang, J. (1988). Some properties of Hoelter's CN. *Sociological Methods and Research, 16*, 492–503.

Bollen, K. A., & Long, S. J. (1993). *Testing structural equation models.* Newbury Park, CA: Sage.

Browne, M. W. (1984). Asymptotically distribution-free methods for the analysis of covariance structures. *British Journal of Mathematical and Statistical Psychology, 37*, 62–83.

Browne, M. W., & Cudeck, R. (1993). Alternative ways of assessing model fit. In K. A. Bollen & J. S. Long (Eds.), *Testing structural equation models* (pp. 132–162). Beverly Hills, CA: Sage.

Byrne, B. M., & Watkins, D. (2003). The issue of measurement invariance revisited. *Journal of Cross-Cultural Psychology, 34*(2), 155–175.

Byrne, B., & Sunita, M. S. (2006). The MACS approach to testing for multigroup invariance of a second-order structure-A walk through the process. *Structural Equation Modeling: A Multidisciplinary Journal, 13*(2), 287–321.

Cheung, G. W., & Rensvold, R. B. (2002). Evaluating goodness-of-fit indexes for testing measurement invariance. *Structural Equation Modeling, 9*, 233–255.

Cliff, N. (1983). Some cautions concerning the application of causal modeling methods. *Multivariate Behavioral Research, 18*, 115–126.

Cohen, J. (1988). *Statistical power analysis for the behavioral sciences* (2nd ed.). Hillsdale, NJ: Lawrence Erlbaum.

Costello, A. B., & Osborne, J. (2005). Best practices in exploratory factor analysis: Four recommendations for getting the most from your analysis. *Practical Assessment Research & Evaluation, 10*(7), 1–9.

Cudeck, R., & Henly, S. J. (1991). Model selection in covariance structure analysis and the "problem" of sample size: A clarification. *Psychological Bulletin, 109*, 512–519.

Davey, A., & Savla, J. (2010). *Statistical Power analysis with missing data: A structural equation modeling approach*. Routledge: Taylor & Francis, New York.

Faul, F., Erdfelder, E., Lang, A.-G., & Buchner, A. (2007). G*Power 3: A flexible statistical power analysis program for the social, behavioral, and biomedical sciences. *Behavior Research Methods, 39*, 175–191.

Gerbing, D. W., & Hamilton, J. G. (1996). Viability of exploratory factor analysis as a precursor to confirmatory factor analysis, *Structural Equation Modeling, 3*(1), 62–72.

Gonzalez, R., & Griffin, D. (2001). Testing parameters in structural equation modeling: Every "one" matters. *Psychological Methods, 6*(3), 258–269.

Gorsuch, R. L. (1983). *Factor analysis* (2nd ed.). Hillsdale, NJ: Lawrence Erlbaum.

Hair, J. F., Jr., Anderson, R. E., Tatham, R. L., & Black, W. C. (1992). *Multivariate data analysis with readings* (3rd ed.). New York: Macmillan.

Harmon, H. H. (1976). *Modern factor analysis* (3rd ed.). Chicago, IL: University of Chicago Press.

Hoelter, J. W. (1983). The analysis of covariance structures: Goodness-of-fit indices. *Sociological Methods and Research, 11*, 325–344.

Holzinger, K. J., & Swineford, F. A. (1939). *A study in factor analysis: The stability of a bi-factor solution*. Supplementary Educational Monographs, No. 48. Chicago: University of Chicago, Dept. of Education.

Hu, L., & Bentler, P. M. (1995). Evaluating model fit. In R. H. Hoyle (Ed.), *Structural equation modeling: Concepts, issues, and applications* (pp. 76–99). Thousand Oaks, CA: Sage.

Hu, L., Bentler, P. M., & Kano, Y. (1992). Can test statistics in covariance structure analysis be trusted? *Psychological Bulletin, 112*, 351–362.

James, L. R., Mulaik, S. A., & Brett, J. M. (1982). *Causal analysis: Assumptions, models, and data*. Beverly Hills, CA: Sage.

Jöreskog, K. G. (1969). A general approach to confirmatory maximum likelihood factor analysis. *Psychometrika, 34*, 183–202.

Jöreskog, K. G., & Sörbom, D. (1993). *LISREL 8: Structural equation modeling with the SIMPLIS command language*. Hillsdale, NJ: Lawrence Erlbaum.

Kaplan, D. (1995). Statistical power in structural equation modeling. In R. H. Hoyle (Ed.), *Structural equation modeling: Concepts, issues, and applications* (pp. 100–117). Thousand Oaks, CA: Sage.

Kenny, D. A., & McCoach, D. B. (2003). Effect of the number of variables on measures of fit in structural equation modeling. *Structural Equation Modeling, 10*, 333–351.

Loehlin, J. C. (1987). *Latent variable models: An introduction to factor, path, and structural analysis*. Hillsdale, NJ: Lawrence Erlbaum.

Lomax, R. G. (1982). A guide to LISREL-type structural equation modeling. *Behavior Research Methods and Instrumentation, 14*, 1–8.

Lunneborg, C. E. (1987). *Bootstrap applications for the behavioral sciences. Vol. 1.* Seattle: University of Washington, Psychology Department.

MacCallum, R. C., Browne, M. W., & Sugawara, H. M. (1996). Power analysis and determination of sample size for covariance structure modeling. *Psychological Methods, 1*, 130–149.

MacCallum, R. C., Browne, M. W., & Cai, L. (2006). Testing differences between nested covariance structure models: Power analysis and null hypotheses. *Psychological Methods, 11*, 19–35.

Marcoulides, G. A., & Drezner, Z. (2001). Specification searches in structural equation modeling with a genetic algorithm. In G. A. Marcoulides & R. E. Schumacker (Eds.), *New developments and techniques in structural equation modeling* (pp. 247–268). Mahwah, NJ: Lawrence Erlbaum.

Marcoulides, G. A., & Drezner, Z. (2003). Model specification searches using ant colony optimization algorithms. *Structural Equation Modeling, 10*, 154–164.

Marcoulides, G. A., Drezner, Z., & Schumacker, R. E. (1998). Model specification searches in structural equation modeling using Tabu search. *Structural Equation Modeling, 5*, 365–376.

Marsh, H. W., Balla, J. R., & Hau, K.-T. (1996). An evaluation of incremental fit indices: A clarification of mathematical and empirical properties. In G. A. Marcoulides & R. E. Schumacker (Eds.), *Advanced structural equation modeling: Issues and techniques* (pp. 315–353). Mahwah, NJ: Lawrence Erlbaum.

Marsh, H. W., Balla, J. R., & McDonald, R. P. (1988). Goodness-of-fit indexes in confirmatory factor analysis: The effect of sample size. *Psychological Bulletin, 103*, 391–410.

McDonald, R. P. (1989). An index of goodness-of-fit based on noncentrality. *Journal of Classification, 6*, 97–103.

McDonald, R. P., & Marsh, H. W. (1990). Choosing a multivariate model: Noncentrality and goodness of fit. *Psychological Bulletin, 107*, 247–255.

Mulaik, S. A., James, L. R., Alstine, J. V., Bennett, N., Lind, S., & Stilwell, C. D. (1989). Evaluation of goodness-of-fit indices for structural equation models. *Psychological Bulletin, 105*, 430–445.

Mulaik, S. A., & Millsap, R. E. (2000). Doing the four-step right. *Structural Equation Modeling, 7*, 36–73.

Muthén, B., & Muthén, L. (2002). How to use a Monte Carlo study to decide on sample size and determine power. *Structural Equation Modeling, 9*, 599–620.

Saris, W. E., & Satorra, A. (1993). Power evaluation in structural equation models. In K. Bollen & J. S. Long (Eds.), *Testing structural equation models* (pp. 181–204). Newbury Park, CA: Sage.

Satorra, A. (1993). Multi-sample analysis of moment structures: Asymptotic validity of inferences based on second-order moments. In K. Haagen, D. J. Bartholomew, & M. Deistler (Eds.), *Statistical modeling and latent variables* (pp. 283–298). Amsterdam: Elsevier.

Satorra, A., & Bentler, P. M. (1994). Corrections for test statistics and standard errors in covariance structure analysis. In A. Von Eye & C. C. Clogg (Eds.), *Latent variable analysis: Applications for developmental research* (pp. 399–419). Thousand Oaks, CA: Sage.

Soper, D., Statistics Calculators. Retrieved January 2010 from http://www.danielsoper.com/statcalc/.

SPSS (2009). Statistics 17.0. SPSS, Inc.: Chicago, IL.

Steiger, J. H. (1990). Structural model evaluation and modification: An interval estimation approach. *Multivariate Behavioral Research, 25*, 173–180.

Steiger, J. H., & Lind, J. M. (1980, May). *Statistically-based tests for the number of common factors*. Paper presented at Psychometric Society Meeting, Iowa City, IA.

Tucker, L. R., & Lewis, C. (1973). The reliability coefficient for maximum likelihood factor analysis. *Psychometrika, 38*, 1–10.

Williams, L. J., & Holahan, P. J. (1994). Parsimony-based fit indices of multiple indicator models: Do they work? *Structural Equation Modeling: A Multidisciplinary Journal, 1*, 161–189.

Yuan, K.-H., & Bentler, P. M. (1997). Mean and covariance structure analysis: Theoretical and practical improvements. *Journal of the American Statistical Association, 92*, 767–774.

6

Regression Models

Key Concepts

Explanation versus prediction

Standardized partial regression coefficients

Coefficient of determination

Squared multiple correlation coefficient

Full versus restricted models

Confidence intervals around R^2

Measurement error

Additive versus relational model

In this chapter, we consider multiple regression models as a method for modeling multiple observed variables. Multiple regression, a general linear modeling approach to the analysis of data, has become increasingly popular since 1967 (Bashaw & Findley, 1968). In fact, it has become recognized as an approach that bridges the gap between correlation and analysis of variance in answering research hypotheses (McNeil, Kelly, & McNeil, 1975). Many statistical textbooks elaborate the relationship between multiple regression and analysis of variance (Draper & Smith, 1966; Edwards, 1979; Hinkle, Wiersma, & Jurs, 2003; Lomax, 2007).

Graduate students who take an advanced statistics course are typically provided with the multiple linear regression framework for data analysis. Given knowledge of multiple linear regression techniques (one dependent variable), understanding can be extended to various multivariable statistical techniques (Newman, 1988). A basic knowledge of multiple regression concepts is therefore important in further understanding path analysis as presented in Chapter 7. This chapter shows how beta weights (standardized partial regression coefficients) are computed in multiple regression using a structural equation modeling software program. More specifically, we illustrate how the structural equation modeling approach can be used to compute parameter estimates in multiple regression and what model-fit criteria are reported. We begin with a brief overview of multiple regression concepts followed by an example that illustrates model specification, model identification, model estimation, model testing, and model modification.

6.1 Overview

Multiple regression techniques require a basic understanding of sample statistics (sample size, mean, and variance), standardized variables, correlation (Pedhazur, 1982), and partial correlation (Cohen & Cohen, 1983; Houston & Bolding, 1974). In standard score form (z scores), the simple linear regression equation for predicting the dependent variable Y from a single independent variable X is

$$\hat{z}_y = \beta\, z_x,$$

where β is the standardized regression coefficient. The basic rationale for using the standard-score formula is that variables are converted to the same scale of measurement, the z scale. Conversion back to the raw-score scale is easily accomplished by using the raw score, the mean and the standard deviation.

The relationship connecting the Pearson product-moment correlation coefficient, the unstandardized regression coefficient b and the standardized regression coefficient β is

$$\beta = \frac{\sum z_x z_y}{\sum z_x^2} = b\,\frac{s_x}{s_y} = r_{xy},$$

where s_x and s_y are the sample standard deviations for variables X and Y, respectively. For two independent variables, the multiple linear regression equation with standard scores is

$$\hat{z}_y = \beta_1 z_1 + \beta_2 z_2$$

and the standardized partial regression coefficients β_1 and β_2 are computed from

$$\beta_1 = \frac{r_{y1} - r_{y2} r_{12}}{1 - r_{12}^2} \quad \text{and} \quad \beta_2 = \frac{r_{y2} - r_{y1} r_{12}}{1 - r_{12}^2}.$$

The correlation between the dependent observed variable Y and the predicted scores $\hat{Y}$ is given the special name *multiple correlation coefficient*. It is written as

$$R_{y\hat{y}} = R_{y.12} \, ,$$

where the latter subscripts indicate that the dependent variable Y is being predicted by two independent variables, X_1 and X_2. The *squared multiple correlation coefficient* is computed as

$$R_{y\hat{y}}^2 = R_{y.12}^2 = \beta_1 r_{Y+1} + \beta_2 r_{Y2} \, .$$

The squared multiple correlation coefficient indicates the amount of variance explained, predicted, or accounted for in the dependent variable by the set of independent predictor variables. The R^2 value is used as a model-fit criterion in multiple regression analysis.

Kerlinger and Pedhazur (1973) indicated that multiple regression analysis can play an important role in prediction and explanation. Prediction and explanation reflect different research questions, study designs, inferential approaches, analysis strategies, and reported information. In prediction, the main emphasis is on practical application such that independent variables are chosen by their effectiveness in enhancing prediction of the dependent variable. In explanation, the main emphasis is on the variability in the dependent variable explained by a theoretically meaningful set of independent variables. Huberty (2003) established a clear distinction between prediction and explanation when referring to multiple correlation analysis (MCA) and multiple regression analysis (MRA). In MCA, a parameter of interest is the correlation between the dependent variable Y and a composite of the independent variables X_p. The adjusted formula using sample size n and the number of independent predictors p is

$$R_{Adj}^2 = R^2 - \frac{p}{n-p-1}(1-R^2).$$

In MRA, regression weights are also estimated to achieve a composite for the independent variables X_p, but the index of fit R^2 is computed differently as

$$R_{Adj^*}^2 = R^2 - \frac{2p}{n-p}(1-R^2).$$

When comparing these two formulas, we see that $R_{Adj^*}^2$ has a larger adjustment. For example, given $R^2 = .50$, $p = 10$ predictor variables and $n = 100$ subjects, these two different fit indices are

$$R_{Adj}^2 = R^2 - \frac{p}{n-p-1}(1-R^2) = .50 - .11(.50) = .50 - .055 = .45$$

$$R^2_{Adj^*} = R^2 - \frac{2p}{n-p}(1-R^2) = .50 - .22(.50) = .50 - .11 = .39.$$

Hypothesis testing would involve using the *expected value* or chance value of R^2 for testing the null hypothesis, which is $p/(n-1)$, not 0 as typically indicated. In our example, the expected or chance value for $R^2 = 10/99 = .10$, so the null hypothesis is H_0: $\rho^2 = .10$. An F test used to test the statistical significance of the R^2 value is

$$F = \frac{R^2/p}{(1-R^2)/n-p-1}.$$

In our example,

$$F = \frac{R^2/p}{(1-R^2)/n-p-1} = \frac{.50/10}{(1-.50)/89} = \frac{.05}{.0056} = 8.9,$$

which is statistically significant when compared to the tabled $F = 1.93$, $df = 10,89$, $p < .05$ (Table A.5). In addition to the statistical significance test, a researcher should calculate *effect sizes* and *confidence intervals* to aid understanding and interpretation (Soper, 2010).

The *effect size* (ES) is computed as ES = $R^2 - [p/(n-1)]$. In our example, ES $R^2_{Adj} = .45 - .10 = .35$ and ES $R^2_{Adj^*} = .39 - .10 = .29$. This indicates a moderate to large effect size according to Cohen (1988), who gave a general reference for effect sizes (small = .1, medium = .25, and large = .4).

Confidence intervals (CIs) around the R^2 value can also help our interpretation of multiple regression analysis. Steiger and Fouladi (1992) reported an R^2 CI DOS program that computes confidence intervals, power, and sample size. Steiger and Fouladi (1997) and Cumming and Finch (2001) both discussed the importance of converting the central F value to an estimate of the noncentral F before computing a confidence interval around R^2. Smithson (2001) wrote an R^2 SPSS program to compute confidence intervals.

We use the Steiger and Fouladi (1997) R^2 CI DOS program with our hypothetical example. After entering the program, Option is selected from the tool bar menu and then Confidence Interval is selected from the dropdown menu. To obtain R^2 CI, the number of subjects ($n = 100$), the number of variables ($K = 10$), the R^2 value ($R = .35$), and the desired confidence level ($C = .95$) are entered by using the arrow keys (mouse not supported), and then **GO** is selected to compute the values. The 95% confidence interval around $R^2 = .35$ is .133 to .449 at the $p = .0001$ level of significance for a null hypothesis that $R^2 = 0$ in the population.

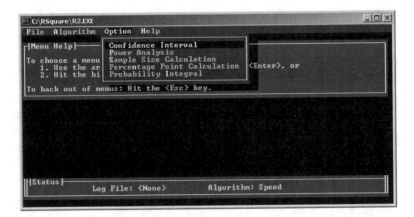

After assessing our initial regression model fit, we might want to determine whether adding or deleting an independent variable would improve the index of fit R^2, but we avoid using stepwise regression methods (Huberty, 1989). We run a second multiple regression equation where a single independent variable is added or deleted to obtain a second R^2 value. We then compute a different F test to determine the statistical significance between the two regression models as follows

$$F = \frac{(R_F^2 - R_R^2)/(p_1 - p_2)}{(1 - R_F^2)/n - p_1 - 1},$$

where R^2_F is from the multiple regression equation with the full original set of independent variables p_1 and R_R^2 is from the multiple regression equation with the reduced set of independent variables p_2. In our heuristic example, we drop a single independent variable and obtain $R_R^2 = .49$ with $p_2 = 9$ predictor variables. The F test is computed as:

$$F = \frac{(R_F^2 - R_R^2)/(p_1 - p_2)}{(1 - R_F^2)/n - p_1 - 1} = \frac{(.50 - .49)/(10 - 9)}{(1 - .50)/100 - 10 - 1} = \frac{.01}{.0056} = 1.78.$$

The F value is not significant at the .05 level, so the variable we dropped does not statistically add to the prediction of Y, which supports our dropping the single predictor variable; that is, a 1% decrease in R^2 is not statistically significant. The nine-variable regression model therefore provides a more parsimonious model.

It is important to understand the basic concepts of multiple regression and correlation because they provide a better understanding of path analysis in chapter 7, and structural equation modeling in general. An example is presented next to further clarify these basic multiple regression computations.

6.2 An Example

A multiple linear regression analysis is conducted using data from Chatterjee and Yilmaz (1992). The data file contains scores from 24 patients on four variables (Var1 = patient's age in years, Var2 = severity of illness, Var3 = level of anxiety, and Var4 = satisfaction level). Given raw data, two different approaches are possible in LISREL: (a) a system file in LISREL–PRELIS using regression statistics from the pull-down menu or (b) a cor-relation or covariance matrix input in the LISREL–SIMPLIS command syntax file. We choose to compute and input a covariance matrix into a LISREL–SIMPLIS program.

6.3 Model Specification

Model specification involves finding relevant theory and prior research to formulate a theoretical regression model. The researcher is interested in specifying a regression model that should be confirmed with sample variance–covariance data, thus yielding a high R^2 value and statisti-cally significant F value. Model specification directly involves deciding which variables to include or not to include in the theoretical regression model.

If the researcher does not select the right variables, then the regression model could be misspecified and lack validity (Tracz, Brown, & Kopriva, 1991). The problem is that a misspecified model may result in biased parameter estimates or estimates that are systematically different from what they really are in the true population model. This bias is known as *specification error*.

The researcher's goal is to determine whether the theoretical regression model fits the sample variance–covariance structure in the data, that is, whether the sample variance–covariance matrix implies some underlying theoretical regression model. The multiple regression model of theoretical interest in our example is to predict the satisfaction level of patients based on patient's age, severity of illness, and level of anxiety (independent vari-ables). This would be characteristic of a *MCA* model because a particular set of variables were selected based on theory. The dependent variable Var4 is therefore predicted by the three independent variables (Var1, Var2, and Var3). The path diagram of the implied regression model is shown in Figure 6.1.

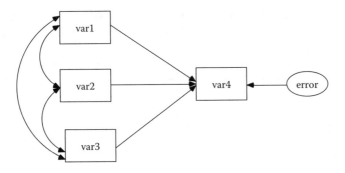

FIGURE 6.1
Satisfaction regression model.

6.4 Model Identification

Once a theoretical regression model is specified, the next concern is *model identification*. Model identification refers to deciding whether a set of unique parameter estimates can be computed for the regression equation. Algebraically, every free parameter in the multiple regression equation can be estimated from the sample variance–covariance matrix (a free parameter is an unknown parameter that you want to estimate). The number of distinct values in the sample variance–covariance matrix equals the number of parameters to be estimated; thus, multiple regression models are always considered *just-identified* (see chapter 4). SEM computer output will therefore indicate that regression analyses are *saturated* models; thus, $\chi^2 = 0$ and degrees of freedom = 0. There are 3 variances, 3 covariance terms, 3 regression weights, and 1 error term so all parameters in the regression equation are being estimated.

6.5 Model Estimation

Model estimation involves estimating the parameters in the regression model—that is, computing the sample regression weights for the independent predictor variables. The squared multiple correlation with three predictor variables (VAR1, VAR2, VAR3) predicting the dependent variable Y (VAR4) is

$$R^2_{y.123} = \beta_1 r_{y1} + \beta_2 r_{y2} + \beta_3 r_{y3} \ .$$

The correlation coefficients are multiplied by their respective standardized partial regression weights and summed to yield the squared multiple regression coefficient $R^2_{y \cdot 123}$.

In LISREL–SIMPLIS, we select *File, New,* and then *Syntax Only* in the dialog box to write the following SIMPLIS program:

```
Regression Analysis Example (no intercept term)
Observed variables: VAR1 VAR2 VAR3 VAR4
Covariance matrix:
 91.384
 30.641 27.288
 0.584  0.641 0.100
 -122.616 -52.576 -2.399 281.210
Sample size: 24
Equation: VAR4 = VAR1 VAR2 VAR3
Number of decimals = 3
Path Diagram
End of Problem
```

You will be prompted to save the program with a file name (*.spl) before the program runs.

The critical portion of the LISREL–SIMPLIS regression output without an *intercept* term in the regression equation looks like:

VAR4 = − 1.153*VAR1 − 0.267*VAR2 − 15.546*VAR3, Errorvar.= 88.515, R^2 = 0.685

(0.279)	(0.544)	(7.232)	(27.991)
−4.129	−0.491	−2.150	3.162

```
Goodness-of-Fit Statistics
Degrees of Freedom = 0
Minimum Fit Function Chi-Square = 0.0 (P = 1.000)
Normal Theory Weighted Least Squares Chi-Square =
0.00 (P = 1.000)
The model is saturated, the fit is perfect!
```

We notice that the regression weights are identified for each independent variable (VAR1 – VAR3). Below each regression weight is the standard error in parenthesis, for example, VAR1 regression weight has a standard error of .279; with the *T* or *Z* value indicated below that, and a p-value listed below the *T* or *Z* value. (*Note:* LISREL 8.8 Student version lists the parameter estimate, standerd error, z value, and associated p-value.) Recall that T = parameter divided by standard error (T = −1.153/.279 = −4.129). If testing each regression weight at the critical t = 1.96, α = .05 level of significance, then VAR1 and VAR3 are statistically significant, but VAR2 is not (T = −.491). We also notice that R^2 = .685 or 69% of the variability in Y scores (VAR4) is predicted by knowledge of VAR1, VAR2, and VAR3.

We will later discuss modifying this regression model—that is, dropping VAR2 (see section 6.7). This example is further explained in Jöreskog and Sörbom (1993, pp. 1–6).

6.6 Model Testing

Model testing involves determining the fit of the theoretical model. Therefore, we will present how to hand calculate the R^2 value from the correlation matrix output by LISREL, as follows:

```
CORRELATION MATRIX
            VAR1        VAR2        VAR3        VAR4
VAR1       1.0000
VAR2       0.6136      1.0000
VAR3       0.1935      0.3888      1.0000
VAR4      -0.7649     -0.6002     -0.4530      1.0000
```

The standardized regression coefficients can be obtained from selecting the *standardized solution* in the pull down menu of the path diagram window of the LISREL–SIMPLIS program. We can now verify the R^2 value using the standardized regression formula:

(**NOTE:** This matches the R^2 value in the LISREL–SIMPLIS output as shown above). The adjusted R^2 value for the MCA theoretical regression model approach is

$$R_{y.123}^2 = \beta_1 r_{y1} + \beta_2 r_{y2} + \beta_3 r_{y3} = -.657(-.7649) + -.083(-.6002)$$

$$+ -.294(-.4530) = .685.$$

$$R_{Adj}^2 = R^2 - \frac{p}{n-p-1}(1 - R^2) = .685 - .15(.315) = .685 - .047 = .638.$$

The F test for the significance of the R^2 value is

$$F = \frac{R^2/p}{(1 - R^2)/n - p - 1} = \frac{.685/3}{(1 - .685)/20} = \frac{.228}{.0157} = 14.52.$$

The *effect size* is

$$R^2 - [p/(n-1)] = .685 - [3/23] = .685 - .130 = .554.$$

This is a large effect size. The 95% *confidence interval* around $R^2 = .685$ using the R^2 CI program is (.33, .83).

The results indicate that a patient's age, severity of illness, and level of anxiety make up a statistically significant set of predictors of a patient's satisfaction level. There is a large effect size and the confidence interval reveals the range of R^2 values one can expect in conducting a regression analysis on another sample of data. The negative standardized regression coefficients indicate that as patient age, severity of illness, and anxiety increase, patient satisfaction decreases.

6.7 Model Modification

The theoretical regression model included a set of three independent explanatory variables, which resulted in a statistically significant $R^2 = .685$. This implies that 69% of the patient satisfaction level score variance is explained by knowledge of a patient's age, severity of illness, and level of anxiety. The regression analysis, however, indicated that the regression weight for *Var2* was not statistically different from zero ($t = -0.491, p > .10$). Thus, one might consider *model modification* where the theoretical regression model is modified to produce a two-variable regression equation, thus allowing for the F test of the difference between the two regression analysis R^2 values.

We repeat the steps for the regression analysis, but this time only including *Var1* and *Var3* in the analysis. The results for the regression equation with these two variables, *Var1* and *Var3* in the LISREL–SIMPLIS program, are:

VAR4 = $- 1.235$*VAR1 $- 16.780$*VAR3, Errorvar. $= 89.581$, $R^2 = 0.681$

$\qquad$ (0.220) $\qquad\qquad$ (6.657) $\qquad\qquad$ (27.645)
$\qquad$ -5.606 $\qquad\qquad$ -2.521 $\qquad\qquad$ 3.240

The F test for a difference between the two models is

$$F = \frac{(R_F^2 - R_R^2)/(p_1 - p_2)}{(1 - R_F^2)/n - p_1 - 1} = \frac{(.685 - .681)/(3 - 2)}{(1 - .685)/24 - 3 - 1} = \frac{.004}{.016} = .25.$$

The F test for the difference in the two R^2 values was nonsignificant indicating that dropping *Var2* does not affect the explanation of a patient's satisfaction level ($R2 = .685$ vs. $R2 = .681$). We therefore use the more parsimonious two-variable regression model (68% of the variance in a patient's satisfaction level is explained by knowledge of a patient's age and level of anxiety, that is, 68% of $281.210 = 191.22$).

Because the R^2 value is not 1.0 (perfect explanation or prediction), additional variables could be added if more recent research indicated that another variable was relevant to a patient's satisfaction level, for example, the number of psychological assessment visits. Obviously, more variables can be added in the model modification process, but a theoretical basis should be established by the researcher for the additional variables.

6.8 Summary

This chapter illustrated the important statistics to report when conducting a regression analysis. We found that the model-fit statistics in chapter 5 do not apply because regression models are saturated just-identified models. We also showed that the selection of independent variables in the regression model (model specification) and the subsequent regression model modification are key issues not easily resolved without a good sound theoretical justification.

The selection of a set of independent variables and the subsequent regression model modification are important issues in multiple regression. How does a researcher determine the best set of independent variables for explanation or prediction? It is highly recommended that a regression model be based on some theoretical framework that can be used to guide the decision of what variables to include. Model specification consists of determining what variables to include in the model and which variables are independent or dependent. A systematic determination of the most important set of variables can then be accomplished by setting the partial regression weight of a single variable to zero, thus testing full and restricted models for a difference in the R^2 values (F test). This approach and other alternative methods were presented by Darlington (1968).

In multiple regression, the selection of a wrong set of variables can yield erroneous and inflated R^2 values. The process of determining which set of variables yields the best prediction, given time, cost, and staffing, is often problematic because several methods and criteria are available to choose from. Recent methodological reviews have indicated that stepwise methods are not preferred, and that an *all-possible-subset* approach is recommended (Huberty, 1989; Thompson, Smith, Miller, & Thomson, 1991). In addition, the Mallows C_P statistic is advocated by some rather than R^2 for selecting the best set of predictors (Mallows, 1966; Schumacker, 1994; Zuccaro, 1992). Overall, which variables are included in a regression equation will determine the validity of the model and be determined by the rationale for the model by the researcher (see Chapter Note, for inclusion of an intercept term).

Because multiple regression techniques have been shown to be robust to violations of assumptions (Bohrnstedt & Carter, 1971) and applicable to contrast coding, dichotomous coding, ordinal coding (Lyons, 1971), and criterion scaling (Schumacker, 1993), they have been used in a variety of research designs. In fact, multiple regression equations can be used to address several different types of research questions. The model specification issue, however, is paramount in achieving a valid multiple regression model. Replication, cross-validation, and bootstrapping have all been applied in multiple regression to determine the validity of a regression model (see chapter 12 for further discussion of these methods in SEM).

There are other issues related to using the regression method, namely, variable measurement error and the additive nature of the equation. These two issues are described next.

6.8.1 Measurement Error

The issue of unreliable variable measurements and their effect on multiple regression has been previously discussed (Cleary, 1969; Cochran, 1968; Fuller & Hidiroglou, 1978; Subkoviak & Levin, 1977; Sutcliffe, 1958). A recommended solution was to multiply the dependent variable reliability and/or average of the independent variable reliabilities by the R^2 value (Cochran, 1968, 1970). The basic equation using only the reliability of the dependent variable is

$$\hat{R}^2_{y.123} = R^2_{y.123} * r_{yy} \, ,$$

or, including the dependent variable reliability and the average of the independent variable reliabilities,

$$\hat{R}^2_{y.123} = R^2_{y.123} * r_{yy} * \bar{r}_{xx} \, .$$

This is not always possible if reliabilities of the dependent and independent variables are unknown. This correction to R^2 for measurement error (unreliability) has intuitive appeal given the definition of classical reliability, namely the proportion of true score variance accounted for given the observed scores. In our previous example, $R^2 = .68$. If the dependent variable reliability is .80, then only 54% of the variance in patient's satisfaction level is true variance, rather than 68%. Similarly, if the average of the two independent variable reliabilities was .90, then multiplying .68 by .80 by .90 yields only 49% variance as true variance. Obviously, unreliable variables (measurement error) can have a dramatic effect on statistics and our interpretation of the results. Werts, Rock, Linn, and Jöreskog (1976) examined correlations, variances, covariances, and regression weights with and without measurement error and developed a program to correct the regression weights for attenuation. Our basic concern is that unreliable measured variables coupled with a potential misspecified model do not represent theory well.

The impact of measurement error on statistical analyses is not new, but is often forgotten by researchers. Fuller (1987) extensively covered structural equation modeling, and especially extended regression analysis to the case where the variables were measured with error. Cochran (1968) studied four different aspects of how measurement error affected statistics: (a) types of mathematical models, (b) standard techniques of analysis that take measurement error into account, (c) effect of errors of measurement in producing bias and reduced precision and what remedial procedures are available, and (d) techniques for studying error of measurement. Cochran (1970) also studied the effects of measurement error on the squared multiple correlation coefficient.

The validity and reliability issues in measurement have traditionally been handled by first examining the validity and reliability of scores on instruments used in a particular research design. Given an acceptable level of score validity and reliability, the scores are then used in a statistical analysis. The traditional statistical analysis of these scores using multiple regression, however, did not adjust for measurement error, so it is not surprising that an approach such as SEM was developed to incorporate measurement error adjustments into statistical analyses (Loehlin, 1992).

6.8.2 Additive Equation

The multiple regression equation is by definition additive ($Y = X_1 + X_2$) and thus does not permit any other relationships among the variables to be specified. This limits the potential for variables to have direct, indirect, and total effects on each other as described in chapter 7 (path models). In fact, a researcher's interest should not be with the Pearson product-moment correlations, but rather with partial or part correlations that reflect the unique additive contribution of each variable, that is, standardized partial regression weights. Even with this emphasis, the basic problem is that variables are typically added in a regression model, a process that functions ideally only if all independent variables are highly correlated with the dependent variable and uncorrelated among themselves. Path models, in contrast, provide theoretically meaningful relationships in a manner not restricted to an additive model (Schumacker, 1991).

Multiple regression as a general data-analytic technique is widely accepted and used by educational researchers, behavioral scientists, and biostatisticians. Multiple regression methods basically determine the overall contribution of a set of observed variables to explanation or prediction, test full and restricted models for the significant contribution of a variable in a model, and delineate the best subset of multiple independent predictors. Multiple regression equations also permit the use of nominal, ordinal, effect, contrast, or polynomial coded variables (Pedhazur, 1982; Pedhazur & Schmelkin, 1992). The multiple regression approach, however, is not robust to measurement error and model misspecification (Bohrnstedt & Carter, 1971) and gives an additive model rather than a relational model; hence, path models play an important role in defining more meaningful theoretical models to test.

Chapter Footnote

Regression Model with Intercept Term

In the LISREL–SIMPLIS GUIDE (Jöreskog & Sörbom, 1993) we see our first use of the CONST command which uses a mean value, thus includes an intercept term in the model. The SEM modeling type *structured means* makes use of this command to test the mean values between models (see Chapter 13). The following LISREL–SIMPLIS Program includes the command, CONST, to produce an intercept term in the regression equation:

LISREL–SIMPLIS Program (Intercept Term)

Regression Analysis

Raw Data from file chatter.psf

Equation: VAR4 = VAR1 VAR2 VAR3 CONST

Path Diagram

End of Problem

The LISREL–SIMPLIS output would look like this:

VAR4 = 156.62 − 1.15*VAR1 − 0.27*VAR2 − 15.59*VAR3, Errorvar. = 88.46, $R^2 = 0.69$

$$\begin{array}{ccccc} (22.61) & (0.28) & (0.54) & (7.24) & (27.97) \\ 6.93 & -4.13 & -0.49 & -2.15 & 3.16 \end{array}$$

In the LISREL 8.8 Student Examples folder, *SPLEX*, the program **EX1A.SPL** computes the regression equation *without* an intercept term, while the program **EX1B.SPL** computes the regression equation *with* an intercept term. In general, if you include sample means, then an intercept term is included in the equation. These examples are further explained in the *LISREL8: Structural Equation Modeling with the SIMPLIS Command Language* (Jöreskog & Sörbom, 1993, p. 1–6).

Exercises

1. Analyze the regression model in LISREL–SIMPLIS using the covariance matrix below with a sample size of 23 as described in Jöreskog and Sörbom (1993, pp. 3–6). The theoretical regression model specifies that the dependent variable, gross national product (GNP), is predicted by labor, capital, and time (three independent variables).

Covariance Matrix

GNP	4256.530			
Labor	449.016	52.984		
Capital	1535.097	139.449	1114.447	
Time	537.482	53.291	170.024	73.747

2. Is there an alternative regression model that predicts GNP better? Report the *F*, effect size, and confidence interval for the revised model. The regression model is shown in Figure 6.2

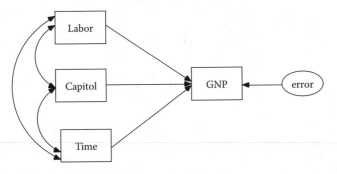

FIGURE 6.2
GNP regression model.

References

Bashaw, W. L., & Findley, W. G. (1968). *Symposium on general linear model approach to the analysis of experimental data in educational research.* (Project No. 7-8096). Washington, DC: U.S. Department of Health, Education, and Welfare.

Bohrnstedt, G. W., & Carter, T. M. (1971). Robustness in regression analysis. In H. L. Costner (Ed.), *Sociological methodology* (pp. 118–146). San Francisco, CA: Jossey-Bass.

Chatterjee, S., & Yilmaz, M. (1992). A review of regression diagnostics for behavioral research. *Applied Psychological Measurement, 16,* 209–227.

Cleary, T. A. (1969). Error of measurement and the power of a statistical test. *British Journal of Mathematical and Statistical Psychology, 22,* 49–55.

Cochran, W. G. (1968). Errors of measurement in statistics. *Technometrics, 10,* 637–666.

Cochran, W. G. (1970). Some effects of errors of measurement on multiple correlation. *Journal of the American Statistical Association, 65,* 22–34.

Cohen, J. (1988). *Statistical power analysis for the behavioral sciences* (2nd ed.). Hillsdale, NJ: Lawrence Erlbaum.

Cohen, J., & Cohen, P. (1983). *Applied multiple regression/correlation analysis for the behavioral sciences* (2nd ed.). Hillsdale, NJ: Lawrence Erlbaum.

Cumming, G., & Finch, S. (2001). A primer on the understanding, use and calculation of confidence intervals that are based on central and noncentral distributions. *Educational and Psychological Measurement, 61,* 532–574.

Darlington, R. B. (1968). Multiple regression in psychological research and practice. *Psychological Bulletin, 69,* 161–182.

Draper, N. R., & Smith, H. (1966). *Applied regression analysis.* New York: Wiley.

Edwards, A. L. (1979). *Multiple regression and the analysis of variance and covariance.* San Francisco, CA: Freeman.

Fuller, W. A. (1987). *Measurement error models.* New York: Wiley.

Fuller, W. A., & Hidiroglou, M. A. (1978). Regression estimates after correcting for attenuation. *Journal of the American Statistical Association, 73,* 99–104.

Hinkle, D. E., Wiersma, W., & Jurs, S.G. (2003). *Applied statistics for the behavioral sciences* (5th ed.). Boston, MA: Houghton Mifflin.

Houston, S. R., & Bolding, J. T., Jr. (1974). Part, partial, and multiple correlation in commonality analysis of multiple regression models. *Multiple Linear Regression Viewpoints, 5,* 36–40.

Huberty, C. J. (1989). Problems with stepwise methods—Better alternatives. In B. Thompson (Ed.), *Advances in social science methodology* (Vol. 1, pp. 43–70). Greenwich, CT: JAI.

Huberty, C. J. (2003). Multiple correlation versus multiple regression. *Educational and Psychological Measurement, 63,* 271–278.

Jöreskog, K. G., & Sörbom, D. (1993). *LISREL8: Structural equation modeling with the SIMPLIS command language.* Chicago, IL: Scientific Software International.

Kerlinger, F. N., & Pedhazur, E. J. (1973). *Multiple regression in behavioral research.* New York: Holt, Rinehart, & Winston.

Loehlin, J. C. (1992). *Latent variable models: An introduction to factor, path, and structural analysis* (2nd ed.). Mahwah, NJ: Lawrence Erlbaum.

Lomax, R. G. (2007). *Statistical concepts: A second course* (3rd ed.). Mahwah, NJ: Lawrence Erlbaum.

Lyons, M. (1971). Techniques for using ordinal measures in regression and path analysis. In H. L. Costner (Ed.), *Sociological methodology* (pp. 147–171). San Francisco, CA: Jossey-Bass.

Mallows, C. L. (1966, March). *Choosing a subset regression.* Paper presented at the Joint Meetings of the American Statistical Association, Los Angeles.

McNeil, K. A., Kelly, F. J., & McNeil, J. T. (1975). *Testing research hypotheses using multiple linear regression.* Carbondale: Southern Illinois University Press.

Newman, I. (1988, October). *There is no such thing as multivariate analysis: All analyses are univariate.* President's address at Mid-Western Educational Research Association, Chicago.

Pedhazur, E. J. (1982). *Multiple regression in behavioral research: Explanation and prediction* (2nd ed.). New York: Holt, Rinehart, & Winston.

Pedhazur, E. J., & Schmelkin, L. P. (1992). *Measurement, design, and analysis: An integrated approach.* Hillsdale, NJ: Lawrence Erlbaum.

Schumacker, R. E. (1991). Relationship between multiple regression, path, factor, and LISREL analyses. *Multiple Linear Regression Viewpoints, 18,* 28–46.

Schumacker, R. E. (1993). Teaching ordinal and criterion scaling in multiple regression. *Multiple Linear Regression Viewpoints, 20,* 25–31.

Schumacker, R. E. (1994). A comparison of the Mallows C_p and principal component regression criteria for best model selection. *Multiple Linear Regression Viewpoints, 21,* 12–22.

Smithson, M. (2001). Correct confidence intervals for various regression effect sizes and parameters: The importance of noncentral distributions in computing intervals. *Educational and Psychological Measurement, 61,* 605–632.

Soper, D. Statistics Calculators. Retrieved January 2010 from http://www.danielsoper.com/statcalc/.

Steiger, J. H., & Fouladi, T. (1992). R2: A computer program for interval estimation, power calculation, and hypothesis testing for the squared multiple correlation. *Behavior Research Methods, Instruments, and Computers, 4,* 581–582.

Steiger, J. H., & Fouladi, T. (1997). *Noncentrality interval estimation and the evaluation of statistical models.* In L. Harlow, S. Mulaik, & J.H. Steiger (Eds.), *What if there were no significance tests?* (pp. 222–257). Mahwah, NJ: Lawrence Erlbaum.

Subkoviak, M. J., & Levin, J. R. (1977). Fallibility of measurement and the power of a statistical test. *Journal of Educational Measurement, 14,* 47–52.

Sutcliffe, J. P. (1958). Error of measurement and the sensitivity of a test of significance. *Psychometrika, 23,* 9–17.

Thompson, B., Smith, Q. W., Miller, L. M., & Thomson, W. A. (1991, January). *Stepwise methods lead to bad interpretations: Better alternatives.* Paper presented at the annual meeting of the Southwest Educational Research Association, San Antonio, TX.

Tracz, S. M., Brown, R., & Kopriva, R. (1991). Considerations, issues, and comparisons in variable selection and interpretation in multiple regression. *Multiple Linear Regression Viewpoints, 18,* 55–66.

Werts, C. E., Rock, D. A., Linn, R. L., & Jöreskog, K. G. (1976). Comparison of correlations, variances, covariances, and regression weights with or without measurement error. *Psychological Bulletin, 83,* 1007–1013.

Zuccaro, C. (1992). Mallows C_p statistic and model selection in multiple linear regression. *Journal of the Market Research Society, 34,* 163–172.

7

Path Models

Key Concepts

Path model diagrams

Direct effects, indirect effects, and correlated independent variables

Path (structure) coefficients and standardized partial regression coefficients

Decomposition of correlations

Original and reproduced correlation coefficients

Full versus limited information function

Residual and standardized residual matrix

In this chapter we consider path models, the logical extension of multiple regression models. Although path analysis still uses models involving multiple observed variables, there may be any number of independent and dependent variables and any number of equations. Thus, as we shall see, path models require the analysis of several multiple regression equations using observed variables.

Sewall Wright is credited with the development of path analysis as a method for studying the direct and indirect effects of variables (Wright, 1921, 1934, 1960). Path analysis is not actually a method for discovering causes; rather, it tests theoretical relationships, which historically has been termed *causal modeling*. A specified path model might actually establish causal relationships among two variables when:

1. Temporal ordering of variables exists.

2. Covariation or correlation is present among variables.

3. Other causes are controlled for.

4. A variable X is manipulated, which causes a change in Y.

Obviously, a theoretical model that is tested over time (longitudinal research) and manipulates certain variables to assess the change in other variables (experimental research) more closely approaches our idea of causation. In the social and behavioral sciences, the issue of causation is not as straightforward as in the hard sciences, but it has the potential to be modeled.

Pearl (2009) has renewed a discussion of causation in the behavioral sciences with model examples and rationale for causation as a process (model) that can be expressed in mathematical expressions ready for computer analysis, which fits into the testing of theoretical path models.

This chapter begins with an example path model, and then proceeds with sections on model specification, model identification, model estimation, model testing, and model modification.

7.1 An Example

We begin with a path model that will be followed throughout the chapter. McDonald and Clelland (1984) collected data on the sentiments toward unions of Southern nonunion textile laborers ($n = 173$). This example is presented in the LISREL manual (Jöreskog & Sörbom, 1993, pp. 12–15, example 3); included in the data files of the LISREL program; and was utilized by Bollen (1989, pp. 82–83). The model consists of five observed variables; the independent variables are the number of years worked in the textile mill (actually log of years, denoted simply as years) and worker age (age); the dependent variables are deference to managers (deference), support for labor activism (support), and sentiment toward unions (sentiment). The original variance–covariance matrix, implied model (reproduced) variance–covariance matrix, residual matrix, and standardized residual matrix are given in Table 7.1. The path diagram of the theoretical proposed model is shown in Figure 7.1.

Path models adhere to certain common drawing conventions that are utilized in SEM models (Figure 7.2). The observed variables are enclosed by boxes or rectangles. Lines directed from one observed variable to another observed variable denote *direct effects*, in other words, the direct influence of one variable on another. For example, it is hypothesized that age has a direct influence on support, meaning that the age of the worker may influence an increase (or decrease) in support. A curved, double-headed line between two independent observed variables indicates *covariance*; that is, they are correlated. In this example, age and years are specified to correlate. The rationale for such relationships is that there are influences on both of these independent variables outside of the path model. Because these influences are not studied in this path model, it is reasonable to expect that the same unmeasured variables may influence both independent variables.

TABLE 7.1

Original, Reproduced, Residual, and Standardized Residual Covariance
Matrices for the Initial Union Sentiment Model

Original Matrix

Variable	Deference	Support	Sentiment	Years	Age
Deference	14.610				
Support	−5.250	11.017			
Sentiment	−8.057	11.087	31.971		
Years	−0.482	0.677	1.559	1.021	
Age	−18.857	17.861	28.250	7.139	215.662

Reproduced Matrix

Variable	Deference	Support	Sentiment	Years	Age
Deference	14.610				
Support	−1.562	11.017			
Sentiment	−5.045	10.210	30.534		
Years	−0.624	0.591	1.517	1.021	
Age	−18.857	17.861	25.427	7.139	215.662

Residual Matrix

Variable	Deference	Support	Sentiment	Years	Age
Deference	0.000				
Support	−3.688	0.000			
Sentiment	−3.012	0.877	1.437		
Years	0.142	0.086	0.042	0.000	
Age	0.000	0.000	2.823	0.000	0.000

Standardized Residual Matrix

Variable	Deference	Support	Sentiment	Years	Age
Deference	0.000				
Support	−4.325	0.000			
Sentiment	−3.991	3.385	3.196		
Years	0.581	0.409	0.225	0.000	
Age	0.000	0.000	0.715	0.000	0.000

Finally, each dependent variable has an error term, denoted by a circle
around the error term pointing toward the proper dependent variable.
Take deference, for example, some variance in deference scores will be predicted or explained by age and some variance will not. The unexplained
variance will become the error term, which indicates other possible influences on deference that are not contained in the specified path model.

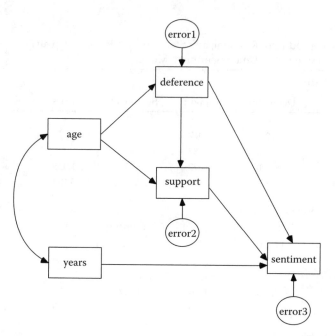

FIGURE 7.1
Union sentiment model.

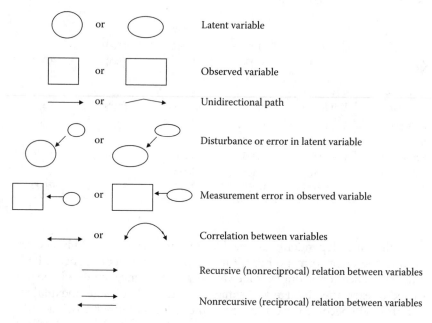

FIGURE 7.2
Common path diagram symbols.

7.2 Model Specification

Model specification is necessary in examining multiple variable relationships in path models, just as in the case of multiple regression. Many different relationships among a set of variables can be hypothesized with many different parameters being estimated. In a simple three-variable model, for example, many possible path models can be postulated on the basis of different hypothesized relationships among the three variables.

For example, in Figure 7.3a–c we see three different path models where X1 influences X2. In Model (a), X1 influences X2, which in turn influences Y. Here, X2 serves as a mediator between X1 and Y. In Model (b), an additional path is drawn from X1 to Y, such that X1 has both a direct and an indirect effect upon Y. The direct effect is that X1 has a direct influence on Y (no variables intervene between X1 and Y), whereas the indirect effect is that X1 influences Y through X2, that is, X2 intervenes between X1 and Y. In Model (c), X1 influences both X2 and Y; however, X2 and Y are not related. If we were to switch X1 and X2 around, this would generate three more plausible path models.

Other path models are also possible. For example, in Figure 7.4(a,b), X1 does not influence X2. In Model (a), X1 and X2 influence Y, but are uncorrelated. In Model (b), X1 and X2 influence Y and are correlated. How can one determine which model is correct? This is known as model specification and shows the important role that theory and previous research plays in justifying a hypothesized model. Path analysis does not provide a way to specify the model, but rather estimates the effects among the variables once the model has been specified a priori by the researcher on the basis of theoretical considerations. For this reason, model specification is a critical part of SEM modeling.

Path coefficients in path models are usually derived from the values of a Pearson product moment correlation coefficient (r) and/or a standardized partial regression coefficient (β) (Wolfle, 1977). For example, in the path model of Figure 7.4b, the path coefficients (p) are depicted by arrows from X1 to Y and X2 to Y, respectively, as:

$$\beta_1 = p_{Y1}$$
$$\beta_2 = p_{Y2}$$

and the curved arrow between X1 and X2 is denoted as:

$$r_{X1,X2} = p_{12}.$$

The variable relationships, once specified in standard score form, become standardized partial regression coefficients. In multiple regression, a

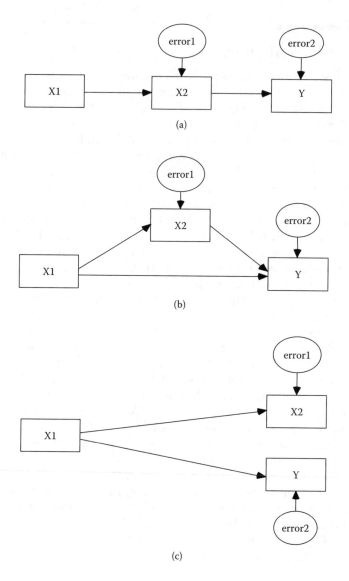

FIGURE 7.3
Possible three-variable models (X1 influences X2).

dependent variable is regressed in a single analysis on all of the independent variables. In path analysis, one or more multiple regression analyses
are performed depending on the variable relationships specified in the
path model. Path coefficients are therefore computed only on the basis
of the particular set of independent variables that lead to the dependent

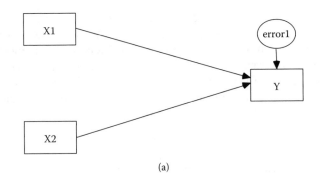

(a)

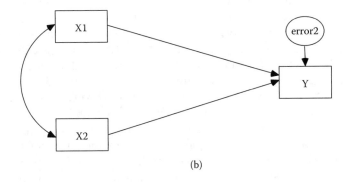

(b)

FIGURE 7.4
Possible three-variable models (X1 does not influence X2).

variable under consideration. In the path model of Figure 7.4b, two standardized partial regression coefficients (path coefficients) are computed, p_{Y1} and p_{Y2}. The curved arrow represents the covariance or correlation between the two independent variables p_{12} in predicting the dependent variable.

For the union sentiment model, the model specification is as follows. There are three structural equations in the model, one for each of the three dependent variables, deference, support, and sentiment. In terms of variable names, the structural equations are as follows.

$$deference = age + error1$$

$$support = age + deference + error2$$

$$sentiment = years + support + deference + error3 .$$

Substantive information from prior research suggested that those six paths be included in the specified model; and that other possible paths, for example from age to sentiment, not be included. This model includes direct effects, for example from age to support, indirect effects, for example from age to support through deference, and correlated independent variables, for example age and years. Obviously many possible path models could be specified for this set of observed variables.

7.3 Model Identification

Once a particular path model has been specified, the next concern is whether the model is identified. In structural equation modeling, it is crucial that the researcher resolve the *identification problem* prior to the estimation of parameters. The general notion of identification was discussed in Chapter 4. Here, we consider model identification in the context of path models, and in particular, for our union sentiment example.

As described in Chapter 4, for the identification problem, we ask the following question: On the basis of the sample data contained in the sample covariance matrix S and the theoretical model implied by the population covariance matrix Σ, can a unique set of parameter estimates be found? For the union sentiment model, for example, we would like to know if the path between age and deference is identified; an example of one parameter to be estimated.

In the union sentiment model, some parameters are fixed and others are free. An example of a fixed parameter is that there is no path or direct relationship between age and sentiment. An example of a free parameter is that there is a path or direct relationship between age and deference.

In determining identification, first consider the order condition. Here, the number of free parameters to be estimated must be less than or equal to the number of distinct values in the matrix S. In our path model we specified the following:

6 path coefficients

3 equation error variances

1 correlation among the independent variables

2 independent variable variances

Thus, there are a total of 12 free parameters that we wish to estimate. The number of distinct values in the matrix S is equal to:

$$[p\,(p+1)]/2 = [5\,(5+1)]/2 = 15,$$

where p is the number of observed variables in the matrix. Thus, the number of distinct values in the sample matrix S, 15 is indeed greater than the number of free parameters, 12. However, this is only a necessary condition and does not guarantee that the model is identified. According to the order condition, the model is also overidentified because there are more values in S than parameters to be estimated.

Although the order condition is easy to assess, other sufficient conditions are not, for example, the rank condition. The sufficient conditions require us to algebraically determine whether each parameter in the model can be estimated from the covariance matrix S. According to the LISREL computer program, which checks on identification, the union sentiment model is identified.

7.4 Model Estimation

Once the identification problem has been addressed, the next step is to estimate the parameters of the specified model. In this section, we consider the following topics: decomposition of the correlation matrix, parameter estimation in general, and parameter estimation of the union sentiment model.

In path analysis, the traditional method of intuitively thinking about estimation is to decompose the correlation matrix. This harkens back to the early days of path analysis in the 1960s when sociologists like Arthur S. Goldberger and Otis D. Duncan were rediscovering and further developing the procedure. The decomposition idea is that the original correlation matrix can be completely reproduced if all of the effects are accounted for in a specified path model. In other words, if all of the possible unidirectional (or recursive) paths are included in a path model, then the observed correlation matrix can be completely reproduced from the obtained standardized estimates of the model.

For example, take the model in Figure 7.4b. Here there are two direct effects, from X1 to Y and from X2 to Y. There are also indirect effects due to the correlation between X1 and X2. In other words, X1 indirectly influences Y through X2, and also X2 indirectly affects Y through X1. The correlations among these three variables can be decomposed as follows:

$$r_{12} = p_{12} \tag{1}$$
$$\text{(CO)}$$

$$r_{Y1} = p_{Y1} + p_{12}p_{Y2} \tag{2}$$
$$\text{(DE)} \qquad \text{(IE)}$$

$$r_{Y2} = p_{Y2} + p_{12}p_{Y1}, \tag{3}$$
$$\text{(DE)} \qquad \text{(IE)}$$

where the r values are the actual observed correlations and the p values are the path coefficients (standardized estimates). Thus, in equation (1), the correlation between X1 and X2 is simply a function of the path, or correlation relationship (CO), between X1 and X2. In equation (2), the correlation between X1 and Y is a function of (a) the direct effect (DE) of X1 on Y, and (b) the indirect effect (IE) of X1 on Y through X2 [the product of the path or correlation between X1 and X2 (p_{12}) and the path or direct effect from X2 to Y (p_{Y2})]. Equation (3) is similar to equation (2) except that X1 and X2 are reversed; there is both a direct effect and an indirect effect.

Let us illustrate how this works with an actual set of correlations. The observed correlations are as follows: $r_{12} = .224$, $r_{Y1} = .507$, and $r_{Y2} = .480$. The specified path model and correlation matrix were run in LISREL. The path coefficients and the complete reproduction of the correlations are:

$$r_{12} = p_{12} = .224 \tag{4}$$
$$\text{(CO)}$$

$$r_{Y1} = p_{Y1} + p_{12}p_{Y2} = .421 + (.224)(.386) = .507 \tag{5}$$
$$\text{(DE)} \quad \text{(IE)}$$

$$r_{Y2} = p_{Y2} + p_{12}p_{Y1} = .386 + (.224)(.421) = .480. \tag{6}$$
$$\text{(DE)} \quad \text{(IE)}$$

Here, the original correlations are completely reproduced by the model because all of the effects are accounted for, direct, indirect, and correlated. If a path were left out of the model, for example p_{12}, then the correlations would not be completely reproduced. Thus, the correlation decomposition approach is a nice conceptual way of thinking about the estimation process in path analysis. For further details on the correlation decomposition approach, we highly recommend reading Duncan (1975).

In chapter 4, we presented the problem of estimation in general. Parameters can be estimated by different estimation procedures, such as maximum likelihood (ML), generalized least squares (GLS), and unweighted least squares (ULS), which are all unstandardized types of estimates, as well as standardized estimates (the path coefficients previously described in this chapter were standardized estimates). In addition to different methods of estimation of the parameter estimates, *full* versus *limited* information estimation functions are invoked based on the software chosen for the analysis. *Full information* estimation computes all of the parameters simultaneously, whereas *limited information* estimation computes parameters for each equation separately. The parameters estimated in structural equation modeling software (LISREL) use full information estimation and therefore differ from parameter estimates computed in

SPSS or SAS, where each equation in the path model is estimated separately (limited information estimation). In limited information estimation, the parameter estimates are determined uniquely in each separate equation to meet the least squares criterion of minimized residuals.

In the union sentiment example we see the estimation process at work. In order to utilize the model modification procedures discussed in section 7.6, we have slightly changed the model specification in Figure 7.1. We remove the path from deference to support and call this the initial model. We evaluate this initial model, and hope, through the model modification process, we will obtain the model as originally specified in Figure 7.1. The intentionally misspecified model was run using LISREL (*Note*: The LISREL program for the correctly specified model is given at the end of the chapter).

The maximum likelihood estimates for the initial model are shown in the first column of Table 7.2. All of the parameter estimates are significantly

TABLE 7.2

Maximum Likelihood Estimates[a] and Selected Fit Indices for the Initial and Final Union Sentiment Models

Paths	Initial Model	Final Model
Age → deference	−.09	−.09
Age → support	0.08	0.06
Deference → support	—	−.28
Years → sentiment	0.86	0.86
Deference → sentiment	−.22	−.22
Support → sentiment	0.85	0.85
Equation error variances		
Deference	12.96	12.96
Support	9.54	8.49
Sentiment	19.45	19.45
Independent variables		
Variance (age)	215.66	215.66
Variance (years)	1.02	1.02
Covariance (age, years)	7.14	7.14
Selected fit indices		
χ^2	19.96	1.25
df	4	3
p value	.00	.74
RMSEA	.15	.00
SRMR	.087	.015
GFI	.96	1.00

[a] All estimates significantly different from zero ($p < .05$).

different from zero, $p < .05$ (the fit of the model is discussed next in section 7.5). Age has a direct effect on both deference and support; deference has a direct effect on sentiment; years has a direct effect on sentiment; and support has a direct effect on sentiment. Numerous indirect effects are also part of the path model, such as the indirect effect of age on sentiment through support. Age and years also have a significant covariance, indicating that one or more common unmeasured variables influence both age and years.

7.5 Model Testing

An important result of any path analysis is the fit of the specified model. If the fit of the path model is good, then the specified model has been supported by the sample data. If the fit of the path model is not so good, then the specified model has not been supported by the sample data, and the researcher typically attempts to modify the path model to achieve a better fit (as described in section 7.6). As discussed in chapter 5, LISREL provides modification indices and expected parameter changes values to guide modifying a model to obtain better model-fit criteria.*

For purposes of the union sentiment example, we include a few model-fit indices at the bottom of Table 7.2. For the initial path model, the χ^2 statistic, technically a measure of badness of fit, is equal to 19.96, with four degrees of freedom, and $p < .01$. As the p value is very small and the χ^2 value is nowhere near the number of degrees of freedom, then according to this measure of fit, the initial path model is poorly specified. The root-mean-square error of approximation (RMSEA) is equal to .15, somewhat below the acceptable level for this measure of fit (RMSEA $< .08$ or .05). The standardized root-mean-square residual (SRMR) is .087, also below the usual acceptable level of fit (SRMR $< .08$ or .05). Finally, the goodness-of-fit index (GFI) is .96 for the initial model, which is an acceptable level for this measure of fit (GFI $> .95$). Across this particular set of model-fit indices, the conclusion is that the data to model fit is approaching a reasonable level, but that some model modifications might allow us to achieve a better model fit between the sample variance–covariance matrix S and the implied model (reproduced) variance–covariance matrix Σ. Model modification is considered in the next section.

---

* Another traditional non-SEM path model-fit index is described in the Chapter Footnote.

7.6 Model Modification

The final step in structural equation modeling is model modification. In other words, if the fit of the model is less than satisfactory, then the researcher typically performs a *specification search* to seek a better fitting model. As described in chapters 4 and 5, several different procedures can be used to assist in this search. One may eliminate parameters that are not significantly different from zero and/or include additional parameters to arrive at a modified model. For the elimination of parameters, the most commonly used procedure in LISREL is to compare the *t* statistic for each parameter to a tabled *t* value (e.g., $t > 1.96$) to determine statistical significance.

For the inclusion of additional parameters, the most commonly used techniques in LISREL are (a) the modification index (MI) (the expected value that χ^2 would decrease if such a parameter were to be included; large values indicate potentially useful parameters), and (b) the expected parameter change statistic (EPC) (the approximate value of the new parameter if added to the model).

In addition, an examination of the residual matrix, or the more useful standardized residual matrix, often gives clues as to which original covariance or correlations are not well accounted for by the model. Recall that the residual matrix is the difference between the observed variance-covariance S and the model implied (reproduced) variance-covariance matrix Σ. Large residuals indicate values not well accounted for by the model. Standardized residuals are like z scores in that large values (greater than 1.96 or 2.58) indicate that a particular relationship is not well accounted for by the path model (Table A.1).

For the initial union sentiment example, the original, model implied (reproduced), residual, and standardized residual covariance matrices are given in Table 7.1. Here we see that the largest standardized residual is between deference and support (–4.325). The *t* statistics do not suggest the elimination of any existing parameters from the initial path model because every parameter is statistically different from zero. With regard to the possible inclusion of new parameters, the largest modification index is for the path from deference to support (MI = 18.9). For that potential path, the estimated value, or expected parameter change (EPC), is –0.28.

Taken together, these statistics indicate that there is something misspecified between deference and support that is not captured by the initial model. Specifically, adding a path is recommended from deference to support. This is precisely the path from the originally specified path model that we intentionally eliminated from the initial path model. Thus, the specification search was successful in obtaining the original model. The ML estimates and selected fit indices for the final model, where this path is now included, are shown in the second column of Table 7.2. All of the parameters included are significantly different from zero ($p < .05$), all of the fit indices now indicate an acceptable level of fit, and no additional modification indices are indicated for any further recommended changes. Thus, we deem this as the final path model for the union sentiment example.

7.7 Summary

This chapter presented a detailed discussion of path models. We began by presenting the union sentiment path model and then followed it throughout the chapter. We moved on to model specification, first with several possible three-variable models, and then with the union sentiment model. The next step was to consider model identification of the union sentiment model for both the order and rank conditions. Next, we discussed estimation. Here, we introduced the notion of correlation decomposition with a three-variable model, and the difference between full versus limited estimation functions, and then considered the full information estimation results for the union sentiment model. Model testing of the misspecified union sentiment model was the next step, where the fit of the model was deemed not acceptable. The misspecified model (altered initial model) was then modified through the addition of one path, thereby arriving at a final, best-fitting theoretical model, which was the same as our initial model.

We learned that path models permit theoretically meaningful relationships among variables that cannot be specified in a single additive regression model. However, the issue of measurement error in observed variables is not treated in either regression or path models (Wolfle, 1979). The next chapter helps us to understand how measurement error is addressed in structural equation modeling via factor models.

Appendix: LISREL–SIMPLIS Path Model Program (Figure 7.1)

```
Union Sentiment of Textile Workers
Observed Variables: Deference Support Sentiment Years Age
Covariance matrix:
 14.610
 -5.250 11.017
 -8.057 11.087 31.971
 -0.482 0.677 1.559 1.021
 -18.857 17.861 28.250 7.139 215.662
```

```
Sample Size: 173
Relationships
Deference = Age
Support = Age Deference
Sentiment = Years Deference Support
Print Residuals
Options: ND = 3
Path Diagram
End of Problem
```

Exercise

1. Analyze the following achievement path model (Figure 7.5) using the LISREL software program. The path model indicates that income and ability predict aspire, and income, ability, and aspire predict achieve.

    Sample size = 100

    Observed variables: quantitative achievement (Ach), family income (Inc), quantitative ability (Abl), educational aspiration (Asp)
    Variance–covariance matrix:

	Ach	Inc	Abl	Asp
Ach	25.500			
Inc	20.500	38.100		
Abl	22.480	24.200	42.750	
Asp	16.275	13.600	13.500	17.000

    Equations:

    $$Asp = Inc\ Abl$$

    $$Ach = Inc\ Abl\ Asp$$

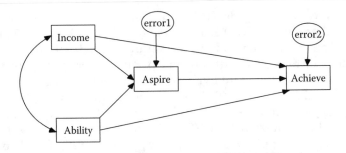

FIGURE 7.5
Achievement path model.

Chapter Footnote

Another Traditional Non-SEM Path Model-Fit Index

The relationship between the original and reproduced correlation matrices is essential for testing the significance of the path model (Specht, 1975). The relationship between the two matrices is tested by calculating a chi-square statistic. A *significant* χ^2 value for a specified level of significance ($\alpha = .05$) indicates that the path model does not fit the data. If $\chi^2 = 0$, then the original and reproduced correlations in the matrices are identical; in other words, the correlations are perfectly reproduced by the path model. Also, if the residuals, for example P_{e1} and P_{e2}, are uncorrelated in a path model, then the sum of squared residual path coefficients will equal the chi-square value. A *non-significant* chi-square value therefore indicates a good path model to data fit in SEM. Another traditional non-SEM path model-fit index, Q, has been reported in the research literature and therefore presented here using a LISREL–SIMPLIS program example with heuristic data.

LISREL–SIMPLIS program

```
Path analysis of Y
Observed variables Y X1 X2 X3
Sample size 100
Correlation Matrix
1.000
.507 1.000
.480 .224 1.000
.275 .062 .577 1.000
Equation:
Y = X1 X2 X3
X3 = X1 X2
End of Problem
```

The theoretical path model in Figure 7.6 indicates that two variables, X1 and X2 predict X3; X1, X2, and X3 predict Y; and X1 and X2 are correlated. This original path model is a saturated model because all paths are included, thus $\chi^2 = 0$, df = 0, and p = 0. The original path model, however, has two R-squared values for each regression equation: $R^2_{X3.X1,X2} = .34$ and $R^2_{Y.X3,X1,X2} = .40$. The path model diagram only shows the $1 - R^2_{X3.X1,X2} = .66$ and $1 - R^2_{Y.X3,X1,X2} = .60$ values. Computer output indicated that the path from X1 to X3 was non-significant ($p_{31} = -.071$) and the path from X3 to Y was non-significant ($p_{3Y} = .040$). For theoretical reason, we only dropped path p_{31} resulting in the modified path model in Figure 7.7.

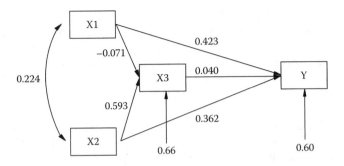

FIGURE 7.6
Original path model.

The modified path model reported a *non-significant* $\chi^2 = .71$, df = 1, and $p = .40$ which indicates that the data fits the path model, although the path coefficient from X3 to Y is still non-significant, but kept in the model for theoretical reasons.

The other traditional non-SEM path model-fit indices can be accomplished by computing the generalized squared multiple correlation (Pedhazur, 1982) as follows:

$$R_m^2 = 1 - (1 - R_1^2)(1 - R_2^2).....(1 - R_p^2).$$

The *R*-squared values are the squared multiple correlation coefficients from each of the separate regression analyses in the path model. In the original path model, the two regression analyses yielded R-squared values of .34 and .40, respectively. The path model-fit R_m^2 would be computed as:

$$R_m^2 = 1 - (1 - .34)(1 - .40) = .604$$

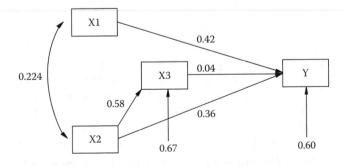

FIGURE 7.7
Modified path model.

An analogous statistic to R^2_m, M, and a large sample measure of model fit, Q, are also presented in Pedhazur (1982). *Q is oftentimes recommended because chi-square is affected by sample size.* Q varies between zero and one and is not a function of sample size. The formula for Q is:

$$Q = (1 - R^2_m)/(1 - M)$$

M is calculated in the same manner as R^2_m, but with a non-significant path deleted. In our example, we dropped the path from X1 to X3 because it yielded a non-significant path coefficient and therefore M calculated from the modified path model would have a different value from R^2_m in the original path model (M values range between zero and R^2_m).

In our example, the path from X1 to X3 in the program was dropped by changing the first LISREL–SIMPLIS equation command to read:

Equation: X3 = X2

The M value is computed as:

$$M = 1 - (1 - .33)(1 - .40) = .598.$$

Q is now computed as:

$$Q = [(1 - .604)/(1 - .598)] = [.396/.402] = .98.$$

Remember, the closer the value of Q to 1.0, the better the model fit. Q can be tested for significance using W, which is computed as:

$$W = -(N - d) \log_e Q,$$

where N = sample size, d = number of path coefficients hypothesized to be zero, $\log_e$ = natural logarithm (ln). For our example,

$$W = -(100 - 1) \log_e (.98) = 2.00.$$

Since W approximates the χ^2 distribution with degrees of freedom = d, the tabled critical chi-square value for $d = 1$, $\alpha = 05$, is 3.841 (Table A.4). W is less than the tabled critical value, therefore nonsignificant, suggesting a good path model fit to the data. The W value fell between $p = .20$ ($\chi^2 = 1.642$) and $p = .10$ ($\chi^2 = 2.706$) in Table A.4.

Prior to SEM, Q and the W path model-fit index were reported to test whether a path model significantly reproduced the correlation matrix. The R^2_m value was reported to indicate the amount of variation in Y predicted by the direct and indirect effects of the independent variables. Individual tests of path coefficients were also computed and reported by dividing the path coefficient by its standard error. We used the path coefficient, standard error, and associated t-value provided in the computer output to determine if a path coefficient was nonsignificant, thus dropping it from the path model.

References

Bollen, K. A. (1989). *Structural equations with latent variables*. New York: Wiley.

Duncan, O. D. (1975). *Introduction to structural equation models*. New York: Academic.

Jöreskog, K. G., & Sörbom, D. (1993). *LISREL 8: Structural equation modeling with the SIMPLIS command language*. Chicago, IL: Scientific Software International.

McDonald, J. A., & Clelland, D. A. (1984). Textile workers and union sentiment. *Social Forces, 63*, 502–521.

Pearl, J. (2009). *Causality: Models, reasoning, and inference* (2nd ed.). Cambridge University Press: London.

Pedhazur, E. J. (1982). *Multiple regression in behavioral research: Explanation and prediction* (2nd ed.). New York: Holt, Rinehart & Winston.

Specht, D. A. (1975). On the evaluation of causal models. *Social Science Research, 4*, 113–133.

Wolfle, L. M. (1977). An introduction to path analysis. *Multiple Linear Regression Viewpoints, 8*, 36–61.

Wolfle, L. M. (1979). Unmeasured variables in path analysis. *Multiple Linear Regression Viewpoints, 9*, 20–56.

Wright, S. (1921). Correlation and causation. *Journal of Agricultural Research, 20*, 557–585.

Wright, S. (1934). The method of path coefficients. *Annals of Mathematical Statistics, 5*, 161–215.

Wright, S. (1960). Path coefficients and path regression: Alternative or complementary concepts? *Biometrics, 16*, 189–202.

8

Confirmatory Factor Models

Key Concepts

Confirmatory factor analysis versus exploratory factor analysis

Latent variables (factors) and observed variables

Factor loadings and measurement errors

Correlated factors and correlated measurement errors

In chapter 7 we examined path models as the logical extension of multiple regression models (chapter 6) to show more meaningful theoretical relationships among our observed variables. Thus, the two previous chapters dealt exclusively with models involving observed variables. In this chapter we begin developing models involving factors or latent variables and continue latent variable modeling throughout the remainder of the book. As we see in this chapter, a major limitation of models involving only observed variables is that measurement error is not taken into account. The use of observed variables in statistics assumes that all of the measured variables are perfectly valid and reliable, which is unlikely in many applications. For example, father's educational level is not a perfect measure of a socioeconomic status factor and amount of exercise per week is not a perfect measure of a fitness factor.

The validity and reliability issues in measurement have traditionally been handled by first examining the validity and reliability of scores on instruments used in a particular context. Given an acceptable level of score validity and reliability, the scores are then used in a statistical analysis. However, the traditional statistical analysis of these scores—for example, in multiple regression and path analysis—does not adjust for measurement error. The impact of measurement error has been investigated and found to have serious consequences—for example, biased parameter estimates (Cochran, 1968; Fuller, 1987). Structural equation modeling software that accounts for the measurement error of variables was therefore developed—that is, factor analysis—which creates latent variables used in structural equation modeling.

Factor analysis attempts to determine which sets of observed variables share common variance–covariance characteristics that define theoretical constructs or factors (latent variables). Factor analysis presumes that some factors that are smaller in number than the number of observed variables are responsible for the shared variance–covariance among the observed variables. In practice, one collects data on observed variables and uses factor-analytic techniques to either *confirm* that a particular subset of observed variables define each construct or factor, or *explore* which observed variables relate to factors. In exploratory factor model approaches, we seek to find a model that fits the data, so we specify different alternative models, hoping to ultimately find a model that fits the data and has theoretical support. This is the primary rationale for exploratory factor analysis (EFA). In confirmatory factor model approaches, we seek to statistically test the significance of a hypothesized factor model—that is, whether the sample data confirm that model. Additional samples of data that fit the model further confirm the validity of the hypothesized model. This is the primary rationale for confirmatory factor analysis (CFA).

In CFA, the researcher specifies a certain number of factors, which factors are correlated, and which observed variables measure each factor. In EFA, the researcher explores how many factors there are, whether the factors are correlated, and which observed variables appear to best measure each factor. In CFA, the researcher has an a priori specified theoretical model; in EFA, the researcher does not have such a model. In this chapter we only concern ourselves with confirmatory factor models because the focus of the book is on testing theoretical models; exploratory factor analysis is covered in depth elsewhere (Comrey & Lee, 1992; Gorsuch, 1983; and Costello & Osborne, 2005). This chapter begins with a classic example of a confirmatory factor model and then proceeds with sections on model specification, model identification, model estimation, model testing, and model modification.

8.1 An Example

We use a classic confirmatory factor model that will be followed throughout the chapter. Holzinger and Swineford (1939) collected data on 26 psychological tests from seventh- and eighth-grade children in a suburban school district of Chicago. Over the years, different subsamples of the children and different subsets of the variables of this dataset have been analyzed and presented in various multivariate statistics textbooks—for example, Harmon (1976) and Gorsuch (1983)—and SEM software program guides—for example, Jöreskog and Sörbom (1993; example 5, pp. 23–28).

The raw data analyzed here are on the first six psychological variables for all 301 subjects (see chapter 5); the resulting sample covariance matrix

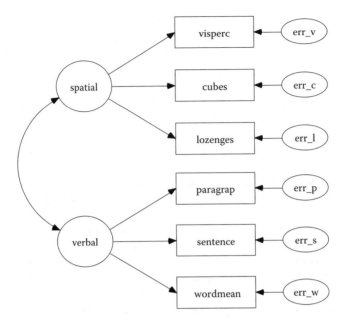

FIGURE 8.1
Confirmatory factor model. (From Holzinger, K. J., & Swineford, F. A. [1939]. *A study in factor analysis: The stability of a bi-factor solution.* [Supplementary Educational Monographs, No. 48]. Chicago, IL: University of Chicago, Department of Education.)

S is given in the Appendix. The confirmatory factor model consists of the following six observed variables: *Visual Perception, Cubes, Lozenges, Paragraph Comprehension, Sentence Completion,* and *Word Meaning.* The first three measures were hypothesized to measure a *spatial* ability factor and the second three measures to measure a *verbal* ability factor.

The path diagram of the theoretical proposed model is shown in Figure 8.1. The drawing conventions utilized in Figure 8.1 were described in chapter 7. The observed variables are enclosed by boxes or rectangles, and the factors (latent variables) are enclosed by circles or ellipses—that is, *spatial* and *verbal.* Conceptually, a factor represents the common variation among a set of observed variables. Thus, for example, the *spatial* ability factor represents the common variation among the *Visual Perception, Cubes,* and *Lozenges* tasks. Lines directed from a factor to a particular observed variable denote the relationship between that factor and that measure. These relationships are interpreted as factor loadings with the square of the factor loading called the commonality estimate of the variable.

The measurement errors are enclosed by smaller ellipses and indicate that some portion of each observed variable is measuring something other than the hypothesized factor. Conceptually, a measurement error represents the unique variation for a particular observed variable beyond the variation due to the relevant factor. For example, the *Cubes* task is largely a measure of *spatial* ability, but may also be assessing other characteristics such as a different common factor or unreliability. To assess measurement error, the variance of each measurement error is estimated (known as measurement error variance).

A curved, double-headed line between two factors indicates that they have shared variance or are correlated. In this example, *spatial* and *verbal* ability are specified to covary or correlate. The rationale for this particular factor correlation is that *spatial* ability and *verbal* ability are related to a more general ability factor and thus should be theoretically related.

A curved, double-headed line between two measurement error variances indicates that they also have shared variance or are correlated. Although not shown in this example, two measurement error variances could be correlated if they shared something in common such as (a) common method variance where the method of measurement is the same, such as the same scale of measurement, or they are both part of the same global instrument, or (b) the same measure is being used at different points in time, that is, the *Cubes* task is measured at Time 1 and again at Time 2.

8.2 Model Specification

Model specification is a necessary first step in analyzing a confirmatory factor model, just as it was for multiple regression and path models. Many different relationships among a set of variables can be postulated with many different parameters being estimated. Thus, many different factor models can be postulated on the basis of different hypothesized relationships between the observed variables and the factors.

In our example, there are six observed variables with two different latent variables (factors) being hypothesized. Given this, many different confirmatory factor models are possible. First, each observed variable can load on either one or both factors. Thus, there could be anywhere from 6 to 12 total factor loadings. Second, the two factors may or may not be correlated. Third, there may or may not be correlations or covariance terms among the measurement error variances. Thus, there could be anywhere from 0 to 15 total correlated measurement error variances.

From the model in Figure 8.1, each observed variable is hypothesized to measure only a single factor—that is, three observed variables per factor with six factor loadings; the factors are believed to be correlated (a single factor correlation); and the measurement error variances are not related (zero correlated measurement errors. Obviously, we could have hypothesized a single factor with six observed variables or six factors each with a single observed variable. When all of this is taken into account, many different confirmatory factor models are possible with these six observed variables.

How does the researcher determine which factor model is correct? We already know that *model specification* is important in this process and indicates the important role that theory and prior research play in justifying a specified model. Confirmatory factor analysis does not tell us how to specify the model, but rather estimates the parameters of the model once the model has been specified a priori by the researcher on the basis of theoretical and research based knowledge. Once again, model specification is the hardest part of structural equation modeling.

For our confirmatory factor model, the model specification is diagrammed in Figure 8.1 and contains six measurement equations in the model, one for each of the six observed variables. In terms of the variable names from Figure 8.1, the measurement equations are as follows:

$$visperc = function\ of\ spatial + err\_v$$

$$cubes = function\ of\ spatial + err\_c$$

$$lozenges = function\ of\ spatial + err\_l$$

$$paragrap = function\ of\ verbal + err\_p$$

$$sentence = function\ of\ verbal + err\_s$$

$$wordmean = function\ of\ verbal + err\_w$$

Substantive theory and prior research suggest that these particular factor loadings should be included in the specified model (the functions being the factor loadings), and that other possible factor loadings—for example, *visperc* loading on *verbal*, should not be included in the factor model. Our factor model includes six factor loadings and six measurement error variances, one for each observed variable, and one correlation between the factors *spatial* ability and *verbal* ability with zero correlated measurement errors.

8.3 Model Identification

Once a confirmatory factor model has been specified, the next step is to determine whether the model is identified. As stated in chapter 4, it is crucial that the researcher solve the *identification problem* prior to the estimation of parameters. We first need to revisit model identification in the context of confirmatory factor models and then specifically for our confirmatory factor model example.

In model identification (see chapter 4), we ask the following question: On the basis of the sample data contained in the sample variance–covariance matrix S, and the theoretical model implied by the population variance–covariance matrix Σ, can a unique set of parameter estimates be found? For our confirmatory factor model, we would like to know if the factor loading of *Visual Perception* on *Spatial Ability*, *Cubes* on *Spatial Ability*, *Lozenges* on *Spatial Ability*, *Paragraph Comprehension* on *Verbal Ability*, *Sentence Completion* on *Verbal Ability*, and *Word Meaning* on *Verbal Ability* are identified (can be estimated). In our confirmatory factor model, some parameters are fixed and others are free. An example of a *fixed parameter* is that *Cubes* is not allowed to load on *Verbal Ability*. An example of a *free parameter* is that *Cubes* is allowed to load on *Spatial Ability*.

In determining identification, we first assess the *order condition*. The number of free parameters to be estimated must be less than or equal to the number of distinct values in the matrix S. A count of the free parameters is as follows:

6 factor loadings

6 measurement error variances

0 measurement error covariance terms or correlations

1 correlation among the latent variables

Thus, there are a total of 13 free parameters that we wish to estimate. The number of distinct values in the matrix S is equal to

$$p\,(p+1)/2 = 6\,(6+1)/2 = 21,$$

where p is the number of observed variables in the sample variance–covariance matrix. The number of values in S, 21, is greater than the number of free parameters, 13, with the difference being the degrees of freedom for the specified model, $df = 21 - 13 = 8$. However, this is only a necessary condition and does not guarantee that the model is identified. According to the order condition, this model is *over-identified* because there are more values in S than parameters to be estimated—that is, our degrees of freedom is positive **not** zero (*just-identified*) or negative (*under-identified*).

Although the order condition is easy to assess, other sufficient conditions are not, for example, the *rank condition*. The sufficient conditions require us to algebraically determine whether each parameter in the model can be estimated from the covariance matrix S. According to the LISREL computer program, which checks on identification through the rank test and information matrix, the confirmatory factor model is identified.

8.4 Model Estimation

After the identification problem has been addressed, the next step is to estimate the parameters of the specified factor model. In this section we consider the following topics: decomposition of the correlation (or variance–covariance) matrix, parameter estimation in general, and parameter estimation for the confirmatory factor model example.

In factor analysis the traditional method of intuitively thinking about estimation is to decompose the correlation (or variance–covariance) matrix. The decomposition notion is that the original correlation (or variance–covariance) matrix can be completely reproduced if all of the relations among the observed variables are accounted for by the factors in a properly specified factor model. If the model is not properly specified, then the original correlation (or variance–covariance) matrix will not be completely reproduced. This would occur if (a) the number of factors was not correct, (b) the wrong factor loadings were specified, (c) the factor correlations were not correctly specified, and/or (d) the measurement error variances were not specified correctly.

In chapter 4, under model estimation, we considered the statistical aspects of estimation. We learned, for example, that parameters can be estimated by different estimation procedures, such as maximum likelihood (ML), generalized least squares (GLS), and unweighted least squares (ULS), and reported as unstandardized estimates or standardized estimates. We analyzed our confirmatory factor model using maximum likelihood estimation with a standardized solution to report our statistical estimates of the free parameters.

To better understand model modification in section 8.6, we have slightly changed the confirmatory factor model specified in Figure 8.1. We forced the observed variable *Lozenges* to have a factor loading on the latent variable *Verbal Ability* instead of on the latent variable *Spatial Ability*. This intentionally misspecified model is shown in Figure 8.2. We therefore use the confirmatory factor model in Figure 8.2 as our initial model and through the model modification process in section 8.6 hope to discover the best-fitting model to be the confirmatory factor model originally specified in Figure 8.1.

The misspecified model (Figure 8.2) was run using LISREL (computer program in chapter Appendix). The sample variance-covariance matrix *S*

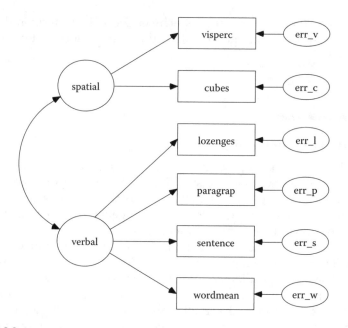

FIGURE 8.2

Misspecified confirmatory factor model. (From Holzinger, K. J., & Swineford, F. A. [1939].
A study in factor analysis: The stability of a bi-factor solution. [Supplementary Educational
Monographs, No. 48]. Chicago, IL: University of Chicago, Department of Education.)

is given at the top of Table 8.1 along with the model implied (reproduced)
matrix, residual matrix, and standardized residual matrix for the misspecified model in Figure 8.2.

    The first column in Table 8.2 contains the standardized estimates for
the misspecified model (Figure 8.2), and the second column contains the
standardized estimates for the original model (Figure 8.1). The parameter
estimates are found to be significantly different from zero ($p < .05$). The fit
of the model is discussed in section 8.5. Of greatest importance is that all
of the factor loadings are statistically significantly different from zero and
have the expected sign, that is, positive factor loadings.

8.5 Model Testing

An important part of the estimation process in analyzing confirmatory
factor models is to fit the sample variance–covariance data to the specified
model. If the fit of the model is good, then the specified model is supported

TABLE 8.1

Original, Reproduced, Residual, and Standardized Residual Covariance
Matrices for the Misspecified Holzinger–Swineford Model

Original Matrix:

Variable	Visperc	Cubes	Lozenges	Parcomp	Sencomp	Wordmean
Visperc	49.064					
Cubes	9.810	22.182				
Lozenges	27.928	14.482	81.863			
Parcomp	9.117	2.515	5.013	12.196		
Sencomp	10.610	3.389	3.605	13.217	26.645	
Wordmean	19.166	6.954	13.716	18.868	28.502	58.817

Reproduced Matrix:

Variable	Visperc	Cubes	Lozenges	Parcomp	Sencomp	Wordmean
Visperc	49.064					
Cubes	9.810	22.182				
Lozenges	5.098	1.646	81.863			
Parcomp	8.595	2.775	5.266	12.196		
Sencomp	12.646	4.083	7.747	13.061	26.645	
Wordmean	18.570	5.996	11.376	19.180	28.218	58.817

Residual Matrix:

Variable	Visperc	Cubes	Lozenges	Parcomp	Sencomp	Wordmean
Visperc	0.000					
Cubes	0.000	0.000				
Lozenges	22.830	12.836	0.000			
Parcomp	0.522	-0.260	-0.253	0.000		
Sencomp	-2.036	-0.694	-4.142	0.155	0.000	
Wordmean	0.596	0.958	2.339	-0.312	0.283	0.000

Standardized Residual Matrix:

Variable	Visperc	Cubes	Lozenges	Parcomp	Sencomp	Wordmean
Visperc	0.000					
Cubes	0.000	0.000				
Lozenges	7.093	5.455	0.000			
Parcomp	1.002	-0.668	-0.336	0.000		
Sencomp	-2.587	-1.182	-3.647	2.310	0.000	
Wordmean	0.484	1.046	1.321	-2.861	1.696	0.000

by the sample data. If the fit of the model is not so good, then the specified
model is not supported by the sample data, and the researcher typically
has to modify the model to achieve a better fit (see section 8.6). As previously discussed in chapter 5, there is a wide variety of model-fit indices
available to the SEM researcher.

TABLE 8.2

Standardized Estimates and Selected Fit Indices for the
Misspecified and Original Holzinger–Swineford Models

	Misspecified Model	Original Model
Factor loadings:		
Visual Perception	.79	.78
Cubes	.38	.43
Lozenges	.20	.57
Paragraph Comprehension	.85	.85
Sentence Completion	.85	.85
Word Meaning	.84	.84
Measurement error variances:		
Visual Perception	.38	.39
Cubes	.86	.81
Lozenges	.96	.68
Paragraph Comprehension	.27	.27
Sentence Completion	.28	.27
Word Meaning	.30	.30
Correlation of independent variables:		
(Spatial, Verbal)	.52	.46
Selected fit Indices:		
χ^2	80.926	24.407
Df	8	8
p value	.001	.002
RMSEA	.174	.083
GFI	.918	.974

For our confirmatory factor model example, we report a few fit indices at the bottom of Table 8.2. For the misspecified model, the χ^2 statistic (technically a measure of badness of fit) is equal to 80.926, with eight degrees of freedom, and $p < .001$. The chi-square statistic is significant, so the specified confirmatory factor model is not supported by the sample variance–covariance data. Another interpretation is that because the χ^2 value is not close to the number of degrees of freedom, the fit of the initial model is poor. Recall that the noncentrality parameter (NCP) is calculated as $\chi^2 - df$, has an expected value of 0 (NCP = 0; perfect fit), and is used in computing several of the model-fit indices. A third criterion is that the root-mean-square error of approximation (RMSEA) is equal to .174, higher than the acceptable level of model fit (RMSEA < .08 or .05). Finally, the goodness-of-fit index (GFI) is .918 for the misspecified model, which is below the acceptable range of model fit (GFI > .95). Across this particular set of model-fit indices, the conclusion is that the model fit is reasonable, although still not acceptable, but that some model modification might allow us to achieve a better sample data (variance–covariance matrix) to confirmatory factor model fit. Determining what change(s) to make to our confirmatory factor model to achieve a better fitting model is considered in the next section.

8.6 Model Modification

A final step in structural equation modeling is to consider changes to a specified model that has poor model-fit indices—that is, model modification. This typically occurs when a researcher discovers that the fit of the specified model is less than satisfactory. The researcher typically performs a *specification search* to find a better fitting model. As discussed in chapter 4, several different procedures can be used to assist in this specification search. One may eliminate parameters that are not significantly different from zero and/or include additional parameters to arrive at a modified model. For the elimination of parameters, the most commonly used procedure in LISREL is to compare the t statistic for each parameter to a tabled t value—for example $t = 1.96$, at $\alpha = .05$, two-tailed test; or $t = 2.58$ at $\alpha = .01$, two-tailed test (see Table A.2), to determine statistical significance.

For the inclusion of additional parameters, the most commonly used techniques in LISREL are (a) the modification index (MI—the expected value that χ^2 would decrease if such a parameter were to be included in the model; large values indicate potentially useful parameters), and (b) the expected parameter change statistic (EPC—the approximate value of the new parameter).

In addition, an examination of the residual matrix, or the more useful standardized residual matrix, often gives clues as to which original covariance terms or correlations are not well accounted for by the model. The residual matrix is the difference between the observed covariance or correlation matrix S and the model implied (reproduced) covariance or correlation matrix Σ. Large residuals indicate values not well accounted for by the model. Standardized residuals are like z scores such that large values (values greater than 1.96 or 2.58) indicate that a particular relationship is not well accounted for by the model.

For the misspecified confirmatory factor model in Figure 8.2, the original, model-implied (reproduced), residual, and standardized residual covariance matrices are given in Table 8.1. Here, we see that the two largest residuals are for the *Lozenges* observed variable (22.830 and 12.836) and the standardized residuals (7.093 and 5.455) are greater than $t = 1.96$ or 2.58. The results also indicate that the *Lozenges* variable should load on the

Spatial Ability factor to reduce error (MI = 60.11) with an expected parameter change (EPC) of 6.30.

The large residuals for *Lozenges*, the statistically significant standardized residuals, the modification index, and the expected change value all indicated that there was something wrong with the *Lozenges* observed variable that is not captured by the misspecified model. Specifically, the factor loading for *Lozenges* should be on the *Spatial Ability* factor rather than the *Verbal Ability* factor. This is precisely the factor loading from the original specified model in Figure 8.1 that we intentionally eliminated to illustrate the model modification process. Thus, the use of several modification criteria in our specification search was successful in obtaining the original model in Figure 8.1.

The standardized estimates and selected model-fit indices for the final model (Figure 8.1), where the modification in the *Lozenges* factor loading is now included, and are shown in the second column of Table 8.2. All of the parameters included are statistically significantly different from zero ($p < .05$), and all of the fit indices now indicate an acceptable level of fit with no additional model modifications indicated. Thus, we consider this to be the final best fitting confirmatory factor model with our sample variance-covariance data. The LISREL–SIMPLIS program is provided at the end of the chapter for this model analysis.

8.7 Summary

This chapter discussed confirmatory factor models using the five basic building blocks from model specification through model modification. We began by analyzing a confirmatory factor model that was misspecified (Figure 8.2) and interpreted a few model-fit criteria where the fit of the model was deemed not acceptable. We then used model modification criteria to modify the model, which yielded the confirmatory factor model in Figure 8.1. This confirmatory factor model was deemed to be our final best fitting model. This final best fitting model can be further validated by testing the same confirmatory factor model with other samples of data (see chapter 12).

Appendix: LISREL–SIMPLIS Confirmatory Factor Model Program

```
Confirmatory Factor Model Figure 8.1
Observed Variables:
VISPERC CUBES LOZENGES PARCOMP SENCOMP WORDMEAN
```

```
Covariance Matrix
      49.064
       9.810   22.182
      27.928   14.482   81.863
       9.117    2.515    5.013   12.196
      10.610    3.389    3.605   13.217   26.645
      19.166    6.954   13.716   18.868   28.502   58.817
Sample Size: 301
Latent Variables: Spatial Verbal
Relationships:
VISPERC - LOZENGES = Spatial
PARCOMP - WORDMEAN = Verbal
Print Residuals
Number of Decimals = 3
Path Diagram
End of problem
```

Exercise

1. Test the following hypothesized confirmatory factor model (Figure 8.3) using the LISREL computer software program:

   Sample Size: 3094

   Observed variables:
   Academic ability (Academic)
   Self-concept (Concept)
   Degree aspirations (Aspire)
   Degree (Degree)
   Occupational prestige (Prestige)
   Income (Income)

   Correlation matrix:

Academic	Concept	Aspire	Degree	Prestige	Income
1.000					
0.487	1.000				
0.236	0.206	1.000			
0.242	0.179	0.253	1.000		
0.163	0.090	0.125	0.481	1.000	
0.064	0.040	0.025	0.106	0.136	1.000

   Hypothesized CFA model: The CFA model indicates that the first three observed variables measure the latent variable Academic Motivation (Motivate) and the last three observed variables measure the latent variable Socioeconomic Status (SES). Motivate and SES are correlated.

   Then modify the model to achieve a better model fit as shown in Figure 8.4.

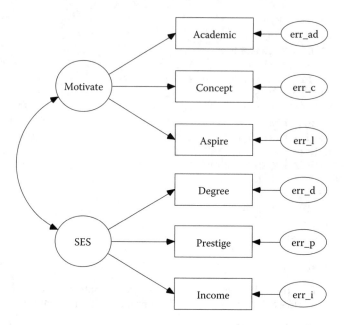

FIGURE 8.3
Hypothesized CFA model for exercise.

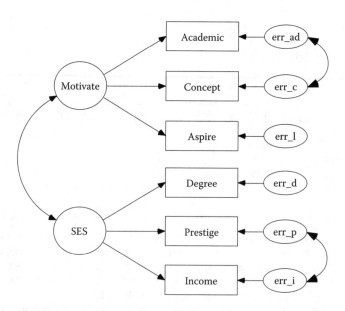

FIGURE 8.4
Final CFA model for exercise.

References

Cochran, W. G. (1968). Errors of measurement in statistics. *Technometrics, 10,* 637–666.

Comrey, A. L., & Lee, H. B. (1992). *A first course in factor analysis.* Hillsdale, NJ: Lawrence Erlbaum.

Costello, A. B., & Osborne, J. (2005). Best practices in exploratory factor analysis: four recommendations for getting the most from your analysis. *Practical Assessment Research and Evaluation, 10*(7), 1–9.

Fuller, W. A. (1987). *Measurement error models.* New York: Wiley.

Gorsuch, R. L. (1983). *Factor analysis* (2nd ed.). Hillsdale, NJ: Lawrence Erlbaum.

Harmon, H. H. (1976). *Modern factor analysis* (3rd ed., rev.). Chicago: University of Chicago Press.

Holzinger, K. J., & Swineford, F. A. (1939). *A study in factor analysis: The stability of a bi-factor solution.* (Supplementary Educational Monographs, No. 48). Chicago, IL: University of Chicago, Department of Education.

Jöreskog, K. G., & Sörbom, D. (1993). *LISREL 8: Structural equation modeling with the SIMPLIS command language.* Chicago, IL: Scientific Software International.

9

Developing Structural Equation Models: Part I

Key Concepts

Latent independent and dependent variables

Observed independent and dependent variables

Developing structural models with latent variables

Establishing relationships between latent variables

Covariance terms

The four-step approach to SEM modeling

Structural equation models have been developed in a number of academic disciplines to substantiate and test theory. Structural equation models have further helped to establish the relationships between latent variables or constructs, given a theoretical perspective. The structural equation modeling approach involves developing measurement models to define latent variables and then establishing relationships or structural equation models with the latent variables. The focus of this chapter is on providing researchers with a better understanding of how to develop structural equation models. An attempt is made to minimize matrix and statistical notation so that the reader can better understand the structural equation modeling approach.

This chapter begins with a more extensive discussion of observed variables and latent variables, and then proceeds with sections on the measurement model, the structural model, variances and covariance terms, and finally the two-step/four-step approaches to structural equation modeling. Chapter 10 extends the development of SEM models in examining model specification, model identification, model estimation, model testing, and model modification.

9.1 Observed Variables and Latent Variables

In structural equation modeling, as in traditional statistics, we use X and Y to denote the observed variables. We use X to refer to independent (or predictor) variables and Y to refer to dependent (or criterion) variables; this is the same in multiple regression, analysis of variance, and all general linear models. In structural equation modeling, however, we further define latent independent variables using observed variables denoted by X and latent dependent variables using observed variables denoted by Y. Latent independent and dependent variables are created with observed variables using confirmatory factor models discussed in the previous chapter.

There are two major types of variables in structural equation modeling: observed (indicator) variables and latent (construct) variables. Latent variables are not directly observable or measured, rather they are observed or measured indirectly, and hence they are inferred constructs based on what observed variables we select to define the latent variable. For example, intelligence is a latent variable and represents a psychological construct. Intelligence cannot be directly observed, for example, through visual inspection of an individual, and thus there is no single agreed upon definition for intelligence. However, intelligence can be indirectly measured through observed or indicator variables, for example, specific IQ tests.

Observed or indicator variables are variables that are directly observable or measured. For example, the Wechsler Intelligence Scale for Children–Revised (WISC-R) is an instrument commonly used to measure children's intelligence. The instrument represents one definition or measure of what we mean by intelligence. Other researchers rely on other definitions or observed measures, and thus on other instruments, for example, the Stanford–Binet Intelligence Scale. Latent variables such as intelligence are not directly observable or measured, but can be indirectly observed or measured by using several observed (indicator) variables, for example, IQ tests such as the WISC-R and the Stanford–Binet Intelligence Scale.

Let us further examine the concept of latent variables as they are used in structural equation models. Consider a basic structural equation model in which we propose that a latent independent variable predicts a latent dependent variable. For instance, *Intelligence* (latent independent variable) is believed to predict subsequent *Scholastic Achievement* (latent dependent variable), which could be depicted as

$$\text{Intelligence} \rightarrow \text{Achievement}$$

Any latent variable that is predicted by other latent variables in a structural equation model is known as a *latent dependent variable*. A latent dependent variable, therefore, must have at least one arrow pointing to it from another latent variable, sometimes referred to as an *endogenous* latent variable. Any latent variable that does not have an arrow pointing to it from another latent variable is known as a *latent independent variable,* sometimes referred to as an *exogenous* latent variable. As shown in the foregoing example, the latent independent variable *Intelligence* does not have any arrows pointing to it from another latent variable. In our basic structural equation model, *Intelligence* is the latent independent variable with no direct lines or arrows pointing to it, and *Achievement* is the latent dependent variable because it has an arrow pointing to it from *Intelligence*.

Consider adding a third latent variable to our basic structural equation model, such that *Achievement* is measured at two points in time. This model would be depicted as follows:

$$\text{Intelligence} \rightarrow \text{Achievement}_1 \rightarrow \text{Achievement}_2.$$

Intelligence is still a latent independent variable. *Achievement$_2$* is clearly a latent dependent variable because there is an arrow pointing to it from *Achievement$_1$*. However, there is an arrow pointing to *Achievement$_1$* from *Intelligence* and another arrow pointing from *Achievement$_1$* to *Achievement$_2$*. This basic structural equation model indicates that *Achievement$_1$* is predicted by *Intelligence,* but then *Achievement$_1$* predicts *Achievement$_2$*. *Achievement$_1$* is first a dependent latent variable and then an independent latent variable. This type of structural equation model is possible and illustrates indirect effects using latent variables. *Achievement$_1$* in this basic structural equation model is a *mediating* latent variable. Our designation of a latent variable as independent or dependent is therefore determined by whether or not an arrow is drawn from one latent variable to another latent variable. If no arrows point to a latent variable from another latent variable in the structural equation model, then it is a latent *independent* variable. If an arrow points to a latent variable from another latent variable in the structural equation model, then it is a latent *dependent* variable.

Next, we consider the concept behind the observed or indicator variables. The latent independent variables are measured by observed independent variables via a confirmatory factor analysis measurement model and traditionally denoted by X. The latent dependent variables are measured by observed dependent variables via a confirmatory factor analysis measurement model and traditionally denoted by Y. Following our example, we might choose the WISC-R and the Stanford–Binet Intelligence Scale as observed independent measures of the latent independent variable *Intelligence*. We can denote these observed variables as X_1 and X_2. For each of the achievement latent variables, we might choose the California Achievement Test and the Metropolitan Achievement Test as our observed dependent measures. If these measures are observed at two points in time, then we can denote the observed variables of *Achievement$_1$* as Y_1 and Y_2, and those of *Achievement*$_2$ as Y_3 and Y_4, respectively. In our SEM model, each latent variable is measured by two observed variables.

What is the benefit of using more than one observed variable to assess a latent variable? In using a single observed variable to assess a latent variable, we assume that no measurement error is associated with the measurement of that latent variable. In other words, it is assumed that the latent variable is perfectly measured by the single observed variable, which is typically not the case. We define measurement error quite generally here to include errors due to reliability and validity issues (see chapter 8).

Reliability is concerned with the ability of a measure (score) to be consistent, commonly referred to as internal consistency, consistency over time, and consistency using similar measures, to denote different types of measurement error associated with observed variable scores. Would Jamie's score on the WISC-R be about the same if measured today as compared with next week? Evidence of score reliability (consistency) could be shown when a measure is given to the same group of individuals at two points in time, and the scores are roughly equivalent. If only a single measure of a latent variable is used and it is not very reliable, then our latent variable is not defined very well. If the reliability of a single observed measure of a latent variable is known, then it is prudent to specify or fix the measurement error in the SEM model. This is accomplished, for example, in LISREL–SIMPLIS by setting the error variance of the single variable. The error variance of a single variable is determined by the following formula:

$$\text{Error Variance of } X1 = (1 - \text{reliability coefficient}) \, (s^2{}_{X1}).$$

If the reliability of scores for *X1* is .85 with a standard deviation of 5.00, then the error variance would be computed as:

$$X1_{\text{error variance}} = (1 - .85) \, (5.00)^2 = .15 \, (25) = 3.75.$$

In the LISREL–SIMPLIS program, you would then add the following command line to set the error variance for X1:

$$\text{Set the error variance of X1 to 3.75}$$

Validity is concerned with the extent to which scores accurately define a construct, which is score inference—commonly referred to as content, factorial, convergent–divergent, and discriminant validity—to denote different types of score inference associated with observed scores. Our interest in validity is how well we can make an inference from the measured scores to the latent variable; that is, how well do test scores indicate what they purport to measure. Does Jamie's score on the WISC-R really measure her intelligence or something else, such as her height? Evidence of validity is shown when two indicators of the same latent variable are substantially correlated. For example, if WISC-R and height were used as indicators of the latent variable *Intelligence*, we would expect them to not be correlated. If only a single measure of a latent variable is used and the score is not valid (for example, if height is used to measure intelligence), then our latent variable is not well defined. Establishing the reliability of scores for our observed variable helps in estimating the validity coefficients (factor loadings) in our measurement model because score validity is limited by the reliability of the observed variable scores; that is, the maximum validity coefficient is less than or equal to the product of the square roots of the two reliability coefficients, $\rho_{XY} \leq \sqrt{\rho_{XX'}} \sqrt{\rho_{YY'}}$.

If we selected WISC-R and height as observed indicator variables for the latent independent variable *Intelligence* it would certainly not be well defined and would include measurement error. The selection of only height as an observed indicator of *Intelligence* would increase the measurement error and poorly define the construct. Consequently, in selecting observed variables to define a latent variable, we need to select observed variables that show evidence of both score reliability and score validity for the intended purpose of our study. Because of the inherent difficulty involved in obtaining reliable and valid measures with a single observed variable, we strongly encourage you to consider multiple indicator variables for each latent independent and dependent variable in the structural equation model.

There are a few obvious exceptions to this recommendation, especially when research indicates that only one observed variable is available. In this case, you have no other choice than to define the latent variable using a single observed variable or use the observed variable in a Multiple Indicator Multiple Indicator Cause (MIMIC) model (see chapter 15). Jöreskog and Sörbom (1993, p. 37, EX7A.SPL) provided the rationale and gave an example for setting the error variance of a single observed variable (*VERBINTM*) in defining the latent variable *Verbint*. The verbal intelligence test (*VERBINTM*) was a fallible (unreliable) measure of the latent variable *Verbint*, and therefore it was unreasonable to assume that the error variance was zero (perfectly reliable). Consequently, the sample reliability coefficient for *VERBINTM* was assumed to be $r_{XX'} = .85$ rather than 1.00 (perfectly reliable, zero error variance). The assumed value of the reliability coefficient, hence designation of the error variance for *VERBINTM*, will affect parameter estimates as well as standard errors. A reliability coefficient of $r_{XX'} = .85$ for *VERBINTM* is equivalent to an error variance of 0.15 times the variance of *VERBINTM* $(3.65)^2$. The assumed error variance of *VERBINTM* was computed as $.15 (3.65)^2 = 1.998$.

If we can assume a reasonable reliability coefficient for an observed variable, then multiplying the observed variable's variance by 1 minus the reliability coefficient provides a reasonable estimate of error variance. In the LISREL–SIMPLIS program EX7B.SPL, the error variance for the single observed variable *VERBINTM* is accomplished by using the *SET* command as follows:

SET the error variance of VERBINTM to 1.998

Later in this chapter we show how measurement error is explicitly a part of any structural equation model. The basic concept, however, is that multiple observed variables used in defining either a latent independent variable or a latent dependent variable permit measurement error to be estimated through structural equation modeling. This provides the researcher with additional information about the measurement characteristics of the observed variables. When there is only a single observed indicator of a latent variable, then measurement error cannot be estimated through structural equation modeling, but can be fixed to a certain value. Most SEM software programs, such as LISREL, permit the specification of error variance for single or multiple variables, whether the values are known or require our best guess. In the next two sections we discuss the two approaches that make up structural equation modeling: the measurement model and the structural model.

9.2 Measurement Model

As previously mentioned, the researcher specifies the measurement model to define the relationships between the latent variables and the observed variables. The measurement model in SEM is a confirmatory factor model. Using our previous example, the latent independent variable *Intelligence* is measured by two observed variables, the WISC-R and the Stanford–Binet Intelligence Scale. Our other latent variables *Achievement*₁ (dependent latent variable) and *Achievement*₂ (dependent latent variable) are each measured by the same two observed variables, the California Achievement Test and the Metropolitan Achievement Test, but at two different times. Both of these observed variables are composite or scale scores from summing numerous individual items. In chapter 8, we pointed out that individual items on an instrument could be used to create a construct (latent variable); hence, confirming the unidimensionality of the construct, while taking into account the observed variable score reliability and fit of the measurement model. The use of many individual items rather than the composite score or item parcels—that is, collections of individual items as the observed measures of a latent variable—increases the degrees of freedom in the measurement model and can cause problems in model fit. Measurement characteristics at the item level might be more appropriate for exploratory data reduction methods than they are for SEM measurement models.

The researcher is typically interested in having the following questions answered about the observed variables: To what extent are the observed variables actually measuring the hypothesized latent variable; for example, how good is the California Achievement Test as a measure of achievement? Which observed variable is the best measure of a particular latent variable; for example, is the California Achievement Test a better measure of achievement than the Metropolitan Achievement Test? To what extent are the observed variables actually measuring something other than the hypothesized latent variable? For example, is the California Achievement Test measuring something other than achievement, such as the quality of education received? These types of questions need to be addressed when creating the measurement models that define the latent variables.

In our measurement model example each latent variable is defined by two indicator variables. The relationships between the observed variables and the latent variables are indicated by factor loadings. The factor loadings provide us with information about the extent to which a given observed variable is able to measure the latent variable (a squared factor loading indicates variable communality or amount of variance shared with the factor). The factor loadings are referred to as validity coefficients because multiplying the factor loading times the observed variable score indicates how much of the observed variable score variance is valid (true score). The observed variable measurement error is defined as that portion of the observed variable score that is measuring something other than what the latent variable is hypothesized to measure. It serves as a measure of error variance, and hence assesses the observed variable score reliability. Measurement error could be the result of (a) an observed variable that is measuring some other latent variable, (b) unreliability, or (c) a higher second order factor. For example, the California Achievement Test may be measuring something besides achievement, or it may not yield very reliable scores. Thus, we would like to know how much measurement error is associated with each observed variable.

In our measurement model there are six measurement equations, one for each observed variable, which can be illustrated as follows:

$$\text{California}_1 = \text{function of Achievement}_1 + \text{error}$$

$$\text{Metropolitan}_1 = \text{function of Achievement}_1 + \text{error}$$

$$\text{California}_2 = \text{function of Achievement}_2 + \text{error}$$

$$\text{Metropolitan}_2 = \text{function of Achievement}_2 + \text{error}$$

$$\text{WISC-R} = \text{function of Intelligence} + \text{error}$$

$$\text{Stanford–Binet} = \text{function of Intelligence} + \text{error}$$

In the LISREL–SIMPLIS program, an explicit definition of the measurement model can be done by specifying measurement equations. One can expand the variable labels in the measurement model equations using up to eight characters; the labels are case-sensitive (upper and lower characters are recognized). The measurement model equations are specified, using either the *Relationships:* or *Paths:* command (both methods are equivalent). For the *Relationships:* command, both the latent variables and the observed variables can be written using eight-character variable names. The observed variables are given on the left-hand side of the equation with spaces between the multiple observed variable names (*Cal1, Metro1, Cal2, Metro2, WISCR,* and *Stanford*) and the latent variables on the right-hand side of the equation (*Achieve1, Achieve2,* and *Intell*). The LISREL–SIMPLIS measurement equations follow where *Achieve1* refers to Achievement$_1$, *Intell* refers to Intelligence, *Achieve2* refers to Achievement$_2$, *Cal1* refers to California$_1$, *Metro1* refers to Metropolitan$_1$, *Cal2* refers to California$_2$, *Metro2* refers to Metropolitan$_2$, *WISCR* refers to WISC-R, and *Stanford* refers to Stanford–Binet). The command line for *Relationships* would be written as:

> *Relationships:*
>
>   *Cal1 Metro1 = Achieve1*
>
>   *Cal2 Metro2 = Achieve2*
>
>   *WISCR Stanford = Intell*

For the *Paths:* command, the latent variables are depicted to the left of the arrow and the observed variables to the right of the arrow with spaces between the multiple observed variable names. The command line for *Paths* in the following measurement equation would be written as:

> *Paths:*
>
>   *Achieve1 → Cal1 Metro1*
>
>   *Achieve2 → Cal2 Metro2*
>
>   *Intell → WISCR Stanford*

9.3 Structural Model

In chapter 8 we discussed the rationale and process for specifying a measurement model to indicate whether the latent variables are measured well, given a set of observed variables. If the latent variables (independent and dependent) are measured well, we then specify a structural model to indicate how these latent variables are related. The researcher specifies the structural model to allow for certain relationships among the latent variables depicted by the direction of the arrows. In our example we hypothesized that intelligence and achievement are related in a specific way. We hypothesized that intelligence predicts later achievement. The hypothesized structural model can now be specified and tested to determine the extent to which these a priori hypothesized relationships are supported by our sample variance–covariance data; that is, Can intelligence predict achievement? Could there be other latent variables that we need to consider to better predict achievement? These types of questions are addressed when specifying the structural model.

At this point we need to provide a more explicit definition of the structural model and a specific notational system for the latent variables under consideration. Let us return to our previous example where we indicated a specific hypothesized relationship for the latent variables:

$$\text{Intelligence} \rightarrow \text{Achievement}_1 \rightarrow \text{Achievement}_2.$$

The hypothesized relationships for the latent variables indicate two latent dependent variables, so there will be two structural equations. The first equation should indicate that *Achievement$_1$* is predicted by *Intelligence*. The second equation should indicate that *Achievement$_2$* is predicted by *Achievement$_1$*. These two equations can be illustrated as follows:

$$Achievement_1 = \text{structure coefficient}_1 * Intelligence + \text{error}$$

$$Achievement_2 = \text{structure coefficient}_2 * Achievement_1 + \text{error}$$

These two equations specify the estimation of two structure coefficients to indicate the magnitude (strength as well as statistical significance) and direction (positive or negative) of the prediction. Each structural equation also contains a prediction error or disturbance term that indicates the portion of the latent dependent variable that is not explained or predicted by the other latent variables in that equation. In our example there are two structure coefficients, one for *Intelligence* predicting *Achievement$_1$* and one for *Achievement$_1$* predicting *Achievement$_2$*. Because there are two structural equations, there are two prediction errors or disturbances.

The LISREL–SIMPLIS command language permits an easy way to specify structural equations among the latent variables. The structural model can be denoted in terms of either the *Relationships:* or *Paths:* commands (both methods are equivalent). For the *Relationships:* command, the latent variables can be written using eight-character variable names with the latent dependent variables on the left side of the equation (where *Achieve1* refers to *Achievement$_1$*, *Intell* refers to *Intelligence*, and *Achieve2* refers to *Achievement$_2$*):

> *Relationships:*
> *Achieve1 = Intell*
> *Achieve2 = Achieve1*

For the *Paths:* command, these latent dependent variables are to the right of the arrow, as in the following structural equations:

> *Paths:*
> *Intell → Achieve1*
> *Achieve1 → Achieve2*

(**NOTE:** You do not need to indicate the prediction error in LISREL–SIMPLIS structural equations for either the *Relationships:* or *Paths:* commands because these are known to exist and automatically estimated by the program.)

The path diagram of the measurement and structural models for our example is shown in Figure 9.1.

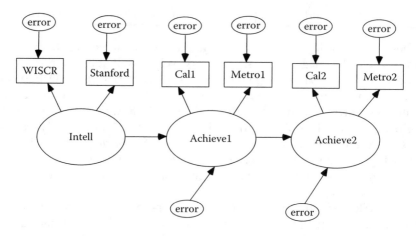

FIGURE 9.1
Achievement path model.

9.4 Variances and Covariance Terms

In structural equation modeling, the term *covariance structure analysis* or *covariance structure modeling* is often used because the estimation of factor loadings and structure coefficients involves the decomposition of a sample variance–covariance matrix. In this section we further explore the notion of variance–covariance as it relates to observed and latent variables. There are three different variance–covariance terms that we need to define and understand. In the structural model there are two variance–covariance terms to consider. First, there is a variance–covariance matrix of the latent independent variables. This consists of the variances for each latent independent variable, as well as the covariance terms among them. Although we are interested in the variances (the amount of variance associated with the latent independent variable intelligence), the covariance terms may or may not be part of our theoretical model. In our model there is only one latent independent variable, so there is only one variance term and no covariance term.

If we specified two latent independent variables in a different structural equation model, for example, *Intelligence* and *Home Background*, we could include a covariance term for them. We would then be hypothesizing that *Intelligence* and *Home Background* are correlated or covary because we believe that some common unmeasured latent variable is influencing both of them. We could hypothesize that a latent variable not included in the model, such as *Parenting Ability*, influences both *Intelligence* and *Home Background*. In other words, *Intelligence* and *Home Background* co-vary, or are correlated, because of their mutual influence from *Parenting Ability*, which has not explicitly been included in the model (but which perhaps could be included).

In the LISREL–SIMPLIS program, the variance term would automatically be given or implied in the output for the latent independent variable *Intelligence*. A covariance term, if one existed, would also automatically be given or implied in the output. If one desired the two latent independent variables, *Intelligence* and *Home Background*, to be uncorrelated or to have a covariance of zero, then one would specify the following in the LISREL–SIMPLIS program:

```
Set the Covariance between Intell and HomeBack to 0
```

The second set of variance–covariance terms that we need to define and understand is in the covariance matrix of the structural equation model for prediction errors. This consists of the variances for each structural equation prediction error (the amount of unexplained variance for each structural equation), as well as covariance terms among them. Although we are interested in the variances, the covariance terms may or may not be part of our model. We could specify that two structural equation prediction errors are correlated, perhaps because some unmeasured latent variable is leading to error in both equations. An example of this might be where *Parental Occupational Status* (parent income) is not included as a latent variable in a model where *Children's Education* (in years) and *Children's Occupational Status* (income at age 30 years) are latent dependent variables. The structural equations for *Children's Education* and *Children's Occupational Status* would then both contain structural equation prediction error due to the omission of *Parental Occupational Status*. Because the same latent variable was not included in both equations, we expect that the structural equation prediction errors would be correlated. (*Note:* Our hypothesized structural model does not contain any such covariance terms.)

In the LISREL–SIMPLIS program, the variance terms are automatically included in the output for each structural equation. Because the covariance terms are assumed by the program to be set to zero, one must specify any covariance terms one wants estimated. A covariance term, if one existed between *Achievement₁* and *Achievement₂*, would be specified using the following command:

```
Set the Error Covariance between Achieve1 and Achieve2 free
```

The third set of variance–covariance terms is from the measurement model. Here, we need to define and understand the variances and covariance terms of the measurement errors. Although we are interested in the variances (the amount of measurement error variance associated with each observed variable), the covariance terms may or may not be part of our model. We could hypothesize that the measurement errors for two observed variables are correlated (known as *correlated measurement error*). This might be expected in our example model where the indicators of the latent variables *Achievement₁* and *Achievement₂* are the same—for example, from using the California Achievement Test at two different times. We might believe that the measurement error associated with the California Achievement Test at Time 1 is related to the measurement error for the California Achievement Test at Time 2.

In the LISREL–SIMPLIS program, the variance terms are automatically specified in the program for each observed variable. Once again, the covariance terms are assumed by the program to be set to zero; so we must specify any covariance term of interest and allow it to be estimated. A covariance term, if one existed between the measurement errors for the California Achievement Test at Times 1 and 2, would be specified using the following command:

```
Set the Error Covariance between Cal1 and Cal2 free
```

There is one final variance–covariance term that we need to mention, and it really represents the ultimate variance–covariance for our combined measurement model and structural model. From the structure coefficient parameters we estimate in the structural model, the factor loadings in the measurement model(s), and all of the variance–covariance terms, we generate an ultimate matrix of variance–covariance terms for the overall SEM model. This variance–covariance matrix is implied by the overall model and is denoted by Σ (see chapter 17 for a representation of all of these matrices). Our goal in structural equation modeling is to estimate all of the parameters in the overall model and test the overall fit of the model to the sample variance–covariance data. In short, the parameters in our overall SEM model create an implied variance–covariance matrix Σ from the sample variance–covariance matrix S, which contains the sample variances and covariance terms among our observed variables. We interpret our model-fit indices (see chapter 5) to determine the level of model fit between Σ and S (closeness of the values in the variance–covariance matrix Σ implied by our hypothesized model, and the sample variance–covariance matrix S given our sample data). We also examine the magnitude (strength as well as statistical significance of parameter estimates) and the direction (positive or negative coefficients) to provide a meaningful interpretation of our SEM model results.

9.5 Two-Step/Four-Step Approach

James, Mulaik, and Brett (1982) proposed a two-step modeling approach that emphasized the analysis of the two conceptually distinct latent variable models: measurement models and structural models. Anderson and Gerbing (1988) described their approach by stating that the measurement model provides an assessment of convergent and discriminant validity, and the structural model provides an assessment of predictive validity. Mulaik et al. (1989) also expanded the idea of assessing the fit of the structural equation model among latent variables (structural model) independently of assessing the fit of the observed variables to the latent variables (measurement model). Their rationale was that even with few latent variables, most parameter estimates define the relationships of the observed variables to the latent variables in the measurement model, rather than the structural relationships of the latent variables themselves. Mulaik and Millsap (2000) further elaborated a four-step approach discussed in chapter 5. Jöreskog and Sörbom (1993, p. 113) had earlier summarized many of their thoughts by stating:

> The testing of the structural model, i.e., the testing of the initially
> specified theory, may be meaningless unless it is first established that
> the measurement model holds. If the chosen indicators for a construct
> do not measure that construct, the specified theory must be modified
> before it can be tested. Therefore, the measurement model should be
> tested before the structural relationships are tested.

We have found it prudent to follow their advice. In the establishment of
measurement models, it is best to identify a few good indicators of each
latent variable with three or four indicators being recommended. In our
example, we intentionally used only a few indicators to define or measure
the latent variables to keep the model simple. We have also found that
when selecting only a few indicator variables, it is easier to check how
well each observed variable defines a latent variable—that is, to examine
the factor loadings, reliability coefficients, and the amount of latent variable variance explained. For example, rather than use individual items
as indicator variables, sum the items to form a total test score or a parcel
score (composite score or scale score). In addition, one can calculate the
reliability of the composite (scale) score and even consider fixing the value
of the relevant measurement error variance in the model (as described in
section 9.1), thus reducing the need to estimate one parameter. It is only
after latent variables are adequately defined (measured) that it makes
sense to examine latent variable relationships in a structural model. We
think a researcher with adequately measured latent variables is in a better position to establish a substantive, meaningful structural model, thus
supporting theory.

9.6 Summary

This chapter focused on how to develop structural equation models. We
began with a more detailed look at both observed and latent variables.
Next, we discussed the measurement and structural models. We extended
some of the basic concepts found in confirmatory factor models (measurement models) and regression/path models (structural models) to structural
equation modeling. We then described three types of variance–covariance
matrices typically utilized in structural equation models. The chapter concluded with a discussion of the popular two-step/four-step approaches
to structural equation modeling. In chapter 10 we extend our discussion
of the development of structural equation models by considering model
specification, model identification, model estimation, model testing, and
model modification, utilizing a more complex hypothesized theoretical
model.

Exercises

1. Diagram two indicator variables *X1* and *X2* of a latent variable *LV*.
2. Diagram two observed variables *X1* and *X2* that predict a third observed variable *Y*. *X1*, and *X2* are correlated.
3. Diagram a latent independent variable *LIV* predicting a latent dependent variable *LDV*.
4. Would you use a single indicator of a latent variable? Why or why not?

References

Anderson, J. C., & Gerbing, D. W. (1988). Structural equation modeling in practice: A review and recommended two-step approach. *Psychological Bulletin, 103,* 411–423.

James, L. R., Mulaik, S. A., & Brett, J. M. (1982). *Causal analysis: Assumptions, models, and data.* Los Angeles, CA: Sage.

Jöreskog, K. G., & Sörbom, D. (1993). *LISREL 8: Structural equation modeling with the SIMPLIS command language.* Chicago: Scientific Software International.

Mulaik, S. A., James, L. R., Alstine, J. V., Bennett, N., Lind, S., & Stilwell, C. D. (1989). Evaluation of goodness-of-fit indices for structural equation models. *Psychological Bulletin, 105,* 430–445.

Mulaik, S. A., & Millsap, R. E. (2000). Doing the four-step right. *Structural Equation Modeling, 7,* 36–73.

10

Developing Structural Equation Models: Part II

Key Concepts

> Factor loadings and measurement errors
>
> Structure coefficients and prediction errors
>
> Variance and covariance terms
>
> Specification search

In chapter 9 we presented the basic framework for the development of structural equation models. We focused on the measurement model, the structural model, and the different variance–covariance terms. These constitute the basic building blocks for analyzing and interpreting a structural equation model. In this chapter we extend our discussion of the development of structural equation models. We present a hypothesized theoretical structural equation model and discuss issues related to model specification, model identification, model estimation, model testing, and model modification in the context of that example.

10.1 An Example

We hypothesized a structural equation model based on predicting educational achievement as a latent dependent variable. The structural model is diagrammed in Figure 10.1 with four latent variables drawn as ellipses: two latent independent variables, home background (*Home*) and *Ability*, and two latent dependent variables, aspirations (*Aspire*) and achievement (*Achieve*).

Three of the latent variables are defined by using two indicator variables, and one latent variable, *Home*, is defined by using three indicator variables in the measurement model. The indicator variables are depicted using rectangles as follows: (a) for *Home*, family income (*FamInc*), father's education (*FaEd*) and mother's education (*MoEd*); (b) for *Ability*, verbal

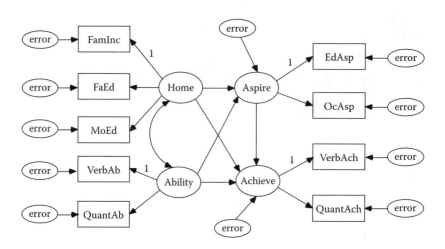

FIGURE 10.1
Structural equation model of educational achievement.

ability (*VerbAb*) and quantitative ability (*QuantAb*); (c) for *Aspire*, educational aspiration (*EdAsp*) and occupational aspiration (*OcAsp*); and (d) for *Achieve*, verbal achievement (*VerbAch*) and quantitative achievement (*QuantAch*).

The measurement models for each latent variable identify which observed variables define that particular latent variable. An arrow is drawn from the latent variable to each of its observed indicator variables. For each arrow, we understand that a factor loading will be computed. For example, the observed measures of family income, father's education and mother's education define the latent variable *Home*, with each observed variable having a factor loading estimated. Figure 10.1 has nine arrows going from the latent variables drawn as ellipses to observed variables drawn as rectangles, thus nine factor loadings will be estimated.

In Figure 10.1 each observed variable has a unique measurement error. This is indicated by an arrow pointing to each observed variable and shows that some portion of each observed variable is measuring something other than the hypothesized latent variable. For example, mother's education (*MoEd*) is hypothesized to define *Home* (home background), but it may also be assessing other latent variables, a function of other variables not in the model, random, or systematic error. The unique measurement error is estimated for each observed variable, so there will be nine unique measurement errors estimated. Each observed variable has a factor loading and a unique measurement error that forms an equation to compute the latent variable score; for example,

MoEd = factor loading * Home + measurement error

Our model diagram does not include any curved arrows for measurement error, but this issue should be discussed. A curved arrow between two measurement error terms is possible and indicates that the measurement error terms are correlated. Two measurement error terms could be correlated if they share something in common, such as common method variance, or if the same measure is being used at different points in time. For example, quantitative ability (*QuantAb*) and quantitative achievement (*QuantAch*) may have correlated measurement error terms, for example, because they represent two measures of quantitative skills. Correlated measurement error terms may also exist for father's education (*FaEd*) and mother's education (*MoEd*), for example, because using the same method of measurement, the errors for one parent might be reflected in the other parent.

A straight arrow leading from a latent variable to a latent dependent variable designates that a structure coefficient is to be estimated. For example, it was hypothesized that *Home* (home background) predicts *Aspire* (aspirations). The structure coefficients we want to estimate in our hypothesized structural model come from a review of prior research and theory. In our hypothesized structural model there are five structure coefficients we want to estimate. Each latent dependent variable has one or more structure coefficients and a unique prediction error that forms an equation; for example,

$$\textit{Aspire} = \text{structure coefficient} * \textit{Home} + \text{structure coefficient} * \textit{Ability} + \text{prediction error}$$

The prediction error for *Aspire* indicates that some portion of *Aspire* (aspiration) is not predicted by the latent independent variables *Home* and *Ability*. There are two equations in our hypothesized structural model, so we estimate two prediction errors, one for *Aspire* and one for *Achieve*:

$$\textit{Aspire} = \text{structure coefficient} * \textit{Home} + \text{structure coefficient} * \textit{Ability} + \text{prediction error}$$

$$\textit{Achieve} = \text{structure coefficient} * \textit{Home} + \text{structure coefficient} * \textit{Ability} + \text{structure coefficient} * \textit{Aspire} + \text{prediction error}$$

10.2 Model Specification

Model specification is the first step in structural equation modeling (also for regression models, path models, and confirmatory factor models). We need theory because a set of observed variables can define a multitude of different latent variables in a measurement model. In addition, many different structural models can be generated on the basis of different hypothesized relationships among the latent variables.

In our theoretical structural equation model to predict *Achieve* (educational achievement) we used nine observed variables and hypothesized four latent variables. Given this, many different measurement models and structural models are possible. First, each observed variable can load on one or more latent variables, so there could be nine or more possible factor loadings (up to 36 in our measurement model). Second, the two latent independent variables may or may not be correlated. Third, there may or may not be correlations or covariance terms among the measurement errors, suggesting there could be anywhere from zero to several possible correlated measurement error terms. Fourth, different structural models could be tested, so we could have more than five or less than five structure coefficients in the different models. Finally, each structural equation has a prediction error—one for each latent dependent variable—so we could have more or less prediction errors, and the prediction errors could be correlated.

How does a researcher determine which model is correct? We have already learned that model specification is complicated, and we must meet certain data conditions with the observed variables (see chapter 2). Basically, structural equation modeling does not determine which model to test; rather, it estimates the parameters in a model once that model has been specified a priori by the researcher based on theoretical knowledge. Consequently, theory plays a major role in formulating structural equation models and guides the researcher's decision on which model(s) to specify and test. Once again, we are reminded that model specification is indeed the hardest part of structural equation modeling.

We used theory to formulate our measurement model and structural model in predicting educational achievement, *Achieve* (Lomax, 1985). In the measurement model there are nine equations, one for each observed variable. From Figure 10.1, we formed the following nine measurement equations:

$$\text{EdAsp} = \text{factor loading} * \text{Aspire} + \text{measurement error}$$

$$\text{OcAsp} = \text{factor loading} * \text{Aspire} + \text{measurement error}$$

$$\text{VerbAch} = \text{factor loading} * \text{Achieve} + \text{measurement error}$$

$$\text{QuantAch} = \text{factor loading} * \text{Achieve} + \text{measurement error}$$

$$\text{FamInc} = \text{factor loading} * \text{Home} + \text{measurement error}$$

$$\text{FaEd} = \text{factor loading} * \text{Home} + \text{measurement error}$$

$$\text{MoEd} = \text{factor loading} * \text{Home} + \text{measurement error}$$

VerbAb = factor loading * Ability + measurement error

QuantAb = factor loading * Ability + measurement error

Our latent variables are unobserved and have no definite scale of measurement (origin and unit of measurement are arbitrary). To define the measurement model correctly, the origin and unit of measurement for each latent variable must be defined. The origin of a latent variable is usually assumed to have a mean of 0. The unit of measurement (variance) of a latent variable can be set using two different approaches. To compare our factor loadings (interpret the parameter estimates), we need to define a common unit of measurement for the latent variables. This is accomplished by setting a single observed variable factor loading to 1 for the latent variable, for example, *EdAsp* = 1 * *Aspire* + measurement error. The observed variable selected usually represents the best indicator of the latent variable and is called a *reference variable* because all other observed variables for that latent variable are interpreted in relation to its unit of measurement. Another option is to assume that the latent variables have a standardized unit of measurement and fix the latent variable variance to 1 (see Jöreskog & Sörbom, 1993, p. 173, 174).

In the LISREL–SIMPLIS command language (Jöreskog & Sörbom, 1993), the measurement model equations are typically written using variable names. In the *Relationships:* command, the observed variables are specified on the left-hand side of the equation with spaces between the multiple observed variable names and the latent variables on the right-hand side. The LISREL–SIMPLIS measurement equations are specified using variable names as follows:

Relationships:
 EdAsp = 1*Aspire
 OcAsp = Aspire
 VerbAch = 1*Achieve
 QuantAch = Achieve
 FamInc = 1*Home
 FaEd MoEd = Home
 VerbAb = 1*Ability
 QuantAb = Ability

(**NOTE:** The 1* notation in LISREL–SIMPLIS indicates parameters that are fixed to 1.)

The equations for the structural model are

Aspire = structure coefficient * *Home* + structure coefficient * *Ability*
          + prediction error

Achieve = structure coefficient * *Home* + structure coefficient * *Ability*
          + structure coefficient * *Aspire* + prediction error

In LISREL–SIMPLIS, the structural model can be specified using a *Relationships:* command. The latent variables can be written as eight-character variable names with either spaces or plus signs (+) used between the latent variables. The prediction error terms for the two equations are assumed, so they are not included. The two structural equations in LISREL–SIMPLIS are:

Relationships:
  Aspire = Home Ability
  Achieve = Aspire Home Ability

Finally, we must consider the three different types of variance–covariance term terms. First, we check for variances and covariance terms among the latent independent variables. For our model, there are separate variance terms for *Home* and *Ability* and a correlation term for the covariance between *Home* and *Ability*. All of these parameter estimates are automatically specified in the LISREL–SIMPLIS program. Second, we check for variances and covariance terms among the prediction errors. In our model there are separate variance terms for each of the two structural equations—that is, *Aspire* and *Achieve*—and no covariance term. These variance terms are also automatically specified in the LISREL–SIMPLIS program. Finally, we need to check for variance and covariance terms among the measurement errors of the observed variables. In our measurement model equations there are nine variance terms for the observed variables and no covariance terms. These are also automatically specified in the LISREL–SIMPLIS program. Our careful attention to these details assists in the specification of our structural equation model.

10.3 Model Identification

Once a structural equation model has been specified, the next step is to determine whether the model is identified. In chapter 4 we pointed out that the researcher must solve the *identification problem* prior to the estimation of parameters. For the identification problem, we ask the following question: On the basis of the sample data contained in the sample variance–covariance matrix S and the theoretical model implied by the population variance–covariance matrix Σ, can a unique set of parameter estimates be found? For the prediction of *Achieve* (educational achievement) specified in our theoretical model, we would like to know whether the factor loadings, measurement errors, structure coefficients, and prediction errors can be estimated (identified). In our model we fixed certain parameters to resolve the origin and unit of measurement problem (factor loading = 1) while leaving other parameters free to be estimated. An example of a fixed parameter was setting the factor loading for *FamInc* (family income) on the latent independent variable *Home* (home background) to 1. An example of a free parameter was the factor loading for *FaEd* (father's education) on *Home* (home background) because it was not fixed, but rather free to be estimated.

We determine model identification by first checking the order condition. The number of free parameters to be estimated must be less than or equal to the number of distinct values in the matrix S. A count of the free parameters is as follows:

5 factor loadings (with 4 other factor loadings fixed to 1)

9 measurement error variances

0 measurement error covariance terms

2 latent independent variable variances

1 latent independent variable covariance

5 structure coefficients

2 equation prediction error variances

0 equation prediction error covariance terms

There are a total of 24 free parameters in our structural model that we want to estimate. The number of distinct values in the matrix S is equal to

$$p\,(p + 1)/2 = 9\,(9 + 1)/2 = 45,$$

where p is the number of observed variables in the sample variance–covariance matrix. The number of values in S, 45, is greater than the number of free parameters, 24, so the model is probably identified, and we should be able to estimate the number of free parameters that we specified. The degrees of freedom for our structural equation model is the difference between the number of distinct values in the matrix S and the number of free parameters we want to estimate, $df = 45 - 24 = 21$. Thus, according to the order condition, the model is *overidentified*, as there are more values in S than parameters to be estimated.

However, the order condition is only a necessary condition and is no guarantee that the model is identified. Although the order condition is easy to assess, other sufficient conditions are not, for example, the rank condition. These other sufficient conditions require us to algebraically determine whether each parameter in the model can be estimated from the sample variance–covariance matrix S. According to the LISREL–SIMPLIS computer program, which checks on identification through the rank test and/or information matrix, the hypothesized structural equation model for predicting *Achieve* (educational achievement) is identified.

10.4 Model Estimation

Once the identification problem has been resolved, the next step is to estimate the parameters in the hypothesized structural equation model. Once again, we can consider the traditional method of intuitively thinking about estimation by decomposing the variance–covariance (or correlation) matrix. The decomposition notion is that the original sample variance–covariance (or correlation) matrix can be completely reproduced if the relations among the observed variables are totally accounted for by the theoretical model. If the model is not properly specified, the original sample variance–covariance matrix will not be completely reproduced.

We now consider the estimation of the parameters for our hypothesized structural model in Figure 10.1. The sample variance–covariance matrix S is shown in Table 10.1 and the standardized residual matrix is shown in Table 10.2. Our initial model was run in LISREL–SIMPLIS (LISREL–SIMPLIS program in chapter Appendix).

TABLE 10.1

Sample Variance–Covariance Matrix for Example Data

Variable		1	2	3	4	5	6	7	8	9
1	EdAsp	1.024								
2	OcAsp	.792	1.077							
3	VerbAch	1.027	.919	1.844						
4	QuantAch	.756	.697	1.244	1.286					
5	FamInc	.567	.537	.876	.632	.852				
6	FaEd	.445	.424	.677	.526	.518	.670			
7	MoEd	.434	.389	.635	.498	.475	.545	.716		
8	VerbAb	.580	.564	.893	.716	.546	.422	.373	.851	
9	QuantAb	.491	.499	.888	.646	.508	.389	.339	.629	.871

TABLE 10.2

Standardized Residual Matrix for Model 1

	1	2	3	4	5	6	7	8	9
1. EdAsp	.000								
2. OcAsp	.000	.000							
3. VerbAch	1.420	-.797	.000						
4. QuantAch	-.776	-.363	.000	.000					
5. FamInc	3.541	3.106	5.354	2.803	.000				
6. FaEd	-2.247	-.578	-2.631	-.863	-2.809	.000			
7. MoEd	-1.031	-1.034	-2.151	-.841	-3.240	6.338	.000		
8. VerbAb	.877	1.956	-2.276	1.314	4.590	-.903	-2.144	.000	
9. QuantAb	-2.558	.185	1.820	-.574	3.473	-1.293	-2.366	.000	.000

The maximum likelihood estimates for the initial model are shown in the first column of Table 10.3. All of the parameter estimates are within the expected magnitude and direction based on previous research (Lomax, 1985). All of the parameter estimates are significantly different from zero ($p < .05$), except the structure coefficient of *Home* predicting *Achieve* (achievement) (standardized estimate = .139, $t = 1.896$, unstandardized estimate = .242). Because this structure coefficient is of substantive theoretical interest, we will not remove it from the model. *Aspire* was statistically significantly predicted, $R^2 = .612$, and *Achieve* was statistically significantly, predicted $R^2 = .863$, for both structural model equations. *Home* and *Ability* latent variables were highly correlated, $r = .728$.

10.5 Model Testing

Model testing is the next crucial step in interpreting our results for the hypothesized structural equation model. When the model-fit indices are acceptable, the hypothesized model has been supported by the sample variance–covariance data. When the model-fit indices are not acceptable, we usually attempt to modify the model by adding or deleting paths to achieve a better model to data fit (see section 10.6).

For our initial model, we include several model-fit indices at the bottom of Table 10.3 (see chapter 5). For the initial model, the χ^2 statistic, a measure of badness of fit, is equal to 58.85, 21 degrees of freedom, and $p < .001$. Because the χ^2 value is statistically significant ($p < .001$) and is not close in value to the number of degrees of freedom (recall NCP = 0, based on $\chi^2 - df = 0$), this model-fit index indicates that the initial model is unacceptable. The root-mean-square error of approximation (RMSEA) is equal to .095,

TABLE 10.3

Maximum Likelihood Estimates for Models 1 and 2

Estimates	Model 1	Model 2 (modified)
OcAsp factor loading	.917	.918
QuantAch factor loading	.759	.753
FaEd factor loading	1.007	.782
MoEd factor loading	.964	.720
QuantAb factor loading	.949	.949
Aspire -> Achieve coefficient	.548	.526
Home -> Aspire coefficient	.410	.506
Home -> Achieve coefficient	.242[a]	.302[a]
Ability -> Aspire coefficient	.590	.447
Ability -> Achieve coefficient	.751	.685
Home variance	.532	.662
Ability variance	.663	.663
Home, Ability covariance	.432	.537
Aspire equation error variance	.335	.319
Achieve equation error variance	.225	.228
EdAsp error variance	.160	.161
OcAsp error variance	.351	.350
VerbAch error variance	.205	.193
QuantAch error variance	.342	.349
FamInc error variance	.320	.190
FaEd error variance	.130	.265
MoEd error variance	.222	.373
VerbAb error variance	.188	.188
QuantAb error variance	.274	.274
FaEd, MoEd error covariance	—	.173
Goodness-of-fit indices:		
χ^2	58.85	18.60
df	21	20
p value	.000	.548
GFI	.938	.980
AGFI	.868	.954
RMSR	.049	.015
RMSEA	.095	.000

[a] Estimates are not statistically significantly different from zero ($p < .05$). The χ^2 values for Model 1 and Model 2 can be checked for significance using Table A.4 in the Appendix.

which is below the typical acceptable level of model fit (criterion RMSEA < .08 or .05). The goodness-of-fit index (GFI) is .938 for the initial model, which is around our acceptable range of model fit (criterion GFI > .95). Finally, the adjusted goodness-of-fit index (AGFI) is .868 for this model, not an acceptable level of fit (criterion AGFI > .95). From this particular set of model-fit indices, we conclude that the hypothesized structural equation model is reasonable, but that some model modification might allow us to achieve a more acceptable model to data fit. Model modification is discussed in the next section.

10.6 Model Modification

The final step in structural equation modeling is to consider model modification to achieve a better model to data fit. If the hypothesized structural equation model has model-fit indices that are less than satisfactory, a researcher typically performs a *specification search* to find a better fitting model to the sample variance–covariance matrix. In chapter 4 we discussed the different procedures one can use in the specification search process. For example, the researcher might eliminate parameters that are not significantly different from zero and/or include additional parameters. To eliminate parameters, the most commonly used procedure in LISREL–SIMPLIS is to compare the t statistic for each parameter to a tabled t value, for example, $t > 1.96$, $\alpha = .05$, two-tailed test, or $t > 2.58$, $\alpha = .01$, two-tailed test (Table A.2) for statistical significance. To include additional parameters, the most commonly used techniques in LISREL–SIMPLIS are to (a) select the highest modification index (MI; the expected value that χ^2 would decrease if such a parameter were to be included), and (b) select the highest expected parameter change statistic (EPC; the approximate value of the new parameter added to the model).

A researcher could also examine the residual matrix (or the more useful standardized residual matrix) to obtain clues as to which original variances and covariance terms are not well accounted for by the model (the residual matrix is the difference between the observed variance–covariance terms in S and the corresponding model implied (reproduced) variance–covariance terms in Σ). Large standardized residuals—for example, greater than 1.96 or 2.58—indicate that a particular variable relationship is not well accounted for in the model.

For our hypothesized structural equation model, the original sample variance–covariance matrix is shown in Table 10.1 and the standardized residual variance–covariance matrix is given in Table 10.2. The largest standardized residual is for the relationship between FaEd (father's education) and MoEd (mother's education), which is 6.338. (*Note*: the *t* statistics do not suggest the elimination of existing parameters, except one, from the initial model.) When considering the addition of new parameters in the model, the largest modification index is for the measurement error covariance between FaEd (father's education) and MoEd (mother's education), which is MI = 40.176. If we were to estimate that parameter (correlation between FaEd and MoEd measurement errors), the expected parameter change would be EPC = 0.205.

In our specification search, the standardized residual and EPC values indicated that something was wrong with how we specified the relationship between *FaEd* (father's education) and *MoEd* (mother's education), because it was not specified well in the initial model. Consequently, we decided to specify a measurement error covariance (correlation) between *FaEd* (father's education) and *MoEd* (mother's education) because, upon further reflection, there should be common method variance on measures using the same scale with two different parents.

The ML estimates and selected model-fit indices for the modified model, where the measurement error covariance is now included, are shown in the second column of Table 10.3 and diagrammed in Figure 10.2. All of the parameters are statistically significantly different from zero (*p* < .05), except for the path between *Home* (home background) and *Achieve* (achievement), but once again, for substantive theoretical reasons, we chose to leave this relationship specified in the model. Our selected model-fit indices now all indicate an acceptable level of fit, and a second specification search did not result in any further recommended changes. Thus, we consider our modified model to be our final structural equation model for the prediction

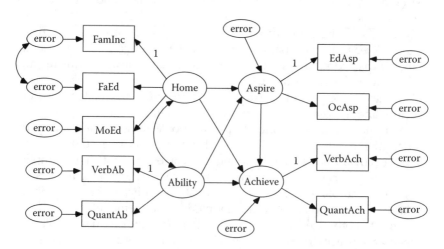

FIGURE 10.2
Modified structural equation model of educational achievement.

of educational achievement. Applying this structural equation model to other samples of data will, we hope, provide further validation that this is a theoretically meaningful structural model (see chapter 12).

10.7 Summary

This chapter completes the basic discussion of structural equation modeling we began in chapter 9. We hypothesized a structural equation model to predict educational achievement and described it in further detail. We followed the recommended steps a researcher should take in the structural equation modeling process, namely model specification, model identification, model estimation, model testing, and finally model modification. We did not obtain acceptable model-fit indices with our initial theoretical model, so we conducted a specification search. The specification search suggested adding a parameter estimate for the correlation between the measurement error terms of father's and mother's education level. The modified model resulted in acceptable model-fit indices, so this was determined to be our best model to data fit. In chapter 11 we provide suggestions and recommendations for how structural equation modeling studies should be reported in the literature.

Appendix: LISREL–SIMPLIS Structural Equation Model Program

```
Educational Achievement Example—Model 2 Respecified
Observed variables: EdAsp OcAsp VerbAch QuantAch FamInc FaEd
MoEd VerbAb QuantAb
Covariance matrix:
1.024
 .792  1.077
1.027   .919  1.844
 .756   .697  1.244  1.286
 .567   .537   .876   .632   .852
 .445   .424   .677   .526   .518   .670
 .434   .389   .635   .498   .475   .545   .716
 .580   .564   .893   .716   .546   .422   .373   .851
 .491   .499   .888   .646   .508   .389   .339   .629   .871
Sample size: 200
```

```
Latent variables: ASPIRE ACHIEVE HOME ABILITY
Relationships:
 EdAsp = 1*ASPIRE
 OcAsp = ASPIRE
 VerbAch = 1*ACHIEVE
 QuantAch = ACHIEVE
 FamInc = 1*HOME
 FaEd MoEd = HOME
 VerbAb = 1*ABILITY
 QuantAb = ABILITY
 ASPIRE = HOME ABILITY
 ACHIEVE = ASPIRE HOME ABILITY
Let the error covariances of FaEd and MoEd correlate
Path diagram
End of problem
```

Exercise

1. Conduct the following structural equation model analysis using the LISREL–SIMPLIS program:
   Sample size = 500
   Observed X variables:
       ACT score (ACT)
       College Grade Point Average (CGPA)
       Company entry-level skills test score (ENTRY)
   Observed Y variables:
       Beginning salary (SALARY)
       Current salary due to promotions (PROMO)
   Latent dependent variable: Job Success (JOB)
   Latent independent variable: Academic Success (ACAD)
   Structural model:
       ACAD -> JOB

   Variance-covariance matrix:

ACT	1.024				
CGPA	.792	1.077			
ENTRY	.567	.537	.852		
SALARY	.445	.424	.518	.670	
PROMO	.434	.389	.475	.545	.716

References

Jöreskog, K. G., & Sörbom, D. (1993). *LISREL 8: Structural equation modeling with the SIMPLIS command language.* Chicago, IL: Scientific Software International.

Lomax, R. G. (1985). A structural model of public and private schools. *Journal of Experimental Education, 53*, 216–226.

11

Reporting SEM Research: Guidelines and Recommendations

Key Concepts

    Theoretical models and data preparation

    Sample matrix in SPSS or Excel

    Model specification and identification

    Model estimation and testing

    Model modification and specification search

Breckler (1990) reviewed the personality and social psychology research literature and found several shortcomings of structural equation modeling, namely that model-fit indices can be identical for a potentially large number of models, that assumptions of multivariate normality are required, that sample size affects results, and that cross-validation of models was infrequently addressed or mentioned. Many of the studies only reported a single model-fit index. Breckler concluded that there was cause for concern in the reporting of structural equation modeling results. Raykov, Tomer, and Nesselroade (1991) proposed guidelines for reporting SEM results in the journal *Psychology and Aging*. Maxwell and Cole (1995) offered some general tips for writing methodological articles, and Hoyle and Panter (1995) published a chapter on reporting SEM research with an emphasis on describing the results and what model-fit criteria to include.

    The Publication Manual of the American Psychological Association (American Psychological Association, 2001, pp. 161, 164–167, and 185) specifically states that researchers should include the means, standard deviations, and correlations of the entire set of variables so that others can replicate and confirm the analysis, as well as provide example tables and figures for reporting structural equation modeling research. Unfortunately, the guidelines do not go far enough in outlining the basic information that should be included to afford an evaluation of the research study and some fundamental points that should be addressed when conducting

SEM studies. A few other scholars have previously offered their advice, as follows.

Boomsma (2000) discussed how to write a research paper when structural equation models were used in empirical research and how to decide what information to report. His basic premise was that all information necessary for someone else to replicate the analysis should be reported. He provided recommendations along the lines of our basic steps in structural equation modeling, namely model specification, model identification, model estimation, model testing, and model modification. Boomsma found that many studies lacked a theoretical foundation for the theoretical model, gave a poor description of the model tested, provided no discussion of the psychometric properties of the variables and level of measurement, did not include sample data, and had a poor delineation or justification for the model modification process. He pointed out how difficult it can be to evaluate or judge the quality of published SEM research.

MacCallum and Austin (2000) provided an excellent survey of problems in applications of SEM. Thompson (2000) provided guidance for conducting structural equation modeling by citing key issues and including the following list of 10 commandments for good structural equation modeling behavior: (a) do not conclude that a model is the only model to fit the data, (b) cross-validate any modified model with split-sample data or new data, (c) test multiple rival models, (d) evaluate measurement models first, then structural models, (e) evaluate models by fit, theory, and practical concerns, (f) report multiple model-fit indices, (g) meet multivariate normality assumptions, (h) seek parsimonious models, (i) consider variable scale of measurement and distribution, and (j) do not use small samples.

McDonald and Ringo Ho (2002) examined 41 of 100 articles in 13 psychological journals from 1995 to 1997. They stated that SEM researchers should give a detailed justification of the SEM model tested along with alternative models, account for identification, address nonnormality and missing data concerns, and include a complete set of parameter estimates with standard errors, correlation matrix (and perhaps residuals), and goodness-of-fit indices.

We further elaborate several key issues in SEM. First, in structural equation model analyses several different types of sample data matrices can be used (e.g., variance-covariance matrix, asymptotic variance-covariance matrix, Pearson correlation matrix, or polyserial, polychoric, or tetrachoric matrices). As previously described in chapter 3, the type of matrix used depends on several factors such as nonnormality and type of variables.

A second issue concerns model identification, that is, the number of distinct values in the sample variance-covariance matrix should equal or exceed the number of free parameters estimated in the model (degrees of freedom should not be negative for the model; the order condition) and the rank of the matrix should yield a non-zero determinant value (the rank condition). A researcher must also select from various parameter estimation techniques in model estimation, for example, unweighted least squares, maximum likelihood, or generalized least squares estimation under the assumption of multivariate normality, or asymptotically distribution-free estimation using ADF or CVM techniques when the multivariate normality assumption is not met. Obviously, many factors discussed in chapters 2 and 3 affect multivariate normality.

A researcher should also be aware that equivalent models and alternative models may exist in an over-identified model (more distinct values in the matrix than free parameters estimated), and rarely are we able to perfectly reproduce the sample variance-covariance matrix, given the implied theoretical model. We use model-fit indices and specification searches to obtain an acceptable model to data fit, given alternative models. Model-fit statistics should guide our search for a better fitting model. Chapter 5 outlined different model-fit criteria depending on the focus of the research. Under some situations, for example, use of large sample sizes, the chi-square values will be inflated leading to statistically significance, thus erroneously implying a poor data to model fit. A more appropriate use of the chi-square statistic in this situation would be to compare alternative models with the same sample data (nested models). The specification search process involves finding whether a variable should be added (parameter estimated) or a variable deleted (parameter not estimated). A researcher, when modifying an initial model, should make one modification at a time, that is, add or delete one parameter estimate, and give a theoretical justification for the model change.

Ironically, structural equation modeling requires larger sample sizes as models become more complex or the researcher desires to conduct cross-validation with split samples. In traditional multivariate statistics the rule of thumb is 20 subjects per variable (20:1). The rules of thumb used in structural equation modeling vary from 100, 200, to 500 or more subjects per study, depending on model complexity and cross-validation requirements. Sample size and power are also important considerations in structural equation modeling (see chapter 5). Finally, a two-step/four-step approach is important because if measurement models do not fit the observed variables, then relationships among the latent variables in structural models are not very meaningful.

We find the following checklist to be valuable when publishing SEM research and hopefully journal editors will embrace the importance of this information when published. Our checklist is:

1. Provide a review of literature that supports your theoretical model.
2. Provide the software program used along with the version.
3. Indicate the type of SEM model analysis (multi-level, structured means, etc.).

4. Include correlation matrix, sample size, means, and standard deviations of variables.

5. Include a diagram of your theoretical model.

6. For interpretation of results, describe fit indices used and why; include power and sample size determination; and effect size measure.

Our checklist is important because the SEM software, model, data, and program will be archived in the journal. The power, sample size, and effect size will permit future use in meta-analysis studies. Providing this research information will also permit future cross-cultural research, multi-sample or multi-group comparisons, replication, or validation by others in the research community because the analysis can be further examined.

We have made many of these same suggestions in our previous chapters, so our intentions in this chapter are to succinctly summarize guidelines and recommendations for SEM researchers.

11.1 Data Preparation

A researcher should begin a SEM research study with a rationale and purpose for the study, followed by a sound theoretical foundation of the measurement model and the structural model. This includes a discussion of the latent variables and how they are defined in the measurement model. The hypothesis should involve the testing of the structural model and/or a difference between alternative models.

An applied SEM research study typically involves using sample data, in contrast to a methodological simulation study. The sample matrix should be described as to the type (augmented, asymptotic, covariance, or correlation), whether multivariate normality assumptions have been met, the scale of measurement for the observed variables, and be related to an appropriate estimation technique, for example, maximum likelihood. Regression analysis, path analysis, factor analysis, and structural equation modeling all use data as input into a computer program (see SPSS and Microsoft Excel examples at the end of the chapter). The SEM program should include the sample matrix, and for certain models, means and standard deviations of the observed variables.

To show another way to input data, we can create special data file types in SPSS by designating special *rowtype_* and *varname_* fields in the SPSS Data Editor and entering variable names, an example of which follows from the Holzinger and Swineford (1939) data previously presented in chapter 8.

We then enter the individual sample size, correlation coefficients, standard deviations, and means for the girls' data. We saved this file as *girls_cor.sav*.

A set of recommendations for data preparation is given in SEM Checklist Box 11.1.

11.2 Model Specification

Model specification involves determining every relationship and parameter in the model that is of interest to the researcher. Moreover, the goal of the researcher is to determine, as best possible, the theoretical model that generates the sample variance–covariance matrix. If the theoretical model is misspecified, it could yield biased parameter estimates; parameter estimates that are different from what they are in the true population model, that is, specification error. We do not typically know the true population model, so bias in parameter estimates is generally attributed

SEM CHECKLIST BOX 11.1—DATA PREPARATION

1. Have you adequately described the population from which the random sample data was drawn?
2. Did you report the measurement level and psychometric properties (i.e., reliability and validity) of your variables?
3. Did you report the descriptive statistics on your variables?
4. Did you create a table with correlations, means and standard deviations?
5. Did you consider and treat any missing data (e.g., can result in data analysis issues)? What was the sample size both before and after treating the missing data?
6. Did you consider and treat any outliers (e.g., can affect sample statistics)?
7. Did you consider the range of values obtained for variables, as restricted range of one or more variables can reduce the magnitude of correlations?
8. Did you consider and treat any nonnormality of the data (e.g., skewness and kurtosis, data transformations)?
9. Did you consider and treat any multicollinearity among the variables?
10. Did you consider whether variables are linearly related, which can reduce the magnitude of correlations?
11. Did you resolve any correlation attenuation (e.g., can result in reduced magnitude of correlations and error messages)?
12. Did you take the measurement scale of the variables into account when computing statistics such as means, standard deviations, and correlations?
13. Did you specify the type of matrix used in the analysis (e.g., covariance, correlation (Pearson, polychoric, polyserial), augmented moment, or asymptotic matrices)?
14. When using the correlation matrix, did you include standard deviations of the variables in order to obtain correct estimates of standard errors for the parameter estimates?
15. How can others access your data and SEM program (e.g., appendix, Web site, email)?

to specification error. The model should be developed from the available theory and research in the substantive area. This should be the main purpose of the literature review.

Recommendations for model modification are provided in SEM Checklist Box 11.2.

SEM CHECKLIST BOX 11.2—MODEL SPECIFICATION

1. Did you provide a rationale and purpose for your study, including why SEM rather than another statistical analysis approach was required?
2. Did you describe your latent variables, thus providing a substantive background to how they are measured?
3. Did you establish a sound theoretical basis for your measurement models and structural models?
4. Did you theoretically justify alternative models for comparison (e.g., nested models)?
5. Did you use a reasonable sample size, thus sufficient power in testing your hypotheses?
6. Did you clearly state the hypotheses for testing the structural models?
7. Did you discuss the expected magnitude and direction of expected parameter estimates?
8. Did you include a figure or diagram of your measurement and structural models?
9. Have you described every free parameter in the models that you want to estimate? In contrast, have you considered why other parameters are not included in the models and/or why you included constraints or fixed certain parameters?

11.3 Model Identification

In structural equation modeling it is crucial that the researcher resolve the *identification problem* prior to the estimation of parameters in measurement models and/or structural models. In the identification problem, we ask the following question: On the basis of the sample data contained in the sample covariance matrix S, and the theoretical model implied by the population covariance matrix Σ, can a unique set of parameter estimates be found?

A set of recommendations for model identification includes the following shown in SEM Checklist Box 11.3.

SEM CHECKLIST BOX 11.3—MODEL IDENTIFICATION

1. Did you specify the number of distinct values in your sample covariance matrix?
2. Did you indicate the number of free parameters to be estimated?
3. Did you inform the reader that the order and/or rank condition was satisfied?
4. Did you report the number of degrees of freedom and thereby the level of identification of the model?
5. How did you scale the latent variables (i.e., fix either one factor loading per latent variable or the latent variable variances to 1.0)?
6. Did you avoid non-recursive models until identification has been assured?
7. Did you utilize parsimonious models to assist with identification?

11.4 Model Estimation

In *model estimation* we need to decide which estimation technique to select for estimating the parameters in our measurement model and structural model, that is, our estimates of the population parameters from sample data. For example, we might choose the maximum likelihood estimation technique because we meet the multivariate normality assumption (acceptable skewness and kurtosis); there are no missing data; no outliers; and continuous variable data. If the observed variables are interval scaled and multivariate normal, then the ML estimates, standard errors and chi-square test are appropriate.

Our experience is that model estimation often does not work because of messy data. In chapters 2 and 3 we outlined many of the factors that can affect parameter estimation in general, and structural equation modeling specifically. Missing data, outliers, multicollinearity, and nonnormality of data distributions can seriously affect the estimation process and often result in fatal error messages pertaining to Heywood variables (variables with negative variance), non-positive definite matrices (determinant of matrix is zero), or failure to reach convergence (unable to compute a final set of parameter estimates). SEM is a correlation research method and all of the factors that affect correlation coefficients, the general linear model (regression, path, and factor models), and statistics in general are compounded in structural equation modeling. *Do not overlook the problems caused by messy data!*

Recommendations for model estimation are given in SEM Checklist Box 11.4.

SEM CHECKLIST BOX 11.4—MODEL ESTIMATION

1. What is the ratio of chi-square to the degrees of freedom?
2. What is the ratio of sample size to number of parameters?
3. Did you consider tests of parameter estimates?
4. Did you identify the estimation technique based on the type of data matrix?
5. What estimation technique is appropriate for the distribution of the sample data (ML and GLS for multivariate normal data with small to moderate sample sizes; ADF or CVM for non-normal, asymptotic covariance data, and WLS for non-normal with large sample sizes)?
6. Did you encounter Heywood cases (negative variance), multicollinearity, or non-positive definite matrices?
7. Did you encounter and resolve any convergence problems or inadmissible solution problems by using start values, setting the admissibility check off, using a larger sample size, or using a different method of estimation?
8. Which SEM program and version did you use?
9. Did you report the R^2 values to indicate the fit of each separate equation?
10. Do parameter estimates have the expected magnitude and direction?

11.5 Model Testing

Having provided the SEM program and sample data along with our measurement and structural models, anyone can check our results and verify our findings. In interpreting our measurement model and structural model, we establish how well the data fit the models. In other words, we examine the extent to which the theoretical model is supported by the sample data. In model testing we consider model-fit indices for the fit of the entire model and examine the specific tests for the statistical significance of individual parameters in the model.

A set of recommendations for model testing includes the following as shown in SEM Checklist Box 11.5.

SEM CHECKLIST BOX 11.5—MODEL TESTING

1. Did you report several model-fit indices (e.g., for a single model: chi-square, *df*, GFI, NFI, RMSEA; for a nested model: LR test, CFI, AIC; for cross-validation indices: CVI, ECVI; and for parameter estimates, *t* values and standard errors)?
2. Did you specify separate measurement models and structural models?
3. Did you check for measurement invariance in the factor loadings prior to testing between-group parameter estimates in the structural model?
4. Did you provide a table of estimates, standard errors, statistical significance (possibly including effect sizes and confidence intervals)?

11.6 Model Modification

If the fit of an implied theoretical model is not acceptable, which is typically the case with an initial model, the next step is *model modification* and subsequent evaluation of the new, modified model. Most of model modifications occur in the measurement model rather than the structural model. Model modification occurs more in the measurement model because that is where the main source of misspecification occurs and measurement models are the foundation for the structural model.

After we are satisfied with our final best-fitting model, future research should undertake *model validation* by replicating the study (using multiple sample analysis, chapter 13), performing cross-validation (randomly splitting the sample and running the analysis on both sets of data), or bootstrapping the parameter estimates to determine the amount of bias. These model validation topics are covered in chapter 12.

A set of recommendations for model modification is given in SEM Checklist Box 11.6. Although not fully discussed until chapter 12, a set

SEM CHECKLIST BOX 11.6 —MODEL MODIFICATION

1. Did you compare alternative models or equivalent models?
2. Did you clearly indicate how you modified the initial model?

3. Did you provide a theoretical justification for the modified model?
4. Did you add or delete one parameter at a time? What parameters were trimmed?
5. Did you provide parameter estimates and model-fit indices for both the initial model and the modified model?
6. Did you report statistical significance of free parameters, modification indices and expected change statistics of fixed parameters, and residual information for all models?
7. How did you evaluate and select the best model?

SEM CHECKLIST BOX 11.7—MODEL VALIDATION

1. Did you replicate your SEM model analysis using another sample of data (e.g., conduct a multiple sample analysis)?
2. Did you cross-validate your SEM model by splitting your original sample of data?
3. Did you use bootstrapping to determine the bias in your parameter estimates?

---

of recommendations for model validation is provided in SEM Checklist Box 11.7.

11.7 Summary

In this chapter we showed that model fit is a subjective approach that requires substantive theory because there is no single best model (other models may be equally plausible given the sample data and/or equivalent models). In structural equation modeling the researcher follows the steps of model specification, identification, estimation, testing, and modification, so we advise the researcher to base measurement and structural models on *sound theory*, utilize the *two-step/four-step approach*, and establish measurement model fit and measurement invariance before *model testing* the latent variables in the structural model. We also recommend that theoretical models need to be *replicated*, *cross-validated*, and/or *bootstrapped* to determine the stability of the parameter estimates (see chapter 12). Finally, we stated that researchers should include their SEM program, data, and path diagram in any article. This permits a replication of the analysis and verification of the results. We do not advocate using specification searches to find the best fitting model without having a theoretically justified reason for modifying the initial model. We further advocate using another sample of data to validate that the modified model is a meaningful and substantive theoretical structural model. Most importantly, we provide the researcher with checklists to follow when doing structural equation modeling. These checklists follow a logical progression from data preparation through model specification, identification, estimation, testing, modification, and validation.

Exercise

1. Enter the following data in special matrix format in SPSS and save as *Fels_fem.sav*. Use special variable names *rowtype_* and *varname_* along with *n, corr, stddev,* and *mean* in these special data sets.

   $N = 209$

   Correlation Matrix

Academic	1.00						
Athletic	.43	1.00					
Attract	.50	.48	1.00				
GPA	.49	.22	.32	1.00			
Height	.10	− .04	−.03	.18	1.00		
Weight	.04	.02	−.16	−.10	.34	1.00	
Rating	.09	.14	.43	.15	−.16	−.27	1.00
s.d.	.16	.07	.49	3.49	2.91	19.32	1.01
means	.12	.05	.42	10.34	.00	94.13	2.65

References

American Psychological Association (2001). *Publication manual of the American Psychological Association* (5th ed.). Washington, DC: Author.

Boomsma, A. (2000). Reporting analyses of covariance structure. *Structural Equation Modeling, 7,* 461–483.

Breckler, S. J. (1990). Applications of covariance structure modeling in psychology: Cause for concern? *Psychological Bulletin, 107,* 260–273.

Holzinger, K. J., & Swineford, F. A. (1939). *A study in factor analysis: The stability of a bi-factor solution.* (Supplementary Educational Monographs, No. 48). Chicago: University of Chicago, Department of Education.

Hoyle, R. H., & Panter, A. T. (1995). Writing about structural equation models. In R. H. Hoyle (Ed.), *Structural equation modeling: Concepts, issues, and applications* (pp. 158–176). Thousand Oaks, CA: Sage.

MacCallum, R. C., & Austin, J. T. (2000). Applications of structural equation modeling in psychological research. *Annual Review of Psychology, 51,* 201–226.

Maxwell, S. E., & Cole, D. A. (1995). Tips for writing (and reading) methodological articles. *Psychological Bulletin, 118,* 193–198.

McDonald, R. P., & Ringo Ho, M. (2002). Principles and practice in reporting structural equation analyses. *Psychological Methods, 7,* 64–82.

Raykov, T., Tomer, A., & Nesselroade, J. R. (1991). Reporting structural equation modeling results in *Psychology and Aging*: Some proposed guidelines. *Psychology and Aging, 6,* 499–533.

Thompson, B. (2000). Ten commandments of structural equation modeling. In L. Grimm & P. Yarnold (Eds.), *Reading and understanding more multivariate statistics* (pp. 261–284). Washington, DC: American Psychological Association.

12

Model Validation

Key Concepts

Replication: multiple samples

Cross validation: randomly split subsamples

Cross validation indexes: ECVI, CVI, and MECVI

Bootstrap via LISREL and PRELIS

Bootstrap via program menu

In previous chapters we learned about the *basics* of structural equation modeling using the following steps: model specification, identification, estimation, testing, and modification. In this chapter we consider a selection of topics related to model validation. However, our discussion only scratches the surface of these approaches in structural equation modeling, so you should check out the references in this chapter for more information.

We begin by presenting the topic of replication, which uses multiple samples. In our first example, the validation of a theoretical confirmatory factor model using two samples of data is presented. Cross validation is presented next, where a larger sample is randomly split into two subsamples. Then, we present the basics of how to determine the stability of parameter estimates using the bootstrap method. Ideally, a researcher should seek model validation with additional samples of data (replication). The other methods are not as rigorous, but in the absence of replication, provide evidence of model validity—that is, the viability of the theoretical framework suggested by the measurement and/or structural models.

12.1 Multiple Samples

A nice feature of structural equation modeling, although not frequently used, is the possibility of studying a theoretical model and then validating it using one or more additional samples of data. Theoretical models can therefore be examined across samples to determine the degree of invariance in fit indices, parameter estimates, and standard errors.

SEM also permits the use of multiple samples in the analysis of quasi-experimental, experimental, cross-sectional, and/or longitudinal data. With multiple samples it is possible to estimate separately the parameters for each independent sample, to test whether specified parameters or parameter matrices are equivalent across the samples (that is, for any of the parameters in the measurement and/or structural equation models), or to test whether there are sample mean differences for the indicator variables and/or for any of the structural equations.

We can obviously estimate parameters in each sample of data separately. We would fit a theoretical model to the first sample of data and then apply the model to the other samples of data. It is possible that a confirmatory factor model will fit all samples of data (multiple samples), indicating measurement invariance, and yet have different values for error covariance, factor loadings, or factor correlations. We can also statistically determine whether certain specified parameters or parameter matrices are equivalent across samples of data. For instance, one may be interested in whether factor loadings and factor correlations are stable across random samples of data applied to a theoretical model. We could also randomly split a large national sample of data into several subsamples.

SEM also permits the testing of the equivalence of matrices or parameter estimates across several samples taken randomly from a population. A researcher indicates the specific hypothesis to be tested, for example, equal factor loadings and factor correlation. For a measurement model, we could test whether the factor loadings are equal across the samples, or whether the factor variances and covariance terms are equal across the samples, or even whether the unique error variances and covariance terms are equal across samples. For a structural model, we could test whether the structure coefficients are equal across the samples. For a combined structural equation model, all parameters in the entire model are tested for equivalence across the samples. Obviously, in this instance both the covariance matrix and the coefficients are tested for equality across the samples, lending itself to a more complex model requiring adequate sample size and power.

In this chapter, we present four models: Model A with all parameters invariant; Model B with only error variance and factor correlation invariant; Model C with only factor correlation invariant; and finally Model D with factor loadings and factor correlation invariant. These examples should give you a better understanding of how different model attributes can be tested using multiple samples.

We now demonstrate how to conduct these multiple sample analyses in LISREL–SIMPLIS using the example in Jöreskog and Sörbom (1996c,

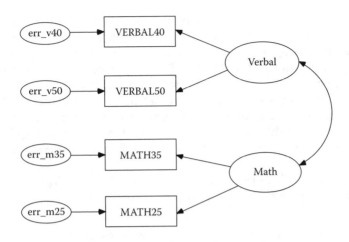

FIGURE 12.1
Path Diagram for SAT Verbal and Math. (From Jöreskog, K. G., & Sörbom, D., 1993. *Bootstrapping and Monte Carlo experimenting with PRELIS2 and LISREL8.* Chicago: Scientific Software International; example 10, p. 52.)

example 10, p. 52) that indicated two samples of data on candidates who took the Scholastic Aptitude Test (SAT) in 1971 (Figure 12.1).

In LISREL–SIMPLIS, measurement and/or structural models can be specified and tested across samples of data for model validation. The LISREL–SIMPLIS program stacks separate programs, but does not require that the observed variables, latent variables, and equations be repeated in each program when the parameters in the theoretical model are assumed identical in subsequent individual programs. The second and subsequent individual programs only need to include their sample size and variance–covariance matrix. Each individual program, however, must be designated by use of the special command, **Group 1:** and **Group 2:** etc. (*Note:* Do not use Sample 1: and Sample 2: etc. to designate the individual programs).

The computer output indicates results for each individual program with chi-square contributions to the overall global chi-square value. Each individual program outputs a chi-square value that sums to the global chi-square value. A percent contribution to the global chi-square value is also indicated for each individual program. In a multiple sample analysis, the global chi-square is a measure of fit in all samples to the theoretical model. (*Note:* Individual sample parameter values can be obtained by including the latent variable and equation statements in each subsequent stacked program.)

LISREL–SIMPLIS generally requires running different multiple sample program models to determine which parameters are different or similar among factor loadings, error variances, and factor correlations. In LISREL–SIMPLIS, Model A (EX10A.SPL) tests the equality of all parameters across both samples (factor loadings, error variances, and factor correlation). Model B (EX10B.SPL) allows the factor loadings to be different, but maintains equal error variances and factor correlation. Model C (EX10C.SPL) allows the factor loadings and error variances to be different, but maintains equal factor correlation across the two samples. Finally, Model D (EX10D.SPL) specifies that the factor loadings and the factor correlation are the same for both samples with the error variances different.

The LISREL–SIMPLIS Model A program (EX10A.SPL), which tests equality of all parameters (invariant) across both samples, is:

```
Group 1: Testing Equality of all model parameters
Model A: Factor Loadings, Correlation, Error Variances Invariant
Observed Variables: VERBAL40 VERBAL50 MATH35 MATH25
Covariance Matrix from File EX10.COV
Sample Size = 865
Latent Variables: Verbal Math
Relationships:
        VERBAL40 VERBAL50 = Verbal
        MATH35 MATH25 = Math
Group 2: Testing Equality of all model parameters
Covariance Matrix from File EX10.COV
Sample Size = 900
Path diagram
End of problem
```

12.1.1 Model A Computer Output

```
Group 1:
        Contribution to Chi-Square = 19.16
        Percentage Contribution to Chi-Square = 54.92
Group 2:
        Contribution to Chi-Square = 15.73
        Percentage Contribution to Chi-Square = 45.08
Global Goodness-of-Fit Statistics
Degrees of Freedom = 11
Minimum Fit Function Chi-Square = 34.89 (P = 0.00026)
```

The global chi-square is significant, so having all parameters equal (invariant) is not a tenable solution. Some parameters are therefore different in the two samples.

The LISREL–SIMPLIS Model B program (EX10B.SPL), which tests differences in factor loadings with equal error variance and factor correlation, is:

```
Group 1: Testing Equality Of Factor Structures
Model B : Factor Correlation and Error Variances Invariant
Observed Variables: VERBAL40 VERBAL50 MATH35 MATH25
Covariance Matrix from File EX10.COV
Sample Size = 865
Latent Variables: Verbal Math
Relationships:
        VERBAL40 VERBAL50 = Verbal
        MATH35 MATH25 = Math
Group 2: Testing Equality Of Factor Correlations
Covariance Matrix from File EX10.COV
Sample Size = 900
Relationships:
        VERBAL40 VERBAL50 = Verbal
        MATH35 MATH25 = Math
Path diagram
End of problem
```

12.1.2 Model B Computer Output

```
Group 1:
        Contribution to Chi-Square = 15.62
        Percentage Contribution to Chi-Square = 52.65
Group 2:
        Contribution to Chi-Square = 14.05
        Percentage Contribution to Chi-Square = 47.35
Global Goodness-of-Fit Statistics
Degrees of Freedom = 7
Minimum Fit Function Chi-Square = 29.67 (P = 0.00011)
```

The global chi-square was significant, which indicates that equal error variance and equal factor correlation are not tenable results with factor loadings being different.

The LISREL–SIMPLIS Model C program (EX10C.SPL), which tests differences in factor loadings and error variance, but equal in factor correlation, is:

```
Group 1: Testing Equality of Factor Structures
Model C: Factor Correlation Invariant
Observed Variables: VERBAL40 VERBAL50 MATH35 MATH25
Covariance Matrix from File EX10.COV
Sample Size = 865
Latent Variables: Verbal Math
Relationships:
        VERBAL40 VERBAL50 = Verbal
        MATH35 MATH25 = Math
Group 2: Testing Equality of Factor Correlations
Covariance Matrix from File EX10.COV
Sample Size = 900
```

```
Relationships:
        VERBAL40 VERBAL50 = Verbal
        MATH35 MATH25 = Math
Set the Error Variances of VERBAL40 - MATH25 free
Path diagram
End of problem
```

12.1.3 Model C Computer Output

```
Group 1:
        Contribution to Chi-Square = 2.21
        Percentage Contribution to Chi-Square = 55.02
Group 2:
        Contribution to Chi-Square = 1.81
        Percentage Contribution to Chi-Square = 44.98
Global Goodness-of-Fit Statistics
Degrees of Freedom = 3
Minimum Fit Function Chi-Square = 4.03 (P = 0.26)
```

The factor correlation was $r = .76$ for both samples. This is tenable, given the nonsignificant global chi-square statistic ($\chi^2 = 4.03$, $df = 3$, $p = .26$).

The LISREL–SIMPLIS Model D program (EX10D.SPL), which tests factor loadings and factor correlation the same (invariant), but allows for differences in error variance is:

```
Group 1: Testing Equality of Factor Structures
Model D: Factor Loadings and Factor Correlation Invariant
Observed Variables: VERBAL40 VERBAL50 MATH35 MATH25
Covariance Matrix
        63.382
        70.984 110.237
        41.710 52.747 60.584
        30.218 37.489 36.392 32.295
Sample Size = 865
Latent Variables: Verbal Math
Relationships:
        VERBAL40 VERBAL50 = Verbal
        MATH35 MATH25 = Math
Group 2: Testing Equality of Factor Correlations
Covariance Matrix
        67.898
        72.301 107.330
        40.549 55.347 63.203
        28.976 38.896 39.261 35.403
Sample Size = 900
Set the Error Variances of VERBAL40 - MATH25 free
Path diagram
End of problem
```

12.1.4 Model D Computer Output

```
Group 1:
      Contribution to Chi-Square = 5.48
      Percentage Contribution to Chi-Square = 50.40
Group 2:
      Contribution to Chi-Square = 5.39
      Percentage Contribution to Chi-Square = 49.60
Global Goodness-of-Fit Statistics
Degrees of Freedom = 7
Minimum Fit Function Chi-Square = 10.87 (P = 0.14)
```

The global chi-square indicated a good fit of the measurement model across both samples of data. Therefore, equal factor loadings and factor correlation with unequal error variances is tenable. Error variances would typically be different in a measurement model, so assuming equal factor loadings and factor correlation was theoretically reasonable to test.

12.1.5 Summary

Although the multiple sample programs provide the individual and global chi-square values, the researcher should consider creating a table with the parameter values and standard errors. This would provide an easier comparison of the intended parameter estimates that were modeled in the different programs.

More complex model comparisons are possible. For example, we could test the equality of both factor loadings and factor correlations across three samples of data. Many different measurement and structural models using the multiple sample approach are possible and have been illustrated in journal articles, software manuals, and books. The interested reader is referred to Jöreskog and Sörbom (1993), Muthén (1987) and Bentler and Wu (2002), as well as books by Hayduk (1987) and Bollen (1989), for more details on running these various multiple sample models. Other empirical examples using multiple-sample models are given by Lomax (1983, 1985), Cole and Maxwell (1985), Faulbaum (1987), and McArdle and Epstein (1987). A suggested strategy for testing models in the multiple sample case is also given by Lomax (1983).

12.2 Cross Validation

The replication of a study with a second set of data is often prohibitive given the time, money, or resources available. An alternative is to randomly split an original sample, given that the sample size is sufficient, and run the SEM analysis on one set of data while using the other in a multiple-sample analysis to compare the results. Cudeck and Browne (1983) created a split sample cross-validation index (CVI), while Browne and Cudeck (1989, 1993) developed a single sample cross-validation (ECVI) and further explained CVI and ECVI in structural equation modeling. Except for a constant scale factor, ECVI is similar to the AIC index $[(1/n)^*$ (AIC)]. Arbuckle and Wothke (1999, p. 406) also report MECVI, which, except for a scale factor, is similar to BCC $[(1/n) * (BCC)]$. The Browne–Cudeck criterion (BCC) imposes a slightly greater penalty for model complexity than AIC, and is a fit index developed specifically for the analysis of moment structures. These fit indices are intended for model comparisons, and thus indicate *badness of fit*; with simple models that fit well receiving low values and poorly fitting models receiving high values.

12.2.1 ECVI

Browne and Cudeck (1989) proposed a single-sample expected cross-validation index (ECVI) for comparing alternative models using only one sample of data. The alternative model that results in the *smallest* ECVI value should be the most stable in the population. The ECVI is a function of chi-square and degrees of freedom. It is computed in LISREL as ECVI = $(c/n) + 2(p/n)$, where c is the chi-square value for the overall fitted model, p is the number of independent parameters estimated, and $n = N - 1$ (sample size). Alternatively, ECVI can be reported as similar to the Akaike Information Criterion, except for a scale factor—that is, $(1/n) * $ AIC, where $n = N - r$ (N = sample size; r = number of groups). Browne and Cudeck (1989, 1993) also provided a confidence interval for ECVI. The 90% lower and upper limits(c_L; c_U) = $[(\delta_L + d + 2q)/n; (\delta_U + d + 2q)/n]$, where c_L = lower limit, c_U = upper limit, δ_L = parameter estimate for lower limit, δ_U = parameter estimate for upper limit, d = degrees of freedom, and q = the number of parameters. When sample size is small, it is important to compare the confidence intervals of the ECVI for the alternative competing models. The ECVI is also not very useful for choosing a parsimonious model when the sample size is large. In this instance, we recommend one of the parsimonious model-fit indices and/or the comparative fit index if comparing alternative models (see chapter 5).

Bandalos (1993), in a simulation study, further examined the use of the one-sample expected cross-validation index and found it to be quite accurate in confirmatory factor models. Other research also indicated that the one-sample expected cross validation index yielded highly similar results to those of the two-sample approach (Benson & Bandalos, 1992; Benson &

El-Zahhar, 1994; Benson, Moulin-Julian, Schwarzer, Seipp, & El-Zahhar, 1992).

The ECVI is routinely printed among the fit indices reported by LISREL–SIMPLIS. We used our previous multiple-sample programs in LISREL–SIMPLIS, but this time ran them separately to obtain the ECVI values. The ECVI for sample one was close to zero, indicating a measurement model that would be expected to cross-validate; likewise similar findings were reported for the second sample of data. The confidence intervals around ECVI in both programs further supported that ECVI would probably range between .02 and .03 for this model. (*Note*: We would not interpret the ECVI in the multiple-sample model.)

LISREL–SIMPLIS ECVI Output

Sample 1

```
Expected Cross-Validation Index (ECVI) = 0.021
90 Percent Confidence Interval for ECVI = (0.019 ; 0.028)
ECVI for Saturated Model = 0.011
ECVI for Independence Model = 3.05
```

Sample 2

```
Expected Cross-Validation Index (ECVI) = 0.021
90 Percent Confidence Interval for ECVI = (0.021 ; 0.029)
ECVI for Saturated Model = 0.022
ECVI for Independence Model = 3.00
```

The AIC and BCC values can be computed to show the scale factor relationship to ECVI. AIC = $\chi^2 + 2q$ = 1.3 + 2(9) = 19.3, that is, reported as 19.255 for the first sample, where q = number of parameters in the model. AIC = $\chi^2 + 2q$ = .9 + 2(9) = 18.922 for the second sample. ECVI = $[1/(N - r)](\text{AIC})$ = $[1/(865 - 2)](19.255)$ = .022 for sample 1 and ECVI = $[1/(N - r)]$ (AIC) = $[1/(900 - 2)](18.922)$ = .021 for sample 2. N is the sample size in each group and r is the number of groups. MECVI doesn't apply in this model analysis, but is computed as: $[1/(N - r)]$ (BCC) or $[1/(865 - 2)]$ (19.36) and $[1/(900 - 2)]$ (19.023), respectively.

12.2.2 CVI

Cudeck and Browne (1983) also proposed a cross-validation index (CVI) for covariance structure analysis that incorporated splitting a sample into two subsamples. Subsample **A** is used as a *calibration* sample, and subsample **B** is used as the *validation* sample. The model implied (reproduced) covariance matrix, Σ_a, from the calibration sample is then compared with the covariance matrix derived from Subsample **B**, S_b. A CVI value near zero indicates that the model cross-validates or is the same in the two subsamples. The cross validation index is denoted as CVI = $F(S_b, \Sigma_a)$. The choice among alternative models can also be based on the model that yields the smallest CVI value. One could further *double-cross-validate* by using Subsample **B** as the calibration sample and Subsample **A** as the validation sample. In this instance, the cross validation index is denoted as CVI = $F(S_a, \Sigma_b)$. If the same model holds regardless of which subsample is used as the calibration sample, greater confidence in the model validity is achieved. An obvious drawback to splitting a sample into two subsamples is that sufficient subsample sizes may not exist to provide stable parameter estimates. Obviously, this approach requires an initial large sample that can be randomly split into two subsamples of equal and sufficient size.

The CVI can be computed using LISREL–SIMPLIS command language, but requires two programs with randomly split data and the cross-validate command. In the following example, two LISREL–SIMPLIS programs are run to compute the CVI. The first program reads in the covariance matrix of the calibration sample (S_a), then generates and saves the model implied covariance matrix, Σ_a. The second program uses the covariance matrix of Subsample **B** and then outputs the CVI value. The CVI cross validation example involved randomly splitting an original sample of size 400 and calculating two separate covariance matrices.

```
Program One Calibration Sample
Observed Variables: X1 X2 X3
Covariance Matrix
5.86
3.12 3.32
35.28 23.85 622.09
Latent Variables: Factor1
Relationships:
 X1-X3 = Factor1
Sample Size: 200
Save Sigma in File MODEL1C
End of problem
Program Two Validation Sample and Compute CVI
Observed Variables: X1 X2 X3
Covariance Matrix
5.74
3.47 4.36
45.65 22.58 611.63
Sample Size: 200
Crossvalidate File MODEL1C
End of problem
```

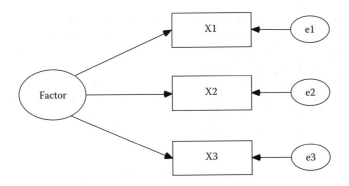

FIGURE 12.2
Single Factor Model (cross validation).

A single factor measurement model with three indicator variables is being tested to see if it cross-validates using a randomly split sample of data (Figure 12.2).

The low CVI value indicated that the measurement model holds for both subsamples. The reduced computer output from the CVI cross validation program is:

```
PROGRAM ONE CALIBRATION SAMPLE
COVARIANCE MATRIX TO BE ANALYZED
         X1      X2      X3
X1     5.86
X2     3.12    3.32
X3     35.28   23.85   622.09
SI was written to file MODEL1C
PROGRAM TWO VALIDATION SAMPLE AND COMPUTE CVI
COVARIANCE MATRIX TO BE ANALYZED
         X1      X2      X3
X1     5.74
X2     3.47    4.36
X3     45.65   22.58   611.63
 MATRIX SIGMA
         X1      X2      X3
X1     5.86
X2     3.12    3.32
X3     35.28   23.85   622.09
CROSS-VALIDATION INDEX (CVI) = 0.38
```

The ECVI and CVI are most useful after a theoretically implied model has an acceptable model fit, that is, when a specified model yields model-fit indices and parameter estimates that are meaningful with sufficient sample size and power. The number of parameters, model complexity, and sample size affect these cross validation indices; therefore, you should not routinely discard other modeling considerations when you select the smaller ECVI of two competing models, report the CVI from two subsamples, or report the CVI across samples taken from a population. Currently, LISREL–SIMPLIS computes ECVI for single sample expected cross validation, however, only LISREL–SIMPLIS computes CVI for split sample cross validation.

12.3 Bootstrap

The bootstrap method treats a random sample of data as a substitute for the population (pseudo population) and re-samples from it a specified number of times, to generate sample bootstrap estimates and standard errors. These sample bootstrap estimates and standard errors are averaged and used to obtain a confidence interval around the average of the bootstrap estimates. This average is termed a *bootstrap estimator*. The bootstrap estimator and associated confidence interval are used to determine how stable or good the sample statistic is as an estimate of the population parameter. Obviously, if the random sample initially drawn from the population is not representative, then the sample statistic and corresponding bootstrap estimator obtained from re-sampling will yield misleading results. The bootstrap approach is used in research when replication with additional sample data and/or cross validation with a split sample is not possible. Fan (2003) demonstrates how the bootstrap method is implemented in various software packages and its utility in correlation, regression, analysis of variance, and reliability. We present examples using PRELIS.

12.3.1 PRELIS Graphical User Interface

Bootstrapping can be accomplished in two different ways using PRELIS (Jöreskog & Sörbom, 1993; 1996b); LISREL–SIMPLIS program does not provide bootstrap capabilities. Our first example will demonstrate the use of the PRELIS graphical user interface. The second example will use the PRELIS command language syntax (Jöreskog & Sörbom, 1996b, pp. 185–190). In our first bootstrap example, we select File, then Import Data to import the SPSS saved file, dataex7.sav, located in the SPSSEX subfolder in LISREL 8 Student Examples directory and save the PRELIS SYSTEM FILE, dataex7.psf.

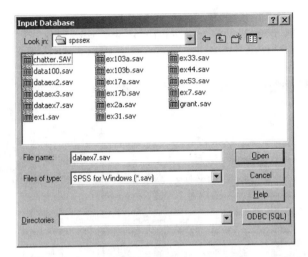

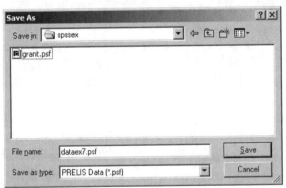

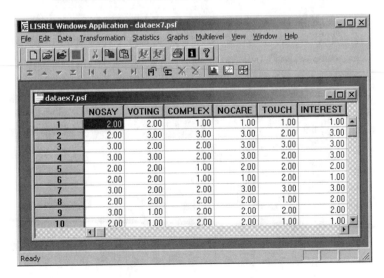

We now see the PRELIS SPREADSHEET with the raw data and the PRELIS tool bar menu with several options from which to choose. We select Statistics from the toolbar menu, and then Bootstrapping.

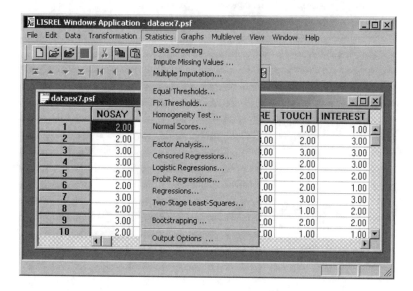

Once we select Bootstrapping, a dialog appears that permits us to specify the number of bootstrap samples, bootstrap fraction, and names for saving the bootstrap matrix, means and standard deviations. The *Syntax* button will create a PRELIS program that you can edit and save. The *Output Options* button provides other formats for saving the data.

The output provides us with the PRELIS command language syntax program and descriptive statistics, as follows.

```
!PRELIS SYNTAX: Can be edited
 SY='C:\lisrel854\spssex\dataex7.PSF'
 OU MA=KM SM=data7.cor ME=data7.me SD=data7.sd XM BS=100 SF=50
 BM=data7.cor ME=data7.me SD=data7.sd
```

Bootstrap Correlation Matrix

	NOSAY	VOTING	COMPLEX	NOCARE	TOUCH	INTEREST
NOSAY	1.000					
VOTING	0.292	1.000				
COMPLEX	0.259	0.276	1.000			
NOCARE	0.462	0.263	0.442	1.000		
TOUCH	0.386	0.180	0.294	0.669	1.000	
INTEREST	0.408	0.239	0.368	0.710	0.640	1.000

Descriptive Statistics

Variable	Mean	St. Dev.
NOSAY	0.000	1.000
VOTING	0.000	1.000
COMPLEX	0.000	1.000
NOCARE	0.000	1.000
TOUCH	0.000	1.000
INTEREST	0.000	1.000

12.3.2 LISREL and PRELIS Program Syntax

In our second example, we use *LISREL* and *PRELIS* command language syntax in various programs to further elaborate the bootstrap method. We first run a LISREL program using the original sample data. The raw-data file, *efficacy.raw*, is provided with *LISREL* and used in other examples in the *PRELIS2 User's Reference Guide* (Jöreskog & Sörbom, 1996b). A two-factor model is specified with six factor loadings estimated; three for each of the factors (see the MO and FR command lines). The LISREL program is written as:

```
Estimate factor loadings for model from file efficacy.raw
DA NI=6 NO=297 ME=GLS
RA=efficacy.raw FO;(6F1.0)
CO ALL
MO NX=6 NK=2
FR LX(1,1) LX(2,1) LX(3,1) LX(4,2) LX(5,2) LX(6,2)
OU MA=CM
```

The variance-covariance matrix to be analyzed is indicated as:

```
VAR     1     0.60
VAR     2     0.16     0.59
VAR     3     0.11     0.14     0.59
VAR     4     0.23     0.14     0.21     0.57
VAR     5     0.16     0.08     0.14     0.30     0.49
VAR     6     0.19     0.11     0.17     0.34     0.27     0.53
```

The six factor loadings for the two factor model specified are estimated as:

	Estimate	Standard Error
LX(1,1)	0.43	0.05
LX(2,1)	0.30	0.05
LX(3,1)	0.37	0.05
LX(4,2)	0.63	0.04
LX(5,2)	0.48	0.04
LX(6,2)	0.55	0.04

Then, to compute bootstrap estimates of the factor loadings for the two-factor model with three indicators per factor, the raw data file is read into a PRELIS program with the number of variables, number of cases, and estimation method specified (DA NI=6 NO=297, ME=GLS). In this example, the PRELIS program reads in a raw data file containing 6 variables and 297 cases with the generalized least-squares estimation method selected [RA = *efficacy.raw* FO;(6F1.0)]. The PRELIS program then generates 10 covariance matrices using the generalized least-squares estimation method. The number of bootstrap samples to be taken is specified (BS=10), and these samples are randomly drawn from the raw data file with replacement. A 100% resampling (SF=100) of the raw data file is specified. The 10 covariance matrices are output into a bootstrap save file (BM = *efficacy. cm*) for further analysis by another LISREL program. This output file is in ASCII format and can be examined. The PRELIS program is:

```
Generate 10 covariance matrices from file efficacy.raw
DA NI=6 NO=297 ME=GLS
RA=efficacy.raw FO; (6F2.0)
OU MA=CM BS=10 SF=100 BM=efficacy.cm
```

The first two variance-covariance matrices output into the file *efficacy.cm* are:

```
VAR     1     1.00
VAR     2     0.27     1.00
VAR     3     0.26     0.26     1.00
VAR     4     0.46     0.25     0.42     1.00
```

VAR	5	0.38	0.16	0.27	0.64	1.00	
VAR	6	0.43	0.26	0.36	0.72	0.63	1.00

VAR	1	1.00					
VAR	2	0.32	1.00				
VAR	3	0.11	0.22	1.00			
VAR	4	0.40	0.26	0.45	1.00		
VAR	5	0.35	0.18	0.36	0.68	1.00	
VAR	6	0.34	0.22	0.32	0.72	0.68	1.00

Notice that the diagonal values indicate variances equal to 1.0, whereas the off-diagonal values indicate the covariance terms. The manipulation of raw data (recoding variables, selecting cases, transformations) and the treatment of missing data (imputation method and/or deleting cases listwise) should be specified and handled in this program prior to bootstrap estimation. The researcher can also specify the type of matrix and estimation method desired in the PRELIS program.

The saved file, *efficacy.cm*, is next read by a LISREL program (CM = *efficacy.cm*) to estimate 10 sets of six factor loadings for the two-factor model. The output from this program indicates the 10 different bootstrap sampled covariance matrices read from the file, as well as parameter estimates, fit indices, and so forth. (*Note*: The output is no different from running 10 separate stacked programs.)

The LISREL program is written as:

```
Estimate 10 sets of 6 factor loadings for two factor model
DA NI=6 NO=297 RP=10
CM=efficacy.cm
MO NX=6 NK=2
FR LX(1,1) LX(2,1) LX(3,1) LX(4,2) LX(5,2) LX(6,2)
OU LX=efficacy.lx
```

The LISREL program indicates that 6 variables and 297 cases were used to compute the 10 covariance matrices that are read in from the saved file (CM = *efficacy.cm*). The program is run 10 times (RP = 10), once for each covariance matrix saved in the file. The model specifies six variables and two factors (MO NX=6 NK=2). The parameters (factor loadings) to be estimated indicate that the first three variables define one factor and the last three variables define a second factor (see the FR command line, which indicates elements in the matrix to be free or estimated). The 10 sets of six factor loadings are computed and output in a saved file (OU LX=*efficacy.lx*).

The saved file is then read by the following PRELIS program to generate the bootstrap estimates and standard errors for the six factor loadings in the model:

```
Analyze 10 sets of 6 factor loadings from file efficacy.lx
DA NI=12
```

```
LA
 'LX(1,1)'  'LX(1,2)'  'LX(2,1)'  'LX(2,2)'  'LX(3,1)'  'LX(3,2)'
 'LX(4,1)'  'LX(4,2)'  'LX(5,1)'  'LX(5,2)'  'LX(6,1)'  'LX(6,2)'
RA=efficacy.lx
SD 'LX(1,2)'  'LX(2,2)'  'LX(3,2)'  'LX(4,1)'  'LX(5,1)'  'LX(6,1)'
CO ALL
OU MA=CM
```

The PRELIS program analyzes the 10 sets of six factor-loading bootstrap estimates and outputs summary statistics. Notice that we used the **SD** command to delete the other six factor loadings that were set to zero in the two-factor model. For our example, the bootstrap estimator and standard deviation for the six factor loadings (three-factor loadings for each factor) were:

```
UNIVARIATE SUMMARY STATISTICS FOR CONTINUOUS VARIABLES
VARIABLE      MEAN     S. D.
 LX(1,1)      0.298    0.322
 LX(2,1)      0.447    0.459
 LX(3,1)      0.207    0.230
 LX(4,2)      0.373    0.384
 LX(5,2)      0.251    0.260
 LX(6,2)      0.403    0.415
```

These values can be used to form confidence intervals around the original sample factor-loading estimates to indicate how stable or good the estimates are as estimates of population values. Rather than further discuss the PRELIS and LISREL command language syntax program setups for bootstrapping, we refer you to the manual and excellent help examples in the software for various straightforward data set examples and output explanations. These two examples were intended only to provide a basic presentation of the bootstrap method in structural equation modeling. Lunneborg (1987) provided additional software to compute bootstrap estimates for means, correlations (bivariate, multivariate, part, and partial), regression weights, and analysis-of-variance designs, to name a few. Stine (1990) provided a basic introduction to bootstrapping methods, and Bollen and Stine (1993) gave a more in-depth discussion of bootstrap in structural equation modeling. Mooney and Duval (1993) also provided an overview of bootstrapping methods, gave a basic algorithm and program for bootstrapping, and indicated other statistical packages that have bootstrap routines. We therefore refer you to these references, as well as others presented in this section, for a better coverage of the background, rationale, and appropriateness of using bootstrap techniques.

12.4 Summary

In this chapter, our concern was model validation. A theoretical model requires validation on additional random samples of data. We refer to this as *replication* and demonstrated how multiple samples could be tested against the specified theoretical model. In the absence of replication, cross validation and bootstrap techniques were discussed as a means of validating a theoretical model.

The chapter began with a look at replication involving the testing of the multiple samples of data against the theoretical model, followed by single sample (ECVI) and split-sample (CVI) cross-validation techniques. We also introduced the bootstrap method to assess the stability of our parameter estimates and standard errors, especially given different distributional assumptions.

We hope that our discussion of these model validation topics in structural equation modeling has provided you with a basic overview and introduction to these methods. We encourage you to read the references provided at the end of the chapter and run some of the program setups provided in the chapter. We further hope that the basic introduction in this chapter will permit you to read the research literature and better understand the topics presented in the chapter. We now turn our attention to chapters 13 to 16 where we present various advanced SEM applications to demonstrate the variety of research designs and research questions that can be addressed using structural equation modeling.

Exercises

1. Test whether the following three variance-covariance matrices fit the theoretical confirmatory factor model in Figure 12.3 using LISREL–SIMPLIS. The sample size is 80 for each sample. The variables are entered in order as: SOFED (father's education), SOMED (mothers' education), SOFOC (father's occupation), FAFED (father's education), MOMED (mother's education), and FAFOC (father's occupation).

   Sample 1
      5.86
      3.12 3.32
      35.28 23.85 622.09
      4.02 2.14 29.42 5.33
      2.99 2.55 19.20 3.17 4.64
      35.30 26.91 465.62 31.22 23.38 546.01
   Sample 2
      8.20
      3.47 4.36

45.65　22.58　611.63
6.39　3.16　44.62　7.32
3.22　3.77　23.47　3.33　4.02
45.58　22.01　548.00　40.99　21.43　585.14
Sample 3
5.74
1.35　2.49
39.24　12.73　535.30
4.94　1.65　37.36　5.39
1.67　2.32　15.71　1.85　3.06
40.11　12.94　496.86　38.09　14.91　538.76

a. Run individual program for sample 1 to determine CFA model and report CFA parameters.
b. Run individual programs with CFA model on sample 2 and sample 3 and report CFA parameters.
c. Run multiple-sample program to test factor loadings and factor correlations invariant (equal) with unequal error variances and report individual and global chi-square values.
d. Interpret your results.

2. For Exercise #1, Report the single sample expected cross validation index (ECVI). Given a sample size of 80, would you split the sample and cross validate the model using CVI?

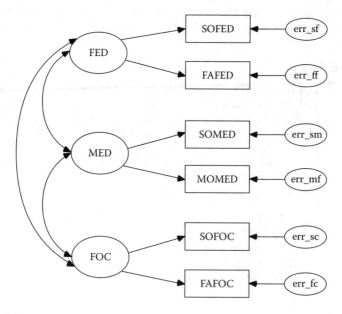

FIGURE 12.3
Multiple Sample Confirmatory Factor Model.

References

Arbuckle, J. L., & Wothke, W. (1999). *AMOS 4.0 User's Guide.* Chicago, IL: Smallwaters Corporation.

Bandalos, D. (1993). Factors influencing the cross-validation of confirmatory factor analysis models. *Multivariate Behavioral Research, 28,* 351–374.

Benson, J., & Bandalos, D. (1992). Second-order confirmatory factor analysis of the reactions to tests' scale with cross-validation. *Multivariate Behavioral Research, 27,* 459–487.

Benson, J, Moulin-Julian, M., Schwarzer, C., Seipp, B., & El-Zahhar, N. (1992). Cross-validation of a revised test anxiety scale using multi-national samples. In K. Hagtvet (Ed.), *Advances in test anxiety research: Vol. 7* (pp. 62–83). Lisse, Netherlands: Swets & Zeitlinger.

Benson, J., & El-Zahhar, N. (1994). Further refinement and validation of the revised test anxiety scale. *Structural Equation Modeling: A Multidisciplinary Journal, 1*(3), 203–221.

Bentler, P. M., & Wu, E. (2002). *EQS for Windows User's Guide.* Encino, CA: Multivariate Software.

Bollen, K. A. (1989). *Structural equations with latent variables.* New York: Wiley.

Bollen, K. A., & Stine, R. A. (1993). Bootstrapping goodness-of-fit measures in structural equation models. In K. A. Bollen, & J. S. Long (Eds.), *Testing structural equation models* (pp. 66–110). Newbury Park, CA: Sage.

Browne, M., & Cudeck, R. (1989). Single sample cross-validation indices for covariance structures. *Multivariate Behavioral Research, 24,* 445–455.

Browne, M., & Cudeck, R. (1993). Alternative ways of assessing model fit. In K. A. Bollen & J. S. Long (Eds.), *Testing structural equation models.* Newbury Park, CA: Sage.

Cole, D. A., & Maxwell, S. E. (1985). Multitrait-multimethod comparisons across populations: A confirmatory factor analytic approach. *Multivariate Behavioral Research, 20,* 389–417.

Cudeck, R., & Browne, M. W. (1983). Cross-validation of covariance structures. *Multivariate Behavioral Research, 18,* 147–167.

Fan, X. (2003). Using commonly available software for bootstrapping in both substantive and measurement analysis. *Educational and Psychological Measurement, 63*(1), 24–50.

Faulbaum, F. (1987). Intergroup comparisons of latent means across waves. *Sociological Methods and Research, 15,* 317–335.

Hayduk, L. A. (1987). *Structural equation modeling with LISREL: Essentials and advances.* Baltimore: Johns Hopkins University Press.

Jöreskog, K. G., & Sörbom, D. (1993). *Bootstrapping and Monte Carlo experimenting with PRELIS2 and LISREL8.* Chicago: Scientific Software International.

Jöreskog, K. G., & Sörbom, D. (1996a). *LISREL8 user's reference guide.* Chicago: Scientific Software International.

Jöreskog, K. G., & Sörbom, D. (1996b). *PRELIS2: User's reference guide.* Chicago: Scientific Software International.

Jöreskog, K. G., & Sörbom, D. (1996c). *LISREL8: Structural equation modeling with the SIMPLIS command language.* Hillsdale, NJ: Lawrence Erlbaum.

Lomax, R. G. (1983). A guide to multiple sample equation modeling. *Behavior Research Methods and Instrumentation, 15*, 580–584.

Lomax, R. G. (1985). A structural model of public and private schools. *Journal of Experimental Education, 53*, 216–236.

Lunneborg, C. E. (1987). *Bootstrap applications for the behavioral sciences: Vol. 1.* Psychology Department, University of Washington, Seattle.

McArdle, J. J., & Epstein, D. (1987). Latent growth curves within developmental structural equation models. *Child Development, 58*, 110–133.

Mooney, C. Z., & Duval, R. D. (1993). *Bootstrapping: A nonparametric approach to statistical inference.* Sage University Series on Quantitative Applications in the Social Sciences, 07-097. Beverly Hills, CA: Sage.

Stine, R. (1990). An introduction to bootstrap methods: Examples and ideas. In J. Fox. & J. S. Long (Eds.), *Modern methods of data analysis* (pp. 325–373). Beverly Hills, CA: SAGE.

13

Multiple Sample, Multiple Group, and Structured Means Models

Key Concepts

Testing for parameter differences between samples of data

Testing parameter differences between groups

Testing hierarchical intercept and slope differences in nested groups

In previous chapters, we have learned about the *basics* of structural equation modeling. In this chapter and subsequent chapters, we will consider other SEM models that demonstrate the variety of applications suitable for structural equation modeling. You should be aware, however, that our discussion will only introduce these SEM models. You are encouraged to explore other examples and applications reported in books (Marcoulides & Schumacker, 1996; Marcoulides & Schumacker, 2001), LISREL software examples, and the references at the end of this chapter. Our intention is to provide a basic understanding of the applications in this chapter to further your interest in the structural equation modeling approach. We have used LISREL–SIMPLIS program examples to better illustrate each application.

13.1 Multiple Sample Models

The multiple samples approach was explained in a previous chapter, but related to testing measurement invariance in a measurement model. We expand on the multiple sample approach here to include testing a model for differences in parameter estimates across samples of data. The theoretical model is in Figure 13.1a.

The data set we used for our multiple sample approach can be found in SPSS 16 Sample folder: *C:\Program Files\SPSSInc\SPSS16\Samples*

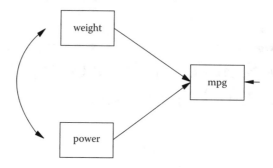

FIGURE 13.1a
Multiple Samples Model.

Cars.sav. The *Cars.sav* data set estimates miles per gallon (mpg) based on various vehicle characteristics (weight, horsepower, engine displacement, year of vehicle, etc.). For our purposes we selected mile per gallon as the dependent variable with vehicle weight and horsepower as independent predictor variables. The original data set contains N = 406; however, only N = 392 are useable because of 14 missing cases (8 due to dependent variable missingness and 6 due to independent variable missingness).

The descriptive statistics for the dependent and independent variables are shown in Table 13.1. The average was 23.45 miles per gallon with an approximate +/–7.8 miles per gallon standard deviation.

Table 13.2 reports the multiple regression prediction results that yielded an $R^2 = .675$ ($F = 404.583$; $df = 2, 389$; $p = .0001$). Our interpretation would suggest that two-thirds of the miles per gallon variation can be explained by a vehicles weight and horsepower. The negative beta coefficients are expected because as weight and horsepower increase, miles per gallon decrease.

Our interest in multiple samples is to compare the parameter estimates of each sample to determine whether they differ significantly. We therefore took two random samples without replacement from the *Cars.sav*

TABLE 13.1

Complete Sample Descriptive Statistics (N = 392)

Variable	Miles Per Gallon	Vehicle Weight	Horsepower
Miles per gallon	1.0		
Vehicle weight	–.807	1.0	
Horse power	–.771	.857	1.0
Mean	23.45	2967.38	104.21
SD	7.805	852.294	38.233

TABLE 13.2

Multiple Regression Complete Sample

	Unstandardized Coefficients		Standardized Coefficients			95% Confidence Interval for B	
	b	Std Error	B	t	P	Lower CI	Upper CI
Constant	44.777	.825		54.307	.0001	43.156	46.398
Vehicle Weight	−.005	.001	−.551	−9.818	.0001	−.006	−.004
Horsepower	−.061	.011	−.299	−5.335	.0001	−.084	−.039

data.[*] The descriptive statistics for both samples are indicated below in Table 13.3 and Table 13.4, respectively.

Sample 1

TABLE 13.3

Sample 1 Descriptive Statistics (N = 206)

Variable	Miles Per Gallon	Vehicle Weight	Horsepower
Miles per gallon	1.0		
Vehicle weight	−.821	1.0	
Horse power	−.778	.865	1.0
Mean	23.94	2921.67	104.23
SD	8.140	835.421	41.129

Sample 2

TABLE 13.4

Sample 2 Descriptive Statistics (N = 188)

Variable	Miles Per Gallon	Vehicle Weight	Horsepower
Miles per gallon	1.0		
Vehicle weight	−.823	1.0	
Horse power	−.760	.855	1.0
Mean	23.59	2952.02	102.72
SD	7.395	805.372	36.234

The SPSS multiple regression analyses are in Table 13.5 and Table 13.6, respectively, for the two samples of data. We see from the SPSS multiple

---

[*] See Chapter Footnote for SPSS details on selecting random samples from Cars.sav.

TABLE 13.5

Sample 1 Multiple Regression Results (N = 206)

	Unstandardized Coefficients		Standardized Coefficients			95% Confidence Interval for B	
	b	Std Error	B	t	p	Lower CI	Upper CI
Constant	46.214	1.193		38.723	.0001	43.861	48.568
Vehicle Weight	−.006	.001	−.585	−7.550	.0001	−.007	−.004
Horsepower	−.054	.015	−.272	−3.509	.0001	−.084	−.024

$R^2 = .692$ ($F = 228.206$; $df = 2, 203$; $p = .001$)

regression analysis of the complete data (N = 292) what our sample results provide in terms of R^2 values, F value, and regression coefficients. We also can visually compare our two individual sample SPSS regression analyses. The results appear to be very similar. Structural equation modeling software, however, provides the capability of testing whether our results (parameter estimates) are statistically different.

LISREL provides the ability to compare both samples rather than having to run separate multiple regression programs on each sample and hand calculate a t-test or z-test for differences in the regression weights. The LISREL multiple sample approach is therefore presented to show how to stack or include each program with different samples of data.

TABLE 13.6

Sample 2 Multiple Regression Results (N = 188)

	Unstandardized Coefficients		Standardized Coefficients			95% Confidence Interval for B	
	b	Std Error	B	t	p	Lower CI	Upper CI
Constant	45.412	1.166		38.957	.0001	43.112	47.712
Vehicle weight	−.006	.001	−.642	−8.114	.0001	−.007	−.004
Horsepower	−.043	.016	−.212	−2.675	.0001	−.075	−.011

$R^2 = .689$ ($F = 204.502$; $df = 2, 185$; $p = .001$).

Regression model comparing two samples
Group 1: Sample 1
Observed variables: mpg weight power

Sample Size: 206
Correlation Matrix
    1.0
    −.821 1.0
    −.778 .865 1.0
Means 23.94 2921.67 104.23
Standard Deviations 8.140 835.421 41.129
Equations:
    mpg = weight power
Group 2: Sample 2
Observed variables: mpg weight power
Sample Size: 188
Correlation Matrix
    1.0
    −.823 1.0
    −.760 .855 1.0
Means: 23.59 2952.02 102.72
Standard Deviations: 7.395 805.372 36.234
Path Diagram
End of Problem

The LISREL multisample output in Figure 13.1b reveals that the chi-square test is nonsignificant ($\chi^2 = 2.01$, $df = 3$, $p = .57$), which indicates that the two samples do not have statistically different parameter estimates in the regression model. Another way of thinking about these results is

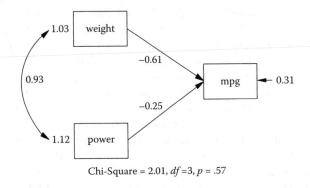

Chi-Square = 2.01, $df = 3$, $p = .57$

FIGURE 13.1b
Multiple Samples Output.

that both samples fit the theoretical model equally. The regression coefficient in common for *weight* predicting *mpg* was –.61; the individual regression weights in SPSS were estimated as –.585 and –.642, respectively. So, it seems reasonable to have a common regression beta weight of –.61. Looking at the regression weight for *power* predicting *mpg*, we find a common regression coefficient of –.25. The individual regression weights in SPSS were estimated as –.272 and –.212, respectively. So, it seems reasonable to have a common regression beta weight of –.25. Also, notice that the error of prediction for *mpg* is .31 $(1 - R^2)$, which means that the common model $R^2 = .69$. We find that for each individual sample, the R^2 values were .692 and .689, respectively. So, once again, the common R^2 value of .69 is reasonable.

The SEM modeling approach is useful for testing whether samples of data yield similar or different parameter estimates, whether comparing multiple regression equations, path models, confirmatory factor models, or structural equation models.

13.2 Multiple Group Models

Multiple group models are set up the same way as multiple sample models. You are basically applying a single specified model to either one or more samples of data or in the case of multiple groups, one or more groups. This type of SEM modeling permits testing for group differences in the specified model or testing for differences in specific parameter estimates by imposing constraints. For example, Lomax (1985) examined a model for schooling using the High School and Beyond (HSB) database. The model included home background, academic orientation, extracurricular activity, achievement, and educational and occupational aspirations as latent variables. The research determined the extent to which the measurement and structural equation models fit both a sample of public school students and a sample of private school students and also examined whether model differences existed between the two groups. The multiple group model analysis should first establish the acceptance of the measurement models and measurement invariance for the groups before hypothesizing any statistically significant difference in coefficients between groups. A LISREL–SIMPLIS multiple group example is presented based on an example in Arbuckle and Wothke (2003). The multiple group model is specified to examine the perceived attractiveness and perceived academic ability differences between a sample of 209 girls and 207 boys.

The LISREL–SIMPLIS program is constructed to include the GROUP command to distinguish between the two groups of data. The observed variables, sample size, means, standard deviations, and correlation matrix are given for each group. The LISREL–SIMPLIS program provides a test of a common model when you only include the EQUATIONS or RELATIONSHIP command in the first group. The computer output yields a common model with the parameter estimates. If you wish to have separate models, hence separate parameter estimates for each group, you would run each program separately with the same EQUATIONS or RELATIONSHIP command in both programs.

13.2.1 Separate Group Models

We will begin by first running a LISREL–SIMPLIS program that provides separate path analysis estimates for girls and boys. The LISREL–SIMPLIS program would be run as follows:

```
Multiple Group Path Model Analysis
Group 1: Girls
Observed Variables academic attract gpa height weight rating
Sample Size = 209
Means .12 .42 10.34 .00 94.13 2.65
Standard Deviation .16 .49 3.49 2.91 19.32 1.01
Correlation Matrix
1.00
.50 1.00
.49 .32 1.00
.10 -.03 .18 1.00
.04 -.16 -.10 .34 1.00
.09 .43 .15 -.16 -.27 1.00
Equation:
academic = gpa attract
attract = academic height weight rating
Let the errors of academic and attract correlate
Group 2: Boys
Observed Variables academic attract gpa height weight rating
Sample Size = 207
Means: .10 .44 8.63 .00 101.91 2.59
Standard Deviations: .16 .49 4.04 3.41 24.32 .97
Correlation Matrix
1.00
```

```
.49 1.00
.58 .30 1.00
-.02 .04 -.11 1.00
-.11 -.19 -.16 .51 1.00
.11 .28 .13 .06 -.18 1.00
Equation:
academic = gpa attract
attract = academic height weight rating
Let the errors of academic and attract correlate
Number of Decimals = 3
Path diagram
End of problem
```

Computer Output

The annotated computer output for girls and boys multiple-group model (Figure 13.2a and Figure 13.2b) results are listed below:

GIRLS

Structural Equations

academic = 0.0257* attract + 0.0212*gpa,   Errorvar.= 0.0175, R^2 = 0.296
         (0.0427)   (0.00329)   (0.00213)
          0.603   6.440   8.196

attract = 1.688*academic − 0.000248*height − 0.00169*weight + 0.175*rating,
        (0.362)   (0.0102)   (0.00154)   (0.0287)
         4.666   −0.0244   −1.097   6.085

   Errorvar.= 0.155 , R^2 = 0.386
            (0.0110)
            14.044

Error Covariance for attract and academic = −0.010
                                          (0.00979)
                                          −0.982

Group Goodness-of-Fit Statistics

```
Contribution to Chi-Square = 3.773
Percentage Contribution to Chi-Square = 66.580
Root Mean Square Residual (RMR) = 0.105
Standardized RMR = 0.0276
Goodness-of-Fit Index (GFI) = 0.994
```

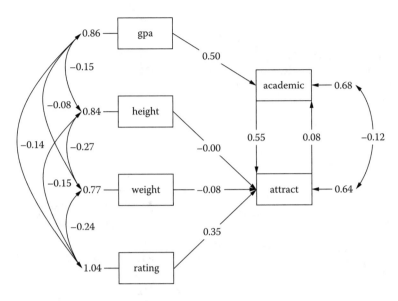

FIGURE 13.2a
Multiple Group Model: girls.

BOYS

Structural Equations

academic = 0.00657*attract + 0.0227*gpa, Errorvar.= 0.0175, R^2 = 0.338
    (0.0481)   (0.00288)   0.00213)
     0.137   7.882   8.196

attract = 1.381*academic + 0.0179*height − 0.00341*weight + 0.0975*rating,
    (0.303)   (0.00955)   (0.00136)   (0.0295)
     4.560   1.875   −2.504   3.301

Errorvar.= 0.155 , R^2 = 0.323
   (0.0110)
   14.044

Error Covariance for attract and academic = −0.001
              (0.00989)
              −0.095

Group Goodness-of-Fit Statistics

```
Contribution to Chi-Square = 1.894
Percentage Contribution to Chi-Square = 33.420
Root Mean Square Residual (RMR) = 0.0223
Standardized RMR = 0.0183
Goodness-of-Fit Index (GFI) = 0.997
```

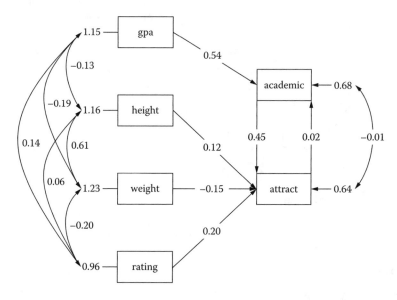

FIGURE 13.2b
Multiple Group Model: boys.

The results indicate different parameter estimates for the girl's data and the boy's data when applied to the model. For example, the reciprocal path coefficients between *academic* and *attract* for the girl's data were $p_{12} = .55$ and $p_{21} = .08$, whereas for the boy's data these same path coefficients were .45 and .02, respectively. The girl's data fit the path model as indicated by the nonsignificant chi-square value ($\chi^2 = 3.773$), and the boy's data also fit the path model as indicated by their nonsignificant chi-square value ($\chi^2 = 1.894$). The Global Fit Statistics indicated a chi-square for the hypothesis of unequal (separate) parameter estimates in the path model ($\chi^2 = 5.667$, $df = 6$, $p = .461$). You will notice that the separate chi-square values for the girls' and boys' path model results will add up to this global chi-square value: $\chi^2 = 3.773$ (girls) + 1.894 (boys) = 5.667. Our primary interest, however, is in testing a hypothesis about whether the groups have equal (same) parameter estimates in the path model.

13.2.2 Similar Group Model

LISREL–SIMPLIS uses the GROUP command (GROUP must be followed by a number) and does not use the EQUATION commands in the second group, when testing whether the two groups share a common path model. The LISREL–SIMPLIS program would now be as follows:

```
Multiple Group Path Model Analysis
Group 1: Girls
Observed Variables academic attract gpa height weight rating
Sample Size = 209
Means .12 .42 10.34 .00 94.13 2.65
Standard Deviation .16 .49 3.49 2.91 19.32 1.01
Correlation Matrix
1.00
.50 1.00
.49 .32 1.00
.10 -.03 .18 1.00
.04 -.16 -.10 .34 1.00
.09 .43 .15 -.16 -.27 1.00
Equation:
academic = gpa attract
attract = academic height weight rating
Let the errors of academic and attract correlate
Group 2: Boys
Observed Variables academic attract gpa height weight rating
Sample Size = 207
Means: .10 .44 8.63 .00 101.91 2.59
Standard Deviations: .16 .49 4.04 3.41 24.32 .97
Correlation Matrix
1.00
.49 1.00
.58 .30 1.00
-.02 .04 -.11 1.00
-.11 -.19 -.16 .51 1.00
.11 .28 .13 .06 -.18 1.00
Number of Decimals = 3
Path diagram
End of problem
```

Computer Output

Structural Equations

academic = 0.0167*attract + 0.0221*gpa, Errorvar. = 0.0174, R^2 = 0.290
            (0.0404)   (0.00237)   (0.00217)
             0.414   9.330   8.039

attract = 1.439*academic + 0.00863*height − 0.00256*weight + 0.142*rating,
      (0.233)   (0.00687)   (0.00102)   (0.0204)
       6.189   1.255   −2.499   6.985

Errorvar. = 0.156 , R^2 = 0.346
(0.0109)
14.309

Error Covariance for attract and academic = −0.003
(0.00796)
−0.429

GIRLS

    Group Goodness-of-Fit Statistics

        Contribution to Chi-Square = 6.739

        Percentage Contribution to Chi-Square = 57.949

        Root Mean Square Residual (RMR) = 0.0920

        Standardized RMR = 0.0320

    Goodness-of-Fit Index (GFI) = 0.989

BOYS

    Group Goodness-of-Fit Statistics

        Contribution to Chi-Square = 4.890

        Percentage Contribution to Chi-Square = 42.051

        Root Mean Square Residual (RMR) = 0.0276

        Standardized RMR = 0.0249

        Goodness-of-Fit Index (GFI) = 0.992

    Global Goodness-of-Fit Statistics

        Degrees of Freedom = 13

        Minimum Fit Function Chi-Square = 11.629 (P = 0.558)

        Normal Theory Weighted Least Squares Chi-Square = 11.699
            (P = 0.552)

        Root Mean Square Error of Approximation (RMSEA) = 0.0

        90 Percent Confidence Interval for RMSEA = (0.0 ; 0.0633)

        P-Value for Test of Close Fit (RMSEA < 0.05) = 0.876
            Normed Fit Index (NFI) = 0.975

When the path diagram window is open you will see a window labeled, *Groups: Multiple Group Path Model*. The first path model is for GIRLS. All of the parameters specified in the EQUATIONS command are set equal between the two groups. Only the covariance among the observed variables is free to vary.

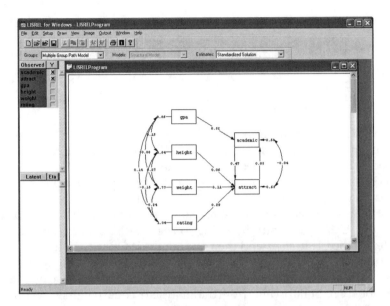

When you scroll down to select *Group 2: Boys* in the Groups window, you will then see the path diagram for the boys. You will see that the parameter estimates are equal for all the paths specified in the EQUATIONS command. The only parameters free to vary (be different) are the covariance among the observed variables.

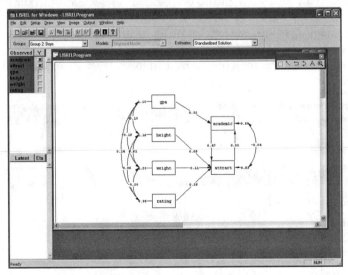

You will notice that the parameter estimates are the same in both groups. For example, $p_{12} = .47$ and $p_{21} = .05$. The individual chi-square values for each group also add up to the global chi-square statistic for this common model.

The chi-square for the girls was $\chi^2 = 6.739$ and the chi-square for the boys was $\chi^2 = 4.890$, which yield the global chi-square value of $\chi^2 = 11.629$, $df = 13$, $p = .558$. These results indicated that both sets of data fit the path model based on the hypothesis of similar path coefficients in the path model.

13.2.3 Chi-Square Difference Test

It is possible to compute a chi-square difference test between the two path model analyses. Recall that the first LISREL–SIMPLIS program analysis tested a hypothesis of unequal parameter estimates, while the second LISREL–SIMPLIS program analysis tested a hypothesis of equal parameter estimates. You can compute a chi-square difference test between these two models by using an EXCEL spreadsheet program, CV.XLS. You will find this EXCEL program by going to the *LISREL 8.8 Student Examples* folder on the *C:/directory*, and then finding the WORKSHOP folder.

Open the *CV.XLS* program outside the LISREL–SIMPLIS program, otherwise it will crash and cause an error message. All you have to do is enter the Global Chi-Square value from the analysis of equal parameter estimates ($\chi^2 = 11.629$, $df = 13$) and the Global Chi-Square value from the analysis of unequal parameter estimates ($\chi^2 = 5.667$, $df = 6$). The program calculates the difference in the chi-square values and associated p-values.

The chi-square difference was $\chi^2 = 5.962$, $df = 7$, $p = .544$, which indicated no difference between the two model analyses. This implies that the girls' and boys' data separately fit the path model, as well as both data sets fit a common path model. A different path model analysis might examine other variables besides *gender* that produce different results, for example, Caucasian versus African-American path models.

The dialog box for the chi-square difference test should look like the one below.

13.3 Structured Means Models

The structured means model is yet another special type of SEM application that is used to test group mean differences in observed and/or latent variables. Mean differences between observed variables in SEM is similar to analysis of variance and covariance techniques. However, mean difference in latent variables is unique to SEM.

13.3.1 Model Specification and Identification

The structured means model example (Figure 13.3) is from LISREL–SIMPLIS and uses the program EX13B.SPL (Jöreskog & Sörbom, 1993, EX13B.SPL). The structured means model examines the mean difference between academic and nonacademic boys in 5th and 7th grades on a latent variable, *verbal ability*. The structured means model is diagrammed below where writing and reading scores measure each latent variable at the 5th grade (Writing5 and Reading5) and 7th grade (Writing7 and Reading7).

Two LISREL–SIMPLIS programs will need to be run to test the mean difference between the latent variables, *Verbal5* and *Verbal7*. The first program indicates the observed variables and equations that relate to the structured means model diagram. The coefficient **CONST** is used to designate the means in the equations for the observed variables and the latent variables, respectively. The first program also includes the sample size, covariance matrix, and means for the first group (academic boys). The second program includes the sample size, covariance matrix, and means for the second group (nonacademic boys). In addition, the second program

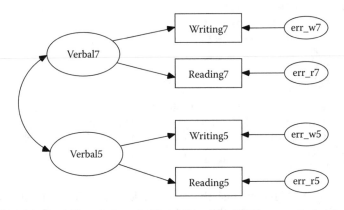

FIGURE 13.3
Structured Means Model.

establishes a test of the mean differences between the latent variables in
the **Relationship** command:

Relationships:
    Verbal5 = CONST
    Verbal7 = CONST

The first and second LISREL–SIMPLIS programs are both stacked into
one complete program, but identified separately using the *GROUP* command, as follows:

```
Group ACADEMIC: Reading and Writing, Grades 5 and 7
Observed Variables: READING5 WRITING5 READING7 WRITING7
Covariance Matrix
281.349
184.219 182.821
216.739 171.699 283.289
198.376 153.201 208.837 246.069
Means 262.236 258.788 275.630 269.075
Sample Size: 373
Latent Variables: Verbal5 Verbal7
Relationships:
 READING5 = CONST + 1*Verbal5
 WRITING5 = CONST + Verbal5
 READING7 = CONST + 1*Verbal7
 WRITING7 = CONST + Verbal7
Group NONACADEMIC: Reading and Writing, Grades 5 and 7
Covariance Matrix
174.485
134.468 161.869
129.840 118.836 228.449
102.194 97.767 136.058 180.460
Means 248.675 246.896 258.546 253.349
Sample Size: 249
Relationships:
 Verbal5 = CONST
 Verbal7 = CONST
Set the Error Variances of READING5 - WRITING7 free
Set the Variances of Verbal5 - Verbal7 free
Set the Covariance between Verbal5 and Verbal7 free
Path diagram
End of problem
```

(*Note*: You should first establish that the data fit a theoretical model before testing for mean differences in the latent variable. Acceptable model-fit indices
for each group, as well as for both groups combined, should be obtained.)

13.3.2 Model Fit

The current example had individual group and combined group model-fit indices that were acceptable.

Academic Boys

Group Goodness-of-Fit Statistics
    Contribution to Chi-Square = 4.15
    Standardized RMR = 0.025
Goodness-of-Fit Index (GFI) = 0.99

Nonacademic Boys

Group Goodness-of-Fit Statistics
    Contribution to Chi-Square = 5.97
    Standardized RMR = 0.042
Goodness-of-Fit Index (GFI) = 0.99

Global Goodness-of-Fit Statistics

Degrees of Freedom = 6
Minimum Fit Function Chi-Square = 10.11 (P = 0.12)
Root Mean Square Error of Approximation (RMSEA) = 0.046
90 Percent Confidence Interval for RMSEA = (0.0 ; 0.095)
P-Value for Test of Close Fit (RMSEA < 0.05) = 0.27
Comparative Fit Index (CFI) = 1.00

13.3.3 Model Estimation and Testing

The LISREL–SIMPLIS computer output reflects the structured mean equations by replacing the **CONST** term with the mean value for each group in the measurement equations.

Measurement Equations: Academic Group

```
READING5 = 262.37 + 1.00*Verbal5, Errorvar .= 50.15, R² = 0.81
            (0.84)                                (6.02)
            312.58                                8.34
WRITING5 = 258.67 + 0.84*Verbal5, Errorvar. = 36.48, R² = 0.81
            (0.70)    (0.024)                   (4.28)
            366.96    34.35                      8.52
READING7 = 275.71 + 1.00*Verbal7, Errorvar. = 51.72, R² = 0.82
            (0.87)                               (6.62)
            317.77                               7.82
```

```
WRITING7 = 268.98 + 0.89*Verbal7, Errorvar. = 57.78, R² = 0.76
           (0.80)    (0.028)                    (6.05)
           338.00    31.95                      9.55
```

Measurement Equations: Nonacademic Group

```
READING5 = 262.37 + 1.00*Verbal5, Errorvar.= 23.25, R² = 0.87
           (0.84)                            (6.23)
           312.58                            3.73
WRITING5 = 258.67 + 0.84*Verbal5, Errorvar. = 42.80, R² = 0.72
           (0.70)    (0.024)                  (5.64)
           366.96    34.35                    7.59
READING7 = 275.71 + 1.00*Verbal7, Errorvar. = 65.67, R² = 0.70
           (0.87)                             (9.87)
           317.77                             6.65
WRITING7 = 268.98 + 0.89*Verbal7, Errorvar. = 67.36, R² = 0.65
           (0.80)    (0.028)                  (8.74)
           338.00    31.95                    7.71
```

The structured means model is testing the mean latent variable difference, which is indicated by the *Mean Vector of Independent Variables*. Results are interpreted based on the knowledge that the mean latent value on *Verbal5* and *Verbal7* are set to zero (0) in the first group (academic boys), so the values reported here are going to indicate that the second group was either greater than (positive) or less than (negative) the first group on the latent variables.

The latent variable mean difference value of –13.80 is indicated for the first latent variable, which indicates the mean difference was less than the first group, that is, nonacademic boys scored below academic boys on verbal ability in the 5th grade.

The latent variable mean difference value of –17.31 is indicated for the second latent variable, which indicates the mean difference was less than the first group; that is, nonacademic boys scored below academic boys on verbal ability in the 7th grade.

Overall, nonacademic boys are scoring below academic boys in the 5th and 7th grades. The latent variable mean differences are divided by their standard error to yield a one-sample T value, that is, $T = -13.80/1.18 = -11.71$ (within rounding error).

Mean Vector of Independent Variables

Verbal5	Verbal7
–13.80	–17.31
(1.18)	(1.24)
–11.71	–13.99

13.4 Summary

In this chapter we have described multiple samples, multiple group, and structured means modeling to demonstrate the versatility of structural equation modeling. The first application involved comparing structure coefficients across samples of data. We referred to this as a *Multiple Sample Model*. The second application involved testing the difference between parameter estimates given multiple groups, for example, different grade levels, different countries, or different schools. We referred to this as a Multiple Group Model. Our third application demonstrated how to test for mean differences between groups on latent variables. We referred to this as a Structured Means Model. This extends the basic analysis of variance approach where mean differences on observed variables are tested but, more importantly, mean differences in latent variables can be tested (Cole, Maxwell, Arvey, & Salas, 1993).

The chapter presented only one example for each of the applications because a more in depth coverage is beyond the scope of this book. However, the LISREL software *HELP* library provides other examples and can be searched by using keywords to find other software examples and explanations. The LISREL User Guide is another excellent reference for other examples of these applications. We now turn our attention to the next chapter where other SEM applications are presented and discussed.

Exercises

1. MULTIPLE SAMPLE MODEL

Nursing programs are interested in knowing if their outcomes are similar from one semester to the next. Two semesters of data were obtained on how student effort and learning environment predicted clinical competence in nursing. The regression model is:

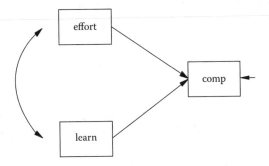

FIGURE 13.4
Nursing Multiple Sample Model.

Create a LISREL–SIMPLIS program to test whether the regression coefficients in the model are the same or statistically significantly different for the two semester samples of data. Semester 1 had 250 nurses and Semester 2 had 205 nurses. (*Note:* The means and standard deviations were not available, so assume the data is in standardized form and only use the correlation matrix in your analysis.)

Semester 1 (N = 250)

	Clinical	Effort	Learn
Clinical	1.0		
Effort	.28	1.0	
Learn	.23	.25	1.0

Semester 2 (N = 205)

	Clinical	Effort	Learn
Clinical	1.0		
Effort	.21	1.0	
Learn	.16	.15	1.0

2. MULTIPLE GROUP MODEL

Create a LISREL–SIMPLIS program that produces output to determine if path coefficients are statistically significantly different. You will need the LISREL–SIMPLIS software and separate data set information provided below to perform this task. Also, provide the path diagrams with interpretation of results using the Excel program.

The path model tests that job satisfaction (satis) is indicated by boss attitude (boss) and the number of hours worked (hrs). The boss attitude (boss) is in turn indicated by the employee satisfaction (satis). The boss attitude (boss) is also indicated by the type of work performed (type), level of assistance provided (assist), and evaluation of the work (eval). The Equation command would therefore be specified as follows:

Equation:
    satis = boss hrs
    boss = type assist eval satis

(**NOTE:** Since a reciprocal relation exists between boss and satis, the errors would need to be correlated to obtain the correct path coefficients.)

The data set information to be used to test hypotheses of equal or unequal parameter estimates in a path model between Germany and the United States are listed below.

Germany

Path Model Analysis for Germany
Observed Variables satis boss hrs type assist eval
Sample Size = 400
Means 1.12 2.42 10.34 4.00 54.13 12.65
Standard Deviation 1.25 2.50 3.94 2.91 9.32 2.01
Correlation Matrix
  1.00
  .55 1.00
  .49 .42 1.00
  .10 .35 .08 1.00
  .04 .46 .18 .14 1.00
  .01 .43 .05 .19 .17 1.00

United States

Path Model Analysis for United States
Observed Variables satis boss hrs type assist eval
Sample Size = 400
Means: 1.10 2.44 8.65 5.00 61.91 12.59
Standard Deviations: 1.16 2.49 4.04 4.41 4.32 1.97
Correlation Matrix
  1.00
  .69 1.00
  .48 .35 1.00
  .02 .24 .11 1.00
  .11 .19 .16 .31 1.00
  .10 .28 .13 .26 .18 1.00

3. STRUCTURED MEANS MODEL

A researcher is interested in testing whether a low-motivation group and a high-motivation group in two different cities (Los Angeles and Chicago) have a production rate mean difference on the production line. Create and run the two stacked LISREL–SIMPLIS programs for a test of latent variable mean differences. Explain results.

The structured means model is diagrammed in Figure 13.5.

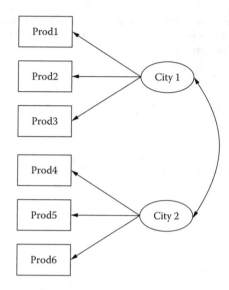

FIGURE 13.5
Motivation Structured Means Model.

The Low-Motivation data information is:

Group Low Motivation:
Observed Variables: Prod1 Prod2 Prod3 Prod4 Prod5 Prod6
Correlation Matrix
    1.00
    .64 1.00
    .78 .73 1.00
    .68 .63 .69 1.00
    .43 .55 .50 .59 1.00
    .65 .63 .67 .81 .60 1.00

Means 4.27 5.02 4.48 4.69 4.53 4.66
Sample Size: 300

The High-Motivation data information is:

Group High Motivation:
Correlation Matrix
    1.00
    .72 1.00
    .76 .74 1.00
    .51 .46 .57 1.00
    .32 .33 .39 .40 1.00
    .54 .45 .60 .73 .45 1.00

Means 14.35 14.93 14.59 14.86 14.71 14.74
Sample Size: 300

Suggested Readings

Multiple Samples

Geary, D. C. & Whitworth, R. H. (1988). Dimensional structure of the Wais-R: A simultaneous multi-sample analysis. *Educational and Psychological Measurement*, *48*(4), 945–956.

Tschanz, B. T., Morf, C. C., & Turner, C. W. (1998). Gender differences in the structure of Narcissism: A multi-sample analysis of the narcissistic personality inventory. *Sex Roles: A Journal of Research*, *38*, 863–868.

Poon, W. Y., & Tang, F. C. (2002). Multisample analysis of multivariate ordinal categorical variables. *Multivariate Behavioral Research*, *37*, 479–500.

Multiple Group Models

Conner, B. T., Stein, J. A., Longshore, D. (2005). Are cognitive AIDS risk-reduction model equally applicable among high- and low-risk seekers? *Personality & Individual Differences*, *38*, 379–393.

Long, B. (1998). Coping with workplace stress: A multiple-group comparison of female managers and clerical workers. *Journal of Counseling Psychology*, *45*, 65–78.

Unrau, N. & Schlackman, J. (2006, November/December). Motivation and its relationship with reading achievement in an urban middle school. *The Journal of Educational Research*, *100*(2), 81–101.

Structured Means Models

Anderson, N., & Lievens, F. (2006). A construct-driven investigation of gender differences in a leadership-role assessment center. *Journal of Applied Psychology*, *91*, 555–566.

Hancock, G. (2001). Effect size, power, and sampling size determination for structured means modeling and mimic approaches to between groups hypothesis testing of means on a testing of means on a single latent construct. *Psychometrika*, *66*, 3, 373–388.

Hayashi, N., Igarashi, Y., Yamashina, M., & Suda, K. (2002, January/February). Is there a gender difference in a factorial structure of the positive and negative syndrome scale? *Psychopathology*, *35*(1), 28–35.

Wei, M. F., Russell, D. W., Mallinckrodt, B., & Zakalik, R. A. (2004). Cultural equivalence of adult attachment across four ethnic groups: factor structure, structured means, and associations with negative mood. *Journal of Counseling Psychology*, *51*, 408–417.

Chapter Footnote

SPSS

Select Cases: Random Sample

This dialog box allows you to select a random sample based on an approximate percentage or an exact number of cases. Sampling is performed without replacement; so, the same case cannot be selected more than once.

Approximately: Generates a random sample of approximately the specified percentage of cases. Since this routine makes an independent pseudo-random decision for each case, the percentage of cases selected can only approximate the specified percentage. The more cases there are in the data file, the closer the percentage of cases selected is to the specified percentage.

Exactly: A user-specified number of cases. You must also specify the number of cases from which to generate the sample. This second number should be less than or equal to the total number of cases in the data file. If the number exceeds the total number of cases in the data file, the sample will contain proportionally fewer cases than the requested number.

From the menu choose:
Data
  Select Cases
    Select Random sample of cases.
    Click Sample.
Select the sampling method and enter the percentage or number of cases.

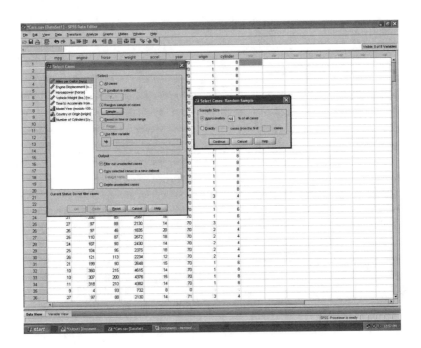

References

Arbuckle, J. L., & Wothke, W. (2003). *Amos 5.0 user's guide.* Chicago, IL: Smallwaters Corporation.

Cole, D. A., Maxwell, S. E., Arvey, R., & Salas, E. (1993). Multivariate group comparisons of variable systems: MANOVA and structural equation modeling. *Psychological Bulletin, 114,* 174–184.

Jöreskog, K., & Sörbom, D. (1993). *LISREL 8: Structural equation modeling with the SIMPLIS command language.* Chicago, IL: Scientific Software International.

Lomax, R. G. (1985). A structural model of public and private schools. *Journal of Experimental Education, 53,* 216–226.

Marcoulides, G., & Schumacker, R. E. (Eds.). (1996). *Advanced structural equation modeling: Issues and techniques.* Mahwah, NJ: Lawrence Erlbaum.

Marcoulides, G., & Schumacker, R. E. (Eds.). (2001). *New developments and techniques in structural equation modeling: Issues and techniques.* Mahwah, NJ: Lawrence Erlbaum.

14

Second-Order, Dynamic, and Multitrait Multimethod Models

Key Concepts

Second-order factors

Dynamic models: measuring factors over time

Establishing reliability and validity when measuring multiple traits and methods

In the previous chapter we learned about comparing samples or groups using structural equation modeling applications. In this chapter we present additional applications that expand our understanding of SEM models, but now related to measurement models. Please be aware that our discussion will only scratch the surface of the many exciting new developments in structural equation modeling related to measurement models. Some of these new applications have been included in chapters of books (Marcoulides & Schumacker, 1996; Marcoulides & Schumacker, 2001; and Schumacker & Marcoulides, 1998) and journal articles. In addition, the newest version of LISREL has included these capabilities with software examples and further explanations. Our intention is to provide a basic understanding of these topics to further your interest in the structural equation modeling approach. We have included computer program examples to better illustrate each type of SEM model.

14.1 Second-Order Factor Model

14.1.1 Model Specification and Identification

A second-order factor model is indicated when first-order factors are explained by some higher-order factor structure. Theory plays an important role in justifying a higher-order factor. *Visual, verbal,* and *speed* are three psychological factors

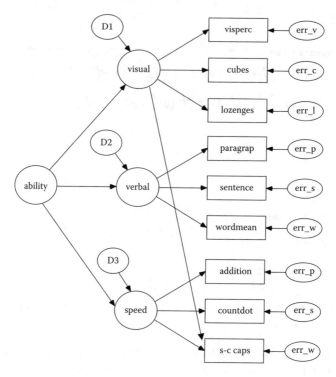

FIGURE 14.1
Second-Order Factor Model.

that most likely indicate a second-order factor, namely *Ability*. A second-order factor model is therefore hypothesized and diagrammed in Figure 14.1.

14.1.2 Model Estimation and Testing

The data used for testing the second-order factor model is based on an example in the LISREL 8 Student Examples, *SPLEX* folder (EX5.spl). The data are nine psychological variables that identified three common factors (*Visual*, *Verbal*, and *Speed*). The second-order factor model hypothesizes that these three common factors indicate a higher-order second factor, *Ability*.

The LISREL–SIMPLIS program includes the *Ability* latent variable and sets the variance of this higher-order second factor to 1.0. (*Note: S-C CAPS* loads on both latent variables Visual and Speed, and a single quote is used when variable names have a space between them.) The LISREL–SIMPLIS program is therefore written as:

```
Second-Order Factor Analysis (EX5.SPL)
Observed Variables
  'VIS PERC' CUBES LOZENGES 'PAR COMP' 'SEN COMP' WORDMEAN
```

```
ADDITION COUNTDOT 'S-C CAPS'
Correlation Matrix
1.000
 .318 1.000
 .436 .419 1.000
 .335 .234 .323 1.000
 .304 .157 .283 .722 1.000
 .326 .195 .350 .714 .685 1.000
 .116 .057 .056 .203 .246 .170 1.000
 .314 .145 .229 .095 .181 .113 .585 1.000
 .489 .239 .361 .309 .345 .280 .408 .512 1.000
Sample Size 145
Latent Variables: Visual Verbal Speed Ability
Relationships:
 'VIS PERC' - LOZENGES 'S-C CAPS' = Visual
 'PAR COMP' - WORDMEAN = Verbal
 ADDITION - 'S-C CAPS' = Speed
Visual = Ability
Verbal = Ability
Speed = Ability
Set variance of Ability = 1.0
Number of Decimals = 3
Wide Print
Print Residuals
Path diagram
End of problem
```

The *selected* LISREL–SIMPLIS model-fit indices listed below indicated that the hypothesized second-order factor model has an acceptable fit (χ^2 = 28.744, p = .189, df = 23; RMSEA = .04; GFI = .958).

```
Goodness-of-Fit Statistics
Degrees of Freedom = 23
Minimum Fit Function Chi-Square = 29.008 (P = 0.180)
Normal Theory Weighted Least Squares Chi-Square = 28.744
(P = 0.189)
Estimated Noncentrality Parameter (NCP) = 5.744
90 Percent Confidence Interval for NCP = (0.0; 23.597)
Root Mean Square Error of Approximation (RMSEA) = 0.0416
90 Percent Confidence Interval for RMSEA = (0.0; 0.0844)
P-Value for Test of Close Fit (RMSEA < 0.05) = 0.580
Root Mean Square Residual (RMR) = 0.0451
Standardized RMR = 0.0451
Expected Cross-Validation Index (ECVI) = 0.505
90 Percent Confidence Interval for ECVI = (0.465; 0.629)
ECVI for Saturated Model = 0.625
ECVI for Independence Model = 4.695
Normed Fit Index (NFI) = 0.956
Goodness-of-Fit Index (GFI) = 0.958
```

The structural equations in the computer output indicate the strength of relationship between the first-order factors and the second-order factor, *Ability*. *Visual* (.987) is indicated as a stronger measure of *Ability*, followed by *Verbal* (.565) and *Speed* (.395), with all three being statistically significant ($t > 1.96$). Therefore, student *Ability* is predominantly a function of visual perception of geometric configurations with complementary verbal skills and speed in completing numerical tasks, which enhance a students' overall ability.

```
Structural Equations
 Visual = 0.987*Ability, Errorvar.= 0.0257, R² = 0.974
        (0.229)                (0.401)
         4.309                  0.0640
 Verbal = 0.565*Ability, Errorvar.= 0.681 , R² = 0.319
        (0.141)                (0.170)
         4.015                  3.997
  Speed = 0.395*Ability, Errorvar.= 0.844 , R² = 0.156
       (0.132)                 (0.227)
        2.999                   3.717
```

14.2 Dynamic Factor Model

A class of SEM applications that involve stationary and nonstationary latent variables across time with lagged (correlated) measurement error has been called dynamic factor analysis (Hershberger, Molenaar, & Corneal, 1996). A characteristic of the SEM dynamic factor model is that the same measurement instruments are administered to the same subject on two or more occasions. The purpose of the analysis is to assess change in the latent variable between the ordered occasions due to some event or treatment. When the same measurement instruments are used over two or more occasions, there is a tendency for the measurement errors to correlate (autocorrelation); for example, a specific sequence of correlated error, where error at Time 1 correlates with error at Time 2, and error at Time 2 correlates with error at Time 3, is called an ARIMA model in econometrics.

Educational research has indicated that anxiety increases the level of student achievement and performance. Psychological research in contrast indicates that anxiety has a negative effect upon individuals, thus should interfere or have a decreasing impact on the level of achievement and performance. Is it possible that both areas of research are correct?

A dynamic factor model was hypothesized to indicate student achievement and performance measures at three equal time points two weeks apart (time 1, time 2, and time 3). The student data indicates achievement (A1) and performance (P1) at time 1, achievement (A2) and performance (P2) at time 2, and achievement (A3) and performance (P3) at time 3. The errors at time 1 were hypothesized to correlate with errors at time 2 and errors at time 2 were hypothesized to correlate with errors at time 3, indicating an ARIMA model. Time 1 predicts time 2 and time 2 predicts time 3. The dynamic factor model is diagrammed in Figure 14.2a:

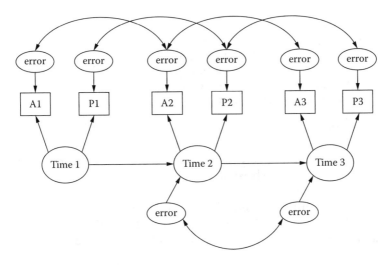

FIGURE 14.2a
Dynamic Factor Model (Wheaton et al., 1977).

The data set contains 600 students who were measured on the same achievement and performance measures at three different points in time. The two variables, achievement and performance, defined the factor *time*. Thus, the latent variable, *time*, was represented as time1, time2, and time3, with two indicator variables at each time point. How well students did at time 2 was predicted by the time 1 latent variable. Likewise, how well students did at time 3 was predicted by time 2. Students were given a high level of anxiety by having to meet deadlines, take frequent quizzes, and turn in extra assignments. A LISREL–SIMPLIS program was created to test this dynamic factor model.

```
Dynamic Factor Model
Observed Variables: A1 P1 A2 P2 A3 P3
Covariance Matrix
 11.834
 6.947 9.364
 6.819 5.091 12.532
```

```
 4.783 5.028 7.495 9.986
-3.839 -3.889 -3.841 -3.625 9.610
-2.190 -1.883 -2.175 -1.878 3.552 4.503
Sample Size: 600
Latent Variables: Time1 Time2 Time3
Relationships:
 A1 P1 = Time1
 A2 P2 = Time2
 A3 P3 = Time3
 Time2 = Time1
 Time3 = Time2
Let the Errors of A1 and A2 correlate
Let the Errors of P1 and P2 correlate
Let the Errors of A2 and A3 correlate
Let the Errors of P2 and P3 correlate
Let the Errors of Time2 and Time3 correlate
Path Diagram
End of Problem
```

The dynamic factor model results indicated an acceptable model fit (χ^2 = 2.76, df = 2, and p = .25). The structural equations indicate the prediction across the three time intervals for the latent variable, *time*. Time 1 was a statistically significant predictor of time 2; coefficient was statistically significant (T = 12.36) and R^2 = .47. Time 2 was a statistically significant predictor of time 3; however, the result indicated a negative coefficient (–.82).

Structural Equations
```
Time2 = 0.68*Time1, Errorvar. = 0.53 , R² = 0.47
         (0.055)                     (0.071)
          12.36                       7.50
Time3 = - 0.82*Time2, Errorvar. = 0.80 , R² = 0.20
         (0.085)                     (0.12)
         -9.66                        6.52
```

The dynamic factor model would therefore be interpreted as follows: anxiety increased the level of student achievement and performance from time 1 to time 2, but then decreased the level of student achievement and performance from time 2 to time 3. Anxiety increased levels of achievement and performance, but only for a certain amount of time, then it had a negative effect. So, it appears educational researchers and psychologists are both correct to some extent. The dynamic factor model clarifies how anxiety affects the level of student achievement and performance, given a time continuum.

The dynamic factor model output with standardized coefficients is listed in Figure 14.2b with standardized coefficients:

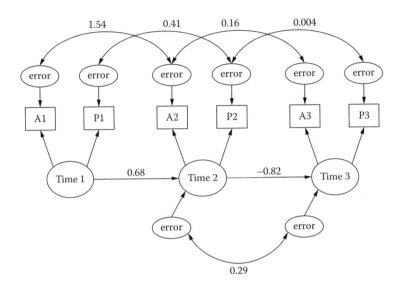

FIGURE 14.2b
Dynamic Factor Model Output.

14.3 Multitrait Multimethod Model (MTMM)

The Multitrait Multimethod model (MTMM) is used to indicate multiple traits assessed by multiple measures—for example, student achievement and student motivation (traits) assessed by teacher ratings and student self ratings (methods). MTMM models, however, are problematic to analyze as noted by Lomax and Algina (1979) who compared two procedures for analyzing MTMM matrices. The MTMM matrix does provide a convenient way to report reliability and construct validity coefficients (Campbell & Fiske, 1959). Construct validity involves providing psychometric evidence of convergent validity, discriminant validity, trait, and method effects, even across populations (Cole & Maxwell, 1985). The Multitrait Multimethod matrix conveniently displays the convergent validity coefficients, discriminant validity coefficients, and the reliability coefficients along the diagonal. A two-trait/two-method matrix is displayed in Table 14.1.

Reliability coefficients (1) indicate the internal consistency of scores on the instrument, and therefore should be in the range .85 to .95 or higher. Convergent validity coefficients (2) are correlations between measures of the same trait (construct) using different methods (instruments), and therefore should also be in the range .85 to .95 or higher. Discriminant validity coefficients (3) are correlations between measures of different

TABLE 14.1

Two-Trait/Two-Method Multitrait Multimethod Matrix

	Method 1		Method 2	
Trait	A	B	A	B
Method 1. Self Ratings				
A. Achievement	(1)			
B. Motivation	(3)	(1)		
Method 2. Teacher Ratings				
A. Achievement	(2)	—	(1)	
B. Motivation	—	(2)	(3)	(1)

Note: (1) = reliability coefficients; (2) = convergent validity coefficients; (3) = discriminant validity coefficients; and (—) = correlations between ratings that
share neither trait nor method.

traits (constructs) using the same method (instrument), and should be much lower than the convergent validity coefficients and/or the instrument reliability coefficients. The basic MTMM model for two traits/two methods is diagrammed in Figure 14.3a:

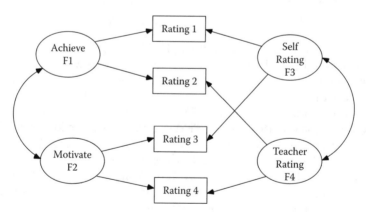

FIGURE 14.3a
Basic MTMM Model (two traits/two methods).

The correlation of ratings from different methods of the same trait should be statistically significant—that is, having convergent validity (2). The convergent validity coefficients should also be greater than the correlations of ratings from different traits using the same method—that is, discriminant validity (3), and the correlations between ratings that share neither trait nor method (–).

14.3.1 Model Specification and Identification

The Multitrait Multimethod (MTMM) model example indicates three methods (self-ratings, peer ratings, and observer ratings) used to assess four traits of leadership (prominence, achievement, affiliation, and leader). The sample size is N = 240 subjects.

MTMM models are problematic to analyze and typically will require specifying start values (initial parameter values) and setting AD = OFF (admissibility check) to obtain convergence—that is, obtain parameter estimates. (*Note*: Start values are typically chosen between .1 and .9 so that the estimation process does not have to start with a zero value for parameters in the model; the 2SLS estimates also provide reasonable start values). The Multitrait Multimethod models are difficult to analyze because they lack model identification (initially have negative degrees of freedom) and can have convergence problems (nonpositive definite matrix). Consequently, latent variable variances should be set to 1.0, and factor correlations between traits and methods set to zero, otherwise, the PHI matrix will be nonpositive definite. Additionally, certain error variances need to be set equal to prevent negative error variance (Heywood case).

In MTMM models, the different methods are uncorrelated with the different traits, so a model diagram helps to visually display the specified model (Figure 14.3b).

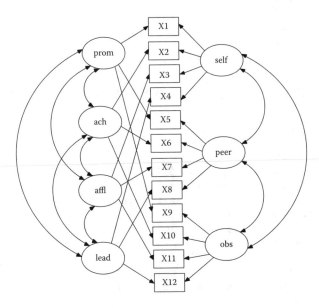

FIGURE 14.3b
Multitrait Multimethod Model. (From Bollen, K. A. [1989]. *Structural equations with latent variables*. New York: John Wiley & Sons.)

14.3.2 Model Estimation and Testing

The LISREL–SIMPLIS program to analyze the three sets of ratings on the four traits as a MTMM model is:

```
Multitrait-Multimethod Bollen (1989)
!Start Values Added (.5) and Admissibility Check Off (AD=OFF)
Observed Variables: X1 X2 X3 X4 X5 X6 X7 X8 X9 X10 X11 X12
Correlation Matrix
1.0
 .50 1.0
 .41 .48 1.0
 .67 .59 .40 1.0
 .45 .33 .26 .55 1.0
 .36 .32 .31 .43 .72 1.0
 .25 .21 .25 .30 .59 .72 1.0
 .46 .36 .28 .51 .85 .80 .69 1.0
 .53 .41 .34 .56 .71 .58 .43 .72 1.0
 .50 .45 .29 .52 .59 .55 .42 .63 .84 1.0
 .36 .30 .28 .37 .53 .51 .43 .57 .62 .57 1.0
 .52 .43 .31 .59 .68 .60 .46 .73 .92 .89 .63 1.0
Sample Size: 240
Latent Variables: prom ach affl lead self peer obs
Relationships:
X1 = (.3)*self + (.5)*prom
X2 = (.3)*self + (.5)*ach
X3 = (.3)*self + (.5)*affl
X4 = (.3)*self + (.5)*lead
X5 = (.3)*peer + (.5)*prom
X6 = (.2)*peer + (.5)*ach
X7 = (.2)*peer + (.5)*affl
X8 = (.2)*peer + (.5)*lead
X9 = (.2)*obs + (.5)*prom
X10 = (.3)*obs + (.5)*ach
X11 = (.3)*obs + (.5)*affl
X12 = (.3)*obs + (.5)*lead
Set Variance of prom - obs to 1.0
Set correlation of prom and self to 0
Set correlation of ach and self to 0
Set correlation of affl and self to 0
Set correlation of lead and self to 0
Set correlation of prom and peer to 0
Set correlation of ach and peer to 0
Set correlation of affl and peer to 0
Set correlation of lead and peer to 0
Set correlation of prom and obs to 0
Set correlation of ach and obs to 0
Set correlation of affl and obs to 0
```

```
Set correlation of lead and obs to 0
Let the error variance of X10 and X12 be equal
OPTIONS: AD = OFF
LISREL OUTPUT
End of Problem
```

Results from the computer output are summarized in Table 14.2 to demonstrate the interpretation of trait and method effects. The assessment of *Affiliation* (Affl) had the highest error variance when using *Self* ratings (error = .67) and *Observer* ratings (error = .39), thus *Affiliation* was the most difficult trait to assess using either of these two methods. The self rating worked best for leadership assessment (factor loading = .61; error variance = .30). The peer rating method worked best with assessing affiliation (factor loading = .79; error variance = .14). The observer rating method worked best with assessing achievement (factor loading = .68; error variance = .07).

(**NOTE:** Most attempts at running MTMM models will result in unidentified models or lack convergence (unable to estimate parameters). Other types of MTMM models—for example, correlated uniqueness model or a composite direct product model—generally work better. A correlated uniqueness model will therefore be presented next.

14.3.3 Correlated Uniqueness Model

We present an example of a correlated uniqueness model, since it seems to have less convergence problems with meaningful results, and is

TABLE 14.2

MTMM Estimates of Four Traits Using Three Methods (N = 240)

	Traits				Methods			
	Prom	**Ach**	**Affl**	**Lead**	**Self**	**Peer**	**Obs**	**Error**
Prom	.52				.58			.41
Ach		.42			.61			.46
Affl			.35		.47			.67
Lead				.58	.61			.30
Prom	.84					.32		.19
Ach		.69				.53		.23
Affl			.48			.79		.14
Lead				.84		.43		.09
Prom	.80						.53	.09
Ach		.69					.68	.07
Affl			.75				.23	.39
Lead				.78			.59	.07

recommended by Marsh and Grayson (1995) and Wothke (1996) as an alternative to traditional MTMM models. In correlated uniqueness models, each variable is affected by one trait factor and one error term, and there are no method factors. The method effects are accounted for by the correlated error terms of each variable. The correlated error terms only occur between variables measured by the same method.

Different types of correlated uniqueness models can be analyzed (Huelsman, Furr, & Nemanick, 2003). For example, one general factor with correlated uniqueness, two correlated factors with correlated uniqueness, two correlated factors with uncorrelated uniqueness, or two uncorrelated factors with correlated uniqueness. Marsh and Grayson (1995) indicated that a significant decrease in fit between a model with correlated traits, but no correlated error terms and a model with correlated traits and correlated error terms, indicated the presence of method effects. Following this approach, you can test method effects by analyzing a correlated trait correlated uniqueness model (CTCU) and a correlated trait (CT) only model.

Figure 14.3c displays the correlated trait–correlated uniqueness (CTCU) model with three traits and three methods. The CTCU model represents the method effects through the correlated error terms of the observed variables. Figure 14.3d displays the correlated trait (CT) only model with no correlated error terms. In the CT model, the variables measured by the same method are grouped under each trait factor.

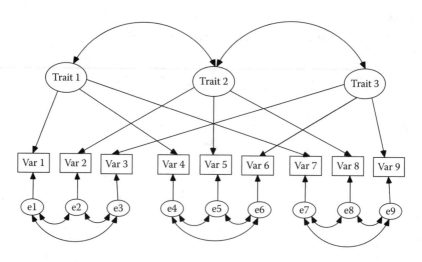

FIGURE 14.3c
Correlated Trait–Correlated Uniqueness Model.

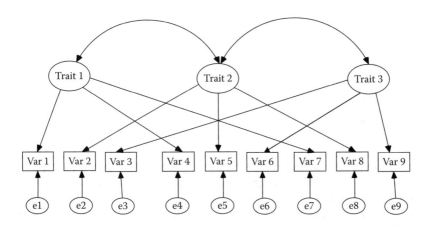

FIGURE 14.3d
Correlated Trait Model.

The data from Bollen (1989) was used again, but this time only three traits (*prom, ach,* and *affl*) with three methods (*self, peer,* and *obs*) were analyzed. The LISREL–SIMPLIS program for the CTCU model with correlated traits and correlated error terms is:

```
Correlated Traits—Correlated Uniqueness Model - Bollen (1989)
Observed Variables: Var1 Var2 Var3 Var4 Var5 Var6 Var7
Var8 Var9
Correlation Matrix
1.0
 .50 1.0
 .41 .48 1.0
 .45 .33 .26 1.0
 .36 .32 .31 .72 1.0
 .25 .21 .25 .59 .72 1.0
 .53 .41 .34 .71 .58 .43 1.0
 .50 .45 .29 .59 .55 .42 .84 1.0
 .36 .30 .28 .53 .51 .43 .62 .57 1.0
Sample Size: 240
Latent Variables: prom ach affl
Relationships:
Var1 = prom
Var2 = ach
Var3 = affl
Var4 = prom
Var5 = ach
Var6 = affl
```

```
Var7 = prom
Var8 = ach
Var9 = affl
Set Variance of prom-affl to 1.0
Let Error Covariance of Var1 - Var3 Correlate
Let Error Covariance of Var4 - Var6 Correlate
Let Error Covariance of Var7 - Var9 Correlate
Path Diagram
End of Problem
```

The results from the computer output are presented in Table 14.3. Findings indicated that all three traits were statistically significantly correlated. More importantly, the *observation* method was the best for assessing any of the three traits, as indicated by the higher trait factor loadings and lower correlated uniqueness error terms. The data also had an acceptable fit to the CTCU model ($\chi^2 = 17.38$, $p = .30$, $df = 15$; RMSEA = .026).

The LISREL program was run again to estimate a correlated trait (CT)-only model with no correlated error terms. To accomplish this, you simply delete the following command lines:

```
Let Error Covariance of Var1 - Var3 Correlate
Let Error Covariance of Var4 - Var6 Correlate
Let Error Covariance of Var7 - Var9 Correlate
```

TABLE 14.3

Correlated Uniqueness Model with Correlated Traits and Errors

Method	Trait	Factor Loading	Uniqueness	R^2	Correlated Uniqueness of Error Terms		
Self	Prom	.58	.67	.33	1.0		
	Ach	.48	.77	.23	.24	1.0	
	Affl	.40	.85	.16	.20	.30	1.0
Peer	Prom	.78	.40	.61	1.0		
	Ach	.68	.54	.46	.23	1.0	
	Affl	.55	.70	.30	.23	.37	1.0
Observe	Prom	.92	.16	.84	1.0		
	Ach	.84	.30	.70	.12	1.0	
	Affl	.76	.42	.58	.007	−.03	1.0

Trait correlations

Prom	1.0		
Ach	.93	1.0	
Affl	.88	.93	1.0

Note: $\chi^2 = 17.38$, $p = .30$, $df = 15$; RMSEA = .026; n = 240.

TABLE 14.4

Correlated Uniqueness Model with Correlated Traits Only

Method	Trait	Factor Loading	Uniqueness	R^2
Self	Prom	.58	.66	.34
	Ach	.45	.79	.21
	Affl	.41	.83	.17
Peer	Prom	.79	.37	.63
	Ach	.72	.48	.52
	Affl	.62	.61	.39
Observe	Prom	.90	.20	.80
	Ach	.80	.35	.65
	Affl	.68	.53	.47

Trait Correlations[a]

Prom	1.0		
Ach	**1.05**	1.0	
Affl	.95	**1.06**	1.0

Note: $\chi^2 = 270.63$, $p = .0000$, $df = 24$; RMSEA $= .21$; $n = 240$.

[a] Trait correlation matrix is a nonpositive definite matrix because correlations are greater than 1.0.

The results from the computer output are presented in Table 14.4. The trait factor loadings, uniqueness, and R^2 values are not substantially different from the previous CTCU model; however, the data is not an acceptable fit to the CT model ($\chi^2 = 270.63$, $p = .00001$, $df = 24$; RMSEA $= .21$). Comparing the previous CTCU model ($\chi^2 = 17.38$, $p = .30$) to this CT model ($\chi^2 = 270.63$, $p = .00001$) indicates a method effect. The method that was suggested as more effective was the *observation* method. Some trait correlations in the CT model were greater than 1.0 indicating a nonpositive definite matrix (1.05 and 1.06—**boldfaced**). The CT model modification indices also suggested adding the specific unique error covariance terms which, if added, would result in the CTCU model.

```
The Modification Indices Suggest to Add an Error Covariance
Between and Decrease in Chi-Square New Estimate
Var2    Var1    21.4            0.22
Var3    Var1    15.4            0.19
Var3    Var2    27.8            0.28
Var5    Var4    30.4            0.19
Var6    Var4    23.0            0.17
Var6    Var5    76.3            0.35
Var7    Var5    41.0           -0.21
Var7    Var6    27.5           -0.16
```

Var8	Var4	33.7	−0.18
Var8	Var6	10.3	−0.12
Var8	Var7	70.3	0.26

The MTMM model is problematic to analyze, but can be done given the addition of start values, setting AD = OFF, setting latent variances to 1.0, setting factor correlations to zero, and setting error variances equal. The alternative correlated uniqueness model approach in SEM is easier to obtain convergence (compute parameter estimates), but is not without controversy over how to interpret the results because more than one possible explanation may exist for the observed correlated error terms.

Although Bollen (1989, p. 190–206) and Byrne (1998, p. 228–229) have demonstrated how to conduct a multitrait multmethod model with a taxonomy of nested models suggested by Widaman (1985), Marsh and Grayson (1995) and Wothke (1996) have demonstrated that most attempts at running MTMM models result in unidentified models or lack convergence, and offer suggestions for other types of MTMM models that included the correlated uniqueness model or a composite direct product model. We strongly suggest that you read Marsh and Grayson (1995) or Wothke (1996) for a discussion of these alternative MTMM models and problems with analyzing data using a MTMM model.

Saris and Aalberts (2003) questioned the interpretation of the correlated uniqueness model approach in SEM. They agreed that one possible explanation for the observed correlated terms is the similarity of methods for the different traits; however, they provided other explanations for the correlated error terms. Their alternative models explained the correlated error terms based on method effects, relative answers to questions, acquiescence bias, and/or variation in response patterns when examining characteristics of survey research questions on a questionnaire. We are, therefore, reminded that error terms do not necessarily reflect a single unknown measure, rather contain sampling error, systematic error, and other potentially unknown measures (observed variables).

14.4 Summary

In this chapter, we have considered second-order factor models, dynamic factor models, and multitrait multimethod models, including an alternative correlated uniqueness model. We have learned that the traditional multitrait multimethod model has identification and convergence problems such that Marsh and Grayson (1995) and Wothke (1996) have recommended alternative approaches, namely correlated uniqueness and direct product models.

We hope that our discussion of these SEM applications has provided you with a basic overview and introduction to these methods. We encourage you to read the references provided at the end of the chapter and run some of the program setups provided in the chapter. We further hope that the basic introduction in this chapter will permit you to read the research literature and better understand the resulting models presented, which should support various theoretical perspectives. Attempting a few basic models will help you better understand the approach; afterwards, you may wish to attempt one of these SEM applications in your own research.

Exercises

1. SECOND-ORDER FACTOR ANALYSIS

The psychological research literature tends to suggest that drug use and depression are leading indicators of suicide among teenagers. (*Note*: Set variance of Suicide = 1 for model identification purposes). Given the following data set information, create and run a LISREL–SIMPLIS program to conduct a second-order factor analysis.

```
Observed Variables: drug1 drug2 drug3 drug4 depress1
  depress2 depress3 depress4
Sample Size 200
Correlation Matrix
 1.000
 0.628 1.000
 0.623 0.646 1.000
 0.542 0.656 0.626 1.000
 0.496 0.557 0.579 0.640 1.000
 0.374 0.392 0.425 0.451 0.590 1.000
 0.406 0.439 0.446 0.444 0.668 .488 1.000
 0.489 0.510 0.522 0.467 0.643 .591 .612 1.000
Means 1.879 1.696 1.797 2.198 2.043 1.029 1.947 2.024
Standard Deviations 1.379 1.314 1.288 1.388 1.405 1.269
  1.435 1.423
Latent Variables: drugs depress Suicide
```

The second-order factor model is diagrammed in Figure 14.4:

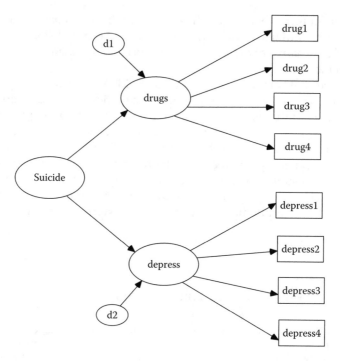

FIGURE 14.4
Siucide Second-Order Factor Model.

2. DYNAMIC FACTOR MODEL

A sports physician was interested in studying heart rate and muscle fatigue of female soccer players. She collected data after three soccer games over a 3-week period. A dynamic factor model was used to determine if heart rate and muscle fatigue were stable across time for the 150 female soccer players.

Create a LISREL–SIMPLIS program to analyze and interpret the dynamic factor model. Include a diagram of the dynamic factor model. The data set information including observed variables, covariance matrix, sample size, and latent variables are provided below:

```
Observed Variables: HR1 MF1 HR2 MF2 HR3 MF3
Covariance Matrix
 10.75
 7.00 9.34
 7.00 5.00 11.50
 5.03 5.00 7.49 9.96
 3.89 4.00 3.84 3.65 9.51
 2.90 2.00 2.15 2.88 3.55 5.50
Sample Size: 150
Latent Variables: Time1 Time2 Time3
```

3. MULTITRAIT MULTIMETHOD (MTMM) MODELS

Students provided ratings of their classroom behavior, motivation to achieve, and attitude toward learning. Teachers, likewise, provided ratings of student classroom behavior, perception of students' motivation to achieve, and attitude toward learning. Finally, other students or peers provided ratings on these three traits. The three ratings (student, teacher, and peer) on three traits (behavior, motivate, attitude) were analyzed in a SEM Multitrait Multimethod model. The Multitrait Multimethod Model is diagrammed in Figure 14.5:

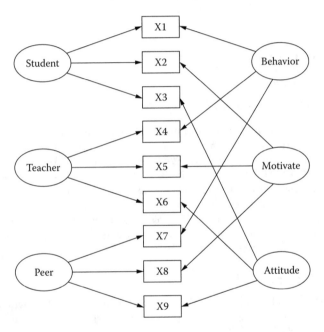

FIGURE 14.5
Classroom MTMM Model.

a. Create and run a LISREL–SIMPLIS program to analyze the three sets of ratings on the three traits as a MTMM model. The observed variables, correlation matrix, sample size, and latent variables are:

```
Observed Variables: X1 X2 X3 X4 X5 X6 X7 X8 X9
Correlation Matrix
1.0
 .40 1.0
 .31 .38 1.0
 .35 .23 .16 1.0
 .26 .22 .21 .62 1.0
 .15 .11 .15 .49 .62 1.0
```

```
.43 .31 .24 .61 .48 .33 1.0
.40 .35 .19 .49 .45 .32 .74 1.0
.26 .20 .18 .43 .41 .33 .52 .47 1.0
Sample Size: 300
Latent Variables: behavior motivate attitude student
teacher peer
```

     b. Create and run a LISREL–SIMPLIS program to compute a CTCU and CU model using the data information from above. Compare the CTCU and CU model results to determine if a method effect exists. Also, compare the CTCU model with the MTMM model above, which provides clearer results?

Suggested Readings

Second-Order Factor Models

Chan, D. W. (2006, Fall). Perceived multiple intelligences among male and female Chinese gifted students in Hong Kong: The structure of the student multiple intelligences profile. *The Gifted Child Quarterly, 50*(4), 325–338.

Cheung, D. (2000). Evidence of a single second-order factor in student ratings of teaching effectiveness. *Structural Equation Modeling: A Multidisciplinary Journal, 7,* 442–460.

Rand, D., Conger, R. D., Patterson, G. R., & Ge, X. (1995). It takes two to replicate: A mediational model for the impact of parents' stress on adolescent adjustment. *Child Development, 66*(1), 80–97.

Dynamic Factor Models

Chow, S. M., Nesselroade, J. R., Shifren, K., & McArdle, J. J. (2004). Dynamic structure of emotions among individuals with Parkinson's disease. *Structural Equation Modeling, 11*(4), 560–582.

Kroonenberg, P. M., van Dam, M., van Uzendoorn, M. H., & Mooijaart, A. (1997, May). Dynamics of behaviour in the strange situation: A structural equation approach. *British Journal of Psychology, 88,* 311–332.

Zuur, A. F., Fryer, R. J., Jolliffe, I. T., Dekker, R., Beukema, J. J. (2003). Estimating common trends in multivariate time series using dynamic factor analysis. *Environmetrics, 14*(7), 665–685.

Multitrait Multimethod Models

Bunting, B. P., Adamson, G., & Mulhall, P. K. (2002). A Monte Carlo examination of an MTMM model with planned incomplete data structures. *Structural Equation Modeling: A Multidisciplinary Journal, 9,* 369–389.

Lim, B., & Ployhart, R. E. (2006, January). Assessing the convergent and discriminant validity of Goldberg's international personality item pool. *Organizational Research Methods, 9*(1), 29–54.

Tildesley, E. A., Hops, H., Ary, D., & Andrews, J. A. (1995). Multitrait-multimethod model of adolescent deviance, drug use, academic, and sexual behaviors. *Journal of Psychopathology and Behavioral Assessment, 17*(2), 185–215.

Correlated Uniqueness Model

Lievens, F., & Van Keer, E. (2001, September). The construct validity of a Belgian assessment centre: A comparison of different models. *Journal of Occupational and Organizational Psychology, 74,* 373–378.

Marsh, H. W., Roche, R. A., Pajares, F., & Miller, M. (1997). Item-specific efficacy judgments in mathematical problem solving: The downside of standing too close to trees in a forest. *Contemporary Educational Psychology, 22,* 363–377.

Quilty, L. C., Oakman, J. M., & Riski, E. (2006). Correlates of the Rosenberg self-esteem scale method effects. *Structural Equation Modeling: A Multidisciplinary Journal. 13,* 99–117.

References

Bollen, K. A. (1989). *Structural equations with latent variables.* New York: John Wiley & Sons.

Byrne, B. M. (1998). *Structural equation modeling with LISREL, PRELIS, and SIMPLIS: Basic concepts, applications, and programming.* Mahwah, NJ: Lawrence Erlbaum.

Campbell, D. T., & Fiske, D. W. (1959). Convergent and discriminant validation by the multitrait-multimethod matrix. *Psychological Bulletin, 56,* 81–105.

Cole, D. A., & Maxwell, S. E. (1985). Multitrait-multimethod comparisons across populations: A confirmatory factor analytic approach. *Multivariate Behavioral Research, 20,* 389–417.

Hershberger, S. L., Molenaar, P. C. M., & Corneal, S. E. (1996). A hierarchy of univariate and multivariate structural times series models (pp. 159–194). In Marcoulides, G. & Schumacker, R. E. (Eds.), *Advanced structural equation modeling: Issues and techniques.* Mahwah, NJ: Lawrence Erlbaum.

Huelsman, T. J., Furr, M. R., Nemanick, Jr., R. C. (2003). Measurement of dispositional affect: Construct validity and convergence with a circumplex model of affect. *Educational and Psychological Measurement, 63*(4), 655–673.

Lomax, R. G., & Algina, J. (1979). Comparison of two procedures for analyzing multitrait multimethod matrices. *Journal of Educational Measurement, 16,* 177–186. [errata: 1980, 17, 80]

Marcoulides, G., & Schumacker, R. E. (Eds.). (1996). *Advanced structural equation modeling: Issues and techniques.* Mahwah, NJ: Lawrence Erlbaum.

Marcoulides, G., & Schumacker, R. E. (Eds.). (2001). *New developments and techniques in structural equation modeling.* Mahwah, NJ: Lawrence Erlbaum.

Marsh, H. W., & Grayson, D. (1995). Latent variable models of multitrait-multimethod data. In Hoyle, R. H. (Ed.). *Structural equation modeling: Concepts, issues, and applications.* Thousand Oaks, CA: Sage Publications.

Saris, W. E., & Aalberts, C. (2003). Different explanations for correlated disturbance terms in MTMM studies. *Structural Equation Modeling, 10*(2), 193–213.

Schumacker, R. E., & Marcoulides, G. A. (1998). *Interaction and nonlinear effects in structural equation modeling.* Mahwah, NJ: Lawrence Erlbaum.

Widaman, K. F. (1985). Hierarchically tested covariance structure models for multitrait-multimethod data. *Applied Psychological Measurement, 9*, 1–26.

Wheaton, B., Muthén, B., Alwin, D. F., & Summers, G. F. (1977). Assessing reliability and stability in panel models. In D. R. Heise (Ed.), *Sociological methodology* (pp 84–136). San Francisco, CA: Jossey-Bass.

Wothke, W. (1996). Models for multitrait-multimethod matrix analysis. In Marcoulides, G. & Schumacker, R. E. (Eds.), *Advanced structural equation modeling: Issues and techniques* (pp. 7–56). Mahwah, NJ: Lawrence Erlbaum.

15

Multiple Indicator–Multiple Indicator Cause, Mixture, and Multilevel Models

Key Concepts

Multiple indicator–multiple cause (MIMIC) models

SEM models with continuous and categorical variables (mixture models)

Testing multilevel intercept and slope differences in nested groups (multilevel models).

In this chapter we continue with our presentation and discussion of SEM model applications. Specifically, we present an example where latent variables are predicted by observed variables (MIMIC model); an example where continuous and categorical variables are included in the model (mixture model); and finally an example where nested design data occur (multilevel model). All three of these SEM applications are unique and are not possible using traditional statistics (analysis of variance, etc.).

15.1 Multiple Indicator–Multiple Cause (MIMIC) Models

The term MIMIC refers to multiple indicators and multiple causes and defines a particular type of SEM model. The MIMIC model involves using latent variables that are predicted by observed variables. An example by Jöreskog and Sörbom (1996a, example 5.4, p. 185–187) is illustrated where a latent variable (*social participation*) is defined by church attendance, memberships, and friends. The *social participation* latent variable is predicted by the observed variables, income, occupation, and education. The MIMIC model is diagrammed in Figure 15.1a.

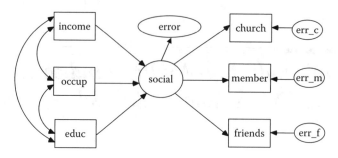

FIGURE 15.1a
MIMIC Model.

The MIMIC model indicates a latent variable, *social*, which has arrows pointing out to the three observed indicator variables (church, member, friends) with separate measurement error terms for each. This is the measurement part of the MIMIC model that defines the latent variable. In the MIMIC model, the latent variable, *social*, also has arrows pointed toward it from the three observed predictor variables, which have implied correlations among them (curved arrows). This is the structural part of the MIMIC model that uses observed variables to predict a latent variable. The MIMIC model diagram also shows the prediction error for the latent variable, *social*.

15.1.1 Model Specification and Identification

Model identification pertains to whether the estimates in the MIMIC model can be calculated, which is quickly gauged by the degrees of freedom. Do you recall how the degrees of freedom are determined? There are a total of 15 free parameters to be estimated in the MIMIC model. The number of distinct values in the variance-covariance matrix S based on 6 observed variables is: $p(p + 1)/2 = 6(6 + 1)/2 = 21$. The degrees of freedom are computed by subtracting the number of free parameters from the number of distinct parameters in the matrix S, which is $21 - 15 = 6$.

15.1.2 Model Estimation and Model Testing

The MIMIC model diagram provides the basis for specifying the LISREL–SIMPLIS program, specifically the *Latent Variable* and *Relationships* command lines in the LISREL–SIMPLIS program. The LISREL–SIMPLIS program that specifies the observed variables, sample size, correlation matrix (standardized variables), and the equations that reflect the MIMIC model is:

```
MIMIC Model
Observed Variables income occup educ church member friends
```

```
Sample Size 530
Correlation Matrix
1.000
 .304 1.000
 .305 .344 1.000
 .100 .156 .158 1.000
 .284 .192 .324 .360 1.000
 .176 .136 .226 .210 .265 1.000
Latent Variable social
Relationships
church = social
member = social
friends= social
social = income occup educ
Path Diagram
End of Problem
```

SEM MIMIC models use goodness-of-fit criteria to determine whether a reasonably good fit of the data to the MIMIC model exists. Some basic fit criteria are printed below from the computer output.

Goodness-of-Fit Statistics

```
Degrees of Freedom = 6
Minimum Fit Function Chi-Square = 12.50 (P = 0.052)
Normal Theory Weighted Least Squares Chi-Square = 12.02
(P = 0.061)
Estimated Noncentrality Parameter (NCP) = 6.02
90 Percent Confidence Interval for NCP = (0.0 ; 20.00)
Root Mean Square Error of Approximation (RMSEA) = 0.044
90 Percent Confidence Interval for RMSEA = (0.0 ; 0.079)
P-Value for Test of Close Fit (RMSEA < 0.05) = 0.56
Expected Cross-Validation Index (ECVI) = 0.079
90 Percent Confidence Interval for ECVI = (0.068 ; 0.11)
Normed Fit Index (NFI) = 0.97
Goodness-of-Fit Index (GFI) = 0.99
```

The Normal Theory Weighted Least Squares χ^2 = 12.02, df = 6, and p = .061 suggests a reasonably good fit of the data to the MIMIC model. The Goodness-of-Fit (GFI) Index suggests that 99% of the variance-covariance in matrix S is reproduced by the MIMIC model. The LISREL software standardized solution indicates factor loadings of .47 * church, .74 * member, and .40 * friends. However, the T-value in the computer output dropped *church* as an important indicator variable in defining the latent variable, *social*.

The observed variables, *member* (T = 6.71) and *friends* (T = 6.03), were therefore selected to define the latent variable *social*. The measurement equations from the computer output are listed below.

Measurement Equations

```
church = 0.47*social, Errorvar. = 0.78 , R² = 0.22
                                  (0.058)
                                  13.61
member = 0.74*social, Errorvar. = 0.46 , R² = 0.54
         (0.11)                   (0.075)
         6.71                     6.10
friends = 0.40*social, Errorvar. = 0.84 , R² = 0.16
          (0.067)                  (0.058)
          6.03                     14.51
```

(**NOTE:** Because a matrix was used rather than raw data, standard error and T-value are not output for the reference indicator variable, *church*. The *HELP* menu offers this explanation: LISREL for Windows uses a reference indicator (indicator with a unit factor loading) to set the scale of each of the endogenous latent (ETA) variables of the model. If you do not specify reference indicators for the endogenous latent variables of your model, LISREL for Windows will select a reference indicator for each endogenous latent variable of your model. Although LISREL for Windows scales the factor loadings to obtain the appropriate estimates for the factor loadings of the reference indicators, it does not use the Delta method to compute the corresponding standard error estimates).

The observed independent variables (income, occup, and educ) in the MIMIC model were correlated amongst themselves as identified in the correlation matrix of the SEM program output:

```
1.000
 .304 1.000
 .305 .344 1.000
```

The structural equation indicated that the latent variable *social* had 26% of its variance predicted (R^2 = .26), with 74% unexplained error variance due random or systematic error, and variables not in the MIMIC model. The T-values for the structural equation coefficients indicated that *occup* (occupation) didn't statistically significantly predict *social* (T = parameter estimate divided by standard error = .097/.056 = 1.73 is less than t = 1.96 at the .05 level of significance, two-tailed test), whereas *income* (T = 3.82) and *educ* (T = 4.93) were statistically significant at the .05 level of significance. The structural equation with coefficients, standard errors in parentheses and associated T values are listed below.

Structural Equation

Social = 0.23*income + 0.097*occup + 0.33*educ, Errorvar.= 0.74 , R² = 0.26
     (0.061)   (0.056)   (0.068)   (0.17)
      3.82   1.73   4.93   4.35

15.1.3 Model Modification

The original MIMIC model was therefore modified by dropping *church* and *occup*. The MIMIC model diagram with these modifications now appears in Figure 15.1b.

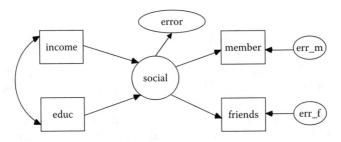

FIGURE 15.1b
Modified MIMIC Model.

The model modification fit criteria are more acceptable, indicating an almost perfect fit of the data to the MIMIC model, since the Minimum Fit Function χ^2 value was close to zero.

Goodness-of-Fit Statistics

```
Degrees of Freedom = 1
Minimum Fit Function Chi-Square = 0.19 (P = 0.66)
Root Mean Square Error of Approximation (RMSEA) = 0.0
90 Percent Confidence Interval for RMSEA = (0.0 ; 0.088)
P-Value for Test of Close Fit (RMSEA < 0.05) = 0.82
Normed Fit Index (NFI) = 1.00
Goodness-of-Fit Index (GFI) = 1.00
```

Measurement Equations

```
member = 0.63*social, Errorvar.= 0.60 , R² = 0.39
                                 (0.08)
                                  7.32
friends = 0.42*social, Errorvar. = 0.82 , R² = 0.17
          (0.07)                   (0.06)
           5.54                     13.66
```

(*NOTE*: Because a matrix was used rather than raw data, standard errors are not output for one of the reference indicator variables, *member* = 0.63*social. The *HELP* menu offers further explanation as noted above.)

Structural Equations

The structural equation now indicated two statistically significant predictor variables with $R^2 = .36$. This also implies that 64 percent of the latent variable variance is left unexplained, mostly due to random or systematic error or other variables not included in the MIMIC model.

```
social = 0.31*income + 0.42*educ, Errorvar. = 0.64 , R² = 0.36
         (0.063)       (0.064)                  (0.19)
          5.01          6.65                      3.39
```

MIMIC models permit the specification of one or more latent variables with one or more observed variables as predictors of the latent variables. This type of SEM model demonstrates how observed variables can be incorporated into theoretical models and tested. We followed the five basic steps in SEM: model specification, model identification, model estimation, model testing, and model modification to obtain our best model to data fit.

15.2 Mixture Models

Mixture models in SEM involve the analysis of observed variables that are categorical and continuous. SEM was originally created using continuous variables in a sample variance–covariance matrix (Pearson correlation matrix with means and standard deviations); however, today SEM models with nominal, ordinal, interval, and ratio-level observed variables can be used in SEM. The use of a mixture of variables, however, requires using other types of matrices than the Pearson correlation matrix and associated variance–covariance matrix in SEM programs. In the LISREL software program, PRELIS (Pre-LISREL) is used to input, edit and handle raw data and produce the type of matrix needed for the LISREL program (Jöreskog & Sorbom, 1996b). In PRELIS, a variable is defined as continuous by the **CO** command (by default the variable must have a minimum of 15 categories), the **OR** command for ordinal variables, or the **CL** command for class or group variables. PRELIS can output normal theory variance–covariance matrices (correlation between continuous variables), polychoric matrices (correlation between ordered categorical variables), polyserial matrices (correlation between continuous and ordered categorical variable), and asymptotic variance–covariance matrices (continuous and/or ordinal variables with nonnormality), and augmented moment matrices (matrices with variable means). Consequently, in LISREL, one would use PRELIS to create and save the appropriate variance–covariance matrix, conduct the analysis as usual, and interpret the fit statistic using a robust model-fit measure (*Note:* The sample variance–covariance matrix and asymptotic covariance matrix with maximum likelihood estimation is required to obtain the Satorra–Bentler robust χ^2 statistic).

15.2.1 Model Specification and Identification

The mixture model example uses variables from the SPSS data set *bankloan.sav*. This is a hypothetical data set that concerns a bank's efforts to reduce the rate of loan defaults. The file contains financial and demographic information on 850 past and prospective customers. The data set is located in the SPSS *Samples* folder, our path location was:

C:\Program Files\SPSSInc\SPSS16\Samples\bankloan.sav

A theoretical model was hypothesized that financial *Ability* was a predictor of *Debt*. The observed variables age, level of education, years with current employer, years at current address, and household income in thousands were used as indicators of the latent independent variable, *Ability*. The observed variables credit card debt in thousands and other debt in thousands were used as indicators of the latent dependent variable, *Debt*.

The SPSS save file (*bankloan.sav*) was imported and saved as a PRELIS System File (*bankloan.psf*). The File, and then Import Data commands, were used along with the Save As command noted in the following two dialog boxes.

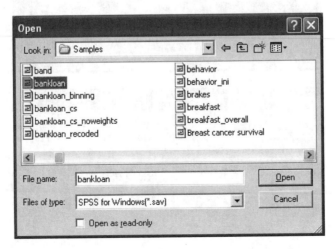

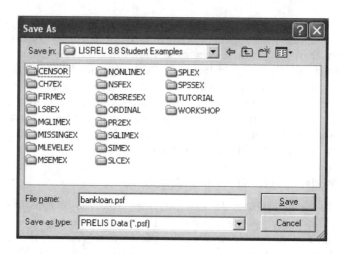

We now opened the PRELIS System File, *bankloan.psf*, and deleted the variable *DEBTINC* by clicking on the variable name using the right mouse button. Next, we deleted the last four variables, *Default, preddef1, pred-def2,* and *preddef3,* leaving seven variables for the theoretical model. We decided that these five variables (DEBTINC, Default, preddef1, preddef2, and preddef3) were not good indicators in our theoretical model. (*Note:* The following dialog boxes will appear if you right mouse click on the variable name).

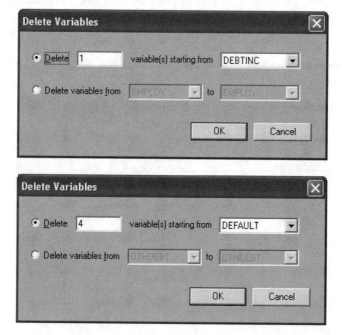

The level of education variable was ordinal (OR), while all other variables were considered continuous (CO). The mixture model for *Ability* predicting *Debt* is therefore represented in Figure 15.2a.

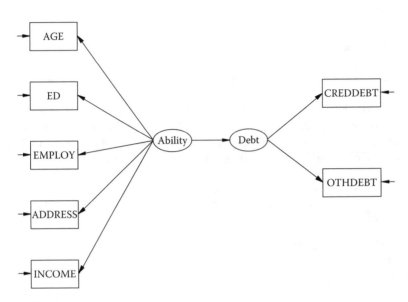

FIGURE 15.2a
Mixture Model.

15.2.2 Model Estimation and Testing

In LISREL, we can now write a PRELIS program that will read in the data and output a polyserial correlation matrix, *bankloan.mat*. (*Note*: The PRELIS program only requires a few lines of code to read in the data and output 8 different types of matrices [Jöreskog & Sörbom, 1996b, p. 92–93]). The title of the program is *Polyserial correlation matrix*. The DA command specifies seven input variables (NI = 7) with 850 observations (NO = 850); missing data is identified by a zero (MI = 0) and treat missing data listwise (TR = LI). The SY command identifies the PRELIS system file (*bankloan.psf*). The OU command identifies the type of matrix to be computed—that is, polyserial matrix (MA = PM)—and the name of the polyserial matrix (PM = *bankloan.mat*). The PRELIS program was entered and saved as *bankloan.pr2*. (*Note*: We click on the run-P icon to execute PRELIS programs.)

```
Polyserial correlation matrix
DA NI = 7 NO=850 MI = 0 TR = LI
SY FI = bankloan.psf
CO AGE
OR ED
CO EMPLOY
CO ADDRESS
CO INCOME
CO CREDDEBT
CO OTHDEBT
OU MA = PM PM = bankloan.mat
```

Two variables, *EMPLOY* and *ADDRESS,* had missing data leaving an effective sample size of $N = 723$. The resulting saved polyserial correlation matrix, *bankloan.mat,* is now used in our mixture model program analysis. The LISREL–SIMPLIS program for the mixture model would be:

```
Mixture Model using Polyserial Correlation Matrix
Observed Variables: AGE ED EMPLOY ADDRESS INCOME CREDDEBT
     OTHDEBT
Sample Size 723
Correlation Matrix
1.000
 0.041 1.000
 0.524 -0.163 1.000
 0.589 0.099 0.335 1.000
 0.454 0.251 0.610 0.299 1.000
 0.261 0.138 0.380 0.150 0.559 1.000
 0.320 0.162 0.411 0.166 0.598 0.647 1.000
Means: 35.903 0.000 9.593 9.216 49.732 1.665 3.271
Standard Deviations: 7.766 1.000 6.588 6.729 40.243 2.227
3.541
Latent Variables Ability Debt
Relationships
AGE ED EMPLOY ADDRESS INCOME = Ability
CREDDEBT OTHDEBT = Debt
Debt = Ability
Number of Decimals = 3
Path Diagram
End of Problem
```

The theoretical model analysis indicated that the normal theory model fit results were **not** adequate ($\chi^2 = 428.22$, $df = 13$, $p = 0.0001$, RMSEA = 0.210). We therefore examined the modification indices to determine any substantive model modifications.

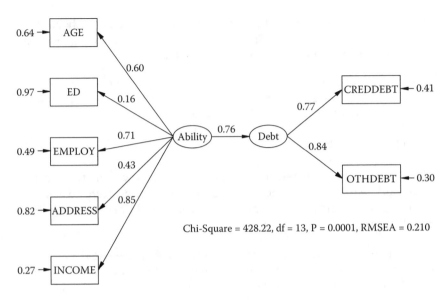

FIGURE 15.2b
Mixture Model output.

15.2.3 Model Modification

The modification indices for Figure 15.2b suggested the following:

```
The Modification Indices Suggest to Add an Error Covariance
  Between       and       Decrease in Chi-Square   New Estimate

  AGE        CREDDEBT            10.0                 -1.30
  EMPLOY     AGE                 34.0                  8.11
  EMPLOY     ED                 144.9                 -2.28
  ADDRESS    OTHDEBT              8.9                 -1.76
  ADDRESS    AGE                182.0                 20.71
  INCOME     CREDDEBT            16.3                  8.41
  INCOME     OTHDEBT             14.8                 12.86
  INCOME     AGE                 60.3                -72.01
  INCOME     ED                  74.6                  9.49
  INCOME     ADDRESS             38.0                -45.95
```

We felt that *EMPLOY* (years with current employer), *ED* (education level), *ADDRESS* (years at current address), and *AGE* were very much related to each other. We therefore added the following commands in the LISREL–SIMPLIS program to correlate their respective error covariance:

```
Let error covariance of EMPLOY and ED correlate
Let error covariance of ADDRESS and AGE correlate
Let error covariance of EMPLOY and AGE correlate
```

Our results continued to indicate a poor model fit (Normal theory χ^2 = 47.73, df = 10, p = 0.0001, RMSEA = 0.072). We therefore examined additional modification indices from our second analysis:

```
The Modification Indices Suggest to Add an Error Covariance
  Between        and     Decrease in Chi-Square    New Estimate
  ED            AGE              12.5                 -0.75
  ADDRESS       ED               14.8                  0.73
  ADDRESS       EMPLOY           30.8                  6.53
```

These modifications also seemed reasonable given how years with current employer; years at current address, age, and education were related. We therefore added the following additional command lines to the LISREL–SIMPLIS program:

```
Let error covariance of EMPLOY and ADDRESS correlate
Let error covariance of ADDRESS and ED correlate
Let error covariance of AGE and ED correlate
```

The final theoretical model was therefore modified to include all of these error covariance correlations with corresponding command lines added to the LISREL–SIMPLIS program (Jöreskog & Sorbom, 1996c). The final LISREL–SIMPLIS program, *bankloan.psf*, was therefore modified as follows:

```
Mixture Model Using Polyserial Correlation Matrix
Observed Variables: AGE ED EMPLOY ADDRESS INCOME CREDDEBT
    OTHDEBT
Sample Size 723
Correlation Matrix
1.000
 0.041 1.000
 0.524 -0.163 1.000
 0.589 0.099 0.335 1.000
 0.454 0.251 0.610 0.299 1.000
 0.261 0.138 0.380 0.150 0.559 1.000
 0.320 0.162 0.411 0.166 0.598 0.647 1.000
Means: 35.903 0.000 9.593 9.216 49.732 1.665 3.271
Standard Deviations: 7.766 1.000 6.588 6.729 40.243 2.227
3.541
Latent Variables Ability Debt
Relationships
AGE ED EMPLOY ADDRESS INCOME = Ability
CREDDEBT OTHDEBT = Debt
Debt = Ability
Let error covariance of EMPLOY and ED correlate
Let error covariance of ADDRESS and AGE correlate
Let error covariance of EMPLOY and AGE correlate
```

```
Let error covariance of EMPLOY and ADDRESS correlate
Let error covariance of ADDRESS and ED correlate
Let error covariance of AGE and ED correlate
Number of Decimals = 3
Path Diagram
End of Problem
```

The theoretical model now had an adequate fit to the bank loan data (Normal Theory $\chi^2 = 5.69$, $df = 7$, $p = 0.57607$, RMSEA = 0.00). However, we recalled that mixture models should report robust statistics which will require using an asymptotic covariance matrix in addition to the sample covariance matrix and maximum likelihood estimation method. So we next describe how to obtain the Satorra–Bentler scaled robust statistic.

15.2.4 Robust Statistic

Our SEM analysis required a polyserial correlation matrix because we had a mixture of variables (ordinal and continuous). We should therefore be reporting a robust chi-square statistic not a normal theory chi-square statistic. How do I obtain the Satorra–Bentler Chi-square robust statistic value? We first open the PRELIS system file, *bankloan.psf,* and then save a covariance matrix (*bankloan.cov*) and an asymptotic covariance matrix (*bankloan.acm*) using the **Statistics** pull down menu and *Output Option* as seen in the dialog box below:

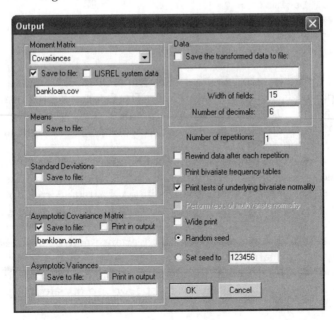

Our LISREL–SIMPLIS program is now modified to include the *Covariance matrix from file*, *Asymptotic Covariance Matrix from File*, and *Method of Estimation: Maximum Likelihood* commands. The computer output under *Goodness-of-Fit* statistics will now include the robust Satorra–Bentler scaled chi-square statistic. The updated LISREL–SIMPLIS program with these commands would be:

```
Mixture Model using Polyserial Correlation Matrix
Observed Variables: AGE ED EMPLOY ADDRESS INCOME CREDDEBT
    OTHDEBT
Sample Size 723
Covariance matrix from file bankloan.cov
Asymptotic Covariance Matrix from File bankloan.acm
Method of Estimation: Maximum Likelihood
Latent Variables Ability Debt
Relationships
AGE ED EMPLOY ADDRESS INCOME = Ability
CREDDEBT OTHDEBT = Debt
Debt = Ability
Let error covariance of EMPLOY and ED correlate
Let error covariance of ADDRESS and AGE correlate
Let error covariance of EMPLOY and AGE correlate
Let error covariance of EMPLOY and ADDRESS correlate
Let error covariance of ADDRESS and ED correlate
Let error covariance of AGE and ED correlate
Number of Decimals = 3
Path Diagram
End of Problem
```

The final theoretical model with the Satorra–Bentler scaled chi-square statistic reported is shown in Figure 15.2c. The Satorra–Bentler Scaled $\chi^2 = 3.419$, $df = 7$, $p = 0.844$ for the theoretical model compared to the Normal Theory $\chi^2 = 5.69$, $df = 7$, $p = 0.57607$. We should expect the robust statistic to indicate a better model fit.

The SEM mixture model permits continuous and categorical variables to be used in a theoretical model. The mixture model however uses a different correlation matrix than the traditional Pearson correlation matrix with means and standard deviations. Consequently, you will need to use PRELIS to read in a data set and output a polyserial correlation matrix. Additionally, you will need to save a covariance matrix and an asymptotic covariance matrix in PRELIS and include it in the SIMPLIS program along with maximum likelihood estimation method to obtain the Satorra–Bentler scaled chi-square statistic for appropriate interpretation of the mixture model.

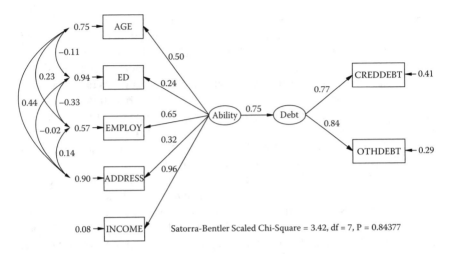

FIGURE 15.2c
Modified Mixture Model (Satorra–Bentler scaled Chi-square).

15.3 Multilevel Models

Multilevel models in SEM are so named because of the hierarchical nature of data in a nested research design. For example, in education a student's academic achievement is based in classrooms, so students are nested in classrooms, teachers are nested within schools, and schools are nested within districts. The nested research design is in contrast to a crossed research design where every level is represented. In multilevel models our interest is in the effects at different levels given the clustered nature of the data. A simple schematic will illustrate multilevel versus crossed designs.

Multilevel Design: Four teachers are indicated at two schools; however, teachers 1 and 2 are in School A, while teachers 3 and 4 are in School B.

School		A		B	
Teacher	1	2	3	4	

Crossed Design: Four teachers are indicated at two schools with all four teachers in both schools.

School	A	B
Teacher	1 2 3 4	1 2 3 4

Several textbooks introduce and present excellent multilevel examples, so we refer you to those for more information on the analysis of multilevel models in SEM (Heck & Thomas, 2000; Hox, 2002). We have also provided a few journal article references that have used the multilevel approach.

LISREL provides an extensive *HELP* library on multilevel modeling that includes an overview of multilevel modeling; differences between OLS and multilevel random coefficient models (MRCM); latent growth curve models; testing of contrasts; analysis of two-level repeated measures data; multivariate analysis of educational data; multilevel models for categorical response variables; and examples using air traffic control data, school, and survey data. Consequently, you are encouraged to use the HELP library in LISREL for more information and examples using PRELIS and SIMPLIS or read about the new statistical features in LISREL by Karl Jöreskog, Dag Sörbom, Stephen du Toit and Mathilda du Toit (2001).

In LISREL, you will be using the **multilevel** tool bar menu to demonstrate *variance decomposition*, which is a basic multilevel model (equivalent to a one-way ANOVA with random effects). The multilevel *null model* is a preliminary first step in a multilevel analysis because it provides important information about the variability of the dependent variable. You should always create a null model (intercept only) to serve as a baseline for comparing additional multilevel models when you add variables to test whether they significantly reduce the unexplained variability in the dependent variable (response or outcome variable).

In LISREL 8.8, student version, find the directory that is labeled, *LISREL 8.8 Student Examples,* then select the *mlevelex* folder, next select the *files of type* which indicates PRELIS DATA (*.psf). You will now see PRELIS SYSTEM FILES (*.psf). Select MOUSE. The dialog box should look like the following:

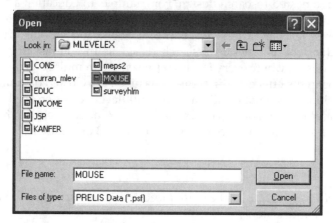

MOUSE.PSF is a nested data set with nine weight measurements taken at nine time periods on 82 mice. The data set should contain $n = 738$ rows of data (9×82), however, the data set only contains $n = 698$ rows of data because some weights are missing for the mice, for example, iden2 = 43, 44, 45, etc. The variables in the *MOUSE.PSF* system file are iden2, iden1, weight, constant, time, timesq, and gender. The dialog box below displays the spreadsheet with these variables.

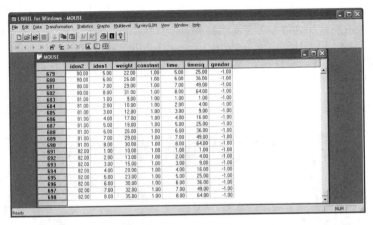

The **multilevel** command now appears on the tool bar menu with linear and nonlinear model options. Now select **Linear Model,** and then **Title and Options**. You will be specifying variables for each of the options shown here, but this is accomplished by selecting **NEXT** after you enter the information for **Title and Options**. You can enter the title *Mouse Data: Variance Decomposition* in the dialog box as indicated below, and then click **NEXT**.

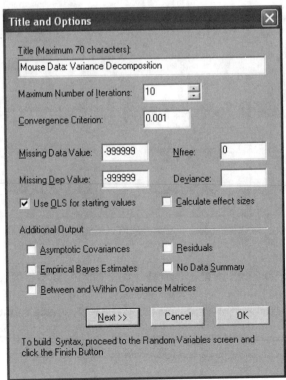

This takes us to the **Identification Variables** dialog box where you will add *ident2* to level 3 and *ident1* to level 2. The variable *ident2* ranges from 1 to 82 and identifies the unique mouse, while *ident1* indicates the 9 time measurements and ranges from 1 to 9. The dialog box should look like the one below:

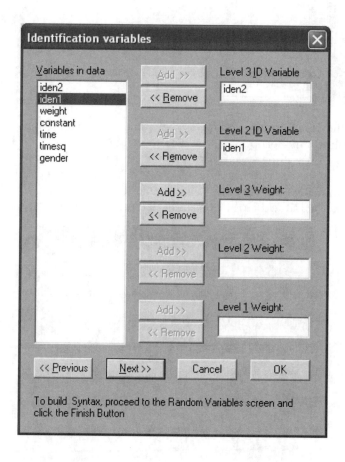

You again click NEXT. This takes us to the Select Response and Fixed Variables dialog box where you add *weight* as the select response (dependent variable and *constant* as a fixed effect to create an intercept only (null) model). Be sure to unselect the *Intercept* box in this dialog box as indicated below:

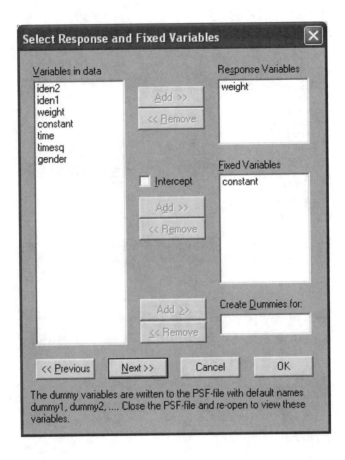

You again click NEXT. This takes you to the Random Variables dialog box where you will add *constant* to both random Level 3 and random Level 2. *Constant* is the intercept term for the response variable (*weight*) and associates an error term for the Level 3 and Level 2 equations. Be sure to unselect the *Intercept* boxes in this dialog box for *ALL RANDOM LEVELS* as indicated below:

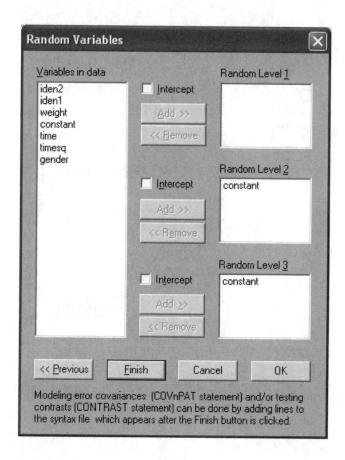

Now click FINISH and a PRELIS program, *mouse.pr2* is written.

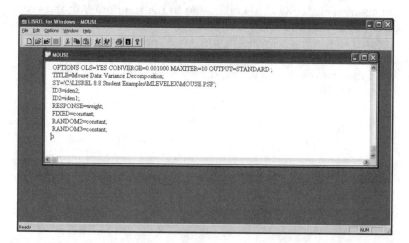

The PRELIS program is executed by clicking the run P (Run PRELIS) on the tool bar menu. The PRELIS computer output will now indicate the fixed and random results for the baseline model (intercept only). (*Note:* Do not use the term *constant* in your model and also select intercept in the dialog boxes.)

15.3.1 Constant Effects

The PRELIS computer output for the baseline model (*constant*) is as follows:

```
        +------------------------------------+
        |  FIXED PART OF MODEL  |
        +------------------------------------+

-------------------------------------------------------------------
COEFFICIENTS    BETA-HAT     STD.ERR.     Z-VALUE     PR > |Z|
-------------------------------------------------------------------
constant        28.63410     0.57021      50.21634    0.00000

        +--------------------------------+
        |  -2 LOG-LIKELIHOOD  |
        +--------------------------------+

DEVIANCE= -2*LOG(LIKELIHOOD)  = 5425.490015929897
NUMBER OF FREE PARAMETERS = 3

        +----------------------------------+
        |  RANDOM PART OF MODEL  |
        +----------------------------------+

-------------------------------------------------------------------
LEVEL 3              TAU-HAT    STD.ERR.   Z-VALUE    PR > |Z|
-------------------------------------------------------------------
constant/constant    11.32910   4.25185    2.66451    0.00771
-------------------------------------------------------------------
LEVEL 2              TAU-HAT    STD.ERR.   Z-VALUE    PR > |Z|
-------------------------------------------------------------------
constant/constant    130.32083  7.42514    17.55130   0.00000
```

15.3.2 Time Effects

The second multilevel analysis includes adding *time* to the fixed variable list. To do so, click on Multilevel, Linear Models, and then Select Response and Fixed Variables in the drop-down menu. Now add *time* to the fixed variable list as indicated in the dialog box below. You will click NEXT. Do not change the *Random Variables* dialog box that appears; simply click FINISH.

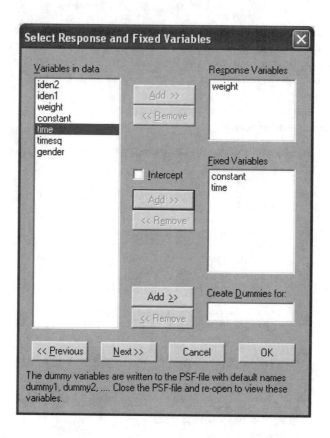

The following PRELIS program will appear in a dialog box with time added to the FIXED command. To run the updated PRELIS file, *mouse.pr2*, click on run P (Run PRELIS).

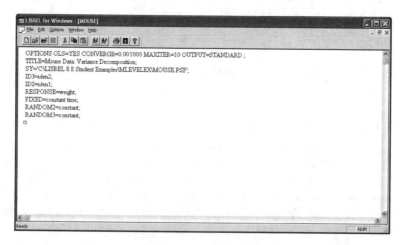

The PRELIS computer output for both *constant* (baseline) plus *time* is as follows:

```
+------------------------------------+
| FIXED PART OF MODEL |
+------------------------------------+
```

```
---------------------------------------------------------------
COEFFICIENTS BETA-HAT STD.ERR. Z-VALUE PR > |Z|
---------------------------------------------------------------
constant 9.09586 0.60387 15.06258 0.00000
time 4.09218 0.06258 65.39108 0.00000
```

```
+------------------------------------+
| -2 LOG-LIKELIHOOD |
+------------------------------------+
```

```
DEVIANCE= -2*LOG(LIKELIHOOD) = 4137.578760208256
NUMBER OF FREE PARAMETERS = 4
```

```
+------------------------------------+
| RANDOM PART OF MODEL |
+------------------------------------+
```

```
---------------------------------------------------------------
LEVEL 3            TAU-HAT    STD.ERR.    Z-VALUE    PR > |Z|
---------------------------------------------------------------
constant/constant  20.69397   3.53655     5.85146    0.00000
---------------------------------------------------------------
LEVEL 2            TAU-HAT    STD.ERR.    Z-VALUE    PR > |Z|
---------------------------------------------------------------
constant/constant  16.46288   0.93806    17.54996    0.00000
```

15.3.3 Gender Effects

We repeat this process a third time to add *gender* to the fixed variables for a final multilevel analysis. To do so, click on Multilevel, Linear Models, and then Select Response and Fixed Variables in the drop-down menu. Now add *gender* to the fixed variable list as indicated in the dialog box below. You will click NEXT. Do not change the *Random Variables* dialog box that appears; simply click FINISH. The *Select Response and Fixed Variables* dialog box should look like the following:

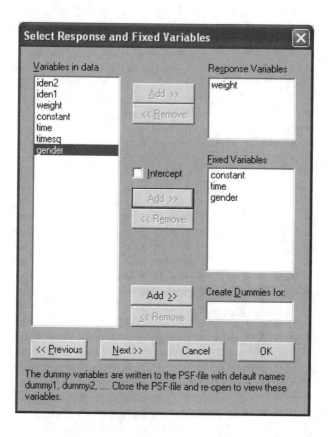

The following PRELIS program will appear in a dialog box with *gender* added to the FIXED command. To run the updated PRELIS file, *mouse.pr2*, click on run P (Run PRELIS). The following PRELIS program should appear:

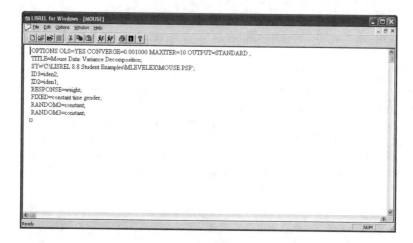

The PRELIS computer output with constant, time, and gender is as follows:

```
+-----------------------------------+
| FIXED PART OF MODEL |
+-----------------------------------+
```

```
-----------------------------------------------------------------
COEFFICIENTS  BETA-HAT      STD.ERR.      Z-VALUE         PR >
|Z|
-----------------------------------------------------------------
constant       9.07800       0.58325      15.56442
0.00000
time    4.08714             0.06261       65.28249        0.00000
gender  1.42015             0.50199        2.82904        0.00467
```

```
+-----------------------------------+
| -2 LOG-LIKELIHOOD |
+-----------------------------------+
```

DEVIANCE = -2*LOG(LIKELIHOOD) = 4129.941071012016
NUMBER OF FREE PARAMETERS = 5

```
+-------------------------------------+
| RANDOM PART OF MODEL |
+-------------------------------------+
```

LEVEL 3	TAU-HAT	STD.ERR.	Z-VALUE	PR > $\|Z\|$
constant/constant	18.68475	3.22290	5.79750	0.00000

LEVEL 2	TAU-HAT	STD.ERR.	Z-VALUE	PR > $\|Z\|$
constant/constant	16.46249	0.93804	17.54996	0.00000

You have now created and run three different PRELIS programs to obtain the multilevel analysis results for an intercept model (model 1), intercept and time model (model 2), and an intercept, time, and gender model (model 3). The PRELIS program, *mouse.pr2*, was updated each time you changed the number of fixed variables. The three PRELIS programs are listed below where it is easily seen that the FIXED command changed as you added additional hypothesized variables to obtain a better prediction of the unexplained variability of the response variable (*weight*).

```
Model 1—Intercept Only
OPTIONS OLS=YES CONVERGE=0.001000 MAXITER=10 OUTPUT=STANDARD ;
 TITLE=Mouse Data: Variance Decomposition;
 SY='C:\LISREL 8.8 Student Examples\MLEVELEX\MOUSE.PSF';
 ID3=iden2;
 ID2=iden1;
 RESPONSE=weight;
 FIXED=constant;
 RANDOM2=constant;
 RANDOM3=constant;
Model 2 - Intercept + Time
OPTIONS OLS=YES CONVERGE=0.001000 MAXITER=10 OUTPUT=STANDARD ;
 TITLE=Mouse Data: Variance Decomposition;
 SY='C:\LISREL 8.8 Student Examples\MLEVELEX\MOUSE.PSF';
 ID3=iden2;
 ID2=iden1;
 RESPONSE=weight;
 FIXED=constant time;
 RANDOM2=constant;
 RANDOM3=constant;
Model 3 - Intercept + Time + Gender
OPTIONS OLS=YES CONVERGE=0.001000 MAXITER=10 OUTPUT=STANDARD ;
 TITLE=Mouse Data: Variance Decomposition;
 SY='C:\LISREL 8.8 Student Examples\MLEVELEX\MOUSE.PSF';
 ID3=iden2;
 ID2=iden1;
 RESPONSE=weight;
 FIXED=constant time gender;
 RANDOM2=constant;
 RANDOM3=constant;
```

The final multilevel equation is specified as:

$$Y_{ij} = \beta_1 + \beta_2\, Time_{ij} + \beta_2\, Gender_{ij} + u_{ij} + e_{ij}.$$

The PRELIS computer results are summarized in Table 15.1 for comparative purposes. (*Note*: Other multilevel models could include random effects rather than only fixed effects.)

15.3.4 Multilevel Model Interpretation

The computer output for the three PRELIS multilevel programs are summarized in Table 15.1 for the variance decomposition of the response variable, *weight*. Model 1 provides a baseline model to determine if additional variables help in reducing the amount of variability in *weight*. Model 2 with *time* added, substantially reduced the unexplained variability in

TABLE 15.1

Summary Results for Multilevel Analysis of Mouse Weight

Multilevel Model Fixed Factors	Model 1 Constant Only	Model 2 Constant + Time	Model 3 Constant + Time + Gender
Intercept Only(B_0)	28.63 (.57)	9.09 (.60)	9.07 (.58)
Time (B_1)		4.09 (.06)	4.08 (.06)
Gender (B_2)			1.42 (.50)
Level 2 error variance (e_{ij})	130.32	16.46	16.46
Level 3 error variance (u_{ij})	11.33	20.69	18.68
ICC	.079 (8%)	.556 (56%)	.532 (53%)
Deviance (-2LL)	5425.49	4137.57	4129.94
Df	3	4	5
Chi-square Difference (df = 1)		1287.92	7.63

Note: $\chi^2 = 3.84$, $df = 1$, $p = .05$.

weight ($\chi^2 = 1287.92$, $df = 1$). Model 3 with *gender* added also significantly reduced the amount of unexplained variability in *weight* ($\chi^2 = 7.63$, $df = 1$). Therefore, mouse *weight* variability is statistically significantly explained by *time* and *gender* fixed variables.

15.3.5 Intraclass Correlation

The intraclass correlation coefficient measures the relative homogeneity within groups in ratio to the total variation. In ANOVA it is computed as (Between-groups MS – Within-groups MS)/(Between-groups MS + $(n - 1)^*$ Within-Groups MS), where n is the average number of cases in each category of the independent variable. SPSS has a drop-down menu option for computing the intraclass correlation coefficient in your data.

If the intraclass correlation coefficient is large and positive, then there is no variation within the groups, but group means differ. It will be at its largest negative value when group means are the same but there is great variation within groups. Its maximum value is 1.0, but its maximum negative value is $(-1/(n - 1))$. A negative intraclass correlation coefficient occurs when between-group variation is less than within-group variation, indicating a third variable is present with nonrandom effects on the different groups.

The presence of a significant intraclass correlation coefficient indicates the need to employ multilevel modeling rather than OLS regression. The main difference is in the standard errors of the parameters, which have smaller estimates in regression analysis if the intraclass correlation coefficient is statistically significant, which can inflate (bias) the regression weights. The intraclass correlation coefficient, using our results, is computed in SEM as:

$$\text{ICC} = \frac{\Phi_3}{\Phi_3 + \Phi_2} = \frac{Tau - Hat(Level - 3)}{Tau - Hat(Level - 3) + Tau - Hat(Level - 2)}$$

$$= \frac{11.33}{11.33 + 130.32} = .079$$

Therefore, 8% of the variance in *weight* is explained in the baseline model. It jumps dramatically when adding *time* as an explanatory variable to 56% variance in *weight*, explained as a function of *time*. It drops modestly to 53% when adding *gender* to the equation. The 3% difference is not enough to infer a nonsignificant effect; therefore *time* and *gender* significantly explain 53% of the variance in mice *weight*.

15.3.6 Deviance Statistic

The deviance statistic is computed as $-2lnL$ (likelihood function), which is used to test for statistical difference in models between Model 1 (constant), Model 2 (constant + time), and Model 3 (constant + time + gender). I chose the chi-square value of 3.84, $df = 1$, at the $p = .05$ level of significance to test whether additional variables in the equation explained variance in mice *weight*. The baseline deviance value was 5425.49. The chi-square difference test between this baseline deviance statistic and the second equation deviance value with time ($-2lnL = 4137.57$) indicated a difference of 1287.92, which is statistically significantly different than the tabled critical chi-square value of 3.84. Consequently, *time* was a significant predictor variable of mice *weight*. The model with *time* and *gender* indicated a deviance statistic of 4129.94 and had a difference from the previous deviance statistic of 7.63, which was also statistically significantly different from the critical tabled chi-square of 3.84. Consequently, *time* and *gender* were statistically significant predictor variables of mice *weight*.

15.4 Summary

In this chapter, we have described MIMIC, mixture, and multilevel modeling, to further demonstrate the versatility of structural equation modeling. The first application presented a SEM model that had multiple indicators of a latent variable where the latent variable was predicted by multiple observed variables. We refer to this type of SEM model as a

Multiple Indicator and Multiple Cause (MIMIC) model. The next application involved models that used ordinal and continuous variables. We refer to this type of SEM model as a Mixture Model. In this application, we learned that normal theory fit indices apply to continuous variables that use a Pearson Correlation Matrix with means and standard deviations of the variables, but that other matrices should be used when ordinal and continuous variables are present in the SEM model (for example, polychoric or polyserial matrices). Our final application involved analyzing nested data, which has become increasingly popular in repeated measures, survey, and education data analysis because of the hierarchical research design. In SEM, we refer to this type of model as a Multilevel model, but in the research literature this type of model is referred to by many different names—for example, hierarchical linear, random-coefficient, variance-component modeling, or HLM.

The chapter presented only one example for each of the applications because a more in depth coverage is beyond the scope of this book. However, the LISREL software *HELP* library and examples can be searched by using keywords to find other software examples and explanations. The LISREL User Guide is also an excellent reference for other examples of these applications. We now turn our attention to the next chapter where other SEM applications are presented and discussed.

Exercises

1. MULTIPLE INDICATOR–MULTIPLE CAUSE (MIMIC) MODEL

Create and run a LISREL–SIMPLIS program given the MIMIC model below. Please interpret the results including any model modification, significance of coefficients, and R^2 value. The data set information is:

```
Observed Variables peer self income shift age
Sample Size 530
Correlation Matrix
1.00
 .42 1.00
 .24 .35 1.00
 .13 .37 .25 1.00
 .33 .51 .66 .20 1.00
```

The following MIMIC Model (next page) includes the latent variable *job satisfaction* (satisfac), which is defined in Figure 15.3 by two observed variables: peer ratings and self ratings. A person's income level, which shift they work, and age are observed predictor variables of *job satisfaction*.

2. MIXTURE MODEL

Given the following Miture Model in Figure 15.4 and data set information, write a LISREL program to test the Mixture Model. (*Note:* Robust

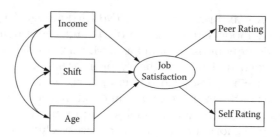

FIGURE 15.3
Job Satisfaction MIMIC model.

statistics require the raw data file, so no Satorra–Bentler scaled chi-square possible). The Mixture Model has six observed variables (*Age, Gender, Degree, Region, Hours,* and *Income*) that define two latent variables (*Person* and *Earning*). A polyserial correlation matrix was created where CO indicates continuous variable and OR indicates a categorical variable. *Age* (CO), *Gender* (OR), and *Degree* (OR) define Personal characteristics, an independent latent variable (*Person*). *Region* (OR), *Hours* (CO), and *Income* (CO) define dependent latent variable Earning Power (*Earning*). Personal Characteristics (*Person*) is hypothesized to predict Earning Power (*Earning*).

The data for the Mixture Model is:

```
Observed Variables: Age Gender Degree Region Hours Income
Correlation Matrix
 1.000
 0.487 1.000
 0.236 0.206 1.000
 0.242 0.179 0.253 1.000
 0.163 0.090 0.125 0.481 1.000
 0.064 0.040 0.025 0.106 0.136 1.000
Means 15.00 10.000 10.000 10.000 7.000 10.000
Standard Deviations 10.615 10.000 8.000 10.000 15.701
10.000
Sample Size 600
```

The Mixture Model diagram is:

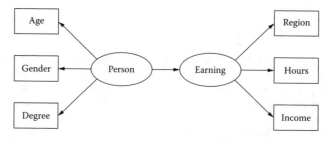

FIGURE 15.4
Earning Power Mixture Model.

3. MULTILEVEL MODEL

You will need to access the directory, *LISREL 8.8 Student Examples*. Click on the *mlevelex* folder and select the PRELIS system file, *income.psf,* which contains the variables *region, state, age, gender, marital,* etc. There are nine regions with 51 states nested within the regions. The sample size is $n = 6062$. It is hypothesized that income varies by state within region.

Open the PRELIS system file, *income.psf,* and run three PRELIS multilevel model programs. The first model will be an intercept only model with *income* as the response variable, Level 3 or ID3 = *region*, and Level 2 or ID2 = *state*. The second PRELIS program will add *gender* as a fixed variable. The third PRELIS program will add an additional variable, *marital,* as a fixed variable. Use the multilevel pull-down menu on the tool bar to create the programs. (*Note:* Unselect the Intercept box in each dialog box).

List Model 1, Model 2, and Model 3 PRELIS programs and summarize the output from the three PRELIS programs in a table. You will need to hand calculate the intraclass correlation coefficient and be sure to interpret the comparative results in the table. The MODEL 1 dialog box should look like the following:

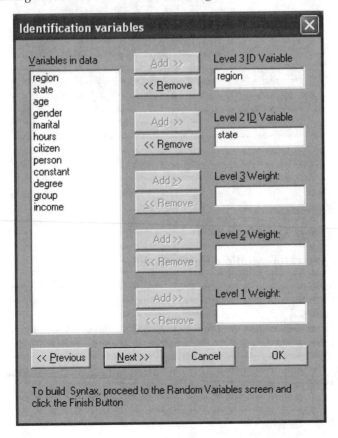

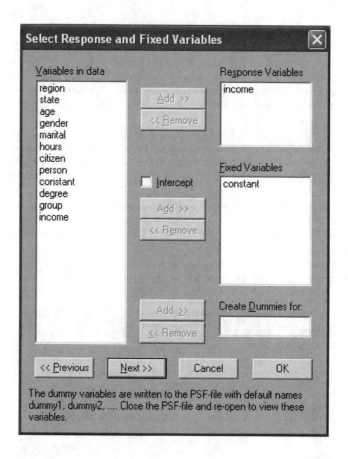

Suggested Readings

Multiple Indicator–Multiple Cause Models

Anderson, K. G., Smith, G. T., & McCarthy, D. M. (2005). Elementary school drinking: The role of temperament and learning. *Psychology of Addictive Behaviors,* 19(1), 21–27.

Sanchez-Perez, M., & Iniesta-Bonillo, M. A. (2004, Winter). Consumers felt commitment towards retailers: Index development and validation. *Journal of Business and Psychology,* 19(2), 141–159.

Shenzad, S. (2006). The determinants of child health in Pakistan: An economic analysis. *Social Indicators Research, 78,* 531–556.

Mixture Models

Bagley, M. N., & Mokhtarian, P. L. (2002). The impact of residential neighborhood type on travel behavior: A structural equations modeling approach. *The Annals of Regional Science, 36*, 279-297.

Loken, E. (2004). Using latent class analysis to model temperament types. *Multivariate Behavioral Research, 39(4)*, 625-652.

Lubke, G. H., & Muthen, B. (2005). Investigating population heterogeneity with factor mixture models. *Psychological Methods, 10*, 21–39.

Multilevel Models

Bryan, A., Schmiege, S. J., & Broaddus, M. R. (2007). Mediational analysis in HIV/AIDS research: Estimating multivariate path analytic models in a structural equation modeling framework. *AIDS Behavior, 11*, 365–383.

Everson, H. T., & Millsap, R. E. (2004). Beyond individual differences: Exploring school effects on SAT scores. *Educational Psychologist, 39(3)*, 157–172.

Trautwein, U., Ludtke, O., Schnyder, I., & Niggli, A. (2006). Predicting homework effect: Support for a domain-specific, multilevel homework model. *Journal of Educational Psychology, 98*, 438–456.

References

Heck, R. H., & Thomas, S. L. (2000). *An introduction to multilevel modeling techniques.* Mahwah, NJ: Lawrence Erlbaum.

Hox, J. (2002). *Multilevel analysis: Techniques and applications.* Mahwah, NJ: Lawrence Erlbaum.

Jöreskog, K., & Sörbom, D. (1996a). *LISREL 8: User's reference guide.* Chicago, IL: Scientific Software International.

Jöreskog, K., & Sörbom, D. (1996b). *PRELIS2: User's reference guide.* Chicago, IL: Scientific Software International.

Jöreskog, K., & Sörbom, D. (1996c). *LISREL 8: Structural equation modeling with the SIMPLIS command language.* Chicago, IL: Scientific Software International.

Jöreskog, K., Sörbom, D., du Toit, S., & du Toit, M. (2001). *LISREL8: New statistical features.* Chicago, IL: Scientific Software International.

16

Interaction, Latent Growth, and Monte Carlo Methods

Key Concepts

Main effects and Interaction Effects

Types of Interaction Effects: continuous nonlinear, categorical, latent variable

Longitudinal data analysis using growth curve models

Monte Carlo methods

16.1 Interaction Models

Most SEM models have assumed that the relations in the models were linear (i.e., the relations among all variables, observed and latent, are represented by linear equations). Several studies have been published where nonlinear and interaction effects are used in multiple regression models; however, these effects have seldom been tested in path models, and you will infrequently find nonlinear factor models. It should not be surprising to find that for several decades structural equation modeling has been based on Linear Structural Relations (LISREL).

SEM models with nonlinear and interaction effects are now possible and can easily be modeled with recent versions of SEM software. However, there are several types of nonlinear and interaction effects: categorical, product indicant, nonlinear, two-stage least squares, and latent variable using normal scores. For continuous observed variables, a nonlinear relationship could exist between two observed variables (i.e., X_1 and X_2 are curvilinear); a quadratic (nonlinear) term in the model (i.e., $X_2 = X_1^2$); or a product of two observed variables (e.g., $X_3 = X_1 X_2$).

These three different types of interaction effects all involve *continuous* observed variables. For *categorical* observed variables, interaction effects are similar to analysis-of-variance and use the multiple-group SEM model (Schumacker & Rigdon, 1995). These continuous variable and categorical variable approaches also apply to latent variables (e.g., latent variable and latent class).

Given that so many different approaches exist, the categorical, latent variable and two-stage least squares examples will be illustrated. Categorical interaction uses a multigroup (multisample) SEM model. The latent variable interaction uses the product of individual latent variable scores that are computed and added to the PRELIS system file.

16.1.1 Categorical Variable Approach

In the categorical variable interaction approach, different groups (samples) are defined by the different levels of the interaction variable. The basic logic is that if interaction effects are present, then certain parameters should have different values in different groups (samples). Both main effects and interaction effects can be determined by using different groups (samples) to test for differences between intercepts and slopes. You accomplish this by running two different SEM categorical variable interaction models: (1) main effects for group differences holding slopes constant, and (2) interaction effects for group differences with both intercepts and slopes estimated. These models are sometimes referred to as intercept only and intercept-slope models.

The following two LISREL–SIMPLIS programs analyze data for two groups: boys versus girls, where *group* represents the categorical variable. Separate covariance matrices and means on the dependent and independent variable are input to estimate the prediction of a math score, given a pretest score. The means are required; otherwise, the intercept values will be zero. The first LISREL–SIMPLIS program includes **Equation: Math = CONST Pretest** for the girls, but only **Equation: Math = CONST** for the boys, which permits different intercept values to be estimated while keeping the slopes equal in the two groups:

```
Group Girls: Math and Pretest Scores
Observed Variables: Math Pretest
Covariance Matrix:
181.349
 84.219 182.821
Means: 82.15 78.35
Sample Size: 373
Equation: Math = CONST Pretest
Group Boys: Math and Pretest Scores
```

```
Covariance Matrix:
174.485
 34.468 161.869
Means: 48.75 46.98
Sample Size: 249
Equation: Math = CONST
End of Problem
```

The results indicated that the slopes were equal (slope = .37), and the intercepts were different (53.26 versus 31.43). The main effect model for differences in intercepts with equal slopes, however, was not an acceptable fit ($\chi^2 = 12.24$, $p = .002$, $df = 2$).

Girls Group:

```
Math = 53.26 + 0.37*Pretest, Errorvar. = 155.07, R² = 0.14
     (3.04)   (0.038)          (8.81)
     17.53     9.73            17.59
```

Boys Group:

```
Math = 31.43 + 0.37*Pretest, Errorvar. = 155.07, R² = 0.12
     (1.95)   (0.038)          (8.81)
     16.13     9.73            17.59
```

The second LISREL–SIMPLIS program uses the **Equation: Math = CONST Pretest** in both groups, thus specifying that both intercepts and slopes are being tested for group differences. Conceptually, this implies a difference in the means (intercept) and a difference in the rate of change (slope).

```
Group Girls: Math and Pretest Scores
Observed Variables: Math Pretest
Covariance Matrix:
181.349
 84.219 182.821
Means: 82.15 78.35
Sample Size: 373
Equation: Math = CONST Pretest
Group Boys: Math and Pretest Scores
Covariance Matrix:
174.485
 34.468 161.869
Means: 48.75 46.98
Sample Size: 249
Equation: Math = CONST Pretest
End of Problem
```

The results indicated that the intercepts (46.06 versus 38.75) and slopes (.46 versus .21) were different in the two groups. This model with main and interaction effects present had an acceptable model fit ($\chi^2 = 1.98$, $p =.16$, $df = 1$). The main effect for group differences in math exam scores is given by the difference in the CONST values: $46.06 - 38.75 = 7.31$. The interaction effect is given by the difference in the slope estimates of pretest values for the two groups: $.46 - .21 = .25$.

Girls group:

```
Math = 46.06 + 0.46*Pretest, Errorvar. = 154.85, R² = 0.20
      (3.80)  (0.048)              (8.80)
      12.13    9.65                17.59
```

Boys group:

```
Math = 38.75 + 0.21*Pretest, Errorvar.= 154.85, R² = 0.045
      (3.03)  (0.062)              (8.80)
      12.81    3.43                17.59
```

A categorical variable interaction model can represent a wide variety of interaction effects, including higher-order interactions, without requiring any substantial new methodological developments. This approach can also be used regardless of whether the interaction intensifies or mutes the effects of the individual variables. Because the interaction effect is represented in the difference between groups (samples), the researcher is able to test linear relations of variables within each group (sample), thus avoiding any potential complications in fitting the model. Finally, multiple group (sample) programs permit parameter constraints across groups thereby permitting many different hypotheses of group differences.

The categorical interaction approach, however, does have certain weaknesses (e.g., smaller subsamples of the total sample size are used). This could be a serious problem if some groups have low sample sizes that affect group parameter estimates. This reduction in sample size could also affect the results of the χ^2 difference tests. Thus, it is possible that the categorical-variable approach may yield group samples that are too small, resulting in a χ^2 test statistic that misleads the researcher into believing that an interaction effect exists, whether it does or not. A possible solution is to minimize the number of distinct parameters being compared in the model by fixing certain parameters to be invariant across the samples being compared.

The categorical-variable interaction approach is not recommended when hypothesizing interaction using continuous variables. The basic logic is that there is a loss of information when reducing a continuous variable to a categorical variable, for purposes of defining a group (i.e., recode age into young and old categories). Group misspecification can also occur when forming groups. Where does one choose the point for dividing a continuous variable into a categorical variable to form the groups? How do you justify the arbitrary cut value (i.e., mean, median, or quartile)? Random-sampling error also ensures that some cases would be misclassified, violating some basic assumptions about subject membership in a particular group.

16.1.2 Latent Variable Interaction Model

A latent variable interaction model would hypothesize that the independent latent variables (*ksi1* and *ksi2*), as well as the product of *ksi1* and *ksi2* (*ksi12*), predict a dependent latent variable (*eta*). The latent variable interaction model is diagrammed in Figure 16.1a.

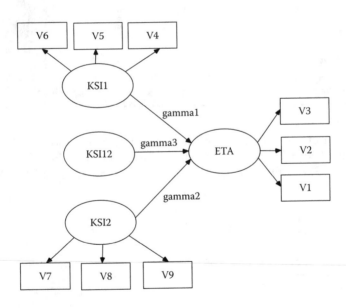

FIGURE 16.1a
Latent Variable Interaction Model (Schumacker, 2002).

16.1.2.1 *Computing Latent Variable Scores*

The latent interaction variable approach uses a PRELIS system file and intermediate steps to create and put latent variable scores into the PRELIS system file (*eta*, *ksi1*, *ksi2*, and *ksi12*).

In LISREL, click on **File, Open,** and then locate the PRELIS SYSTEM FILE, *raw.psf.*

You should see the following PRELIS system file spreadsheet with the 9 variables (V1 –V9). Also, a tool bar menu will appear across the top.

	V1	V2	V3	V4	V5	V6	V7	V8	V9
1	-1.09	0.38	-0.07	-1.26	-2.61	-0.80	0.78	0.04	1.37
2	-0.85	0.46	-0.30	-1.77	-0.88	-0.44	-1.72	-1.26	-1.11
3	-1.88	-0.63	-1.57	-0.95	-1.76	-1.24	0.53	2.00	2.35
4	1.27	0.87	1.61	0.32	-1.81	-1.75	-1.70	-1.12	-3.24
5	-0.12	0.95	0.14	-0.18	0.90	0.59	-0.04	0.38	1.22
6	0.45	-0.29	-0.72	-0.92	-1.79	-2.40	-1.07	-1.34	-0.12
7	1.50	-0.49	0.10	1.67	3.35	3.83	1.10	-1.20	-1.41
8	-1.50	0.13	-0.52	-1.99	-1.10	-0.09	-0.71	0.65	1.22
9	-0.80	-0.86	-2.00	0.05	-1.84	-4.29	-1.43	-2.21	-1.63
10	1.15	-0.25	0.51	0.35	0.11	0.13	-0.16	1.03	2.06
11	-0.08	2.25	1.03	0.46	1.19	1.85	-1.80	-0.72	0.86
12	-0.07	-0.25	0.34	0.91	1.93	1.28	0.77	1.77	0.53
13	-0.22	0.47	0.01	-0.12	1.45	2.10	0.92	1.10	0.89
14	-0.37	-0.08	-1.91	-0.03	0.90	-0.49	-0.40	-0.63	1.05
15	1.01	0.57	1.18	-1.20	-0.55	-0.97	-1.08	-1.56	-1.79
16	-0.37	-0.29	-2.00	-0.21	-0.80	-0.11	-2.08	-0.42	-1.53
17	-1.07	-0.72	-1.88	-1.84	-2.93	-2.59	-3.31	-2.55	-1.60
18	-0.79	-2.39	-2.54	1.00	-0.76	-1.29	-2.67	-2.55	-3.85
19	-0.86	-0.91	-0.86	1.17	1.08	2.20	0.19	1.20	1.90
20	-0.65	-0.33	-0.31	0.07	0.75	-0.55	-1.03	-0.72	0.53
21	1.41	2.22	1.22	-0.22	-0.03	-0.17	-2.58	-2.30	-1.77

You can create a dependent latent variable score and two independent latent variable scores, which will automatically be added to the PRELIS SYSTEM FILE, *raw.psf,* by using the following LISREL–SIMPLIS program:

```
Computing Latent Variable Scores
Observed Variables V1-V9
Raw Data from File raw.psf
Latent Variables : eta ksi1 ksi2
Relationships:
V1 = 1*eta
V2-V3 = eta
V4 = 1*ksi1
V5-V6 = ksi1
V7 = 1*ksi2
V8-V9 = ksi2
PSFfile raw.psf
End of Problem
```

(**NOTE:** You will need to close then open the PRELIS system file, *raw.psf,* before you will see values for the three latent variables: *eta, ksi1,* and *ksi2.*)

The PRELIS system file, *raw.psf*, is displayed below, and it does contain the three latent variables computed using the LISREL–SIMPLIS program above.

The LISREL for Windows - raw window displaying the raw.psf data table:

	V1	V2	V3	V4	V5	V6	V7	V8	V9	eta	ksi1	ksi2
1	-1.09	0.38	-0.07	-1.26	-2.61	-0.80	0.78	0.04	1.37	-0.04	-1.25	0.10
2	-0.85	0.46	-0.30	-1.77	-0.88	-0.44	-1.72	-1.26	2.35	-0.59	-0.45	-0.74
3	-1.88	-0.63	-1.57	-0.95	-1.76	-1.24	0.53	2.00	2.35	-0.59	-0.86	1.18
4	1.27	0.87	1.61	0.32	-1.81	-1.75	-1.70	-1.12	-3.24	0.60	-0.87	-0.74
5	-0.12	0.95	0.14	-0.18	0.90	0.59	-0.04	0.38	1.22	0.14	0.44	0.27
6	0.45	-0.29	-0.72	-0.92	-1.79	-2.40	-1.07	-1.34	-0.12	-0.19	-0.90	-0.74
7	1.50	-0.49	0.10	1.67	3.35	3.83	1.10	-1.20	-1.41	0.08	1.67	-0.62
8	-1.50	0.13	-0.52	-1.99	-1.10	-0.09	-0.71	0.65	1.22	-0.20	-0.54	0.39
9	-0.80	-0.86	-2.00	0.05	-1.84	-4.29	-1.43	-2.21	-1.63	-0.66	-0.94	-1.26
10	1.15	-0.25	0.51	0.35	0.11	0.13	-0.16	1.03	2.06	0.18	0.07	0.63
11	-0.08	2.25	1.03	0.46	1.19	1.85	-1.80	-0.72	0.86	0.53	0.60	-0.39
12	-0.07	-0.25	0.34	0.91	1.93	1.28	0.77	1.77	0.53	0.07	0.95	1.02
13	-0.22	0.47	0.01	-0.12	1.45	2.10	0.92	1.10	0.89	0.05	0.72	0.67
14	-0.37	-0.08	-1.91	-0.03	0.90	-0.49	-0.40	-0.63	1.05	-0.53	0.42	-0.28
15	1.01	0.57	1.18	-1.20	-0.55	-0.97	-1.08	-1.56	-1.79	0.45	-0.29	-0.91
16	-0.37	-0.29	-2.00	-0.21	-0.80	-0.11	-2.08	-0.42	-1.53	-0.58	-0.38	-0.31
17	-1.07	-0.72	-1.88	-1.84	-2.93	-2.59	-3.31	-2.55	-1.60	-0.63	-1.45	-1.50
18	-0.79	-2.39	-2.54	1.00	-0.76	-1.29	-2.67	-2.55	-3.85	-0.95	-0.36	-1.54
19	-0.86	-0.91	-0.86	1.17	1.08	2.20	0.19	1.20	1.90	-0.36	0.57	0.74
20	-0.65	-0.33	-0.31	0.07	0.75	-0.55	-1.03	-0.72	0.53	-0.13	0.35	-0.37
21	1.41	2.22	1.22	-0.22	-0.03	-0.17	-2.58	-2.30	-1.77	0.66	-0.02	-1.35
22	2.76	1.35	2.54	0.70	1.07	0.66	2.09	0.77	2.70	0.98	0.53	0.59

16.1.2.2 Computing Latent Interaction Variable

You create the latent interaction variable by multiplying the latent variable scores *ksi1* and *ksi2*. These latent variable scores are unbiased and produce the same mean and covariance matrix as the latent variables. A PRELIS program can be used to multiply the two independent latent variables to create the interaction latent variable, *ksi12*. The PRELIS **NE** command computes the latent interaction variable, which is automatically added to the PRELIS system file, *raw.psf*. The **CO** command will treat the new latent interaction variable as continuous rather than ordinal level of measurement. The PRELIS program is:

```
Create Latent Interaction Variable
SY = raw.psf
NE ksi12 = ksi1*ksi2
CO ksi12
OU RA = raw.psf
```

NOTE: You will need to close then open the PRELIS system file, *raw.psf*, before you will see the values for the interaction latent variable: *ksi12*. The PRELIS raw.psf file should now contain the latent interaction variable, *ksi12*, as shown below:

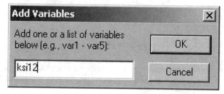

You could alternatively create the latent interaction variable without running a PRELIS program. Simply, open the PRELIS system file, *raw.psf*, select Transformation on the tool bar menu, then click on Compute, and underneath Add Variables, click on Add. You should see the Add Variables dialog box. Now, simply enter the name for the latent interaction variable: *ksi12*.

Click OK and then the COMPUTE dialog box should appear. Now enter the equation to create the new latent interaction variable. Follow the instructions to drag the variable names into an equation in the Compute dialog box. You can also obtain an equal sign (=) and a product sign (*) by using the symbols on the calculator. Click on OK, and the latent interaction variable will instantly appear in the PRELIS system file, *raw.psf*.

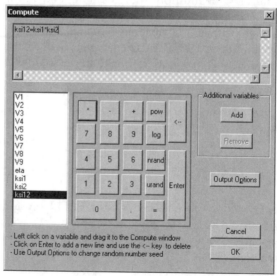

(NOTE: If you do not find the PRELIS System File, *raw.psf*, you can follow these same steps with your own continuous variables.)

16.1.2.3 Interaction Model Output

The PRELIS SYSTEM FILE, *raw.psf*, should now contain the latent interaction variable, *ksi12*. You can run a LISREL–SIMPLIS program to compute the coefficients (gammas) with or without an intercept term in the structural equation. A LISREL–SIMPLIS program to compute the coefficients *without an intercept term* is:

```
Latent Interaction Variable Model - No Intercept Term
Observed Variables: V1-V9 eta ksi1 ksi2 ksi12
Raw Data from File raw.psf
Sample Size = 500
Relationships:
eta = ksi1 ksi2 ksi12
Path Diagram
End of Problem
```

The resultant latent variable interaction model with standardized coefficient is diagrammed in Figure 16.1b.

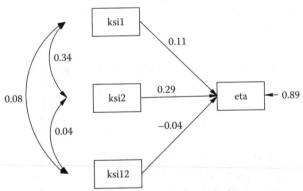

Chi-Square = 0.00, df = 0, P-value = 1.00000, RMSEA = 0.000

FIGURE 16.1b
Interaction Model Output.

The structural equation from the LISREL–SIMPLIS computer output *without the intercept term* is:

eta = 0.078*ksi1 + 0.16*ksi2 – 0.029*ksi12, Errorvar. = 0.21 , R^2 = 0.11
    (0.033)   (0.025)   (0.033)   (0.013)
     2.36   6.36   –0.89   15.75

16.1.2.4 Model Modification

The coefficient for the interaction latent variable, *ksi12*, is not statistically significant ($T = -0.89$). Therefore, you would drop this latent variable from the model and use only *ksi1* and *ksi2*.

The modified model output with standardized estimates would appear as diagrammed in Figure 16.1c.

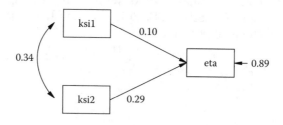

Chi-Square = 0.00, df = 0, P-value = 1.00000, RMSEA = 0.000

FIGURE 16.1c
Interaction Model Modified Output.

The program produces the following output, which yields the same R-squared value, hence the latent interaction variable did not contribute to the prediction of *eta*.

16.1.2.5 Structural Equations—No Latent Interaction Variable

```
eta = 0.076*ksi1 + 0.16*ksi2, Errorvar.= 0.21 , R² = 0.11
      (0.033)        (0.025)                   (0.013)
       2.31           6.35                      15.76
```

(**NOTE 1**: While the PRELIS system file is open, you can use the pull-down menu to run these models. A latent interaction variable is typically nonnormal, even when the latent variables are normally distributed. A solution to this problem is to use the *Normal Score* option in the pull down menu for the ksi1, ksi2, and ksi12 latent variables prior to analysis.

(**NOTE 2**: If *eta, ksi1, ksi2, and ksi12* are variables in the PRELIS data set, another analysis method is available. Select, STATISTICS then use Regressions to enter the variables into the model equation, that is, *RG eta on ksi1 ksi2 ksi12*. Alternatively, the **RG** command in a PRELIS program can be used to conduct univariate or multivariate regression, including ANOVA, ANCOVA, MANOVA, and MANCOVA, as well as other variations of the general multivariate linear model using a list of Y and X variables [i.e., RG Y-Varlist ON X-Varlist]).

16.1.3 Two-Stage Least Squares (TSLS) Approach

Recent developments in nonlinear structural equation modeling have focused on full information methods (e.g., maximum likelihood [ML] or asymptotically distribution free methods [ADF or WLS]) with a concern about estimating parameters and standard errors. We recommend bootstrap estimates of the parameters and standard errors in nonlinear models, given these estimation methods, because the observed and/or latent interaction variables don't meet the multivariate normality assumption. Other problems or sources of error could exist, which is why *start values* are recommended to aid convergence (i.e., the initial TSLS estimates could be replaced with user defined start values). The two-stage least-squares (TSLS) estimates and their standard errors are obtained without iterations and therefore provide the researcher with clues to which parameters exceed their expected values (e.g., correlations with values greater than 1.0 in a nonpositive definite matrix). TSLS estimates therefore provide helpful information to determine whether the specified model is reasonable.

Bollen (1995, 1996) has indicated that nonlinear SEM models can be estimated using instrumental variables in two stage least squares (TSLS). A two-stage least squares analysis using instrumental variables is easily run in LISREL–PRELIS (Jöreskog, Sörbom, du Toit, & du Toit, 2000, pp. 172–174) using the following RG command (see files KJTSLS1.PR2 and KJTSLS2.PR2):

```
Estimating Kenny-Judd Model by Bollen's TSLS
DA NI = 5
LA
Y X1 X2 X3 X4
RA = KJUDD.RAW
CO ALL
NE X1X3 = X1*X3
NE X1X4 = X1*X4
NE X2X3 = X2*X3
NE X2X4 = X2*X4
RG Y ON X1 X3 X1X3 WITH X2 X4 X2X4 RES=U
OU RA = KJRES.RAW
```

The TSLS results are as follows.

Estimated Equations

$$Y = 0.936 + 0.340*X1 + 0.399*X3 + 0.965*X1X3 + \text{Error}, R^2 = 0.594$$
$$(1.011) \quad (0.115) \quad (0.0883) \quad (0.164)$$
$$0.926 \quad 2.948 \quad 4.516 \quad 5.899$$

The latent variable score approach is also easily run using PRELIS and SIMPLIS programs (Jöreskog, Sörbom, du Toit, & du Toit, 2000, pp. 173; see files KJUDD.PR2, KENJUDD.SPL, and KENJUDD.PR2). The following

PRELIS program KJUDD.PR2, creates the PRELIS SYSTEM FILE, *KJUDD. PSF,* the SIMPLIS program *KENJUDD.SPL* computes the latent variable scores, and the PRELIS program *KENJUDD.PR2* computes the parameter estimates in the SEM interaction model. The PRELIS program for computing the PRELIS SYSTEM FILE is:

```
Computing PSF file from KJUDD.RAW
DA NI = 5
LA; Y X1 X2 X3 X4
RA = KJUDD.RAW
CO ALL
OU MA = CM RA=KJUDD.PSF
```

The SIMPLIS program for computing the latent variable scores is:

```
Estimating the Measurement Model in the Kenny-Judd Model
  and Latent Variable Scores
System File from File KJUDD.DSF
Latent Variables Ksi1 Ksi2
Relationships
X1 = 1*Ksi1
X2 = Ksi1
X3 = 1*Ksi2
X4 = Ksi2
PSFfile KJUDD.PSF
Path Diagram
End of Problem
```

The PRELIS program for computing the parameter estimates in the SEM interaction model is:

```
Estimating Kenny-Judd Model from Latent Variable Scores
SY = KJUDD.PSF
CO ALL
NE Ksi1Ksi2 = Ksi1*Ksi2
RG Y ON Ksi1 Ksi2 Ksi1Ksi2
OU
```

Estimated Equations

$Y = 1.082 + 0.232^{*}Ksi1 + 0.290^{*}Ksi2 + 0.431^{*}Ksi1Ksi2 + Error, R^2 = 0.381$
    (0.0207) (0.0297)   (0.0218)   (0.0261)   Error Variance = 0.393
      52.196   7.814   13.281   16.540

Interaction models comprise many different types of models. The use of continuous variables, categorical variables, nonlinear effects, and latent variables has intrigued scholars over the years. The current approaches that appear easy to model are the multigroup categorical approach and the latent variables score approach, because they are not affected by many of the problems discussed next.

The testing of interaction effects can present problems in structural equation modeling. First, you may have the problem of model specification. Linear models simplify the task of determining relations to investigate and distributional assumptions to consider, but this may not be the case in latent variable interaction models. Second, discarding the linearity assumption opens up the possibility of several product indicant variable and latent variable interaction combinations, but this also serves to magnify the critical role of theory in focusing the research effort. Third, a researcher who seeks to model categorical interaction effects must also collect data that spans the range of values in which interaction effects are likely to be evident in the raw data, and must collect a sample size large enough to permit subsamples. Fourth, we have noted that the statistical fit index and parameter standard errors are based on linearity and normality assumptions, and we may not have robust results to recognize the presence of an interaction effect unless it is substantial.

The continuous variable approach does have its good points. It is possible to check for normality of variables, and to standardize them (Normal Score option), and the approach does not require creating subsamples or forming groups where observations could be misclassified, nor does it require the researcher to categorize a variable and thereby lose information. Moreover, the continuous variable approach is parsimonious. Basically, all but one of the additional parameters involved in the interaction model are exact functions of the main-effects parameters, so the only new parameters to be estimated are the structure coefficient for the latent interaction independent variable and the prediction equation error.

The continuous variable approach also has several drawbacks. First, only a few software programs can perform the necessary nonlinear constraints, and the programming for testing interaction effects in the traditional sense is not easy. Second, if you include too many indicator variables of your latent independent variables, this approach can become very cumbersome. For example, if one latent independent variable, Factor 1, has n_1 measures and the other latent independent variable, Factor 2, has n_2 measures, then the interaction term, Factor 1 x Factor 2, could have n_1 x n_2 measures. If each independent latent variable has five indicator variables, then the multiplicative latent independent variable interaction would involve 25 indicators. Including the five measures for each of the two main-effect latent independent variables and two indicators of a latent dependent variable, the model would have 37 indicator variables before any other latent-variable relationships were considered. Third, the functional form of the interaction needs to be specified. The simple multiplicative interaction presented here hardly covers other types of interactions, and for these other types of interactions there is little prior research or available examples to guide the researcher.

A fourth problem to consider is multicollinearity. It is very likely that the interaction factor will be highly correlated with the observed variables used to construct it. This multicollinearity in the measurement model causes the interaction latent independent variable to be more highly correlated with the observed variables of other main effect latent independent variables than each set of observed variables are with their own respective main effect latent independent variables. For multiplicative interactions between normally distributed variables, multicollinearity could be eliminated by centering the observed variables (using scores expressed as deviations from their means) before computing the product variable. However, centering the variables alters the form of the interaction relationship. Researchers who want to model other types of interactions may find no easy answer to the problem of multicollinearity (Smith & Sasaki, 1979).

A fifth concern relates to distributional problems, which are more serious than those associated with linear modeling techniques using observed variables only. If the observed variables are nonnormal, then the variance of the product variable can be very different from the values implied by the basic measurement model, and the interaction effect will perform poorly. Of course, permissible transformations may result in a suitable, normal distribution for the observed variables. The resultant nonnormality, however, in the observed variables violates the distributional assumptions associated with the estimation methods used, for example, maximum-likelihood. Furthermore, estimation methods that do not make distributional assumptions may not work for interaction models. Basically, the asymptotic weight matrix associated with the covariance matrix for an interaction model may be nonpositive definite because of dependencies between moments of different observed variables that are implied by the interaction model. In any case, we would recommend that you bootstrap the parameter estimates and standard errors to achieve a more reasonable estimate of these values.

When using the latent variable score approach you should consider bootstrapping the standard errors because the estimation method used may give inaccurate estimates of standard errors given violation of the distributional assumption for the interaction model. Basically, the asymptotic weight matrix associated with the covariance matrix for an interaction model may be nonpositive definite because of dependencies between moments of different observed variables that are implied by the interaction model. In any case, we would recommend that you bootstrap the parameter estimates and standard errors to achieve a more reasonable estimate of these values (Bollen & Stine, 1993; Mooney & Duval, 1993; Lunneborg, 1987; Stine, 1990; Jöreskog & Sörbom, 1993a; and Yang-Wallentin & Jöreskog, 2001).

In our examples, we have assumed that the relationships in our models have been linear (i.e., the relationships among all variables, observed and latent, could be represented by linear equations). Although the use of nonlinear and interaction effects is popular in regression models (Aiken & West, 1991), the inclusion of interaction hypotheses in path models have been minimal (Newman, Marchant, & Ridenour, 1993), and few examples of non-linear factor models have been provided (McDonald, 1967; Etezadi-Amoli & McDonald, 1983). SEM models with interaction effects are now possible and better understood due to several scholars including Kenny and Judd (1984), Hayduk (1987), Wong and Long (1987), Bollen (1989), Higgins and Judd (1990), Cole, Maxwell, Arvey, and Salas (1993), Mackenzie and Spreng (1992), Ping (1993, 1994, 1995), Jöreskog and Yang (1996), Schumacker and Marcoulides (1998), Algina and Moulder (2001), du Toit and du Toit (2001), Moulder and Algina (2002), and Schumacker (2002), to name only a few.

Jöreskog and Yang (1996) do provide additional insights into model-ing interaction effects, given the problems and concerns discussed here. Jöreskog (2000) discussed many issues related to interaction modeling and included latent variable scores in LISREL that are easy to compute and include in interaction modeling. Schumacker (2002) compared the latent variable score approach to the continuous variable approach using LISREL matrix command language and found the parameter estimates to be similar with standard errors reasonably close. Our recommendation would be to use the latent variable score approach and bootstrap the standard errors. If unfamiliar with the bootstrap approach, then use the Normal Score option with interaction variables to avoid nonnormal issues when testing interac-tion effects.

Structural equation models that include interaction effects are not prev-alent in the research literature, in part, because of all the concerns men-tioned here. The categorical variable approach using multiple samples and constraints has been used most often. The latent variable score approach using normal scores is a useful way to model interaction with latent vari-ables. Hopefully, more SEM research will consider interaction hypotheses given the use of latent variable scores and the use of *Normal Score* data conversion for main effect and interaction variables in LISREL–PRELIS.

16.2 Latent Growth Curve Models

Repeated measures analysis of variance has been widely used with observed variables to statistically test for changes over time. SEM advances the longitudinal analysis of data to include latent variable growth over time while modeling both individual and group changes using slopes and intercepts (McArdle & Epstein, 1987; Stoolmiller, 1995; Byrne & Crombie, 2003). Latent growth curve analysis conceptually involves two different analyses. The first analysis is the repeated measures of each individual across time that is hypothesized to be linear or nonlinear. The second analysis involves using the individual's parameters (slope and intercept values) to determine the difference in growth from a baseline. The latent growth curve model (LGM) represents differences over time that takes into account means (intercepts) and rate of change (slopes), at the individual or group level.

LGM permits an analysis of individual parameter differences, which is critical to any analysis of change. It describes not only an individual's growth over time (linear or nonlinear), but also detects differences in individual parameters over time. LGM using structural equation modeling can test the type of individual growth curve, use time varying covariates, establish the type of group curve, and include interaction effects in latent growth curves (Li, Duncan, T.E., Duncan, S.C., Acock, Yang-Wallentin, & Hops, 2001). The LGM approach, however, requires large samples, multivariate normal data, equal time intervals for all subjects, and change that occurs as a result of the time continuum (Duncan. & Duncan, 1995).

The latent growth curve model illustrates the use of slope and intercept as latent variables to model differences over time. The data set contains 168 adolescent responses over a 5-year period (age 11 to age 15) regarding the tolerance toward deviant behaviors, with higher scores indicating more tolerance of such behavior. The data was transformed (i.e., log X) to create equal interval linear measures from ordinal data. The latent growth curve model is diagrammed in Figure 16.2a.

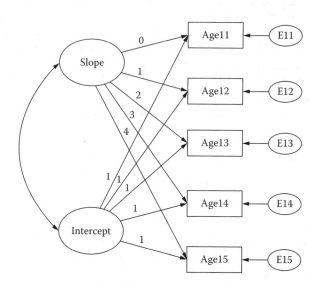

FIGURE 16.2a
Latent Growth Curve Model (Linear).

The slope parameters are coded 0, 1, 2, 3, and 4 to establish a linear trend with zero used as a common starting point. Other polynomial coefficients could be used for quadratic or cubic trend. The intercept parameters are coded 1, 1, 1, 1, and 1 to indicate means for the different age groups. A LISREL–SIMPLIS program was created that shows how these parameters are stipulated for the two latent variables, *slope* and *intercept*. It also includes a command to correlate slope and intercept (curved arrow in diagram) and a special term, CONST, to designate means. The LISREL–SIMPLIS latent growth curve model program is:

16.2.1 Latent Growth Curve Program

```
Latent Growth Model
Observed Variables: age11 age12 age13 age14 age15
Sample size 168
Correlation matrix
1.000
 .161 1.000
 .408 .348 1.000
 .373 .269 .411 1.000
 .254 .143 .276 .705 1.000
Means .201 .226 .326 .417 .446
Standard deviations .178 .199 .269 .293 .296
Latent Variables: slope intercept
Relationships:
age11 = CONST + 0 * slope + 1 * intercept
age12 = CONST + 1 * slope + 1 * intercept
age13 = CONST + 2 * slope + 1 * intercept
age14 = CONST + 3 * slope + 1 * intercept
age15 = CONST + 4 * slope + 1 * intercept
Let slope and intercept correlate
Path Diagram
End of Problem
```

The initial LISREL–SIMPLIS model results indicated a poor model fit (chi-square = 49.74, $df = 7$, $p = 0.00$). The correlation between the intercept values (group means) and the slope (linear growth) was zero indicating that level of tolerance at age 11 did not predict growth in tolerance across the other age groups. However, the group means indicated otherwise, so model modification was conducted; the means for each age are:

age11	age12	age13	age14	age15
0.20	0.23	0.33	0.42	0.45

Modification indices were indicated that recommended correlating the error covariance between age 11 and age 12, as well as between age 14 and age 15. These are apparently the two transition periods in the latent growth curve model were more measurement disturbance was present.

16.2.2 Model Modification

The LISREL–SIMPLIS program was rerun with the following added commands:

```
Let error covariance between age11 and age12 correlate
Let error covariance between age14 and age15 correlate
```

After modification, the latent growth curve model had a more acceptable model fit (chi-square = 11.35, *df* = 5, and *p* = .045).

The final latent growth curve model output with standardized coefficients is diagrammed in Figure 16.2b.

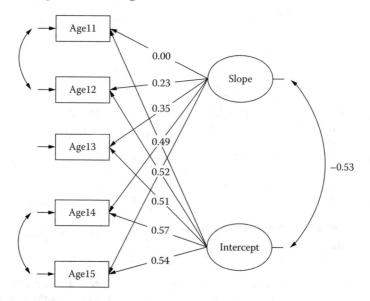

FIGURE 16.2b
Latent Growth Model Output.

The individual slopes increased over time:

Group	Slope
Age 11	.00
Age 12	.23
Age 13	.35
Age 14	.49
Age 15	.62

The intercepts decreased over time:

Group	Intercept
Age 11	.92
Age 12	.80
Age 13	.61
Age 14	.57
Age 15	.54

The negative correlation between the slope and intercept correctly indicates the increase in slope values over time with a corresponding decrease in intercept values over time ($r = -.53$).

(NOTE: The LISREL–SIMPLIS computer output does not list the slope and intercept values, but does display them in the model diagram. They were copied and listed above for convenience.)

A test of linear rate of growth in the latent growth curve model seemed appropriate because the means increased from .20 at age 11 to .45 at age 15. The latent growth curve model is appropriately called a Latent Growth Curve Structured Means Model because group means as well as covariance were specified. There were individual differences in the slopes over time. The negative correlation between the intercept values (group means), and the slope values (linear growth) indicated that as age increased the level of tolerance decreased.

This LGM model indicated a linear rate of growth in adolescent tolerance for deviant behavior using the age 11 as the baseline for assessing linear change over time. You should graph these mean values across the age levels to graphically display the trend. You should also interpret the correlation between the intercept and slope because a positive value would indicate that high initial status at age 11 has a greater rate of change, while a negative correlation would indicate that high initial status at age 11 has a lower rate of change. If the average slope value is zero, then no linear change has occurred. Finally, you can assess how measurement errors across adjacent years are correlated (e.g., lagged correlation in ARIMA models). This ability to model measurement error is a unique advantage of LGM over traditional ANOVA repeated measure designs.

16.3 Monte Carlo Methods

Researchers typically collect a random sample of data and determine if the sample data fit a theoretical model. Model validation (chapter 12) is then conducted to examine stability of parameter estimates and standard errors. Generalizations are then usually made to the population parameters.

We obviously seldom know the population model, data, or parameters, so if we wish to investigate how statistics are affected under violations of assumptions, etc., we need to specify the population model, generate population data (covariance matrix), and now compute model parameters to examine how parameter estimates, standard errors, and fit indices change, when the model is misspecified. Monte Carlo results are made easier by writing parameter estimates, standard error estimates, and measures of fit to a file by using PV (PV = <filename>; stores parameter estimates), SV (SV = <filename>; stores standard errors); and GF (GF = <filename>, stores goodness-of-fit indices) keywords on the LISREL OUTPUT command in the LISREL–SIMPLIS program. The RP command permits replications, which is also useful in Monte Carlo studies to examine how these values change.

The Monte Carlo approach could involve simulating population data, generating variables from a specified population covariance matrix, or generating data from a specified model. Monte Carlo methods involve using a pseudo-random number generator or specifying known population values to produce raw data for a population covariance matrix. (*Note*: Bang, Schumacker, and Schlieve [1998] found that pseudo-random number generators do not perform the same way with many yielding non-random [nonnormal] distributions with sample sizes of less than 10,000). Our interest in Monte Carlo methods is to determine the robustness of our sample statistics, which we can only know when our population model and/or parameters are known. The PRELIS approach to simulation of population data (covariance matrix) is described next for the path model in Figure 16.3.

16.3.1 PRELIS Simulation of Population Data

PRELIS is considered a preprocessor for LISREL and as such screens data, creates different types of matrices, and has other useful features for data creation and data manipulation. PRELIS can easily produce several different types of data distributions—for example, normal and nonnormal. We will create multivariate normally distributed population data. Simply click on **File**, **New**, and then select *PRELIS Data*.

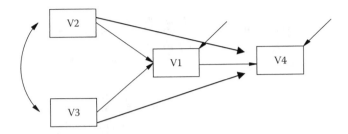

FIGURE 16.3
Path Model (Monte Carlo).

An empty *PRELIS Data* window should appear as indicated below.

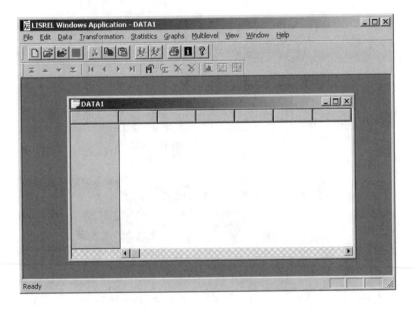

We now need to insert the number of variables and the number of cases that you want to create. We first create the number of variables, which are four in Figure 16.3 (V1–V4). We select Data from the tool bar menu, then Define Variables. A *Define Variables* dialog box appears next and then we click on *Insert*.

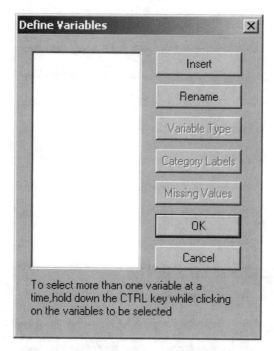

An *Add Variables* dialog box now appears and we enter the names of our variables, that is, V1-V4., and click *OK*. These variables will now appear in the *Define Variables* dialog box. Click *OK* in the *Define Variables* dialog box and they will now appear in the *PRELIS Data* window.

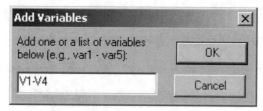

Next, we select *Data* from the Tool Bar menu, then *Insert Cases*. We enter 10000 and click *OK*.

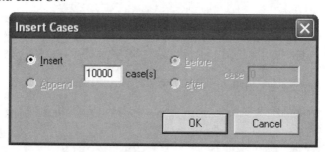

The *PRELIS Data* window now appears with four variables and 10,000 cases, but with zeroes in the cells.

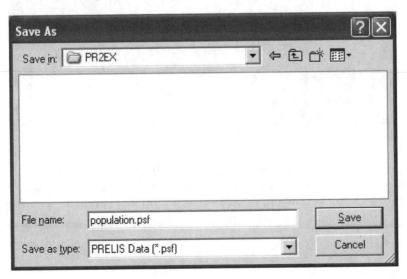

We are now ready to replace the zeroes with numerical values by selecting Transformation from the tool bar menu, then Compute; however, we are first prompted to save our work as a PRELIS SYSTEM FILE (*population. psf*). (*Note*: Choose a directory to save the file in that will also contain your LISREL–SIMPLIS program.)

We can now carefully follow the directions and use the mouse to *drag and drop* variables and click on *n(0,1)* to enter NRAND into the equations. The equations were arbitrarily chosen to have a mean and some correlation with other variables. (*Note*: Navigating this window will involve a learning curve; for example, click on *Next line* to add the next variable via *drag and drop*. You also need to use the mouse to enter numbers and mathematical symbols). When finished, click *OK*.

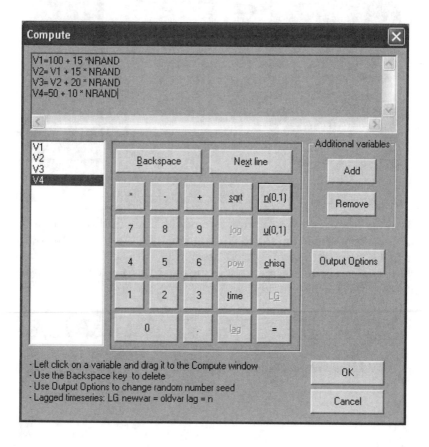

After a few minutes, you will see the computed data values in the PRELIS system file (*population.psf*). Click on the save file icon to save the data file. You can now use many of the PRELIS tool bar menu features to calculate statistics or produces graphs of the variables.

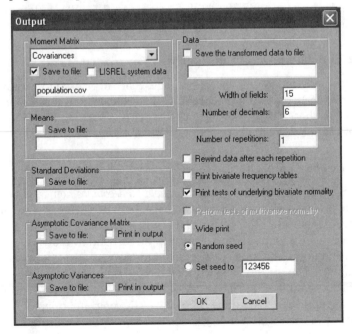

	V1	V2	V3	V4
1	101.80	92.65	72.85	46.86
2	99.68	88.09	106.04	50.30
3	103.34	119.14	99.98	42.27
4	92.82	95.55	77.39	23.43
5	93.77	113.93	115.28	38.29
6	108.78	71.18	66.60	44.53
7	97.27	111.38	133.30	49.01
8	100.24	96.84	75.25	49.04
9	105.05	98.06	86.55	49.05
10	95.61	66.04	87.05	41.25
11	108.83	83.20	67.12	75.23

Click on Statistics in the tool bar menu, and select Output Options to save the raw data from the PRELIS system file (*population.psf*) into a covariance matrix (*population.cov*). (*Note*: A PRELIS program will appear in a dialog box to show that a program was written to output the covariance matrix. It will also indicate that variables are treated as continuous [CO], provide a frequency distribution for each variable, skewness and kurtosis, and the means and standard deviations of the V1 to V4 variables you created as population parameters).

The covariance matrix (*population.cov*) can now be input into a LISREL–SIMPLIS program (*population.spl*) for the model in Figure 16.3. (*Note*: We wanted to treat this covariance matrix as a population matrix to obtain population parameters, so we generated 10,000 cases.) The LISREL–SIMPLIS program (*population.spl*) would be:

```
PRELIS Data as Population Data for Covariance Matrix
Observed variables V1 V2 V3 V4
Sample size 10000
Covariance matrix from file population.cov
Equations:
V1 = V2 V3
V4 = V1 V2 V3
Path Diagram
LISREL OUTPUT SS SC PV=parameter SV=error GF=fit
End of problem
```

We can now use the data set or the covariance matrix in a Monte Carlo study to investigate what parameter estimates and standard errors might be, given a random sample from the 10,000 cases that constitute the population. We can also save the parameter estimates (PV), standard errors (SV), and model goodness-of-fit indices (GF) to separate files using the LISREL OUTPUT command (*Note*: SS = standardized solution; SC = completely standardized solution).

(**NOTE**: Adding the LISREL OUPUT command RP = 10 would repeat the analysis 10 times in a Monte Carlo study).

16.3.2 Population Data from Specified Covariance Matrix

There are many different software packages that can be used to generate data given specification of a population covariance matrix for use in Monte Carlo studies. We chose SPSS, SAS, and LISREL matrix syntax to illustrate how to generate population data from specification of a covariance matrix.

16.3.2.1 SPSS Approach

The SPSS MATRIX routine using the *Cholesky decomposition* can be used to generate raw data and output an SPSS save file. The SPSS save file can then be imported into a LISREL program. The following SPSS MATRIX program only requires the population covariance or correlation matrix (*r*), sample size (*n*), and output file name, Save <filename>. (*Note*: Save corr/outfile = *. ; it will output data into an SPSS Untitled dialog box which you can then save as an SPSS save file.) The SPSS MATRIX program requires a symmetrical matrix as input. To execute the SPSS MATRIX program, open SPSS, select *File, New*, and then *Syntax*. Enter the SPSS Matrix program into the syntax window, save it, and then click on the *run* command on the tool bar menu to execute the program and save the data into an SPSS save file, *sample.sav.*

```
MATRIX.
compute popr =
 {1,  .4,  .3,  .2;
 .4,  1,  .6,  .7;
 .3,  .6,  1,  .8;
 .2,  .7,  .8,  1}.
Print popr.
compute pi = 3.14159.
compute rown = nrow(popr).
compute n = 10000.
compute corr = sqrt(-2*ln(uniform(n,rown)))&*cos((2*pi)*
  uniform(n,rown)).
compute corr=corr*chol(popr).
save corr /outfile = pop.sav.
END MATRIX.
```

We had the SPSS Matrix program print the *popr* matrix to verify it was read correctly. The SPSS output should look like the following:

```
Run MATRIX procedure:
POPR
 1.000000000 .400000000 .300000000 .200000000
 .400000000 1.000000000 .600000000 .700000000
 .300000000 .600000000 1.000000000 .800000000
 .200000000 .700000000 .800000000 1.000000000
------ END MATRIX -----
```

We can now open the SPSS save file, *pop.sav,* and compute the bivariate correlation between the variables, COL1 – COL4, which can be renamed, if desired.

	COL1	COL2	COL3	COL4	var	var
1	1.34	-0.55	0.36	0.20		
2	-1.76	-0.15	0.07	0.56		
3	2.29	1.35	0.93	-0.49		
4	0.18	1.06	0.82	0.98		
5	0.60	-0.84	-0.12	-1.21		
6	-1.73	-0.47	-1.21	0.02		
7	0.78	0.04	-1.25	-1.00		
8	1.45	0.01	0.71	1.42		

The correlation values obtained from SPSS bivariate correlation routine will approximate the ones specified in the *popr* matrix. (*Note*: The correlations should be within .01 of the population correlation/covariance values. Also, every time you run the SPSS MATRIX program you will get slightly different values for the correlations, unless using a random seed number.) The *SPSS Correlation Output* is in Table 16.1.

TABLE 16.1

SPSS Correlation Output

		COLUMN 1	COLUMN 2	COLUMN 3	COLUMN 4
		Correlations			
COL1	Pearson Correlation	1.000	.404[a]	.304[a]	.201[a]
	Sig. (two-tailed)		.000	.000	.000
	N	10000.000	10000	10000	10000
COL2	Pearson Correlation	.404[a]	1.000	.593[a]	.694[a]
	Sig. (two-tailed)	.000		.000	.000
	N	10000	10000.000	10000	10000
COL3	Pearson Correlation	.304[a]	.593[a]	1.000	.800[a]
	Sig. (two-tailed)	.000	.000		.000
	N	10000	10000	10000.000	10000
COL4	Pearson Correlation	.201[a]	.694[a]	.800[a]	1.000
	Sig. (two-tailed)	.000	.000	.000	
	N	10000	10000	10000	10000.000

[a] Correlation is significant at the 0.01 level (two-tailed).

16.3.2.2 SAS Approach

A SAS program can also be written to produce data from a population covariance matrix using a normal distribution function. The SAS program is written as:

```
proc iml;                    /* Generate multivariate normal data in SAS/IML */
cov = {1 .4 .3 .2,
    .4 1 .6 .7,
    .3 .6 1 .8,
    .2 .7 .8 1};
print cov;                   /* population correlation matrix */
    v = nrow(cov);           /* calculate number of variables */
    n = 10000;               /* input number of cases */
    seed = 12345;            /* random seed number */
    l = t(root(cov));        /* calculate cholesky root of cov matrix */
```

```
z = normal(j(v,n, seed));   /* generate nvars*samplesize normal distribution */
x = l*z;                    /* premultiply by cholesky root */
tx = t(x);                  /* transpose of X */
create cor from tx;         /* write out sample data to sas dataset */
append from tx;
quit;
Proc corr data = cor;       /* sample covariance matrix */
var col1 col2 col3 col4;
run;
```

The SAS population matrix and the sample matrix from *Proc corr* should be similar, as desired. Changing the *seed* number, however, will produce slightly different results each time you run the SAS program. Our SAS 9.1 computer output looked like:

```
COV
   1     0.4     0.3     0.2
 0.4      1     0.6     0.7
 0.3     0.6      1     0.8
 0.2     0.7     0.8      1

The CORR Procedure

4 Variables:   COL1    COL2    COL3    COL4

Simple Statistics

Variable    N       Mean    Std Dev    Sum      Minimum   Maximum
COL1     10000    0.00591  1.00676   59.12856  -4.06923  4.13280
COL2     10000   -0.00628  1.00321  -62.81136  -4.47883  3.55955
COL3     10000    0.01407  1.00337  140.74048  -3.50194  3.81102
COL4     10000    0.00662  0.99853   66.17666  -3.45835  3.63828


Pearson Correlation Coefficients, N = 10000
Prob > |r| under H0: Rho=0

                COL1         COL2         COL3         COL4
       COL1   1.00000      0.41708      0.32340      0.22719
       COL2   0.41708      1.00000      0.60942      0.70242
       COL3   0.32340      0.60942      1.00000      0.80413
       COL4   0.22719      0.70242      0.80413      1.00000
```

16.3.2.3 LISREL Approach

It is also possible to generate multivariate normal variables with a desired population covariance matrix using either the *Cholesky decomposition* or *factor pattern matrix* approach in LISREL. We will first input four variables and use the Cholesky decomposed matrix of coefficients to compute four new variables with the desired covariance structure. Secondly, we will use a pattern matrix approach to generate the same Cholesky decomposed matrix of coefficients that one would use to compute the same new multivariate normal variables.

16.3.2.3.1 Cholesky Decomposition Approach

Cholesky decomposition of our symmetric population covariance matrix, S, yields a Lambda Y matrix. The coefficients in the Lambda Y matrix are then used to compute the new variables. You can save either a covariance matrix (RS option) or raw data (RA option); we saved a covariance matrix (POP.CM). You will need to run a series of programs to accomplish the generation of the multivariate normally distributed data for your variables.

Program 1 is a LISREL matrix program which inserts a specified population covariance matrix (CM) with the number of variables, Y1–Y4 (LE), indicated for a model (MO) that has the Lambda Y values to be freely estimated (FR). The model must be saturated ($\chi^2 = 0$) and the residual errors set to zero (TE = ZE). The resulting Lambda Y matrix provides the coefficients to be used to compute the new multivariate normal variables, V1–V4 (LA). (*Note*: You must specify, all Y variables and associated matrices in the MO command line; or correspondingly, all X variables and associated matrices; but not a mix of X and Y variables and associated matrices or the program will not work.)

```
Program 1
! Cholesky decomposition matrix approach
DA NI = 4 NO = 10000
LA
V1 V2 V3 V4
CM
 1.000
 0.41708 1.000
 0.32340 0.60942 1.000
 0.22719 0.70242 0.80413 1.000
MO NY = 4 NE = 4 LY = FU,FI BE = FU,FI PS = SY,FI TE =ZE
LE
 Y1 Y2 Y3 Y4
VA 1.0 PS (1, 1) PS (2, 2) PS (3, 3) PS (4, 4)
FR LY (1, 1) LY (2, 2) LY (3, 3) LY (4, 4)
FR LY (2, 1) LY (3, 1) LY (4, 1)
FR LY (3, 2) LY (4, 2)
FR LY (4, 3)
OU ND = 5 RS
```

```
LAMBDA-Y
                 Y1          Y2          Y3          Y4
             --------    --------    --------    --------
      V1      1.00000       - -         - -         - -
      V2      0.41708     0.90887       - -         - -
      V3      0.32340     0.52212     0.78918       - -
      V4      0.22719     0.66859     0.48351     0.51729
```

Program 2 uses the Lambda Y values in a PRELIS program to compute the new variables, V1-V4. The Y1–Y4 variables are first generated from normally distributed random data (NRAND function) using a seed value (IX = 12345). Next, new variables are created for V1-V4 using the coefficients from the Lambda Y matrix and saved in a covariance matrix (CM = POP.CM). The Y1-Y4 variables are deleted (SD). The RA = <filename> option would save raw data for the variables instead of a matrix if so desired.

Program 2
```
! Compute new multivariate normal variables from Lambda Y
matrix
DA NO = 10000
NE Y1 = NRAND
NE Y2 = NRAND
NE Y3 = NRAND
NE Y4 = NRAND
NE V1 = 1 * Y1
NE V2 = .41708 * Y1 + .90887 * Y2
NE V3 = .32340 * Y1 + .52212 * Y2 + .78918 * Y3
NE V4 = .22719 * Y1 + .66859 * Y2 + .48351 * Y3 + .51729* Y4
CO ALL
SD Y1-Y4
OU CM = POP.CM ND = 5 XM IX = 12345
```

Finally, Program 3 would run a LISREL–SIMPLIS program with the generated population covariance matrix to produce the specified model in Figure 16.3.

Program 3
```
Path model Figure 16.3 with Cholesky decomposed matrix
variables
Observed variables V1 V2 V3 V4
Sample size 10000
!Covariance Matrix from file POP.CM
Covariance Matrix
0.99641
0.42637 1.0185
0.32652 0.62854 1.0379
0.23881 0.72385 0.83883 1.0322
```

```
Equation:
V1 = V2 V3
V4 = V1 V2 V3
Number of Decimals = 5
Path Diagram
End of Problem
```

(**NOTE**: We used sample size of 10,000 and 5 decimal places to avoid rounding error and non-convergence problems.)

16.3.2.3.2 Pattern Matrix Approach

The pattern matrix approach is possible by inputting the pattern matrix (PA) and corresponding lambda X matrix (MA) with the specified covariance matrix (CM). The results would be the same as before. The Lambda X coefficients would be the same as before and used in Program 2 above to compute multivariate normal variables. The LISREL program would be written as:

```
! Pattern Matrix approach
DA NI = 4 NO = 10000
LA
V1 V2 V3 V4
CM
 1.000
 0.41708 1.000
 0.32340 0.60942 1.000
 0.22719 0.70242 0.80413 1.000
MO NX = 4 NK = 4 PH = ID TD =ZE
PA LX
1 0 0 0
1 1 0 0
1 1 1 0
1 1 1 1
MA LX
1 0 0 0
1 1 0 0
1 1 1 0
1 1 1 1
OU ND = 5 RS
```

```
  LAMBDA-X
```

	KSI 1	KSI 2	KSI 3	KSI 4
V1	1.00000	- -	- -	- -
V2	0.41708	0.90887	- -	- -
V3	0.32340	0.52212	0.78918	- -
V4	0.22719	0.66859	0.48351	0.51729

(NOTE: It is also straightforward to compute the Cholesky decomposed matrix using SPSS to check your programming. The SPSS MATRIX procedure with the original population covariance matrix used (*S*) and the resulting Cholesky decomposed matrix [*SCHOL*] is output as follows.)

```
MATRIX.
Compute S = {1.00000,  .41708,  .32340,  .22719;
              .41708, 1.00000,  .60942,  .70242;
              .32340,  .60942, 1.00000,  .80413;
              .22719,  .70242,  .80413, 1.00000}.
Print S.
Compute SCHOL = T(CHOL(S)).
Print SCHOL.
END MATRIX.
```

Run MATRIX procedure:

```
S
 1.000000000 .417080000 .323400000 .227190000
 .417080000 1.000000000 .609420000 .702420000
 .323400000 .609420000 1.000000000 .804130000
 .227190000 .702420000 .804130000 1.000000000
SCHOL
 1.000000000 .000000000 .000000000 .000000000
 .417080000 .908869778 .000000000 .000000000
 .323400000 .522116963 .789180789 .000000000
 .227190000 .668592585 .483505465 .517292107
```

16.3.3 Covariance Matrix from Specified Model

A more appropriate way to generate a population covariance matrix is from a specified population model. This permits a better way to examine how model misspecification affects overall model fit as well as predefined population parameter values. Unfortunately, the population model specification and subsequent generation of population model parameters is not directly possible using LISREL or PRELIS programs. The reason is that not all matrices, especially covariance and certain error terms, can be specified in the programs. The solution is to (1) specify a population model, (2) define what matrices are indicated in the population model, (3) pick values for the population parameters in the matrices, and then (4) use matrix operations to compute the population covariance matrix. In a final step (5), you can verify that the population model with the population parameters was correctly specified by using the population covariance matrix in a LISREL–SIMPLIS program. We will now take you through these steps to illustrate a better way to conduct Monte Carlo

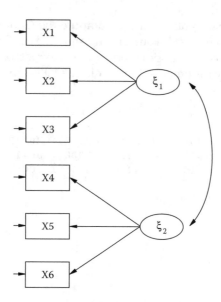

FIGURE 16.4
Population Model (Monte Carlo).

studies (rather than simulation of data or generation of data from a specified correlation/covariance matrix).

Step 1: We begin by specifying a population model in Figure 16.4. The
population model is a confirmatory factor model with two latent independent factors, ξ_1 and ξ_2. Each of the latent independent variables is
measured by three indicator (observed) variables. The indicator variables X1 to X3 define the first latent independent variable and indicator
variables X4 to X6 define the second latent independent variable. Each of
the indicator variables have measurement error, designated as: δ_1 to δ_6.
We also have lambda X values or factor loadings for each of the paths
from the latent independent variables to the indicator variables. Finally,
we have to specify the covariance between the two latent independent
variables.

Step 2: We define what matrices are indicated in this population model.
We described a lambda X matrix (factor loadings), a theta–delta matrix
(measurement error of indicator variables), and a phi matrix (correlation
between the two factors).

Step 3: We specify what we want our population parameters to be in
these matrices. We chose to set factor loadings for X1 to X3 at .6 and factor
loadings for X4 to X6 at .7. We then calculated our measurement errors as
$1 - (.6)^2$ for X1 to X3 and $1 - (.7)^2$ for X4 to X6; .64 and .51, respectively, in

the theta–delta matrix. (*Note*: Failure to have factor loadings and measurement error synchronized—that is, X = T + E—will lead to a nonpositive definite matrix and error warning.) Finally, we set the factor correlation at .70. The matrices with our selected population parameters for the confirmatory factor model would be as follows:

$$
\Lambda_x =
\begin{bmatrix}
.6 & 0 \\
.6 & 0 \\
.6 & 0 \\
0 & .7 \\
0 & .7 \\
0 & .7
\end{bmatrix}
\Theta_\delta =
\begin{bmatrix}
.64 & 0 & 0 & 0 & 0 & 0 \\
0 & .64 & 0 & 0 & 0 & 0 \\
0 & 0 & .64 & 0 & 0 & 0 \\
0 & 0 & 0 & .51 & 0 & 0 \\
0 & 0 & 0 & 0 & .51 & 0 \\
0 & 0 & 0 & 0 & 0 & .51
\end{bmatrix}
\Phi =
\begin{bmatrix}
1.0 & .7 \\
.7 & 1.0
\end{bmatrix}
$$

Please be aware that these matrices in a LISREL program with a pattern matrix or MO commands will not create a population covariance matrix because we cannot specify the measurement errors of the indicator variables exactly (typically created with random number generator) nor the correlation between the factors. Also, there are two other implied matrices that would have zero values: tau matrix of zero mean values for indicator variables (τ_x) and alpha matrix for means of our latent independent variables (α), although these are not used in our calculations of the population covariance matrix that are implicitly set to zero. These two matrices are indicated as:

$$
\tau_x =
\begin{bmatrix}
0 \\
0 \\
0 \\
0 \\
0 \\
0
\end{bmatrix}
\alpha =
\begin{bmatrix}
0 \\
0
\end{bmatrix}
$$

Step 4: We now use matrix operations with these matrices to produce the population covariance matrix (Σ). The covariance matrix equation would multiply the coefficients in the lambda X matrix (LX) times the phi matrix (phi) and post multiply times the transpose of the lambda X matrix (LXT), plus add the measurement error of each indicator variable, which is represented as:

$$
\Sigma = \Lambda_X \Phi \Lambda'_X + \Theta_\delta
$$

We used the SPSS MATRIX procedure to compute the population covariance matrix, which uses full symmetric matrices. The SPSS MATRIX
program is:

```
Matrix.
compute LX= {.6,.0;
             .6,.0;
             .6,.0;
             .0,.7;
             .0,.7;
             .0,.7}.
print LX.
compute phi = {1,.7;
               .7 ,1}.
print phi.
compute thetad={.64,0,0,0,0,0;
                0,.64,0,0,0,0;
                0,0,.64,0,0,0;
                0,0,0,.51,0,0;
                0,0,0,0,.51,0;
                0,0,0,0,0,.51}.
print thetad.
compute LXT = T(LX).
print LXT.
compute sigma = LX * phi * LXT + thetad.
print sigma.
end matrix.
```

The resulting output with a lambda matrix of factor loadings (LX), phi
matrix with factor correlation (PHI), theta–delta matrix with measurement errors for the indicator variables (THETAD), transpose of LX matrix
(LXT) are indicated below, along with the population covariance matrix
(SIGMA):

Run MATRIX procedure:
LX
    .6000000000   .0000000000
    .6000000000   .0000000000
    .6000000000   .0000000000
    .0000000000   .7000000000
    .0000000000   .7000000000
    .0000000000   .7000000000

PHI
    1.000000000   .700000000
    .700000000   1.000000000

THETAD
```
.6400000000 .0000000000 .0000000000 .0000000000 .0000000000 0000000000
.0000000000 .6400000000 .0000000000 .0000000000 .0000000000 .0000000000
.0000000000 .0000000000 .6400000000 .0000000000 .0000000000 .0000000000
.0000000000 .0000000000 .0000000000 .5100000000 .0000000000 .0000000000
.0000000000 .0000000000 .0000000000 .0000000000 .5100000000 .0000000000
.0000000000 .0000000000 .0000000000 .0000000000 .0000000000 .5100000000
```

LXT
```
.6000000000 .6000000000 .6000000000 .0000000000 .0000000000 .0000000000
.0000000000 .0000000000 .0000000000 .7000000000 .7000000000 .7000000000
```

SIGMA
```
1.000000000  .360000000  .360000000  .294000000  .294000000  .294000000
 .360000000 1.000000000  .360000000  .294000000  .294000000  .294000000
 .360000000  .360000000 1.000000000  .294000000  .294000000  .294000000
 .294000000  .294000000  .294000000 1.000000000  .490000000  .490000000
 .294000000  .294000000  .294000000  .490000000 1.000000000  .490000000
 .294000000  .294000000  .294000000  .490000000  .490000000 1.000000000
```

------ END MATRIX -----

Step 5: We now include the population covariance matrix (*SIGMA*) in a LISREL–SIMPLIS program to produce the population confirmatory factor model (Figure 16.5) that should indicate the values we picked for the population parameters. We only need to include the lower triangular matrix in the program. The LISREL–SIMPLIS program with our SIGMA (Σ) covariance matrix is:

```
Confirmatory Factor Model in Figure 16.5
Observed variables X1 X2 X3 X4 X5 X6
Sample size 1000
Covariance Matrix
1.00000
 .360000 1.00000
 .360000 .360000 1.00000
 .294000 .294000 .294000 1.00000
 .294000 .294000 .294000 .490000 1.000000
 .294000 .294000 .294000 .490000 .490000 1.00000
Latent variables KSI1 KSI2
Relationships:
X1 - X3 = KSI1
X4 - X6 = KSI2
Number of Decimals = 5
Path Diagram
End of Problem
```

Figure 16.5 does indeed show the factor loadings, factor correlation, and measurement error for the indicator variables we specified for our

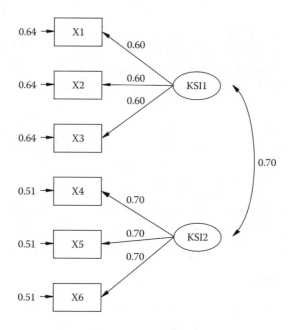

Chi-Square = 0.00, df = 8, P-value = 1.00000, RMSEA = 0.000

FIGURE 16.5
Confirmatory Factor Model (Monte Carlo).

population confirmatory factor model. Please note that the model fits perfectly ($\chi^2 = 0$, $p = 1$). We could now generate data using this population covariance matrix in a SAS or SPSS program and introduce various misspecified models to determine how our population model is affected—for example, model-fit indices, parameters, and standard errors change.

In SEM, the use of a known population covariance matrix permits a comparison with alternative models that produce differing implied covariance matrices that can be compared with the population covariance matrix, as well as an examination of the parameter estimates from the implied model. The variation in the covariance matrices, parameter estimates, and fit indices can be inspected given the new LISREL OUTPUT optional commands; PV, SV, and GF.

Monte Carlo studies are typically conducted to examine model fit, parameter estimates, and standard errors to determine how much they fluctuate or change under certain conditions, for example, different sample sizes, missing data, and/or nonnormal distributions. More complex programs are possible that use data generated from different types of distributions using optional commands other than *normal* when generating data. For example, Enders and Bandalos (2001) studied a three-factor model to compare four methods of missing data estimation. Their experimental condition included different factor loadings, sample size, percent missingness of data, and type of data missingness (MCAR or MAR).

Conducting Monte Carlo studies however can be cumbersome. Paxton, Curran, Bollen, Kirby, and Chen (2001) provided useful steps to follow when conducting a Monte Carlo study. Their basic steps are outlined below, but the reader is encouraged to read their complete journal article.

Step 1: Develop a research question.

Step 2: Create a valid model.

Step 3: Select experimental conditions.

Step 4: Select values of population parameters.

Step 5: Select software package.

Step 6: Conduct simulations.

Step 7: File storage requirements.

Step 8: Troubleshoot and verify results.

Step 9: Summarizing results.

Mooney (1997) provides a basic introduction to Monte Carlo simulation. Skrondal (2000) and Paxton et al. (2001) also offer advice on Monte Carlo methods. Fan, Felsovalyi, Sivo, and Keenan (2002) have written an excellent guide for quantitative researchers who wish to conduct Monte Carlo studies using SAS; a Web site is provided to download a zip file with SAS Monte Carlo programs. Fan (2005) has also published a "Teachers Corner" article on using SAS in structural equation modeling. Bandalos (2006) provides SEM examples generating data from specified models. Long (2008) additionally provided helpful suggestions associated with managing data, although using *STATA* software, the data management suggestions are helpful. We recommend following their suggestions when conducting a Monte Carlo study.

16.4 Summary

In this chapter we have presented many different types of interaction models. The use of continuous variables, categorical variables, nonlinear effects, and latent variables has provided the basis for discussing different interaction models. The two current variable interaction approaches that are easy to model would be the latent variables score approach using normal scores or two-stage least squares approach. We highly recommend either of these two options. Our discussion of latent growth curve models introduced SEM applications for longitudinal data analysis of latent variables. Today, more and more emphasis is being placed on longitudinal data analysis and models. It is a logical extension to expand our thinking into the use of latent variables when applying longitudinal models that heretofore had only used observed variables. Finally, we presented Monte Carlo methods because of the usefulness in creating population models that then permit examination of how parameter estimates, standard errors, and fit indices are affected by missing data sample size, nonnormality, distribution assumptions, and other factors that affect statistical estimation. Specifically, we examined four ways to obtain population data and/or correlation/covariance matrix: (1) simulation of population data, (2) Cholesky decomposition of a specified population matrix to obtain parameter coefficients, (3) pattern matrix of a specified population matrix, which can also be used to obtain parameter coefficients, and finally, (4) obtaining population covariance matrix from a specified population model. We hope these SEM methods have enhanced further your understanding of the usefulness of structural equation modeling.

Exercises

1. INTERACTION MODEL

An organizational psychologist was investigating whether *work tension* and *collegiality* were predictors of *job satisfaction*. However, research indicated that *work tension* and *collegiality* interact, so a SEM Interaction Model was hypothesized and tested. The Interaction Model is diagrammed in Figure 16.6.

Use LISREL to **OPEN** the PRELIS system file, *jobs.psf,* then proceed to follow the necessary steps to create the latent variables (work tension, collegiality, and job satisfaction, interaction) and add them to the PRELIS system file. Next, create and run a LISREL–SIMPLIS program to test the interaction model. What conclusions can you make regarding the interaction of the latent variables *work tension* and *collegiality*?

2. LATENT GROWTH CURVE MODEL

News and radio stations in Dallas, Texas, have apparently convinced the public that a massive crime wave has occurred during the past 4 years, from 2002 to 2005. A criminologist gathered the crime rate data, but needs your help to run a latent growth curve model to test

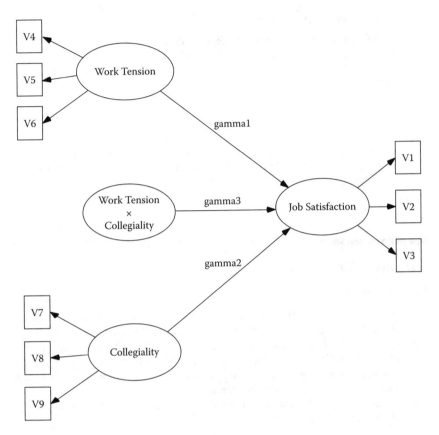

FIGURE 16.6
Job Satisfaction Exercise.

whether a linear trend in crime rates exist for the city. The data set information is:

```
Observed variables: time1 time2 time3 time4
Sample Size 400
Correlation Matrix
1.000
 .799 1.000
 .690 .715 1.000
 .605 .713 .800 1.000
Means 5.417 5.519 5.715 5.83
Standard Deviations .782 .755 .700 .780
```

Create a LISREL–SIMPLIS program, diagram the model with standardized coefficients and interpret your findings. Have crime rates increased in Dallas from 2002 to 2005?

3. MONTE CARLO METHOD

Write a program using either SPSS or SAS for the following population matrix and generate data (N = 10,000 cases):

```
1.00
 .50 1.00
 .30 .70 1.00
 .90 .50 .50 1.00
```

Given the generated data, compute the population correlation matrix. Does the generated data recover the population correlation values in the matrix?

Suggested Readings

Interaction Models

Fielding, D., & Torres, S. (2005). A simultaneous equation model of economic development and income inequality. *Journal of Economic Inequality, 4,* 279–301.

Ritchie, M. D., Hahn, L. W., Roodi, N., Bailey, L. R., Dupont, W. D., Parl, F. F., & Moore, J. H. (2001). Multifactor-dimensionality reduction reveals high-order interactions among estrogen-metabolism genes in sporadic breast cancer. *American Journal of Human Genetics, 69,* 138–147.

Schumacker, R. E. (2002). Latent variable interaction modeling. *Structural Equation Modeling: A Multidisciplinary Journal, 9,* 40–54.

Latent Growth-Curve Models

Duncan, S. C., & Duncan, T. E. (1994). Modeling incomplete longitudinal substance use data using latent variable growth curve methodology. *Multivariate Behavioral Research, 29*(4), 313–338.

Ghisletta, P., & McArdle, J. J. (2001). Latent growth curve analyses of the development of height. *Structural Equation Modeling: A Multidisciplinary Journal, 8,* 531–555.

Shevlin, M., & Millar, R. (2006). Career education: An application of latent growth curve modeling to career information-seeking behavior of school pupils. *British Journal of Educational Psychology, 76,* 141–153.

Monte Carlo Methods

Stephenson, M. T., & Holbert, R. L. (2003). A Monte Carlo simulation of observable versus latent variable structural equation modeling techniques. *Communication Research, 30*(3), 332–354.

Fan, X. (2005). Using SAS for Monte Carlo simulation research in SEM. *Structural Equation Modeling: A Multidisciplinary Journal, 12*(2), 299–33.

Muthèn, L. K., & Muthèn, B. O. (2002). Teacher's corner: How to use a Monte Carlo study to decide on sample size and determine power. *Structural Equation Modeling: A Multidisciplinary Journal, 9*(4), 599–620.

References

Aiken, L. S., & West, S. G. (1991). *Multiple regression: Testing and interpreting interactions*. Newbury Park, CA: Sage.

Algina, J., & Moulder, B. C. (2001). A note on estimating the Jöreskog-Yang model for latent variable interaction using LISREL 8.3. *Structural Equation Modeling, 8*(1), 40–52.

Bandalos, D. L. (2006). The use of Monte Carlo studies in structural equation modeling. In G. R. Hancock & R. O. Mueller (Eds.), *Structural equation modeling: A second course* (pp. 385–426). Greenwich, CT: Information Age.

Bang, J. W., Schumacker, R. E., & Schlieve, P. L. (1998). Random-number generator validity in simulation studies: An investigation of normality. *Educational and Psychological Measurement, 58*(3), 430–450.

Bollen, K. A. (1989). *Structural equations with latent variables*. New York: John Wiley & Sons.

Bollen, K. A., & Stine, R. A. (1993). Bootstrapping goodness-of-fit measures in structural equation models. In K. A. Bollen & J. S. Long (Eds.), *Testing structural equation models* (pp. 66–110). Newbury Park, CA: Sage.

Bollen, K. A. (1995). Structural equation models that are nonlinear in latent variables: A least squares estimator. In P. M. Marsden (Ed.), *Sociological methodology 1995*. Cambridge, MA: Blackwell.

Bollen, K. A. (1996). An alternative two stage least squares (2SLS) estimator for latent variable equations. *Psychometrika, 61*, 109–121.

Byrne, B. M. & Crombie, G. (2003). Modeling and testing change : an introduction to the latent growth curve model. *Understanding Statistics, 2*(3), 177–203.

Cole, D. A., Maxwell, S. E., Arvey, R., & Salas, E. (1993). Multivariate group comparisons of variable systems: MANOVA and structural equation modeling. *Psychological Bulletin, 114*, 174–184.

Duncan, T. E., & Duncan, S. C. (1995). Modeling the processes of development via latent variable growth curve methodology. *Structural Equation Modeling, 2*(3), 187–213.

Du Toit, M., & du Toit, S. (2001). *Interactive LISREL: User's guide*. Lincolnwood, IL: Scientific Software International.

Enders, C. K., & Bandalos, D. L. (2001). The relative performance of full information maximum likelihood estimation for missing data in structural equation models. *Structural Equation Modeling, 8*, 430–457.

Etezadi-Amoli, J., & McDonald, R. P. (1983). A second generation nonlinear factor analysis. *Psychometrika, 48*, 315–342.

Fan, X., Felsovalyi, A., Sivo, S., & Keenan, S. C. (2002). *SAS for Monte Carlo Studies: A Guide for Quantitative Researchers*. Sage Publications: CA. [zip file of SAS Monte Carlo programs available at: http://support.sas.com/publishing/bbu/57323/57323.zip].

Fan, X (2005). Using SAS for Monte Carlo simulation research in SEM. *Structural Equation Modeling: A Multidisciplinary Journal, 12*(2), 299–33.

Hayduk, L. A. (1987). *Structural equation modeling with LISREL.* Baltimore, MD: Johns Hopkins University Press.

Higgins, L. F., & Judd, C. M. (1990). Estimation of non-linear models in the presence of measurement error. *Decision Sciences, 21,* 738–751.

Jöreskog, K. G. (2000). *Latent variable scores and their uses.* Lincolnwood, IL: Scientific Software International.

Jöreskog, K. G., & Sörbom, D. (1993a). *Bootstrapping and Monte Carlo experimenting with PRELIS2 and LISREL8.* Chicago, IL: Scientific Software International.

Jöreskog, K. G., & Sörbom, D. (1993b). *LISREL8 user's reference guide.* Chicago, IL: Scientific Software International, Inc.

Jöreskog, K. G., & Sörbom, D. (1993c). *LISREL 8: Structural equation modeling with the SIMPLIS command language.* Chicago: Scientific Software International.

Jöreskog, K. G., & Sörbom, D. (1993d). *PRELIS2 user's reference guide.* Chicago, IL: Scientific Software International.

Jöreskog, K. G., Sörbom, D., Du Toit, S., & Du Toit, M. (2000). *LISREL8: New statistical features.* Lincolnwood, IL: Scientific Software International.

Jöreskog, K. G., & Yang, F. (1996). Non-linear structural equation models: The Kenny-Judd model with interaction effects. In G. A. Marcoulides, & R. E. Schumacker (Eds.), *New developments and techniques in structural equation modeling* (pp. 57–88). Mahwah, NJ: Lawrence Erlbaum.

Kenny, D. A., & Judd, C. M. (1984). Estimating the non-linear and interactive effects of latent variables. *Psychological Bulletin, 96,* 201–210.

Li, F., Duncan, T. E., Duncan, S. C., Acock, A. C., Yang-Wallentin, F., & Hops, H. (2001). *Interaction models in latent growth curves.* In G. A. Marcoulides, & R. E. Schumacker (Eds.), *New developments and techniques in structural equation modeling* (pp. 173–201). Mahwah, NJ: Lawrence Erlbaum.

Long, J. S. (2008). *The workflow of data analysis using STATA.* College Station, TX: Stata Press.

Lunneborg, C. E. (1987). *Bootstrap applications for the behavioral sciences: Vol. 1.* Psychology Department, University of Washington, Seattle.

Mackenzie, S. B., & Spreng, R. A. (1992). How does motivation moderate the impact of central and peripheral processing on brand attitudes and intentions? *Journal of Consumer Research, 18,* 519–529.

McArdle, J. J., & Epstein, D. (1987). Latent growth curves within developmental structural equation models. *Child Development, 58,* 110–133.

McDonald, R. P. (1967). Nonlinear factor analysis. *Psychometric Monograph,* No. 15.

Moulder, B. C., & Algina, J. (2002). Comparison of method for estimating and testing latent variable interactions. *Structural Equation Modeling, 9*(1), 1–19.

Mooney, C. Z., & Duval, R. D. (1993). *Bootstrapping: A nonparametric approach to statistical inference.* Sage University Series on Quantitative Applications in the Social Sciences, 07-097. Beverly Hills, CA: Sage.

Mooney, C. Z. (1997). *Monte Carlo Simulation.* Sage Series on Quantitative Applications in the Social Sciences. Beverly Hills, CA: Sage.

Newman, I., Marchant, G. J., & Ridenour, T. (1993, April). *Type VI errors in path analysis: Testing for interactions.* Paper presented at the annual meeting of the American Educational Research Association, Atlanta.

Paxton, P., Curran, P. J., Bollen, K. A., Kirby, J., & Chen, F. (2001). Monte Carlo experiments: Design and implementation. *Structural Equation Modeling, 8,* 287–312.

Ping, R. A., Jr. (1993). *Latent variable interaction and quadratic effect estimation: A suggested approach.* Technical Report. Dayton, OH: Wright State University.

Ping, R. A., Jr. (1994). Does satisfaction moderate the association between alternative attractiveness and exit intention in a marketing channel? *Journal of the Academy of Marketing Science, 22*(4), 364–371.

Ping, R. A., Jr. (1995). A parsimonious estimating technique for interaction and quadratic latent variables. *Journal of Marketing Research, 32*(3), 336–347.

Schumacker, R. E., & Marcoulides, G. A. (1998). *Interaction and nonlinear effects in structural equation modeling.* Mahwah, NJ: Lawrence Erlbaum.

Schumacker, R. E., & Rigdon, E. (1995, April). *Testing interaction effects in structural equation modeling.* Paper presented at the annual meeting of the American Educational Research Association, San Francisco.

Schumacker, R. E. (2002). Latent variable interaction modeling. *Structural Equation Modeling, 9*(1), 40–54.

Skrondal, A. (2001). Design and analysis of Monte Carlo experiments: Attacking the conventional wisdom. *Multivariate Behavioral Research, 35,* 137–167.

Smith, K. W., & Sasaki, M. S. (1979). Decreasing multicollinearity: A method for models with multiplicative functions. *Sociological Methods and Research, 8,* 35–56.

Stine, R. (1990). An introduction to bootstrap methods: Examples and ideas. In J. Fox. & J. S. Long (Eds.), *Modern methods of data analysis* (pp. 325–373). Beverly Hills, CA: Sage.

Stoolmiller, M. (1995). Using latent growth curves to study developmental processes. In J. M. Gottman (Ed.), *The analysis of change* (pp. 103–138). Mahwah, NJ: Lawrence Erlbaum.

Wong, S. K., & Long, J. S. (1987). Parameterizing Non-linear Constraints in Models with Latent Variables. Unpublished manuscript, Indiana University, Department of Sociology, Bloomington, IN.

Yang-Wallentin, F., & Joreskog, K. G. (2001). Robust standard errors and chi-squares in interaction models. In G. Marcoulides, & R. E. Schumacker (Eds.), *New developments and techniques in structural equation modeling* (pp. 159–171). Mahwah, NJ: Lawrence Erlbaum.

17

Matrix Approach to Structural Equation Modeling

Key Concepts

Eight matrices in SEM models

Matrix notation: measurement and structural models

Free, fixed, and constrained parameters

Structured means

Mean matrices: tau and kappa

17.1 General Overview of Matrix Notation

We have deliberately delayed presenting the matrix notation used in calculating structural equation models because we wanted to first present the basic concepts, principles, and applications of SEM. SEM models are typically analyzed using the eight different matrices illustrated in Figure 17.1 (Hayduk, 1987); although a few new ones have emerged, for example, tau and kappa. SEM models may use some combination of these matrices, but not use all of the matrices in a given analysis, for example, path analysis or confirmatory factor analysis.

In this chapter we consider the technical matrix notation associated with the LISREL matrix command language. As described in Jöreskog and Sörbom (1996), the structural model is written in terms of the following matrix equation:

$$\eta = B\eta + \Gamma\xi + \zeta \tag{17.1}$$

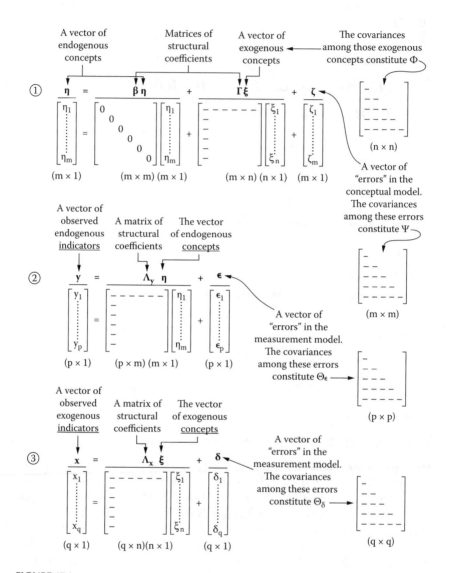

FIGURE 17.1

Summary of the general structural equation model. (From Hayduk, L. A. (1987). *Structural equation modeling with LISREL: Essentials and advances.* Baltimore, MD: Johns Hopkins University Press.)

The latent dependent variables are denoted by η (eta) as a vector ($m \times 1$) of m such variables. The latent independent variables are denoted by ξ (ksi) as a vector ($n \times 1$) of n such variables. A matrix Φ (capital phi) contains the variances and covariance terms among these latent independent variables. The relationships among the latent variables are denoted by B

(capital beta) and Γ (capital gamma), the elements of which are denoted by [β] (lowercase beta) and [γ] (lowercase gamma), respectively. The matrix B is a $m \times m$ matrix of structure coefficients that relate the latent dependent variables to one another. Γ is a $m \times n$ matrix of structure coefficients that relate the latent independent variables to the latent dependent variables. The error term ζ (zeta) in the structural model equation is a vector that contains the equation prediction errors or disturbance terms. The matrix Ψ (capital psi) contains the variances and covariance terms among these latent dependent prediction equation errors.

As described in Jöreskog and Sörbom (1996), the measurement models are written in the following set of matrix equations:

$$Y = \Lambda_y \, \eta + \varepsilon, \qquad (17.2)$$

for the latent dependent variables, and

$$X = \Lambda_x \, \xi + \delta, \qquad (17.3)$$

for the latent independent variables. The observed variables are denoted by the vector Y ($p \times 1$) for the measures of the latent dependent variables η ($m \times 1$), and by the vector X ($q \times 1$) for the measures of the latent independent variables ξ ($n \times 1$). The relationships between the observed variables and the latent variables (typically referred to as *factor loadings*) are denoted by the ($p \times m$) matrix Λ_y (capital lambda sub y) for the Y's, the elements of which are denoted by [λ_y] (lowercase lambda sub y), and by the $q \times n$ matrix Λ_x (capital lambda sub x) for the X's, the elements of which are denoted by [λ_x] (lowercase lambda sub x). Finally, the measurement errors for the Y's are denoted by the $p \times 1$ vector ε (lowercase epsilon) and for the X's by the $q \times 1$ vector δ (lowercase delta). The theta–epsilon matrix Θ_ε contains the variances and covariance terms among the errors for the observed dependent variables. The theta–delta matrix Θ_δ contains the variances and covariance terms among the errors for the observed independent variables.

The summary of the general structural equation model in matrix format depicted by Hayduk (1987) should be studied in great detail. The three equations diagrammed in matrix format correspond to the structural model in Equation 17.1, the measurement model for the Y dependent variables in Equation 17.2, and the measurement model for the X independent variables in Equation 17.3.

Obviously, not all of the matrices are used in every SEM model. We use our examples from chapters 9 and 10 to illustrate the matrix notation for a structural equation model. In our first example in chapter 9 (see Figure 9.1), there were two structure coefficients of interest. The first involved the influence of *Intelligence* on *Achievement*$_1$. The structure coefficient for this influence resides in the matrix Γ because it represents the relationship between the latent independent variable *Intelligence* and the latent dependent variable *Achievement*$_1$. The second structure coefficient involved the influence of *Achievement*$_1$ on *Achievement*$_2$. This coefficient resides in the matrix *B* because it represents the relationship between the latent dependent variable *Achievement*$_1$ and the latent dependent variable *Achievement*$_2$. The final term in the structural model of Equation 17.1 is ζ (zeta), an $m \times 1$ vector of m equation errors or disturbances, which represents that portion of each latent dependent variable that is not explained or predicted by the model.

In LISREL notation our structural equations are written as

$$\eta_1 = \gamma_{11}\xi_1 + \zeta_1,$$

and

$$\eta_2 = \beta_{21}\eta_1 + \zeta_2,$$

respectively, or in the complete matrix equation as

$$\begin{bmatrix} \eta_1 \\ \eta_2 \end{bmatrix} = \begin{bmatrix} 0 & 0 \\ \beta_{21} & 0 \end{bmatrix} \begin{bmatrix} \eta_1 \\ \eta_2 \end{bmatrix} + \begin{bmatrix} \gamma_{11} \\ 0 \end{bmatrix} [\xi_1] + \begin{bmatrix} \zeta_1 \\ \zeta_2 \end{bmatrix},$$

where the subscripts on β represent the rows for a latent dependent variable being predicted and columns for a latent dependent variable as the predictor, respectively. The subscripts for γ represent the rows for a latent dependent variable being predicted and columns for a latent independent variable as the predictor, respectively.

The values of 0 shown in the matrix equations for B and Γ represent structure coefficients that we hypothesize to be equal to 0. For example, because we did not specify that *Intelligence* influenced *Achievement*$_2$, rather than estimate γ_{21}, we set that value to 0. Likewise, we did not specify that *Achievement*$_2$ influenced *Achievement*$_1$, so we set β_{12} to 0. Finally, notice that the diagonal values of B are also 0, that is, β_{11} and β_{22}. The diagonal values of B are always set to 0 because they indicate the extent to which a latent dependent variable influences itself. These influences are never of interest to the SEM researcher. In summary, our matrix equation suggests that there are potentially four structure coefficients of interest, $\beta_{12}, \beta_{21}, \gamma_{11},$ and γ_{21}; however, our model includes only two of these coefficients. Other structural models of these same latent variables can be developed that contain different configurations of structure coefficients.

We now need to provide a more explicit definition of the measurement models in our example. We have two different measurement models in our example, one for the latent dependent variables and one for the latent independent variables. In LISREL matrix notation these equations are written for the Ys as

$$y_1 = \lambda_{y_{11}} \eta_1 + \varepsilon_1$$

$$y_2 = \lambda_{y_{21}} \eta_1 + \varepsilon_2$$

$$y_3 = \lambda_{y_{32}} \eta_2 + \varepsilon_3$$

$$y_4 = \lambda_{y_{42}} \eta_2 + \varepsilon_4$$

and for the Xs as

$$x_1 = \lambda_{x_{11}} \xi_1 + \delta_1$$

$$x_2 = \lambda_{x_{21}} \xi_1 + \delta_2$$

The factor loadings and error terms also appear in their respective error variance–covariance matrices. The complete matrix equation for the Ys is written as

$$
\begin{bmatrix} y_1 \\ y_2 \\ y_3 \\ y_4 \end{bmatrix} =
\begin{bmatrix} \lambda_{y_{11}} & 0 \\ \lambda_{y_{21}} & 0 \\ 0 & \lambda_{y_{32}} \\ 0 & \lambda_{y_{42}} \end{bmatrix}
\begin{bmatrix} \eta_1 \\ \eta_2 \end{bmatrix} +
\begin{bmatrix} \varepsilon_1 \\ \varepsilon_2 \\ \varepsilon_3 \\ \varepsilon_4 \end{bmatrix}
$$

and for the Xs as

$$
\begin{bmatrix} x_1 \\ x_2 \end{bmatrix} =
\begin{bmatrix} \lambda_{x_{11}} \\ \lambda_{x_{21}} \end{bmatrix}
\begin{bmatrix} \xi_1 \end{bmatrix} +
\begin{bmatrix} \delta_1 \\ \delta_2 \end{bmatrix}
$$

where the subscripts in λ_y represent the rows for an observed Y variable and the columns for a latent dependent variable, and those in λ_x represent the rows for an observed X variable and the columns for a latent independent variable, respectively.

The values of 0 shown in the matrix equations for Λ_y (and theoretically for Λ_x, although not for this particular model) represent factor loadings that we hypothesize to be equal to 0. For example, because we did not specify that *California*$_1$ was an indicator of *Achievement*$_2$, rather than estimate λ_{y12}, we set that value to 0. Likewise, we specified that λ_{y22}, λ_{y31}, and λ_{y41} were set to 0.

There are several covariance terms that we need to define. From the structural model, there are two covariance terms to consider. First, we define Φ (capital phi) as an $n \times n$ covariance matrix of the n latent independent variables, the elements of which are denoted by $[\phi]$ (lowercase phi). The diagonal elements of Φ contain the variances of the latent independent variables. In our example, model Φ contains only one element, the variance of Intelligence (denoted by ϕ_{11}).

Second, let us define Ψ (psi) as an $m \times m$ covariance matrix of the m equation errors ζ, the elements of which are denoted by $[\psi]$ (lowercase psi). The diagonal elements of Ψ contain the variances of the equation errors—that is, the amount of unexplained variance for each equation. In our example model Ψ contains two diagonal elements, one for each equation (denoted by ψ_{11} and ψ_{22}).

From the measurement model there are two additional covariance terms to be concerned with. First, we define Θ_ε (capital theta sub epsilon) as a $p \times p$ covariance matrix of the measurement errors for the Ys—that is, ε, the elements of which are denoted by (θ_ε), lowercase theta sub epsilon. The diagonal elements of Θ_ε contain the variances of the measurement errors for the Ys. In our example model Θ_ε contains four diagonal elements, one for each Y. Second, let us define Θ_δ (capital theta sub delta) as a $q \times q$ covariance matrix of the measurement errors for the Xs—that is, δ, the elements of which are denoted by (θ_δ), lowercase theta sub delta. The diagonal elements of Θ_δ contain the variances of the measurement errors for the Xs. In our example model, Θ_δ contains two diagonal elements, one for each X.

There is one more covariance term that we need to define, and it represents the ultimate covariance term. To this point we have defined the following eight different matrices: B, Γ, Λ_y, Λ_x, Φ, Ψ, Θ_δ and Θ_ε. From these matrices we can generate an ultimate matrix of covariance terms that the overall model implies, and this matrix is denoted by Σ (sigma). Officially, Σ is a supermatrix composed of four submatrices, as follows:

$$\begin{bmatrix} \Sigma_{yy} & \Sigma_{yx} \\ \Sigma_{xy} & \Sigma_{xx} \end{bmatrix}$$

(17.4)

This supermatrix certainly looks imposing, but it can be easily understood. First consider the submatrix in the upper left portion of Σ. It deals with the covariance terms among the Ys, and in terms of our model can be written as

$$\Sigma_{yy} = [\Lambda_y[(I-B)^{-1}(\Gamma\Phi\Gamma' + \Psi)(I-B')^{-1}]\Lambda_y' + \Theta_\varepsilon], \tag{17.5}$$

where I is an $m \times m$ identity matrix (i.e., a matrix having 1s on the diagonal and 0s on the off-diagonal). You can see in Equation 17.5 that all of the matrices are involved except for those of the measurement model in the X's. That is, Equation 17.5 contains the matrices for the structural model and for the measurement model in the Ys.

Consider next the submatrix in the lower right portion of Σ. It deals with the covariance terms among the Xs and in terms of our model can be written as

$$\Sigma_{xx} = [\Lambda_x\Phi\Lambda_x' + \Theta_\delta] \tag{17.6}$$

As shown in Equation 17.6, the only matrices included are those that involve the X side of the model. This particular portion of the model is the same as the common factor analysis model, which you may recognize.

Finally, consider the submatrix in the lower left portion of Σ. It deals with the covariance terms between the X's and the Y's and in terms of our model can be written as

$$\Sigma_{xy} = [\Lambda_x\Phi\Gamma'(I-B')^{-1}\Lambda_y']. \tag{17.7}$$

As shown in Equation 17.7, this portion of the model includes all of our matrices except for the error terms, that is, Ψ, Θ_δ and Θ_ε. The submatrix in the upper right portion of Σ is the transposed version of Equation 17.7 (i.e., the matrix of Equation 17.7 with rows and columns switched), so we need not concern ourselves with it.

17.2 Free, Fixed, and Constrained Parameters

Let us return for a moment to our eight structural equation matrices B, Γ, Λ_y, Λ_x, Φ, Ψ, Θ_δ and Θ_ε. In the structural model there are structure coefficients in matrices B and Γ. The covariance terms among structural equation errors are in the matrix Ψ. In the measurement models for latent independent and dependent variables, there are factor loadings in the matrices Λ_x and Λ_y, respectively, for their indicator variables. The covariance terms of measurement errors for the latent independent and dependent variables are in the matrices Θ_δ and Θ_ε, respectively. The covariance terms among the latent independent variables are in the matrix Φ. Each and every element in these eight matrices, if used in a particular model, must be specified to be a free parameter, a fixed parameter, or a constrained parameter. A free parameter is a parameter that is unknown and one that you wish to estimate. A fixed parameter is a parameter that is not free but rather is fixed to a specified value, typically either 0 or 1. A constrained parameter is a parameter that is unknown, but is constrained to be equal to one or more other parameters.

For example, consider the following matrix B:

$$B = \begin{bmatrix} 0 & \beta_{12} \\ \beta_{21} & 0 \end{bmatrix}$$

The βs represent values in B that might be parameters of interest and thus constitute free parameters. The 0s represent values in B that are fixed or constrained to be equal to 0. These diagonal values of B represent the influence of a latent dependent variable on itself, and by definition are always fixed to 0. If our hypothesized model included only β_{21}, then β_{12} would also be fixed to 0. For the model specified in Figure 10.2 in chapter 10, B takes the following form:

$$B = \begin{bmatrix} 0 & 0 \\ \beta_{21} & 0 \end{bmatrix}.$$

For another example, consider the following matrix Λ_y with the factor loadings for the latent dependent variable measurement model:

$$\Lambda_y = \begin{bmatrix} \lambda_{y_{11}} & \lambda_{y_{12}} \\ \lambda_{y_{21}} & \lambda_{y_{22}} \\ \lambda_{y_{31}} & \lambda_{y_{32}} \\ \lambda_{y_{41}} & \lambda_{y_{42}} \end{bmatrix}$$

Here the λ_y represent the values in Λ_y that might be parameters of interest and would constitute free parameters. This specifies that we are allowing all of the parameters in Λ_y to be free so that each of our four indicator variables (the Y's) loads on each of our two latent dependent variables (the η's). However, in order to solve the identification problem for Λ_y, some constraints are usually placed on this matrix whereby some of the parameters are fixed. We might specify that the first two indicator variables are allowed only to load on the first latent dependent variable (η_1) and the latter two indicators on the second latent dependent variable (η_2). Then,

Λ_y appears as

$$\Lambda_y = \begin{bmatrix} \lambda_{y_{11}} & 0 \\ \lambda_{y_{21}} & 0 \\ 0 & \lambda_{y_{32}} \\ 0 & \lambda_{y_{42}} \end{bmatrix}$$

Additional constraints in Λ_y may also be necessary for identification purposes.

For the structural equation model in chapter 10 (Figure 10.2), the following structural equations are specified:

Aspirations = home background + ability + error

Achievement = aspirations + home background + ability + error

The matrix equation would be $\eta = B\eta + \Gamma\xi + \zeta$ and the elements of the matrices are

$$\begin{bmatrix} \eta_1 \\ \eta_2 \end{bmatrix} = \begin{bmatrix} 0 & 0 \\ \beta_{21} & 0 \end{bmatrix} \begin{bmatrix} \eta_1 \\ \eta_2 \end{bmatrix} + \begin{bmatrix} \gamma_{11} & \gamma_{12} \\ \gamma_{21} & \gamma_{22} \end{bmatrix} \begin{bmatrix} \xi_1 \\ \xi_2 \end{bmatrix} + \begin{bmatrix} \zeta_1 \\ \zeta_2 \end{bmatrix}.$$

The matrix equation for the latent dependent variable measurement model is $Y = \Lambda_y \eta + \varepsilon$, and the elements of the matrices are

$$\begin{bmatrix} y_1 \\ y_2 \\ y_3 \\ y_4 \end{bmatrix} = \begin{bmatrix} 1 & 0 \\ \lambda_{y_{21}} & 0 \\ 0 & 1 \\ 0 & \lambda_{y_{42}} \end{bmatrix} \begin{bmatrix} \eta_1 \\ \eta_2 \end{bmatrix} + \begin{bmatrix} \varepsilon_1 \\ \varepsilon_2 \\ \varepsilon_3 \\ \varepsilon_4 \end{bmatrix}.$$

The matrix equation for the latent independent variable measurement model is $X = \Lambda_x \xi + \delta$ and the elements of the matrices are

$$\begin{bmatrix} x_1 \\ x_2 \\ x_3 \\ x_4 \\ x_5 \end{bmatrix} = \begin{bmatrix} 1 & 0 \\ \lambda_{x_{21}} & 0 \\ \lambda_{x_{31}} & 0 \\ 0 & 1 \\ 0 & \lambda_{x_{52}} \end{bmatrix} \begin{bmatrix} \xi_1 \\ \xi_2 \end{bmatrix} + \begin{bmatrix} \delta_1 \\ \delta_2 \\ \delta_3 \\ \delta_4 \\ \delta_5 \end{bmatrix}.$$

Recall that for each dependent and independent latent variable we fixed one factor loading of an observed variable to 1. This was necessary to identify the model and to fix the scale for the latent variables.

The covariance terms are written next. The covariance matrix for the latent independent variables is

$$\Phi = \begin{bmatrix} \phi_{11} & \\ \phi_{21} & \phi_{22} \end{bmatrix}.$$

The covariance matrix for the structural equation errors is

$$\Psi = \begin{bmatrix} \psi_{11} & \\ \psi_{21} & \psi_{22} \end{bmatrix}.$$

The covariance matrices for the measurement errors are written as follows, first for the indicators of the latent independent variables by

$$\Theta_\delta = \begin{bmatrix} \theta_{\delta_{11}} & & & & \\ 0 & \theta_{\delta_{22}} & & & \\ 0 & \theta_{\delta_{32}} & \theta_{\delta_{33}} & & \\ 0 & 0 & 0 & \theta_{\delta_{44}} & \\ 0 & 0 & 0 & 0 & \theta_{\delta_{55}} \end{bmatrix}$$

and second, for the indicators of the latent dependent variables by

$$\Theta_\varepsilon = \begin{bmatrix} \theta_{\varepsilon_{11}} & & & \\ 0 & \theta_{\varepsilon_{22}} & & \\ 0 & 0 & \theta_{\varepsilon_{33}} & \\ 0 & 0 & 0 & \theta_{\varepsilon_{44}} \end{bmatrix}$$

NOTE: This matrix output is possible by including the LISREL OUTPUT command in the LISREL–SIMPLIS program for the model in chapter 10.

17.3 LISREL Model Example in Matrix Notation

The LISREL matrix command language program works directly from the matrix notation previously discussed and is presented here for the example in chapter 10. The basic LISREL matrix command language program includes TITLE, DATA (DA), INPUT, MODEL (MO), and OUTPUT

(OU) program statements. The TITLE lines are optional. The user's guide provides an excellent overview of the various commands and their purpose (Jöreskog & Sörbom, 1996). The DA statement identifies the number of input variables in the variance–covariance matrix, the NO statement indicates the number of observations, and MA identifies the kind of matrix to be *analyzed*, not the kind of matrix to be *inputted*: MA = CM, covariance matrix; MA = KM, correlation matrix based on raw scores or normal scores; MA = MM, matrix of moments (means) about zero; MA = AM, augmented moment matrix; MA = OM, special correlation matrix of optimal scores from PRELIS2; and MA = PM, correlation matrix of polychoric (ordinal variables) or polyserial (ordinal and continuous variables) correlations. The SE statement must be used to select and/or reorder variables used in the analysis of a model (the *Y* variables must be listed first). An external raw score data file can be read using the RA statement with the FI and FO subcommands, for example, RA FI = raw.dat FO. The FO subcommand permits the specification of how observations are to be read (*Note*: for fixed, a FORMAT statement must be enclosed in parentheses; for free-field, an asterisk is placed in the first column, which appears on the line following the RA command). If FI or UN (logical unit number of a FORTRAN file) subcommands are not used, then the data must directly follow the RA command and be included in the program.

In the following LISREL matrix command language program, a lower diagonal variance–covariance matrix is input, hence, the use of the CM statement. The SY subcommand, which reads only the lower diagonal elements of a matrix, has been omitted because it is the default option for matrix input. The LA statement provides for up to eight characters for variable labels, with similar subcommand options for input and specifications as with the RA command for data input. (*Note:* A lower case c permits line continuation for various commands). The LE command permits variable labels for the latent dependent variables, and the LK command permits variable labels for the latent independent variables.

The MO command specifies the model for LISREL analysis. The subcommands specify the number of *Y* variables (*ny*), number of *X* variables (*nx*), number of latent dependent variables (*ne*), and number of latent independent variables (*nk*). The form and mode of the eight LISREL parameter matrices must be specified and are further explained in the user's guide (Jöreskog & Sörbom, 1996). The FU parameter indicates a full non-symmetric matrix form, and FI indicates a fixed matrix mode, in contrast to a free mode (FR). The DI statement indicates a diagonal matrix form, and the SY statement indicates a symmetric matrix form. It is strongly recommended that any designation of a LISREL model for analysis include the presentation of the eight matrices in matrix form. This will greatly ease the writing of the MO command and the identification of fixed or free parameters in the matrices on the FR and VA commands. The VA command assigns numerical values to the fixed parameters. The OU command permits the selection of various output procedures. One feature of interest on the OU command is the AM option, which provides for automatic model specification by freeing at each step the fixed or constrained parameters with the largest modification indices, although, as previously noted, this should not be the sole criterion for model modification.

The LISREL matrix command language program used to analyze the model in Figure 10.2 of chapter 10, using the default maximum likelihood estimation method, is as follows:

Modified Model in Figure 10.2, Chapter 10
da ni=9 no=200 ma=cm
cm sy
1.024
.792   1.077
1.027   .919   1.844
.756   .697   1.244   1.286
.567   .537   .876   .632   .852
.445   .424   .677   .526   .518   .670
.434   .389   .635   .498   .475   .545   .716
.580   .564   .893   .716   .546   .422   .373   .851
.491   .499   .888   .646   .508   .389   .339   .629   .871
la
   EDASP OCASP VERBACH QUANTACH FAMINC FAED MOED VERBAB
c   QUANTAB mo ny=4 nx=5 ne=2 nk=2 be=fu,fi ga=fu,fi ph=sy,fi ps=di,fi

c   ly=fu,fi lx=fu,fi td=fu,fi te=fu,fi
le
  aspire achieve
lk
  home ability
fr be(2,1) ga(1,1) ga(1,2) ga(2,1) ga(2,2)
   c ly(2,1) ly(4,2) lx(2,1) lx(3,1) lx(5,2)
   c te(1,1) te(2,2) te(3,3) te(4,4) td(1,1) td(2,2) td(3,3)
   c td(4,4) td(5,5)
   c ps(1,1) ps(2,2) ph(1,1) ph(2,2) ph(2,1) td(3,2)
va 1.0 ly(1,1) ly(3,2) lx(1,1) lx(4,2)
ou me=ml all

(NOTE: The c values in the LISREL program denote line continuations in program statements.)

The LISREL matrix command language requires the user to specifically understand the nature, form, and mode of the eight matrices, and thereby fully comprehend the model being specified for analysis, even though all eight matrices may not be used in a particular SEM model. We present the LISREL output from this program, but do so in an edited and condensed format. We challenge you to find the various matrices we have described in this chapter in the computer output.

LISREL8 Matrix Program Output (Edited and Condensed)

Modified Model in Figure 10.2, chapter 10

```
            Number of Input Variables   9
            Number of Y - Variables     4
            Number of X - Variables     5
            Number of ETA - Variables   2
            Number of KSI - Variables   2
            Number of Observations    200
```

Covariance Matrix

	EDASP	OCASP	VERBACH	QUANTACH	FAMINC	FAED
EDASP	1.02					
OCASP	0.79	1.08				
VERBACH	1.03	0.92	1.84			
QUANTACH	0.76	0.70	1.24	1.29		
FAMINC	0.57	0.54	0.88	0.63	0.85	
FAED	0.45	0.42	0.68	0.53	0.52	0.67
MOED	0.43	0.39	0.64	0.50	0.47	0.55
VERBAB	0.58	0.56	0.89	0.72	0.55	0.42
QUANTAB	0.49	0.50	0.89	0.65	0.51	0.39

Covariance Matrix

	MOED	VERBAB	QUANTAB
MOED	0.72		
VERBAB	0.37	0.85	
QUANTAB	0.34	0.63	0.87

LISREL Estimates (Maximum Likelihood)

LAMBDA-Y

	aspire	achieve
EDASP	1.00	- -
OCASP	0.92	- -
	(0.06)	
	14.34	
VERBACH	- -	1.00
QUANTACH	- -	0.75
		(0.04)
		18.13

LAMBDA-X

	home	ability
FAMINC	1.00	- -

```
        FAED        0.78           - -
                   (0.06)
                   12.18
        MOED        0.72           - -
                   (0.07)
                   10.37
      VERBAB        - -            1.00
     QUANTAB        - -            0.95
                                  (0.07)
                                  14.10
```

BETA

	aspire	achieve
	--------	--------
aspire	- -	- -
achieve	0.53	- -
	(0.12)	
	4.56	

GAMMA

	home	ability
	--------	--------
aspire	0.51	0.45
	(0.15)	(0.15)
	3.29	2.96
achieve	0.30	0.69
	(0.16)	(0.16)
	1.87	4.27

Covariance Matrix of ETA and KSI

	aspire	achieve	home	ability
	--------	--------	--------	--------
aspire	0.86			
achieve	1.02	1.65		
home	0.57	0.87	0.66	
ability	0.57	0.91	0.54	0.66

PHI

	home	ability
	--------	--------
home		0.66
		(0.09)
		7.32
ability	0.54	0.66
	(0.07)	(0.09)
	7.64	7.51

PSI
Note: This matrix is diagonal.

aspire	achieve
0.32	0.23
(0.06)	(0.06)
5.61	3.97

Squared Multiple Correlations for Structural Equations

aspire	achieve
0.63	0.86

Squared Multiple Correlations for Reduced Form

aspire	achieve
0.63	0.81

THETA-EPS

EDASP	OCASP	VERBACH	QUANTACH
0.16	0.35	0.19	0.35
(0.04)	(0.05)	(0.05)	(0.04)
3.88	7.36	3.81	7.95

Squared Multiple Correlations for Y - Variables

EDASP	OCASP	VERBACH	QUANTACH
0.84	0.67	0.90	0.73

THETA-DELTA

	FAMINC	FAED	MOED	VERBAB	QUANTAB
FAMINC	0.19				
	(0.04)				
	4.74				
FAED	- -	0.27			
		(0.03)			
		7.66			
MOED	- -	0.17	0.37		
		(0.03)	(0.04)		
		5.28	8.50		
VERBAB	- -	- -	- -	0.19	
				(0.03)	
				5.41	
QUANTAB	- -	- -	- -	- -	0.27
					(0.04)
					7.20

Squared Multiple Correlations for X - Variables

FAMINC	FAED	MOED	VERBAB	QUANTAB
0.78	0.60	0.48	0.78	0.69

Goodness-of-Fit Statistics
Degrees of Freedom = 20
Minimum Fit Function Chi-Square = 19.17 (P = 0.51)
Normal Theory Weighted Least Squares Chi-Square = 18.60
(P = 0.55)
Estimated Non-centrality Parameter (NCP) = 0.0
90 Percent Confidence Interval for NCP = (0.0 ; 12.67)

Minimum Fit Function Value = 0.096
Population Discrepancy Function Value (F0) = 0.0
90 Percent Confidence Interval for F0 = (0.0 ; 0.064)
Root Mean Square Error of Approximation (RMSEA) = 0.0
90 Percent Confidence Interval for RMSEA = (0.0 ; 0.056)
P-Value for Test of Close Fit (RMSEA < 0.05) = 0.91

Expected Cross-Validation Index (ECVI) = 0.35
90 Percent Confidence Interval for ECVI = (0.35 ; 0.42)
ECVI for Saturated Model = 0.45
ECVI for Independence Model = 13.72

Chi-Square for Independence Model with 36 Degrees of
Freedom = 2712.06
Independence AIC = 2730.06
Model AIC = 68.60
Saturated AIC = 90.00
Independence CAIC = 2768.74
Model CAIC = 176.05
Saturated CAIC = 283.42

Normed Fit Index (NFI) = 0.99
Non-Normed Fit Index (NNFI) = 1.00
Parsimony Normed Fit Index (PNFI) = 0.55
Comparative Fit Index (CFI) = 1.00
Incremental Fit Index (IFI) = 1.00
Relative Fit Index (RFI) = 0.99

Critical N (CN) = 391.00

Root Mean Square Residual (RMR) = 0.015
Standardized RMR = 0.015
Goodness-of-Fit Index (GFI) = 0.98
Adjusted Goodness-of-Fit Index (AGFI) = 0.95
Parsimony Goodness-of-Fit Index (PGFI) = 0.44

Fitted Covariance Matrix

	EDASP	OCASP	VERBACH	QUANTACH	FAMINC	FAED
EDASP	1.02					
OCASP	0.79	1.08				
VERBACH	1.02	0.93	1.84			
QUANTACH	0.77	0.70	1.24	1.29		
FAMINC	0.57	0.53	0.87	0.66	0.85	
FAED	0.45	0.41	0.68	0.51	0.52	0.67
MOED	0.41	0.38	0.63	0.47	0.48	0.54
VERBAB	0.57	0.52	0.91	0.69	0.54	0.42
QUANTAB	0.54	0.49	0.87	0.65	0.51	0.40

Fitted Covariance Matrix

	MOED	VERBAB	QUANTAB
MOED	0.72		
VERBAB	0.39	0.85	
QUANTAB	0.37	0.63	0.87

Fitted Residuals

	EDASP	OCASP	VERBACH	QUANTACH	FAMINC	FAED
EDASP	0.00					
OCASP	0.00	0.00				
VERBACH	0.01	-0.01	0.00			
QUANTACH	-0.01	-0.01	0.00	0.00		
FAMINC	-0.01	0.01	0.01	-0.02	0.00	
FAED	0.00	0.01	0.00	0.01	0.00	0.00
MOED	0.02	0.01	0.01	0.03	0.00	0.00
VERBAB	0.01	0.04	-0.02	0.03	0.01	0.00
QUANTAB	-0.05	0.00	0.02	-0.01	0.00	-0.01

Fitted Residuals

	MOED	VERBAB	QUANTAB
MOED	0.00		
VERBAB	-0.01	0.00	
QUANTAB	-0.03	0.00	0.00

Summary Statistics for Fitted Residuals

Smallest Fitted Residual = -0.05
 Median Fitted Residual = 0.00
Largest Fitted Residual = 0.04

```
Stemleaf Plot
 - 4|8
 - 3|
 - 2|842
 - 1|4400
 - 0|886542100000000000000000
   0|2469999
   1|1123
   2|0067
   3|
   4|3
```

Standardized Residuals

	EDASP	OCASP	VERBACH	QUANTACH	FAMINC	FAED
EDASP	- -					
OCASP	- -	- -				
VERBACH	1.26	-1.01	- -			
QUANTACH	-0.52	-0.23	- -	- -		
FAMINC	-0.64	0.45	0.55	-1.17	- -	
FAED	-0.25	0.45	-0.23	0.58	0.15	- -
MOED	0.82	0.30	0.36	0.91	-0.15	- -
VERBAB	0.88	1.93	-2.34	1.50	0.72	0.10
QUANTAB	-2.53	0.16	1.59	-0.38	-0.13	-0.50

Standardized Residuals

	MOED	VERBAB	QUANTAB
MOED	- -		
VERBAB	-0.63	- -	
QUANTAB	-1.10	- -	- -

Summary Statistics for Standardized Residuals

```
Smallest Standardized Residual = -2.53
  Median Standardized Residual =  0.00
 Largest Standardized Residual =  1.93
```

Stemleaf Plot

```
 - 2|5
 - 2|3
 - 1|
 - 1|210
 - 0|6655
 - 0|4322210000000000000
   0|122344
   0|5567899
   1|3
   1|569
```

Modification Indices and Expected Change

Modification Indices for LAMBDA-Y

	aspire	achieve
EDASP	- -	0.30
OCASP	- -	0.30
VERBACH	0.32	- -
QUANTACH	0.32	- -

Expected Change for LAMBDA-Y

	aspire	achieve
EDASP	- -	0.28
OCASP	- -	-0.26
VERBACH	0.12	- -
QUANTACH	-0.09	- -

Standardized Expected Change for LAMBDA-Y

	aspire	achieve
EDASP	- -	0.36
OCASP	- -	-0.33
VERBACH	0.11	- -
QUANTACH	-0.09	- -

Modification Indices for LAMBDA-X

	home	ability
FAMINC	- -	0.40
FAED	- -	0.11
MOED	- -	0.49
VERBAB	0.63	- -
QUANTAB	0.63	- -

Expected Change for LAMBDA-X

	home	ability
FAMINC	- -	0.18
FAED	- -	0.04
MOED	- -	-0.08
VERBAB	0.16	- -
QUANTAB	-0.16	- -

Standardized Expected Change for LAMBDA-X

	home	ability
FAMINC	- -	0.15
FAED	- -	0.03
MOED	- -	-0.06
VERBAB	0.13	- -
QUANTAB	-0.13	- -

No Non-Zero Modification Indices for BETA
No Non-Zero Modification Indices for GAMMA
No Non-Zero Modification Indices for PHI
No Non-Zero Modification Indices for PSI

Modification Indices for THETA-EPS

	EDASP	OCASP	VERBACH	QUANTACH
EDASP	- -			
OCASP	- -	- -		
VERBACH	2.32	1.91	- -	
QUANTACH	0.17	0.01	- -	- -

Expected Change for THETA-EPS

	EDASP	OCASP	VERBACH	QUANTACH
EDASP	- -			
OCASP	- -	- -		
VERBACH	0.05	-0.05	- -	
QUANTACH	-0.01	0.00	- -	- -

Modification Indices for THETA-DELTA-EPS

	EDASP	OCASP	VERBACH	QUANTACH
FAMINC	0.12	0.06	0.86	2.09
FAED	0.62	0.32	0.30	0.15
MOED	1.13	0.40	0.02	0.37
VERBAB	0.51	1.13	8.44	3.03
QUANTAB	4.92	0.30	5.47	0.94

Expected Change for THETA-DELTA-EPS

	EDASP	OCASP	VERBACH	QUANTACH
FAMINC	-0.01	0.01	0.03	-0.04
FAED	-0.01	0.01	-0.01	0.01
MOED	0.02	-0.02	0.00	0.01

VERBAB	0.02	0.03	-0.09	0.05
QUANTAB	-0.06	0.02	0.07	-0.03

Modification Indices for THETA-DELTA

	FAMINC	FAED	MOED	VERBAB	QUANTAB
	--------	--------	--------	--------	--------
FAMINC	- -				
FAED	0.02	- -			
MOED	0.02	- -	- -		
VERBAB	0.15	0.14	0.36	- -	
QUANTAB	0.02	0.05	0.59	- -	- -

Expected Change for THETA-DELTA

	FAMINC	FAED	MOED	VERBAB	QUANTAB
	--------	--------	--------	--------	--------
FAMINC	- -				
FAED	0.00	- -			
MOED	0.00	- -	- -		
VERBAB	0.01	0.01	-0.01	- -	
QUANTAB	0.00	0.00	-0.02	- -	- -

Maximum Modification Index is 8.44 for Element (4, 3) of THETA DELTA-EPSILON

Covariances

Y - ETA

	EDASP	OCASP	VERBACH	QUANTACH
	--------	--------	--------	--------
aspire	0.86	0.79	1.02	0.77
achieve	1.02	0.93	1.65	1.24

Y - KSI

	EDASP	OCASP	VERBACH	QUANTACH
	--------	--------	--------	--------
home	0.57	0.53	0.87	0.66
ability	0.57	0.52	0.91	0.69

X - ETA

	FAMINC	FAED	MOED	VERBAB	QUANTAB
	--------	--------	--------	--------	--------
aspire	0.57	0.45	0.41	0.57	0.54
achieve	0.87	0.68	0.63	0.91	0.87

```
X - KSI
```

	FAMINC	FAED	MOED	VERBAB	QUANTAB
home	0.66	0.52	0.48	0.54	0.51
ability	0.54	0.42	0.39	0.66	0.63

First Order Derivatives

LAMBDA-Y

	aspire	achieve
EDASP	0.00	-0.01
OCASP	0.00	0.01
VERBACH	-0.01	0.00
QUANTACH	0.02	0.00

LAMBDA-X

	home	ability
FAMINC	0.00	-0.01
FAED	0.00	-0.01
MOED	0.00	0.03
VERBAB	-0.02	0.00
QUANTAB	0.02	0.00

BETA

	aspire	achieve
aspire	0.00	0.00
achieve	0.00	0.00

GAMMA

	home	ability
aspire	0.00	0.00
achieve	0.00	0.00

PHI

	home	ability
home	0.00	
ability	0.00	0.00

PSI

	aspire	achieve
	-------	-------
aspire	0.00	
achieve	0.00	0.00

THETA-EPS

	EDASP	OCASP	VERBACH	QUANTACH
	-------	-------	-------	--------
EDASP	0.00			
OCASP	0.00	0.00		
VERBACH	-0.24	0.21	0.00	
QUANTACH	0.07	-0.01	0.00	0.00

THETA-DELTA-EPS

	EDASP	OCASP	VERBACH	QUANTACH
	-------	-------	-------	--------
FAMINC	0.07	-0.04	-0.15	0.26
FAED	0.21	-0.13	0.13	-0.09
MOED	-0.26	0.13	-0.03	-0.13
VERBAB	-0.15	-0.20	0.48	-0.32
QUANTAB	0.44	-0.10	-0.38	0.17

THETA-DELTA

	FAMINC	FAED	MOED	VERBAB	QUANTAB
	-------	-------	-------	-------	--------
FAMINC	0.00				
FAED	-0.03	0.00			
MOED	0.03	0.00	0.00		
VERBAB	-0.08	-0.10	0.15	0.00	
QUANTAB	-0.03	-0.06	0.18	0.00	0.00

Factor Scores Regressions

ETA

	EDASP	OCASP	VERBACH	QUANTACH	FAMINC	FAED
	-------	-------	-------	--------	-------	-------
aspire	0.50	0.21	0.10	0.04	0.04	0.02
achieve	0.12	0.05	0.52	0.22	0.07	0.03

ETA

	MOED	VERBAB	QUANTAB
	-------	-------	--------
aspire	0.01	0.02	0.01
achieve	0.01	0.11	0.07

KSI

	EDASP	OCASP	VERBACH	QUANTACH	FAMINC	FAED
home	0.05	0.02	0.07	0.03	0.41	0.19
ability	0.02	0.01	0.11	0.04	0.07	0.03

KSI

	MOED	VERBAB	QUANTAB
home	0.06	0.07	0.04
ability	0.01	0.37	0.24

Standardized Solution

LAMBDA-Y

	aspire	achieve
EDASP	0.93	- -
OCASP	0.85	- -
VERBACH	- -	1.29
QUANTACH	- -	0.97

LAMBDA-X

	home	ability
FAMINC	0.81	- -
FAED	0.64	- -
MOED	0.59	- -
VERBAB	- -	0.81
QUANTAB	- -	0.77

BETA

	aspire	achieve
aspire	- -	- -
achieve	0.38	- -

GAMMA

	home	ability
aspire	0.44	0.39
achieve	0.19	0.43

Correlation Matrix of ETA and KSI

	aspire	achieve	home	ability
aspire	1.00			
achieve	0.85	1.00		
home	0.76	0.83	1.00	
ability	0.75	0.87	0.81	1.00

PSI

Note: This matrix is diagonal.

aspire	achieve
0.37	0.14

Regression Matrix ETA on KSI (Standardized)

	home	ability
aspire	0.44	0.39
achieve	0.36	0.58

Total and Indirect Effects

Total Effects of KSI on ETA

	home	ability
aspire	0.51	0.45
	(0.15)	(0.15)
	3.29	2.96
achieve	0.57	0.92
	(0.17)	(0.18)
	3.26	5.20

Indirect Effects of KSI on ETA

	home	ability
aspire	- -	- -
achieve	0.27	0.23
	(0.10)	(0.09)
	2.63	2.62

Total Effects of ETA on ETA

	aspire	achieve
aspire	- -	- -
achieve	0.53	- -
	(0.12)	
	4.56	

Largest Eigenvalue of B*B' (Stability Index) is 0.276

Total Effects of ETA on Y

	aspire	achieve
EDASP	1.00	- -
OCASP	0.92	- -
	(0.06)	
	14.34	
VERBACH	0.53	1.00
	(0.12)	
	4.56	
QUANTACH	0.40	0.75
	(0.09)	(0.04)
	4.48	18.13

Indirect Effects of ETA on Y

	aspire	achieve
EDASP	- -	- -
OCASP	- -	- -
VERBACH	0.53	- -
	(0.12)	
	4.56	
QUANTACH	0.40	- -
	(0.09)	
	4.48	

Total Effects of KSI on Y

	home	ability
EDASP	0.51	0.45
	(0.15)	(0.15)
	3.29	2.96
OCASP	0.46	0.41
	(0.14)	(0.14)
	3.25	2.93

VERBACH	0.57	0.92
	(0.17)	(0.18)
	3.26	5.20
QUANTACH	0.43	0.69
	(0.13)	(0.14)
	3.23	5.09

Standardized Total and Indirect Effects

Standardized Total Effects of KSI on ETA

	home	ability
	--------	--------
aspire	0.44	0.39
achieve	0.36	0.58

Standardized Indirect Effects of KSI on ETA

	home	ability
	--------	--------
aspire	- -	- -
achieve	0.17	0.15

Standardized Total Effects of ETA on ETA

	aspire	achieve
	--------	--------
aspire	- -	- -
achieve	0.38	- -

Standardized Total Effects of ETA on Y

	aspire	achieve
	--------	--------
EDASP	0.93	- -
OCASP	0.85	- -
VERBACH	0.49	1.29
QUANTACH	0.37	0.97

Standardized Indirect Effects of ETA on Y

	aspire	achieve
	--------	--------
EDASP	- -	- -
OCASP	- -	- -
VERBACH	0.49	- -
QUANTACH	0.37	- -

```
Standardized Total Effects of KSI on Y

                    home                    ability
                  --------                  --------
    EDASP           0.41                      0.36
    OCASP           0.38                      0.33
  VERBACH           0.46                      0.75
 QUANTACH           0.35                      0.56
```

At this point, we leave it up to the reader to extract the factor loadings, error variances, structure coefficients, and disturbance terms from the various matrices indicated in the standardized solution. It is also helpful to determine the direct and indirect effects indicated in the model. The model-fit indices indicated that the data fit the modified theoretical model.

17.4 Other Models in Matrix Notation

This section presents the matrix approach to the path model, the multiple-sample model, the structured means model and two types of interaction models in structural equation modeling. The reader is referred to the previous chapters and references in the book for further detail and explanation of these types of models.

17.4.1 Path Model

The path model in LISREL matrix notation is written as

$$Y = BY + \Gamma X + \zeta,$$

and thus there is no measurement model. Of the eight LISREL matrices, for the path model we only have the following: B, Γ, Φ, and Ψ.

As an example path model, we again consider the union sentiment model as previously shown in Figure 7.1 of Chapter 7. The structural equations in terms of variable names are

$$\text{Deference } (Y_1) = \text{Age } (X_1) + \text{error1}$$

$$\text{Support } (Y_2) = \text{Age } (X_1) + \text{Deference } (Y_1) + \text{error2}$$

$$\text{Sentiment } (Y_3) = \text{Years } (X_2) + \text{Deference } (Y_1) + \text{Support } (Y_2) + \text{error3}.$$

In terms of matrix equations, this translates into the structural equation matrices:

$$\begin{bmatrix} Y_1 \\ Y_2 \\ Y_3 \end{bmatrix} = \begin{bmatrix} 0 & 0 & 0 \\ \beta_{21} & 0 & 0 \\ \beta_{31} & \beta_{32} & 0 \end{bmatrix} \begin{bmatrix} Y_1 \\ Y_2 \\ Y_3 \end{bmatrix} + \begin{bmatrix} \gamma_{11} & 0 \\ \gamma_{21} & 0 \\ 0 & \gamma_{32} \end{bmatrix} \begin{bmatrix} X_1 \\ X_2 \end{bmatrix} + \begin{bmatrix} \zeta_1 \\ \zeta_2 \end{bmatrix}.$$

Finally, the relevant LISREL matrices for this model are as follows:

$$B = \begin{bmatrix} 0 & 0 & 0 \\ \beta_{21} & 0 & 0 \\ \beta_{31} & \beta_{32} & 0 \end{bmatrix}$$

$$\Gamma = \begin{bmatrix} \gamma_{11} & 0 \\ \gamma_{21} & 0 \\ 0 & \gamma_{32} \end{bmatrix}$$

$$\Phi = \begin{bmatrix} \phi_{11} & \\ \phi_{21} & \phi_{22} \end{bmatrix}$$

$$\Psi = \begin{bmatrix} \psi_{11} & & \\ 0 & \psi_{22} & \\ 0 & 0 & \psi_{33} \end{bmatrix}$$

The LISREL path model program would therefore define these matrices as follows:

```
Union Sentiment of Textile Workers
DA NI=5 NO=173 MA=CM
CM SY
  14.610
  -5.250      11.017
  -8.057      11.087      31.971
  -0.482       0.677       1.559       1.021
 -18.857      17.861      28.250       7.139      215.662
LA
Defer Support Sentim Years Age
SE
1 2 3 5 4
MO NY=3 NX=2 BE=FU,FI GA=FU,FI PH=FU,FR PS=DI
FR BE(2,1) BE(3,1) BE(3,2) GA(1,1) GA(2,1) GA(3,2)
OU ND=2
```

Selected computer output from the LISREL path model program would be:

```
Union Sentiment of Textile Workers

  Number of Iterations = 8

  LISREL Estimates (Maximum Likelihood)
      BETA
```

	Defer	Support	Sentim
Defer	- -	- -	- -
Support	-0.28	- -	- -
	(0.06)		
	-4.58		
Sentim	-0.22	0.85	- -
	(0.10)	(0.11)	
	-2.23	7.53	

```
      GAMMA
```

	Age	Years
Defer	-0.09	- -
	(0.02)	
	-4.65	
Support	0.06	- -
	(0.02)	
	3.59	
Sentim	- -	0.86
		(0.34)
		2.52

```
     PHI
```

	Age	Years
Age	215.66	
	(23.39)	
	9.22	
Years	7.14	1.02
	(1.26)	(0.11)
	5.65	9.22

```
     PSI
     Note: This matrix is diagonal.
```

Defer	Support	Sentim
12.96	8.49	19.45
(1.41)	(0.92)	(2.11)
9.22	9.22	9.22

Squared Multiple Correlations for Structural Equations

Defer	Support	Sentim
0.11	0.23	0.39

Goodness-of-Fit Statistics

Degrees of Freedom = 3
Minimum Fit Function Chi-Square = 1.25 (P = 0.74)
Normal Theory Weighted Least Squares Chi-Square = 1.25
(P = 0.74)
Estimated Non-centrality Parameter (NCP) = 0.0
90 Percent Confidence Interval for NCP = (0.0 ; 4.20)

Minimum Fit Function Value = 0.0073
Population Discrepancy Function Value (F0) = 0.0
90 Percent Confidence Interval for F0 = (0.0 ; 0.025)
Root Mean Square Error of Approximation (RMSEA) = 0.0
90 Percent Confidence Interval for RMSEA = (0.0 ; 0.091)
P-Value for Test of Close Fit (RMSEA < 0.05) = 0.84
Expected Cross-Validation Index (ECVI) = 0.16
90 Percent Confidence Interval for ECVI = (0.16 ; 0.18)
ECVI for Saturated Model = 0.18
ECVI for Independence Model = 1.46

Chi-Square for Independence Model with 10 Degrees of Freedom
= 238.10
Independence AIC = 248.10
Model AIC = 25.25
Saturated AIC = 30.00
Independence CAIC = 268.87
Model CAIC = 75.09
Saturated CAIC = 92.30

Normed Fit Index (NFI) = 0.99
Non-Normed Fit Index (NNFI) = 1.03
Parsimony Normed Fit Index (PNFI) = 0.30
Comparative Fit Index (CFI) = 1.00
Incremental Fit Index (IFI) = 1.01
Relative Fit Index (RFI) = 0.98

Critical N (CN) = 1560.66

Root Mean Square Residual (RMR) = 0.73
Standardized RMR = 0.015
Goodness-of-Fit Index (GFI) = 1.00
Adjusted Goodness-of-Fit Index (AGFI) = 0.99
Parsimony Goodness-of-Fit Index (PGFI) = 0.20

17.4.2 Multiple-Sample Model

The multiple-sample model in LISREL matrix notation for the *measurement* model is written as

$$Y = \Lambda_y^{(g)} \eta + \varepsilon$$

for the latent dependent indicator variables, and

$$X = \Lambda_x^{(g)} \xi + \delta$$

for the latent independent indicator variables, where $g = 1$ to G groups and the other terms are as previously defined. The *structural* model can be written as follows:

$$\eta = B^{(g)} \eta + \Gamma^{(g)} \xi + \zeta$$

The four covariance matrices that you are already familiar with are written as: $\Phi^{(g)}$, $\Psi^{(g)}$, $\Theta_\delta^{(g)}$, and $\Theta_\varepsilon^{(g)}$. The measurement and structural equations yield parameter estimates for each of the eight matrices for each group, $B^{(g)}$, $\Gamma^{(g)}$, $\Lambda_y^{(g)}$, $\Lambda_x^{(g)}$, $\Phi^{(g)}$, $\Psi^{(g)}$, $\Theta_\delta^{(g)}$ and $\Theta_\varepsilon^{(g)}$.

For instance, with two groups we may be interested in testing whether the factor loadings are equivalent. These hypotheses for the latent dependent variables are written as

$$\Lambda_y^{(1)} = \Lambda_y^{(2)}$$

and for the latent independent variables as

$$\Lambda_x^{(1)} = \Lambda_x^{(2)}$$

One might also hypothesize that any of the other matrices are equivalent so that

$$\text{Lomax } \delta \text{ corr.} \rightarrow \Theta_\delta^{(1)} = \Theta_\delta^{(2)}$$

$$\text{Schumacker } \delta \text{ corr.} \rightarrow \Theta_\varepsilon^{(1)} = \Theta_\varepsilon^{(2)}$$

$$B^{(1)} = B^{(2)}$$

$$\Gamma^{(1)} = \Gamma^{(2)}$$

$$\Phi^{(1)} = \Phi^{(2)}$$

$$\Psi^{(1)} = \Psi^{(2)}$$

Thus, the groups can be evaluated to determine which matrices are equivalent, and which are different.

17.4.3 Structured Means Model

The structured means model in LISREL matrix notation for the *measurement* model of the latent dependent indicator variables is written as

$$Y = \tau_y^{(g)} + \Lambda_y^{(g)} \eta + \varepsilon,$$

and for the latent independent indicator variables written as

$$X = \tau_x^{(g)} + \Lambda_x^{(g)} \xi + \delta.$$

We denote τ_y and τ_x as vectors of constant intercept terms (means) for the indicator variables, and the other terms are as previously defined (Jöreskog & Sörbom, 1996) denoted these intercept terms as τ; other publications have used v instead]. The structural model is now written as

$$\eta = \alpha^{(g)} + B^{(g)} \eta + \Gamma^{(g)} \xi + \zeta,$$

where α is a vector of constant intercept terms (means) for the structural equations and the other terms are as previously defined. In most SEM models the intercept terms are assumed to be zero, so the structured means model is a special application of SEM used in the analysis of variance as well as slope and intercept models. In the structured means model, the intercept term is not zero and therefore estimated (see chapter 6 for intercept terms in regression using CONST term).

In addition to the means of indicator variables being estimated, other latent variable means can be estimated. The mean of each latent independent variable ξ is given by κ; for example, κ_1 denotes the mean for ξ_1. The mean of each latent dependent variable is given by $(I - B)^{-1}(\alpha + \Gamma\kappa)$.

In addition to the hypotheses given previously for the simple multiple-sample model, the structured means model can also examine α, the group effects for each structural equation, and κ, the group effects for each latent independent variable. We constrain (set equal) the value for one group to be zero, so we can estimate the difference between that group and a second group, which we refer to as a *group effect*.

In the following LISREL matrix program we hypothesize that academic and nonacademic boys are different in their reading and writing ability in fifth and seventh grades. The first structured means program specifies the number of groups (NG = 2), the first group's (academic boys) sample size (NO = 373), the number of observed variables (NI = 4), the type of matrix, that is, a covariance matrix (MA = CM), and the first group's covariance matrix (CM) and means (ME). The second program only has to define the second group's (nonacademic boys) sample size (NO = 249), and the second group's covariance matrix (CM) and means (ME). The means are what defines a structured means program. Special features of this program are

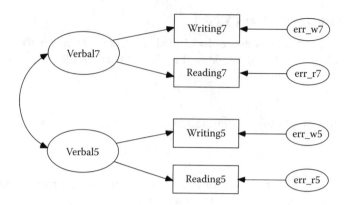

FIGURE 17.2
Structured means model.

setting TX = FR (τ matrix of observed variable means) and KA = FI (κ matrix of latent variable means). This LISREL matrix program parallels the LISREL–SIMPLIS program in chapter 13 for the structured means model, that is, adding the LISREL OUTPUT command in the LISREL–SIMPLIS program yields these same matrices and results (Figure 17.2).

The LISREL matrix structured means program is as follows:

```
Group: ACADEMIC
DA NI=4 NO=373 MA=CM NG=2
CM SY
281.349
184.219 182.821
216.739 171.699 283.289
198.376 153.201 208.837 246.069
ME
262.236 258.788 275.630 269.075
LA
 R5 W5 R7 W7
MO NX=4 NK=2 TX=FR KA=FI
LK
 V5 V7
FR LX(2,1) LX(4,2)
VA 1 LX(1,1) LX(3,2)
OU ND=2 AD=OFF
Group: NONACADEMIC
DA NI=4 NO=249 MA=CM
CM SY
174.485
134.468 161.869
129.840 118.836 228.449
```

```
102.194 97.767 136.058 180.460
ME
248.675 246.896 258.546 253.349
MO LX=IN TX=IN KA=FR TD=FR
LA
 R5 W5 R7 W7
OU
```

The model parameters in the first group for τ are set free (**FR**) and for κ are fixed (**FI**), so that the latent variable intercepts for the first group are fixed to 0. The estimate of the latent variable intercept in the second group (nonacademic boys) is therefore evaluated relative to 0 (academic boys intercept). The structural model is represented as $\eta_2 = \alpha_2 + B_2 \, \eta_1 + \zeta_2$ for both groups separately for the null hypothesis H_0: $\alpha_{academic\,boys} = \alpha_{nonacademic\,boys}$. The edited and condensed structured means program output is as follows.

```
Group: ACADEMIC
LISREL Estimates (Maximum Likelihood)
LAMBDA-X EQUALS LAMBDA-X IN THE FOLLOWING GROUP
```

PHI

	V5	V7
V5	220.06	
	(19.17)	
	11.48	
V7	212.11	233.59
	(17.66)	(20.50)
	12.01	11.40

THETA-DELTA

R5	W5	R7	W7
50.15	36.48	51.72	57.78
(6.02)	(4.28)	(6.62)	(6.05)
8.34	8.52	7.82	9.55

Squared Multiple Correlations for X - Variables

R5	W5	R7	W7
0.81	0.81	0.82	0.76

TAU-X EQUALS TAU-X IN THE FOLLOWING GROUP

```
            Group Goodness-of-Fit Statistics
          Contribution to Chi-Square = 4.15
    Percentage Contribution to Chi-Square = 41.00
```

```
          Root Mean Square Residual (RMR) = 6.07
                    Standardized RMR = 0.025
              Goodness-of-Fit Index (GFI) = 0.99
```

Group: NONACADEMIC

LISREL Estimates (Maximum Likelihood)

```
    LAMBDA-X
              KSI 1            KSI 2
              --------         --------
R5             1.00              - -
W5             0.84              - -
              (0.02)
              34.35
R7             - -              1.00
W7             - -              0.89
                               (0.03)
                               31.95
```

```
    PHI
              KSI 1            KSI 2
              --------         --------
KSI 1         156.34
              (16.19)
               9.66
KSI 2         126.96           153.73
              (14.22)          (18.03)
               8.93             8.53
```

```
    THETA-DELTA
         R5               W5               R7               W7
       --------         --------         --------         --------
        23.25            42.80            65.67            67.36
        (6.23)           (5.64)           (9.87)           (8.74)
         3.73             7.59             6.65             7.71
```

Squared Multiple Correlations for X-Variables

```
         R5               W5               R7               W7
       --------         --------         --------         --------
        0.87             0.72             0.70             0.65
```

```
    TAU-X
         R5               W5               R7               W7
       --------         --------         --------         --------
       262.37           258.67           275.71           268.98
```

```
    (0.84)           (0.70)           (0.87)           (0.80)
    312.58           366.96           317.77           338.00

    KAPPA

      KSI 1            KSI 2
    --------         --------
     -13.80           -17.31
     (1.18)           (1.24)
     -11.71           -13.99
```

We obtain the latent variable mean differences from the kappa matrix, where the nonacademic boys were below the academic boys in reading and writing at both the fifth grade (**KSI 1**) and seventh grade (**KSI 2**). Our model-fit indices indicate an acceptable theoretical model:

```
              Global Goodness-of-Fit Statistics
                   Degrees of Freedom = 6
        Minimum Fit Function Chi-Square = 10.11 (P = 0.12)
   Normal Theory Weighted Least Squares Chi-Square = 9.96
                          (P = 0.13)
         Estimated Noncentrality Parameter (NCP) = 3.96
      90 Percent Confidence Interval for NCP = (0.0 ; 16.79)
                Minimum Fit Function Value = 0.016
      Population Discrepancy Function Value (F0) = 0.0064
       90 Percent Confidence Interval for F0 = (0.0 ; 0.027)
    Root Mean Square Error of Approximation (RMSEA) = 0.046
    90 Percent Confidence Interval for RMSEA = (0.0 ; 0.095)
        P-Value for Test of Close Fit (RMSEA < 0.05) = 0.27
          Expected Cross-Validation Index (ECVI) = 0.087
     90 Percent Confidence Interval for ECVI = (0.068 ; 0.095)
                ECVI for Saturated Model = 0.032
                ECVI for Independence Model = 3.15
       Chi-Square for Independence Model with 12 Degrees of
                       Freedom = 1947.85
                   Independence AIC = 1963.85
                      Model AIC = 53.96
                    Saturated AIC = 40.00
                 Independence CAIC = 2007.31
                    Model CAIC = 173.48
                  Saturated CAIC = 148.66
                Normed Fit Index (NFI) = 0.99
              Nonnormed Fit Index (NNFI) = 1.00
        Parsimony Normed Fit Index (PNFI) = 0.50
            Comparative Fit Index (CFI) = 1.00
            Incremental Fit Index (IFI) = 1.00
              Relative Fit Index (RFI) = 0.99
                 Critical N (CN) = 1031.60
```

```
Group Goodness-of-Fit Statistics
Contribution to Chi-Square = 5.97
Percentage Contribution to Chi-Square = 59.00
Root Mean Square Residual (RMR) = 7.69
Standardized RMR = 0.042
Goodness-of-Fit Index (GFI) = 0.99
```

17.4.4 Interaction Models

In chapter 16 we discussed four different types of interaction models: categorical, nonlinear, continuous observed variable, and latent variable (Schumacker & Marcoulides, 1998). In this chapter we present the LISREL matrix program using latent variables that parallels the interaction latent variable approach in Chapter 16 using LISREL–SIMPLIS, except for slight differences in the standard errors. The matrix approach to latent variable interactions requires the understanding and use of nonlinear constraints, which has made it difficult for most SEM researchers (Jöreskog & Yang, 1996).

The latent variable interaction approach in LISREL matrix notation for Figure 17.3 is $\eta_1 = \gamma_1 \xi_1 + \gamma_2 \xi_2 + \gamma_3 \xi_3 + \zeta_1$, where η_1 is the latent dependent variable, ξ_1 and ξ_2 are the main-effect latent independent variables, ξ_3 is the interaction-effect formed by multiplying ξ_1 and ξ_2, γ_1 and γ_2 are the structure coefficients for the main-effect latent independent variables, γ_3 is

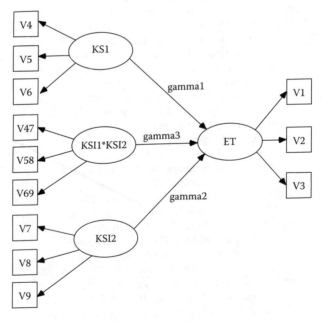

FIGURE 17.3
Latent variable interaction (continuous variable approach).

the structure coefficient for the interaction-effect latent independent variable, and ζ_1 is the error term in the structural equation. Notice that the relationship between η_1 and ξ_3 is itself linear. The structure of the interaction model emerges as a logical extension of the measurement model for ξ_1 and ξ_2. The basic measurement model is $X = \Lambda \xi + \delta$, where X is a vector of observed variables, Λ is a matrix of factor loadings, and δ is a vector of measurement error terms. The covariance matrices of these common and unique factors are Φ and Θ_δ, respectively.

Kenny and Judd (1984) used simple algebraic substitution to develop their model of multiplicative interaction effects (Hayduk, 1987). Basically, given two latent independent variables, the models are $X_1 = \lambda_1 \xi_1 + \delta_1$ and $X_2 = \lambda_2 \xi_2 + \delta_2$. The interaction effect or product is $X_3 = X_1 X_2$, indicated in the model as $X_3 = \lambda_1 \lambda_2 \xi_1 \xi_2 + \lambda_1 \xi_1 \delta_2 + \lambda_2 \xi_2 \delta_1 + \delta_1 \delta_2$, or $X_3 = \lambda_3 \xi_3 + \lambda_1 \xi_4 + \lambda_2 \xi_5 + \delta_3$, where $\xi_3 = \xi_1 \xi_2$, $\xi_4 = \xi_1 \delta_2$, $\xi_5 = \xi_2 \delta_1$, $\delta_3 = \delta_1 \delta_2$, and $\lambda_3 = \lambda_1 \lambda_2$. All of these new latent variables are mutually uncorrelated and uncorrelated with all other latent variables in the model.

In order to incorporate this interaction effect into the structural equation model, we need to specify X_3 as a function of latent variables whose variances and covariance terms reflect these relationships. This involves specifying some model parameters as nonlinear functions of other parameters. In the LISREL program, these types of nonlinear constraints are indicated by using the VA (value), EQ (equality), and CO (constraint) commands. For example, the Kenny–Judd interaction model implies that $\sigma^2(\xi_3) = \sigma^2(\xi_1) \sigma^2(\xi_2) + \sigma(\xi_1 \xi_2)^2$. This relationship using the CO command line is specified as CO PH(3,3) = PH(1,1) * PH(2,2) + PH(2,1) * * 2. Similarly, their model implies that $\sigma^2(\xi_4) = \sigma^2(\xi_1) \sigma^2(\delta_2)$, and this relationship is specified as CO PH(4,4) = PH(1,1) * TD(2,2).

We demonstrate the Kenny and Judd (1984) approach by creating a simulated data set of nine multivariate normal variables and three product indicant variables for 500 participants using a PRELIS program (*mvdata1.pr2*):

Generate multivariate normal variables – LISREL

```
DA NO=500
NE X1=NRAND; NE X2=NRAND; NE X3=NRAND
NE X4=NRAND; NE X5=NRAND; NE X6=NRAND
NE X7=NRAND; NE X8=NRAND; NE X9=NRAND
NE V1=X1
NE V2=.378*X1+.925*X2
NE V3=.320*X1+.603*X2+.890*X3
NE V4=.204*X1+.034*X2+.105*X3+.904*X4
NE V5=.076*X1+.113*X2+.203*X3+.890*X4+.925*X5
NE V6=.111*X1+.312*X2+.125*X3+.706*X4+.865*X5+.905*X6
NE V7=.310*X1+.124*X2+.310*X3+.222*X4+.126*X5+.555*X6+.897*X7
NE V8=.222*X1+.111*X2+.412*X3+.312*X4+.212*X5+.312*X6+.789*X7+.899*X8
```

NE V9=.321*X1+.214*X2+.124*X3+.122*X4+.234*X5+.212*X6+.690*X7+.789*X8+.907*X9
NE V47=V4*V7
NE V58=V5*V8
NE V69=V6*V9
CO ALL
SD X1-X9
OU MA=CM CM=INTERACT.CM ME=INTERACT.ME RA=INTERACT.PSF XM
IX=784123

Although the nine observed variables were created as multivariate normal data, the product indicant variables are typically not multivariate normal. The summary statistics do indicate that the nine observed variables are univariate normal, but that the three product indicant variables have skewness and kurtosis, that is, are nonnormal (**boldfaced**). In LISREL, maximum likelihood estimation (ML) is the default, and it appears to work well under mild violations of multivariate normality in the interaction latent variable model. We used the same random number seed as before so the data could be reproduced (IX = 784123).

PRELIS Computer Output

Univariate Summary Statistics for Continuous Variables

Variable	Mean	St. Dev.	T-Value	Skewness	Kurtosis
V1	-0.061	0.976	-1.394	0.191	0.048
V2	0.007	1.071	0.142	-0.047	0.280
V3	-0.018	1.105	-0.368	0.175	0.441
V4	-0.015	0.956	-0.359	-0.200	-0.158
V5	-0.013	1.351	-0.209	-0.003	0.168
V6	0.011	1.543	0.163	0.171	0.528
V7	-0.065	1.192	-1.222	-0.081	-0.350
V8	-0.041	1.491	-0.615	0.127	0.092
V9	0.005	1.595	0.075	0.058	0.514
V47	0.325	1.143	6.356	**0.958**	**3.861**
V58	0.670	2.179	6.877	**1.916**	**8.938**
V69	0.584	2.754	4.745	**2.304**	**15.266**

Test of Univariate Normality for Continuous Variables

	Skewness		Kurtosis		Skewness and Kurtosis	
					Chi-	
Variable	Z-Score	P-Value	Z-Score	P-Value	Square	P-Value
V1	1.749	0.080	0.321	0.748	3.163	0.206
V2	-0.432	0.666	1.256	0.209	1.764	0.414
V3	1.608	0.108	1.811	0.070	5.866	0.053

V4	-1.833	0.067	-0.695	0.487	3.844	0.146
V5	-0.031	0.975	0.829	0.407	0.688	0.709
V6	1.571	0.116	2.082	0.037	6.802	0.033
V7	-0.746	0.456	-1.865	0.062	4.034	0.133
V8	1.165	0.244	0.513	0.608	1.620	0.445
V9	0.531	0.595	2.039	0.041	4.438	0.109
V47	7.573	0.000	7.085	0.000	**107.539**	**0.000**
V58	12.103	0.000	9.622	0.000	**239.070**	**0.000**
V69	13.428	0.000	11.101	0.000	**303.539**	**0.000**

The PRELIS program saves three files, a covariance matrix (*interact.cm*), means (*interact.me*), and a PRELIS system file (*interact.psf*). The LISREL program inputs the files with the covariance matrix and means.

The LISREL program to run the data for the model in Figure 17.3 is:

```
Fitting Model to Mean Vector and Covariance Matrix
DA NI=12 NO=500
!The three interaction variables are added prior to
program analysis
LA
V1 V2 V3 V4 V5 V6 V7 V8 V9 V47 V58 V69
CM=interact.CM
ME=interact.ME
MO NY=3 NX=9 NE=1 NK=3 TD=SY TY=FR TX=FR KA=FR
FR LY(2) LY(3) GA(1) GA(2) GA(3) LX(2,1) LX(3,1) LX(5,2)
LX(6,2) PH(1,1)-PH(2,2)
FI PH(3,1) PH(3,2)
VA 1 LY(1) LX(1,1) LX(4,2) LX(7,3) !Should be same as
C  SIMPLIS program for comparison
FI KA(1) KA(2)
CO LX(7,1)=TX(4)
CO LX(7,2)=TX(1)
CO LX(8,1)=TX(5)*LX(2,1)
CO LX(8,2)=TX(2)*LX(5,2)
CO LX(8,3)=LX(2,1)*LX(5,2)
CO LX(9,1)=TX(6)*LX(3,1)
CO LX(9,2)=TX(3)*LX(6,2)
CO LX(9,3)=LX(3,1)*LX(6,2)
CO PH(3,3)=PH(1,1)*PH(2,2)+PH(2,1)**2
CO TD(7,1)=TX(4)*TD(1,1)
CO TD(7,4)=TX(1)*TD(4,4)
CO TD(7,7)=TX(1)**2*TD(4,4)+TX(4)**2*TD(1,1)+PH(1,1)*TD(4,4)+
C  PH(2,2)*TD(1,1)+TD(1,1)*TD(4,4)
CO TD(8,2)=TX(5)*TD(2,2)
CO TD(8,5)=TX(2)*TD(5,5)
CO TD(8,8)=TX(2)**2*TD(5,5)+TX(5)**2*TD(2,2)+LX(2,1)**2*PH(1,
1)*TD(5,5)+
C  LX(5,2)**2*PH(2,2)*TD(2,2)+TD(2,2)*TD(5,5)
```

```
CO TD(9,3)=TX(6)*TD(3,3)
CO TD(9,6)=TX(3)*TD(6,6)
CO TD(9,9)=TX(3)**2*TD(4,4)+TX(6)**2*TD(3,3)+LX(3,1)**2*PH(1,
1)*TD(6,6)+
C  LX(6,2)**2*PH(2,2)*TD(3,3)+TD(3,3)*TD(6,6)
CO KA(3)=PH(2,1)
CO TX(7)=TX(1)*TX(4)
CO TX(8)=TX(2)*TX(5)
CO TX(9)=TX(3)*TX(6)
OU AD=OFF IT=500 EP=0.001 IM=3 ND=3
```

The CO command (placing proper constraints in the model) is what becomes difficult to navigate in creating the matrix programs for latent variable interaction models. Discussions of different latent variable interaction models and related issues can be found in Marcoulides and Schumacker (1996, 2001) and Schumacker and Marcoulides (1998).

Given the LISREL matrix program with a latent variable interaction term, several matrices need to be specified. The structural equation with the two main-effect latent variables and the interaction-effect latent variable is as follows:

$$\eta = \alpha + \gamma_1 \xi_1 + \gamma_2 \xi_2 + \gamma_3 \xi_1 \xi_2 + \zeta$$

The measurement model with Y observed variables is defined as follows:

$$Y = T_y + \Lambda_y \eta + \varepsilon$$

The matrices for the Y observed variable measurement model are specified as:

$$\begin{pmatrix} y_1 \\ y_2 \\ y_3 \end{pmatrix} = \begin{pmatrix} \tau_1^{(y)} \\ \tau_2^{(y)} \\ \tau_3^{(y)} \end{pmatrix} + \begin{pmatrix} 1 \\ \lambda_2^{(y)} \\ \lambda_3^{(y)} \end{pmatrix} \eta + \begin{pmatrix} \varepsilon_1 \\ \varepsilon_2 \\ \varepsilon_3 \end{pmatrix},$$

where the theta–epsilon error matrix specified as follows:

$$\Theta_\varepsilon = diag(\theta_1^\varepsilon, \theta_2^\varepsilon, \theta_3^\varepsilon)$$

The measurement model for the X observed variables, which includes both main-effects and the interaction-effect, is defined as follows:

$$X = T_x + \Lambda_x \xi + \delta$$

The matrices for the X observed variable measurement model are specified as follows:

$$
\begin{pmatrix} x_1 \\ x_2 \\ x_3 \\ x_4 \\ x_5 \\ x_6 \\ x_1 x_4 \\ x_2 x_5 \\ x_3 x_6 \end{pmatrix}
=
\begin{pmatrix} \tau_1 \\ \tau_2 \\ \tau_3 \\ \tau_4 \\ \tau_5 \\ \tau_6 \\ \tau_1 \tau_4 \\ \tau_2 \tau_5 \\ \tau_3 \tau_6 \end{pmatrix}
+
\begin{pmatrix}
1 & 0 & 0 \\
\lambda_2 & 0 & 0 \\
\lambda_3 & 0 & 0 \\
0 & 1 & 0 \\
0 & \lambda_5 & 0 \\
0 & \lambda_6 & 0 \\
\tau_4 & \tau_1 & 1 \\
\tau_5 \lambda_2 & \tau_2 \lambda_5 & \lambda_2 \lambda_5 \\
\tau_3 \lambda_3 & \tau_3 \lambda_6 & \lambda_3 \lambda_6
\end{pmatrix}
\begin{pmatrix} \xi_1 \\ \xi_2 \\ \xi_1 \xi_2 \end{pmatrix}
+
\begin{pmatrix} \delta_1 \\ \delta_2 \\ \delta_3 \\ \delta_4 \\ \delta_5 \\ \delta_6 \\ \delta_7 \\ \delta_8 \\ \delta_9 \end{pmatrix}
$$

with errors in the theta delta matrix Θ_δ denoted as follows:

$$
\begin{pmatrix}
\theta_1 & & & & & & & & \\
0 & \theta_2 & & & & & & & \\
0 & 0 & \theta_3 & & & & & & \\
0 & 0 & 0 & \theta_4 & & & & & \\
0 & 0 & 0 & 0 & \theta_5 & & & & \\
0 & 0 & 0 & 0 & 0 & \theta_6 & & & \\
\tau_4 \theta_1 & 0 & 0 & \tau_1 \theta_4 & 0 & 0 & \theta_7 & & \\
0 & \tau_5 \theta_2 & 0 & 0 & \tau_2 \theta_5 & 0 & 0 & \theta_8 & \\
0 & 0 & \tau_6 \theta_3 & 0 & 0 & \tau_3 \theta_6 & 0 & 0 & \theta_9
\end{pmatrix}.
$$

The theta delta values for the observed interaction variables are calculated as follows:

$$\theta_7 = \tau_4^2 \theta_1 + \tau_1^2 \theta_4 + \phi_{11} \theta_4 + \phi_{22} \theta_1 + \theta_1 \theta_4$$

$$\theta_8 = \tau_5^2 \theta_2 + \tau_2^2 \theta_5 + \lambda_5^2 \phi_{11} \theta_5 + \lambda_5^2 \phi_{22} \theta_2 + \theta_2 \theta_5$$

$$\theta_9 = \tau_6^2 \theta_3 + \tau_3^2 \theta_6 + \lambda_3^2 \phi_{11} \theta_6 + \lambda_6^2 \phi_{22} \theta_3 + \theta_3 \theta_6$$

The mean vector implied by the interaction of the exogenous latent variables is defined in the following kappa mean vector matrix:

$$\kappa = \begin{pmatrix} 0 \\ 0 \\ \phi_{21} \end{pmatrix}$$

with the variance–covariance of the latent independent variables (**ksi1 and ksi2**) defined as follows:

$$\Phi = \begin{pmatrix} \phi_{11} & & \\ \phi_{21} & \phi_{22} & \\ 0 & 0 & \phi_{11}\phi_{22} + \phi_{21}^2 \end{pmatrix}$$

We can now look for these matrices and their associated values in the LISREL computer output.

LISREL Interaction Computer Output

The gamma matrix contains the three structure coefficients of interest for the two main-effect latent variables [$\gamma_1 = .077$ (.030), $t = 2.60$ and $\gamma_2 = .155$ (.029), $t = 5.378$] and the interaction latent variable [$\gamma_3 = -.029$ (.029), $t = -1.004$]. The gamma coefficient for the latent variable interaction effect is nonsignificant ($t = -1.004$). We should modify our theoretical model and test main effects only. The edited and condensed LISREL computer output is as follows:

```
LISREL Estimates (Maximum Likelihood)

    LAMBDA-Y

                ETA 1
                --------
V1              1.000
V2              2.080
                (0.257)
                8.097
V3              2.532
                (0.325)
                7.788
```

LAMBDA-X

	KSI 1	KSI 2	KSI 3
V4	1.000	- -	- -
V5	1.981	- -	- -
	(0.091)		
	21.732		
V6	1.925	- -	- -
	(0.090)		
	21.368		
V7	- -	1.000	- -
V8	- -	1.658	- -
		(0.072)	
		22.874	
V9	- -	1.493	- -
	(0.069)		
	21.741		
V47	-0.070	0.013	1.000
	(0.035)	(0.028)	
	-2.027	0.471	
V58	-0.094	-0.010	3.285
	(0.083)	(0.062)	(0.173)
	-1.142	-0.153	18.960
V69	0.020	-0.049	2.875
	(0.090)	(0.067)	(0.152)
	0.226	-0.729	18.940

GAMMA

	KSI 1	KSI 2	KSI 3
ETA 1	0.077	0.155	-0.029
	(0.030)	(0.029)	(0.029)
	2.602	5.378	-1.004

Covariance Matrix of ETA and KSI

	ETA 1	KSI 1	KSI 2	KSI 3
ETA 1	0.150			
KSI 1	0.068	0.463		
KSI 2	0.137	0.211	0.784	
KSI 3	-0.012	- -	- -	0.408

Mean Vector of Eta-Variables

ETA 1
-0.006

```
PHI
            KSI 1            KSI 2            KSI 3
          --------         --------         --------
KSI 1      0.463
          (0.043)
          10.729
KSI 2      0.211            0.784
          (0.021)          (0.069)
          10.236           11.283
KSI 3      - -              - -              0.408
                                            (0.041)
                                            9.953

     PSI

       ETA 1
      --------
       0.123
      (0.029)
       4.193
```

Squared Multiple Correlations for Structural Equations

```
       ETA 1
      --------
       0.179

   THETA-EPS

      V1               V2               V3
   --------         --------         --------
    0.804            0.502            0.267
   (0.053)          (0.058)          (0.074)
   15.166            8.618            3.617
```

Squared Multiple Correlations for Y - Variables

```
      V1               V2               V3
   --------         --------         --------
    0.157            0.563            0.782
```

```
   THETA-DELTA

       V4        V5        V6        V7        V8        V9
   --------  --------  --------  --------  --------  --------
V4  0.458
   (0.029)
   16.044
V5   - -      0.045
             (0.049)
              0.931
V6   - -       - -      0.796
```

	(1)	(2)	(3)	(4)	(5)	(6)
				(0.065) 12.238		
V7	- -	- -	- -	0.647 (0.043) 15.186		
V8	- -	- -	- -	- -	0.105 (0.057) 1.840	
V9	- -	- -	- -	- -	- -	0.936 (0.070) 13.342
V47	-0.032 (0.016) -2.011	- -	- -	0.009 (0.018) 0.471	- -	- -
V58	- -	-0.002 (0.003) -0.722	- -	- -	-0.001 (0.004) -0.152	- -
V69	- -	- -	0.008 (0.037) 0.226	- -	- -	-0.031 (0.042) -0.728

THETA-DELTA

	V47	V58	V69
V47	0.957 (0.047) 20.519		
V58	- -	0.293 (0.138) 2.129	
V69	- -	- -	3.745 (0.200) 18.698

Squared Multiple Correlations for X - Variables

V4	V5	V6	V7	V8	V9
0.503	0.976	0.683	0.548	0.954	0.651

Squared Multiple Correlations for X - Variables

V47	V58	V69
0.300	0.938	0.474

TAU-Y

V1	V2	V3
-0.055	0.019	-0.004
(0.044)	(0.048)	(0.050)
-1.263	0.386	-0.079

TAU-X

V4	V5	V6	V7	V8	V9
0.013	-0.006	-0.033	-0.070	-0.048	0.011
(0.028)	(0.038)	(0.045)	(0.035)	(0.042)	(0.047)
0.471	-0.153	-0.729	-2.027	-1.144	0.226

TAU-X

V47	V58	V69
-0.001	0.000	0.000
(0.002)	(0.002)	(0.002)
-0.456	0.151	-0.215

KAPPA

KSI1	KSI2	KSI3
- -	- -	0.211
		(0.021)
		10.236

Goodness-of-Fit Statistics

Degrees of Freedom = 59
Minimum Fit Function Chi-Square = 403.462 (P = 0.0)
Normal Theory Weighted Least Squares Chi-Square = 365.186
(P = 0.0)
Estimated Non-centrality Parameter (NCP) = 306.186
90 Percent Confidence Interval for NCP = (249.618 ; 370.256)

Minimum Fit Function Value = 0.809
Population Discrepancy Function Value (F0) = 0.614
90 Percent Confidence Interval for F0 = (0.500 ; 0.742)
Root Mean Square Error of Approximation (RMSEA) = 0.102
90 Percent Confidence Interval for RMSEA = (0.0921 ; 0.112)

```
P-Value for Test of Close Fit (RMSEA < 0.05) = 0.000

    Expected Cross-Validation Index (ECVI) = 0.944
90 Percent Confidence Interval for ECVI = (0.763 ; 1.005)
           ECVI for Saturated Model = 0.313
           ECVI for Independence Model = 6.300

Chi-Square for Independence Model with 66 Degrees of
                 Freedom = 3119.580
             Independence AIC = 3143.580
                Model AIC = 471.186
              Saturated AIC = 156.000
           Independence CAIC = 3206.156
               Model CAIC = 747.560
             Saturated CAIC = 562.739

          Normed Fit Index (NFI) = 0.871
        Nonnormed Fit Index (NNFI) = 0.874
    Parsimony Normed Fit Index (PNFI) = 0.778
       Comparative Fit Index (CFI) = 0.887
       Incremental Fit Index (IFI) = 0.887
         Relative Fit Index (RFI) = 0.855

          Critical N (CN) = 108.807

    Root Mean Square Residual (RMR) = 0.142
           Standardized RMR = 0.0636
      Goodness-of-Fit Index (GFI) = 0.893
  Adjusted Goodness-of-Fit Index (AGFI) = 0.859
  Parsimony Goodness-of-Fit Index (PGFI) = 0.676
```

17.5 Summary

This chapter presented the eight basic matrices used in structural equation modeling, plus two new matrices, tau and kappa. We also discussed that for any structural equation model, parameters in these matrices must be free, fixed, or constrained for model identification, model estimation, and model testing. We presented the matrix notation by providing five different SEM models: our theoretical model in chapter 10, a path model, a multiple-sample model, a structured means model, and an interaction model. We presented these same models in earlier chapters using LISREL–SIMPLIS, and displayed them in matrix form in this chapter for comparative purposes. If you wish, simply add the LISREL OUTPUT command to these programs to output the matrices presented in this chapter. We firmly believe that once you master the matrix notation, you will better understand structural equation modeling.

Exercise

1. The National Science Foundation (NSF) is encouraging students to seek academic degrees and careers in science, mathematics, and engineering in the United States. Research has shown a gender difference in science, mathematics, and engineering participation. A key area of study is to investigate what factors influence these gender differences. A latent variable model is hypothesized to investigate factors that influence gender differences because previous research indicated variables such as characteristics of students in science, mathematics, and engineering.

   A structural equation model with two exogenous latent variables measured by six observed variables is hypothesized to predict two endogeneous latent variables measured by five observed variables. The first independent latent variable, $\xi_1 =$ Family Background, is measured by three variables: $X_1 =$ family income, $X_2 =$ father's education, and $X_3 =$ mother's education. The other independent latent variable, $\xi_2 =$ Encouragement, is measured by three variables: $X_4 =$ personal encouragement, $X_5 =$ institutional characteristics, and $X_6 =$ admission status. Students' characteristics, $\eta_1 =$ Students' Characteristics, is measured by three variables: $Y_1 =$ cognitive abilities, $Y_2 =$ interpersonal skills, and $Y_3 =$ motivation. The other endogenous variable, $\eta_2 =$ Aspirations, is measured by two variables: $Y_4 =$ occupational aspiration and $Y_5 =$ educational aspiration.

   The hypothesized structural equation model represents a two-step approach: measurement (confirmatory factor analysis) and structural model. The structural model depicts the relationships between four latent variables: $\xi_1 =$ Family Background, $\xi_2 =$ Encouragement, $\eta_1 =$ Students' Characteristics, and $\eta_2 =$ Aspirations. The structural model is

$$\text{Students' Characteristics} = \text{Family Background} + \text{Encouragement} \\ + \text{Aspirations} + \text{error}$$

$$\text{Aspirations} = \text{Family Background} + \text{Encouragement} + \text{error}.$$

   With this information, you should be able to do the following:

   1. Diagram the structural equation model.
   2. Write the measurement equations using the variable names.

3. Write the measurement equations using LISREL matrix notation.
4. Write the structural equations using the variable names.
5. Write the structural equations using LISREL matrix notation.
6. Create the matrices for the measurement model.
7. Create the matrices for the structural model.

References

Hayduk, L. A. (1987). *Structural equation modeling with LISREL: Essentials and advances.* Baltimore, MD: Johns Hopkins University Press.

Jöreskog, K. G., & Sörbom, D. (1996). *LISREL8 user's reference guide.* Chicago, IL: Scientific Software International.

Jöreskog, K. G., & Yang, F. (1996). Non-linear structural equation models: The Kenny-Judd model with interaction effects. In G. A. Marcoulides & R. E. Schumacker (Eds.), *Advanced structural equation modeling: Issues and techniques* (pp. 57–88). Mahwah, NJ: Lawrence Erlbaum.

Kenny, D. A., & Judd, C. M. (1984). Estimating the non-linear and interactive effects of latent variables. *Psychological Bulletin, 96,* 201–210.

Marcoulides, G., & Schumacker, R. E. (Eds.). (1996). *Advanced structural equation modeling: Issues and techniques.* Mahwah, NJ: Lawrence Erlbaum.

Marcoulides, G., & Schumacker, R. E. (Eds.). (2001). *New developments and techniques in structural equation modeling.* Mahwah, NJ: Lawrence Erlbaum.

Schumacker, R. E., & Marcoulides, G. A. (1998). *Interaction and nonlinear effects in structural equation modeling.* Mahwah, NJ: Lawrence Erlbaum.

Appendix A: Introduction to Matrix Operations

Structural Equation Modeling performs calculations using several different matrices. The matrix operations to perform the calculations involve addition, subtraction, multiplication, and division of elements in the different matrices.* We present these basic matrix operations, followed by a simple multiple regression example.

Matrix Definition

A matrix is indicated by capital letters (e.g., A, B, or R) and takes the form:

$$A_{22} = \begin{bmatrix} 3 & 5 \\ 5 & 6 \end{bmatrix}$$

The matrix can be rectangular or square-shaped, and contains an array of numbers. A correlation matrix would be a square matrix with the value of 1.0 in the diagonal and variable correlations in the off-diagonal. A correlation matrix is symmetrical because the correlation coefficients in the lower half of the matrix are the same as the correlation coefficients in the upper half of the matrix. [*Note*: we usually only report the diagonal values and the correlations in the lower half of the matrix.] For example:

$$R_{33} = \begin{bmatrix} 1.0 & .30 & .50 \\ .30 & 1.0 & .60 \\ .50 & .60 & 1.0 \end{bmatrix},$$

but we report the following as a correlation matrix:

$$\begin{matrix} 1.0 & & \\ .30 & 1.0 & \\ .50 & .60 & 1.0 \end{matrix}$$

---

* Walter L. Sullins (1973). *Matrix algebra for statistical applications*, Danville, IL: The Interstate Printers & Publishers, Inc.

Matrices have a certain number of rows and columns. The A matrix above has two rows and two columns. The order of a matrix is the size of the matrix, or number of rows times the number of columns. The order of the A matrix is 22, and shown as subscripts, where the first subscript is the number of rows, and second subscript is the number of columns.

When we refer to elements in the matrix, we use row and column designations to identify the location of the element in the matrix. The location of an element has a subscript using the row number first, followed by the column number. For example, the correlation $r = .30$ is in the R_{21} matrix location or row 2, column 1.

Matrix Addition and Substraction

Matrix addition adds corresponding elements in two matrices, while matrix subtraction subtracts corresponding elements in two matrices. Consequently, the two matrices must have the same order (number of rows and columns), so we can add $A_{32} + B_{32}$ or subtract $A_{32} - B_{32}$. In the following example, Matrix A elements are added to Matrix B elements:

$$\begin{bmatrix} 3 & 5 & 2 \\ 1 & 6 & 0 \\ 9 & 1 & 2 \end{bmatrix} + \begin{bmatrix} 1 & -3 & 5 \\ 2 & 1 & 3 \\ 0 & 7 & -3 \end{bmatrix} = \begin{bmatrix} 4 & 2 & 7 \\ 3 & 7 & 3 \\ 9 & 8 & -1 \end{bmatrix}$$

Matrix Multiplication

Matrix multiplication is not as straight forward as matrix addition and subtraction. For a product of matrices we indicate $A \bullet B$ or AB. If A is an $m \times n$ matrix and B is an $n \times p$ matrix, then AB is a $m \times p$ matrix of rows and columns. The number of columns in the first matrix must match the number of rows in the second matrix to be compatible and permit multiplication of the elements of the matrices. The following example will illustrate how the row elements in the first matrix (A) are multiplied times the column elements in the second matrix (B) to yield the elements in the third matrix C.

$$c_{11} = 1 \bullet 2 + 2 \bullet 1 = 2 + 2 = 4$$
$$c_{12} = 1 \bullet 4 + 2 \bullet 8 = 4 + 16 = 20$$
$$c_{13} = 1 \bullet 6 + 2 \bullet 7 = 6 + 14 = 20$$

$$c_{21} = 3 \bullet 2 + 5 \bullet 1 = 6 + 5 = 11$$

$$c_{22} = 3 \bullet 4 + 5 \bullet 8 = 12 + 40 = 52$$

$$c_{23} = 3 \bullet 6 + 5 \bullet 7 = 18 + 35 = 53$$

$$A \bullet B = \begin{bmatrix} 1 & 2 \\ 3 & 5 \end{bmatrix} \bullet \begin{bmatrix} 2 & 4 & 6 \\ 1 & 8 & 7 \end{bmatrix} = \begin{bmatrix} 4 & 20 & 20 \\ 11 & 52 & 53 \end{bmatrix}$$

Matrix C is:

$$C = \begin{bmatrix} 4 & 20 & 20 \\ 11 & 52 & 53 \end{bmatrix}$$

It is important to note that matrix multiplication is *noncommutative* (i.e., *AB* ≠ *BA*.) The order of operation in multiplying elements of the matrices is therefore very important. Matrix multiplication, however, is associate [i.e., *A* (*BC*) = (*AB*) *C*] because the order of matrix multiplication is maintained.

A special matrix multiplication is possible when a single number is multiplied times the elements in a matrix. The single number is called a *scalar*. The scalar is simply multiplied times each of the elements in the matrix. For example,

$$D = 2 \begin{bmatrix} 3 & 4 \\ 4 & 6 \end{bmatrix} = \begin{bmatrix} 6 & 8 \\ 8 & 12 \end{bmatrix}$$

Matrix Division

Matrix division is similar to matrix multiplication with a little twist. In regular division, we divide the numerator by the denominator. However, we can also multiply the numerator by the inverse of the denominator. For example, in regular division, 4 is divided by 2; however, we get the same results if we multiply 4 by ½. Therefore, matrix division is simply *A/B* or *A*•1/*B* = *AB*⁻¹. The special designation of the *B*⁻¹ matrix is called the *inverse* of the *B* matrix.

Matrix division requires finding the inverse of a matrix, which involves computing the *determinant* of a matrix, the *matrix of minors*, and the *matrix of cofactors*. We then create a *transposed matrix* and an *inverse matrix*, which when multiplied yield an *identity matrix*. We now turn our attention to finding these values and matrices involved in matrix division.

Determinant of a Matrix

The determinant of a matrix is a unique number (not a matrix) that uses all the elements in the matrix for its calculation, and is a generalized variance for that matrix. For our illustration we will compute the determinant of a 2 by 2 matrix; leaving higher order matrix determinant computations for high-speed computers. The determinant is computed by cross multiplying the elements of the matrix:

$$A = \begin{bmatrix} a & b \\ c & d \end{bmatrix}$$

so, the determinant of A = ad − cb.
    For example,

$$A = \begin{bmatrix} 2 & 5 \\ 3 & 6 \end{bmatrix}$$

so, the determinant of A = 2•6 − 3•5 = −3.

Matrix of Minors

Each element in a matrix has a *minor*. To find the minor of each element, simply draw a vertical and a horizontal line through that element to form a matrix with one less row and column. We next calculate the determinants of these minor matrices, and then place them in a *matrix of minors*. The matrix of minors would have the same number of rows and columns as the original matrix.
    The *matrix of minors* for the following 3 by 3 matrix would be computed as follows:

$$A = \begin{bmatrix} 1 & 6 & -3 \\ -2 & 7 & 1 \\ 3 & -1 & 4 \end{bmatrix}$$

$$M_{11} \begin{bmatrix} 7 & 1 \\ -1 & 4 \end{bmatrix} = (7)(4) - (1)(-1) = 29$$

$$M_{12} \begin{bmatrix} -2 & 1 \\ 3 & 4 \end{bmatrix} = (-2)(4) - (1)(3) = -11$$

$$M_{13} \begin{bmatrix} -2 & 7 \\ 3 & -1 \end{bmatrix} = (-2)(-1) - (7)(3) = -19$$

$$M_{21} \begin{bmatrix} 6 & -3 \\ -1 & 4 \end{bmatrix} = (6)(4) - (-1)(-3) = 21$$

$$M_{22} \begin{bmatrix} 1 & -3 \\ 3 & 4 \end{bmatrix} = (1)(4) - (-3)(3) = 13$$

$$M_{23} \begin{bmatrix} 1 & 6 \\ 3 & -1 \end{bmatrix} = (1)(-1) - (6)(3) = -19$$

$$M_{31} \begin{bmatrix} 6 & -3 \\ 7 & 1 \end{bmatrix} = (6)(1) - (-3)(7) = 27$$

$$M_{32} \begin{bmatrix} 1 & -3 \\ -2 & 1 \end{bmatrix} = (1)(1) - (-3)(-2) = -5$$

$$M_{33} \begin{bmatrix} 1 & 6 \\ -2 & 7 \end{bmatrix} = (1)(7) - (6)(-2) = 19$$

$$A_{Minors} = \begin{bmatrix} 29 & -11 & -19 \\ 21 & 13 & -19 \\ 27 & -5 & 19 \end{bmatrix}$$

Matrix of Cofactors

A *matrix of cofactors* is created by multiplying the elements of the *matrix of minors* by (–1) for $i + j$ elements, where i = row number of the element and j = column number of the element. Place these values in a new matrix, called a *matrix of cofactors*.

An easy way to remember this multiplication rule is to observe the matrix below. Start with the first row and multiply the first entry by (+), second entry by (–), third by (+), and so on to the end of the row. For the second row start multiplying by (–), then (+), then (–), and so on. All odd rows begin with + sign and all even rows begin with – sign.

$$\begin{matrix} + & - & + \\ - & + & - \\ + & - & + \\ - & + & - \end{matrix}$$

We now proceed by multiplying elements in the *matrix of minors* by –1 for the $i + j$ elements.

$$A_{Minors} = \begin{bmatrix} +1 & -1 & +1 \\ -1 & +1 & -1 \\ +1 & -1 & +1 \end{bmatrix} \begin{bmatrix} 29 & -11 & -19 \\ 21 & 13 & -19 \\ 27 & -5 & 19 \end{bmatrix}$$

to obtain the matrix of cofactors:

$$C_{Cofactors} = \begin{bmatrix} 29 & 11 & -19 \\ -21 & 13 & 19 \\ 27 & 5 & 19 \end{bmatrix}$$

Determinant of Matrix Revisited

The matrix of cofactors makes finding the determinant of any size matrix easy. We multiply elements in any row or column of our original A matrix, by any one corresponding row or column in the *matrix of cofactors* to compute the determinant of the matrix. We can compute the determinant using any row or column, so rows with zeroes makes the calculation of the determinant easier. The determinant of our original 3 by 3 matrix (A) using the 3 by 3 matrix of cofactors would be:

$$\det A = a_{11}C_{11} + a_{12}C_{12} + a_{13}C_{13}$$

Recall that matrix A was:

$$A = \begin{bmatrix} 1 & 6 & -3 \\ -2 & 7 & 1 \\ 3 & -1 & 4 \end{bmatrix}$$

The matrix of cofactors was:

$$C_{Cofactors} = \begin{bmatrix} 29 & 11 & -19 \\ -21 & 13 & 19 \\ 27 & 5 & 19 \end{bmatrix}$$

So, the determinant of matrix A, using the first row of both matrices is.

$$\det A = (1)(29) + (6)(11) + (-3)(-19) = 152$$

We also could have used the second columns of both matrices and obtained the same determinant value:

$$\det A = (6)(11) + (7)(13) + (-1)(5) = 152$$

Two special matrices, we have already mentioned, also have determinants: *diagonal matrix* and *triangular matrix*. A *diagonal matrix* is a matrix which contains zero or nonzero elements on its main diagonal, but zeroes everywhere else. A *triangular matrix* has zeros only either above or below the main diagonal. To calculate the determinants of these matrices, we only need to multiply the elements on the main diagonal. For example, the following triangular matrix K has a determinant of 96.

$$K = \begin{bmatrix} 2 & 0 & 0 & 0 \\ 4 & 1 & 0 & 0 \\ -1 & 5 & 6 & 0 \\ 3 & 9 & -2 & 8 \end{bmatrix}$$

This is computed by multiplying the diagonal values in the matrix:

$$\det K = (2)(1)(6)(8) = 96.$$

Transpose of a Matrix

The transpose of a matrix is created by taking the *rows* of an original matrix C and placing them into corresponding *columns* of a transpose matrix, C'. For example:

$$C = \begin{bmatrix} 29 & 11 & -19 \\ -21 & 13 & 19 \\ 27 & 5 & 19 \end{bmatrix}$$

$$C' = \begin{bmatrix} 29 & -21 & 27 \\ 11 & 13 & 5 \\ -19 & 19 & 19 \end{bmatrix}$$

The *transposed matrix* of the *matrix of cofactors* is now given the special term *adjoint matrix*, designated as *Adj(A)*. The *adjoint matrix* is important because we use it to create the inverse of a matrix, our final step in matrix division operations.

Inverse of a Matrix

The general formula for finding an inverse of a matrix is one over the determinant of the matrix times the adjoint of the matrix:

$$A^{-1} = [1 / \det A]\, ADJ(A)$$

Since we have already found the determinant and adjoint of A, we find the inverse of A as follows:

$$A^{-1} = \left(\frac{1}{152}\right) \begin{bmatrix} 29 & -21 & 27 \\ 11 & 13 & 5 \\ -19 & 19 & 19 \end{bmatrix} = \begin{bmatrix} .191 & -.138 & .178 \\ .072 & .086 & .033 \\ -.125 & .125 & .125 \end{bmatrix}$$

An important property of the inverse of a matrix is that if we multiply its elements by the elements in our original matrix, we should obtain an *identity matrix*. An identity matrix will have 1.0 in the diagonal and zeroes in the off-diagonal. The identity matrix is computed as:

$$A\,A^{-1} = I$$

Because we have the original matrix of A and the inverse of matrix A, we multiply elements of the matrices to obtain the *identity* matrix, I:

$$AA^{-1} = \begin{bmatrix} 1 & 6 & -3 \\ -2 & 7 & 1 \\ 3 & -1 & 4 \end{bmatrix} * \begin{bmatrix} .191 & -.138 & .178 \\ .072 & .086 & .033 \\ -.125 & .125 & .125 \end{bmatrix} = \begin{bmatrix} 1 & 0 & 0 \\ 0 & 1 & 0 \\ 0 & 0 & 1 \end{bmatrix}$$

Matrix Operations in Statistics

We now turn our attention to how the matrix operations are used to compute statistics. We will only cover the calculation of the Pearson correlation and provide the matrix approach in multiple regression, leaving more complicated analyses to computer software programs.

Pearson Correlation (Variance–Covariance Matrix)

In the book, we illustrated how to compute the Pearson correlation coefficient from a variance–covariance matrix. Here, we demonstrate the matrix approach. An important matrix in computing correlations is the sums of squares and cross-products matrix (SSCP). We will use the following pairs of scores to create the SSCP matrix.

X1	X2
5	1
4	3
6	5

The mean of X1 is 5 and the mean of X2 is 3. We use these mean values to compute deviation scores from each mean. We first create a matrix of deviation scores, D:

$$D = \begin{bmatrix} 5 & 1 \\ 4 & 3 \\ 6 & 5 \end{bmatrix} - \begin{bmatrix} 5 & 3 \\ 5 & 3 \\ 5 & 3 \end{bmatrix} = \begin{bmatrix} 0 & -2 \\ -1 & 0 \\ 1 & 2 \end{bmatrix}$$

Next, we create the transpose of matrix D, D':

$$D' = \begin{bmatrix} 0 & -1 & 1 \\ -2 & 0 & 2 \end{bmatrix}$$

Finally, we multiply the transpose of matrix D times the matrix of deviation scores to compute the sums of squares and cross-products matrix:

$$SSCP = D' * D$$

$$SSCP = \begin{bmatrix} 0 & -1 & 1 \\ -2 & 0 & 2 \end{bmatrix} * \begin{bmatrix} 0 & -2 \\ -1 & 0 \\ 1 & 2 \end{bmatrix} = \begin{bmatrix} 2 & 2 \\ 2 & 8 \end{bmatrix}$$

The sums of squares are along the diagonal of the matrix, and the sum of squares cross-products are on the off-diagonal. The matrix multiplications are provided below for the interested reader.

$(0)(0) + (-1)(-1) + (1)(1) = 2$ [sums of squares = $(0^2 + -1^2 + 1^2)$]

$(-2)(0) + (0)(-1) + (2)(1) = 2$ [sum of squares cross product]

$(0)(-2) + (-1)(0) + (1)(2) = 2$ [sum of squares cross product]

$(-2)(-2) + (0)(0) + (2)(2) = 8$ [sums of squares = $(-2^2 + 0^2 + 2^2)$]

$$SSCP = \begin{bmatrix} 2 & 2 \\ 2 & 8 \end{bmatrix}$$ Sum of squares in diagonal of matrix

Variance–Covariance Matrix

Structural equation modeling uses a sample variance–covariance matrix in its calculations. The SSCP matrix is used to create the variance–covariance matrix, S:

$$S = \frac{SSCP}{n-1}$$

In matrix notation this becomes ½ times the matrix elements:

$$S = \frac{1}{2} * \begin{bmatrix} 2 & 2 \\ 2 & 8 \end{bmatrix} = \begin{bmatrix} 1 & 1 \\ 1 & 4 \end{bmatrix}$$ Covariance terms in the off-diagonal of matrix
Variance of variables in diagonal of matrix

We can now calculate the Pearson correlation coefficient using the basic formula of covariance divided by the square root of the product of the variances.

$$r = \frac{CovarianceX1X2}{\sqrt{VarianceX1 * VarianceX2}} = \frac{1}{\sqrt{1*4}} = \frac{1}{2} = .50$$

Multiple Regression

The multiple linear regression equation with two predictor variables is:

$$y = \beta_0 + \beta_1 x_1 + \beta_2 x_2 + e_i$$

where y is the dependent variable, $x1$ and $x2$ the two predictor variables, and

β_0 is the regression constant or y-intercept,

β_1 and β_2 are the regression weights to be estimated,

and e is the error of prediction.

Given the data below, we can use matrix algebra to estimate the regression weights:

y	x_1	x_2
3	2	1
2	3	5
4	5	3
5	7	6
8	8	7

We model each subject's y score as a linear function of the betas:

$$y_1 = 3 = 1\beta_0 + 2\ \beta_1 + 1\ \beta_2 + e_1$$

$$y_2 = 2 = 1\beta_0 + 3\ \beta_1 + 5\ \beta_2 + e_2$$

$$y_3 = 4 = 1\beta_0 + 5\ \beta_1 + 3\ \beta_2 + e_3$$

$$y_4 = 5 = 1\beta_0 + 7\ \beta_1 + 6\ \beta_2 + e_4$$

$$y_5 = 8 = 1\beta_0 + 8\ \beta_1 + 7\ \beta_2 + e_5$$

This series of equations can be expressed as a single matrix equation:

$$
y = \quad\quad X \quad\quad \beta + e
$$

$$
y = \begin{bmatrix} 3 \\ 2 \\ 4 \\ 5 \\ 8 \end{bmatrix} = \begin{bmatrix} 1 & 2 & 1 \\ 1 & 3 & 5 \\ 1 & 5 & 3 \\ 1 & 7 & 6 \\ 1 & 8 & 7 \end{bmatrix} \begin{bmatrix} \beta_0 \\ \beta_1 \\ \beta_2 \end{bmatrix} + \begin{bmatrix} e_1 \\ e_2 \\ e_3 \\ e_4 \\ e_5 \end{bmatrix}
$$

The first column of matrix X are 1s, which compute the regression constant. In matrix form, the multiple linear regression equation is $y = X\beta + e$.

Using calculus, we translate this matrix to solve for the regression weights:

$$\hat{\beta} = (X'X)^{-1}X'y$$

The matrix equation is:

$$\hat{\beta} = \left\{ \begin{bmatrix} 1 & 1 & 1 & 1 & 1 \\ 2 & 3 & 5 & 7 & 8 \\ 1 & 5 & 3 & 6 & 7 \end{bmatrix} \begin{bmatrix} 1 & 2 & 1 \\ 1 & 3 & 5 \\ 1 & 5 & 3 \\ 1 & 7 & 6 \\ 1 & 8 & 7 \end{bmatrix} \right\}^{-1} * \begin{bmatrix} 1 & 1 & 1 & 1 & 1 \\ 2 & 3 & 5 & 7 & 8 \\ 1 & 5 & 3 & 6 & 7 \end{bmatrix} \begin{bmatrix} 3 \\ 2 \\ 4 \\ 5 \\ 8 \end{bmatrix}$$

with labels X', X, X', y over the respective matrices.

We first compute $X'X$ and then compute $X'y$

$$X'X = \begin{bmatrix} 5 & 25 & 22 \\ 25 & 151 & 130 \\ 22 & 130 & 120 \end{bmatrix} \quad \text{and} \quad X'y = \begin{bmatrix} 22 \\ 131 \\ 111 \end{bmatrix}$$

Next, we create the inverse of $X'X$, where 1016 is the determinant of $X'X$.

$$(X'X)^{-1} = \frac{1}{1016} \begin{bmatrix} 1220 & -140 & -72 \\ -140 & 116 & -100 \\ -72 & -100 & 130 \end{bmatrix}$$

Finally, we solve for the X1 and X2 regression weights:

$$\hat{\beta} = \frac{1}{1016} \begin{bmatrix} 1220 & -140 & -72 \\ -140 & 116 & -100 \\ -72 & -100 & 130 \end{bmatrix} \begin{bmatrix} 22 \\ 131 \\ 111 \end{bmatrix} = \begin{bmatrix} .50 \\ 1 \\ -.25 \end{bmatrix}$$

The multiple regression equation is:

$$\hat{y}_i = .50 + 1X_1 - .25\,X_2$$

We use the multiple regression equation to compute predicted scores and then compare the predicted values to the original y values to compute the error of prediction values, e. For example, the first y score was 3 with $X1 = 2$ and $X2 = 1$. We substitute the X1 and X2 values in the regression equation and compute a predicted y score of 2.25. The error of prediction is computed as y – this predicted y score or $3 - 2.25 = .75$. These computations are listed below and are repeated for the remaining y values.

$$\hat{y}_1 = .50 + 1(2) - .25\,(1)$$

$$\hat{y}_1 = 2.25$$

$$\hat{e}_1 = 3 - 2.25 = .75$$

$$\hat{y}_2 = .50 + 1(3) - .25\,(5)$$

$$\hat{y}_2 = 2.25$$

$$\hat{e}_2 = 2 - 2.25 = -.25$$

$$\hat{y}_3 = .50 + 1(5) - .25\,(3)$$

$$\hat{y}_3 = 4.75$$

$$\hat{e}_3 = 4 - 4.75 = -.75$$

$$\hat{y}_4 = .50 + 1(7) - .25\,(6)$$

$$\hat{y}_4 = 6.00$$

$$\hat{e}_4 = 5 - 6 = -1.00$$

$$\hat{y}_5 = .50 + 1(8) - .25\,(7)$$

$$\hat{y}_5 = 6.75$$

$$\hat{e}_5 = 8 - 6.75 = 1.25$$

The regression equation is: $\hat{y}_i = .50 + 1.0 X_1 - .25\,X_2$

We can now place the Y values, X values, regression weights, and error terms back into the matrices to yield a complete solution for the Y values. Notice that the error term vector should sum to zero (0.0). Also notice that each y value is uniquely composed of an intercept term (.50), a regression weight (1.0) times an $X1$ value, a regression weight (−.25) times an $X2$ value, and a residual error, e.g., the first y value of $3 = .5 + 1.0(2) - .25\,(1) + .75$.

$$
\begin{bmatrix} 3 \\ 2 \\ 4 \\ 5 \\ 8 \end{bmatrix}
= .5 + 1.0
\begin{bmatrix} 2 \\ 3 \\ 5 \\ 7 \\ 8 \end{bmatrix}
- .25
\begin{bmatrix} 1 \\ 5 \\ 3 \\ 6 \\ 7 \end{bmatrix}
+
\begin{bmatrix} .75 \\ -.25 \\ -.75 \\ -1.00 \\ 1.25 \end{bmatrix}
$$

Appendix B: Statistical Tables

TABLE A.1

Areas under the Normal Curve (z-scores)

z	.00	.01	.02	.03	.04	.05	.06	.07	.08	.09
				Second Decimal Place in z						
.0	.0000	.0040	.0080	.0120	.0160	.0199	.0239	.0279	.0319	.0359
.1	.0398	.0438	.0478	.0517	.0557	.0596	.0636	.0675	.0714	.0753
.2	.0793	.0832	.0871	.0910	.0948	.0987	.1026	.1064	.1103	.1141
.3	.1179	.1217	.1255	.1293	.1331	.1368	.1406	.1443	.1480	.1517
.4	.1554	.1591	.1628	.1664	.1700	.1736	.1772	.1808	.1844	.1879
.5	.1915	.1950	.1985	.2019	.2054	.2088	.2123	.2157	.2190	.2224
.6	.2257	.2291	.2324	.2357	.2389	.2422	.2454	.2486	.2517	.2549
.7	.2580	.2611	.2642	.2673	.2704	.2734	.2764	.2794	.2823	.2852
.8	.2881	.2910	.2939	.2967	.2995	.3023	.3051	.3078	.3106	.3133
.9	.3159	.3186	.3212	.3238	.3264	.3289	.3315	.3340	.3365	.3389
1.0	.3413	.3438	.3461	.3485	.3508	.3531	.3554	.3577	.3599	.3621
1.1	.3643	.3665	.3686	.3708	.3729	.3749	.3770	.3790	.3810	.3830
1.2	.3849	.3869	.3888	.3907	.3925	.3944	.3962	.3980	.3997	.4015
1.3	.4032	.4049	.4066	.4082	.4099	.4115	.4131	.4147	.4162	.4177
1.4	.4192	.4207	.4222	.4236	.4251	.4265	.4279	.4292	.4306	.4319
1.5	.4332	.4345	.4357	.4793	.4382	.4394	.4406	.4418	.4429	.4441
1.6	.4452	.4463	.4474	.4484	.4495	.4505	.4515	.4525	.4535	.4545
1.7	.4554	.4564	.4573	.4582	.4591	.4599	.4608	.4616	.4625	.4633
1.8	.4641	.4649	.4656	.4664	.4671	.4678	.4686	.4693	.4699	.4706
1.9	.4713	.4719	.4726	.4732	.4738	.4744	.4750	.4756	.4761	.4767
2.0	.4772	.4778	.4783	.4788	.4793	.4798	.4803	.4808	.4812	.4817
2.1	.4821	.4826	.4830	.4834	.4838	.4842	.4846	.4850	.4854	.4857
2.2	.4861	.4826	.4868	.4871	.4875	.4878	.4881	.4884	.4887	.4890
2.3	.4893	.4896	.4898	.4901	.4904	.4906	.4909	.4911	.4913	.4916
2.4	.4918	.4920	.4922	.4925	.4927	.4929	.4931	.4932	.4934	.4936
2.5	.4938	.4940	.4941	.4943	.4945	.4946	.4948	.4949	.4951	.4952
2.6	.4953	.4955	.4956	.4957	.4959	.4960	.4961	.4962	.4963	.4964
2.7	.4965	.4966	.4967	.4968	.4969	.4970	.4971	.4972	.4973	.4974
2.8	.4974	.4975	.4976	.4977	.4977	.4978	.4979	.4979	.4980	.4981
2.9	.4981	.4982	.4982	.4983	.4984	.4984	.4985	.4985	.4986	.4986
3.0	.4987	.4987	.4987	.4988	.4988	.4989	.4989	.4989	.4990	.4990
3.1	.4990	.4991	.4991	.4991	.4992	.4922	.4992	.4992	.4993	.4993
3.2	.4993	.4993	.4994	.4994	.4994	.4994	.4994	.4995	.4995	.4995
3.3	.4995	.4995	.4995	.4996	.4996	.4996	.4996	.4996	.4996	.4997
3.4	.4997	.4997	.4997	.4997	.4997	.4997	.4997	.4997	.4997	.4998
3.5	.4998									
4.0	.49997									
4.5	.499997									
5.0	.4999997									

TABLE A.2

Distribution of *t* for Given Probability Levels

	Level of Significance for One-Tailed Test					
	.10	.05	.025	.01	.005	.0005
	Level of Significance for Two-Tailed Test					
df	.20	.10	.05	.02	.01	.001
1	3.078	6.314	12.706	31.821	63.657	636.619
2	1.886	2.920	4.303	6.965	9.925	31.598
3	1.638	2.353	3.182	4.541	5.841	12.941
4	1.533	2.132	2.776	3.747	4.604	8.610
5	1.476	2.015	2.571	3.365	4.032	6.859
6	1.440	1.943	2.447	3.143	3.707	5.959
7	1.415	1.895	2.365	2.998	3.499	5.405
8	1.397	1.860	2.306	2.896	3.355	5.041
9	1.383	1.833	2.262	2.821	3.250	4.781
10	1.372	1.812	2.228	2.764	3.169	4.587
11	1.363	1.796	2.201	2.718	3.106	4.437
12	1.356	1.782	2.179	2.681	3.055	4.318
13	1.350	1.771	2.160	2.650	3.012	4.221
14	1.345	1.761	2.145	2.624	2.977	4.140
15	1.341	1.753	2.131	2.602	2.947	4.073
16	1.337	1.746	2.120	2.583	2.921	4.015
17	1.333	1.740	2.110	2.567	2.898	3.965
18	1.330	1.734	2.101	2.552	2.878	3.992
19	1.328	1.729	2.093	2.539	2.861	3.883
20	1.325	1.725	2.086	2.528	2.845	3.850
21	1.323	1.721	2.080	2.518	2.831	3.819
22	1.321	1.717	2.074	2.508	2.819	3.792
23	1.319	1.714	2.069	2.500	2.807	3.767
24	1.318	1.711	2.064	2.492	2.797	3.745
25	1.316	1.708	2.060	2.485	2.787	3.725
26	1.315	1.706	2.056	2.479	2.779	3.707
27	1.314	1.703	2.052	2.473	2.771	3.690
28	1.313	1.701	2.048	2.467	2.763	3.674
29	1.311	1.699	2.045	2.462	2.756	3.659
30	1.310	1.697	2.042	2.457	2.750	3.646
40	1.303	1.684	2.021	2.423	2.704	3.551
60	1.296	1.671	2.000	2.390	2.660	3.460
120	1.289	1.658	1.980	2.358	2.617	3.373
∞	1.282	1.645	1.960	2.326	2.576	3.291

TABLE A.3

Distribution of *r* for Given Probability Levels

	Level of Significance for One-Tailed Test			
	.05	.025	.01	.005
	Level of Significance for Two-Tailed Test			
df	.10	.05	.02	.01
1	.988	.997	.9995	.9999
2	.900	.950	.980	.990
3	.805	.878	.934	.959
4	.729	.811	.882	.917
5	.669	.754	.833	.874
6	.622	.707	.789	.834
7	.582	.666	.750	.798
8	.540	.632	.716	.765
9	.521	.602	.685	.735
10	.497	.576	.658	.708
11	.576	.553	.634	.684
12	.458	.532	.612	.661
13	.441	.514	.592	.641
14	.426	.497	.574	.623
15	.412	.482	.558	.606
16	.400	.468	.542	.590
17	.389	.456	.528	.575
18	.378	.444	.516	.561
19	.369	.433	.503	.549
20	.360	.423	.492	.537
21	.352	.413	.482	.526
22	.344	.404	.472	.515
23	.337	.396	.462	.505
24	.330	.388	.453	.496
25	.323	.381	.445	.487
26	.317	.374	.437	.479
27	.311	.367	.430	.471
28	.306	.361	.423	.463
29	.301	.355	.416	.486
30	.296	.349	.409	.449
35	.275	.325	.381	.418
40	.257	.304	.358	.393
45	.243	.288	.338	.372
50	.231	.273	.322	.354
60	.211	.250	.295	.325
70	.195	.232	.274	.303
80	.183	.217	.256	.283
90	.173	.205	.242	.267
100	.164	.195	.230	.254

TABLE A.4

Distribution of Chi-Square for Given Probability Levels

df								Probability						
	.99	.98	.95	.90	.80	.70	.50	.30	.20	.10	.05	.02	.01	.001
1	.00016	.00663	.00393	.0158	.0642	.148	.455	1.074	1.642	2.706	3.841	5.412	6.635	10.827
2	.0201	.0404	.103	.211	.446	.713	1.386	2.408	3.219	4.605	5.991	7.824	9.210	13.815
3	.115	.185	.352	.584	1.005	1.424	2.366	3.665	4.642	6.251	7.815	9.837	11.345	16.266
4	.297	.429	.711	1.064	1.649	2.195	3.357	4.878	5.989	7.779	9.488	11.668	13.277	18.467
5	.554	.752	1.145	1.610	2.343	3.000	4.351	6.064	7.289	9.236	11.070	13.388	15.086	20.515
6	.872	1.134	1.635	2.204	3.070	3.828	5.348	7.231	8.558	10.645	12.592	15.033	16.812	22.457
7	1.239	1.564	2.167	2.833	3.822	4.671	6.346	8.383	9.803	12.017	14.067	16.622	18.475	24.322
8	1.646	2.032	2.733	3.490	4.594	5.527	7.344	9.524	11.030	13.362	15.507	18.168	20.090	26.125
9	2.088	2.532	3.325	4.168	5.380	6.393	8.343	10.656	12.242	14.684	16.919	19.679	21.666	27.877
10	2.558	3.059	3.940	4.865	6.179	7.267	9.342	11.781	13.442	15.987	18.307	21.161	23.209	29.588
11	3.053	3.609	4.575	5.578	6.989	8.148	10.341	12.899	14.631	17.275	19.675	22.618	24.725	31.264
12	3.571	4.178	5.226	6.304	7.807	9.034	11.340	14.011	15.812	18.549	21.026	24.054	26.217	32.909
13	4.107	4.765	5.892	7.042	8.634	9.926	12.340	15.119	16.985	19.812	22.362	25.472	27.688	34.528
14	4.660	5.368	6.571	7.790	9.467	10.821	13.339	16.222	18.151	21.064	23.685	26.873	29.141	36.123
15	5.229	5.985	7.261	8.547	10.307	11.721	14.339	17.322	19.311	22.307	24.996	28.259	30.578	37.697
16	5.812	6.614	7.962	9.312	11.152	12.624	15.338	18.418	20.465	23.542	26.296	29.633	32.000	39.252
17	6.408	7.255	8.672	10.085	12.002	13.531	16.338	19.511	21.615	24.769	27.587	30.995	33.409	40.790
18	7.015	7.906	9.390	10.865	12.857	14.440	17.338	20.601	22.760	25.989	28.869	32.346	34.805	42.312
19	7.633	8.567	10.117	11.651	13.716	15.352	18.338	21.689	23.900	27.204	30.144	33.687	36.191	43.820
20	8.260	9.237	10.851	12.443	14.578	16.266	19.337	22.775	25.038	28.412	31.410	35.020	37.566	45.315
21	8.897	9.915	11.591	13.240	15.445	17.182	20.337	23.858	26.171	29.615	32.671	36.343	38.932	46.797
22	9.542	10.600	12.338	14.041	16.314	18.101	21.337	24.939	27.301	30.813	33.924	37.659	40.289	48.268
23	10.196	11.293	13.091	14.848	17.187	19.021	22.337	26.018	28.429	32.007	35.172	38.968	41.638	49.728
24	10.856	11.992	13.848	15.659	18.062	19.943	23.337	27.096	29.553	33.196	36.415	40.270	42.980	51.179
25	11.524	12.697	14.611	16.473	18.940	20.867	24.337	28.172	30.675	34.382	37.652	41.566	44.314	52.620

(continued)

TABLE A.4 (CONTINUED)

Distribution of Chi-Square for Given Probability Levels

df							Probability							
	.99	.98	.95	.90	.80	.70	.50	.30	.20	.10	.05	.02	.01	.001
26	12.198	13.409	15.379	17.292	19.820	21.792	25.336	29.246	31.795	35.563	38.885	42.856	45.642	54.052
27	12.879	14.125	16.151	18.114	20.703	22.719	26.336	30.319	32.912	36.741	40.113	44.140	46.963	55.476
28	13.565	14.847	16.928	18.939	21.588	23.647	27.336	31.391	34.027	37.916	41.337	45.419	48.278	56.893
29	14.256	15.574	17.708	19.768	22.475	24.577	28.336	32.461	35.139	39.087	42.557	46.693	49.588	58.302
30	14.953	16.306	18.493	20.599	23.364	25.508	29.336	33.530	36.250	40.256	43.773	47.962	50.892	59.703
32	16.362	17.783	20.072	22.271	25.148	27.373	31.336	35.665	38.466	42.585	46.194	50.487	53.486	62.487
34	17.789	19.275	21.664	23.952	26.938	29.242	33.336	37.795	40.676	44.903	48.602	52.995	56.061	65.247
36	19.233	20.783	23.269	25.643	28.735	31.115	35.336	39.922	42.879	47.212	50.999	55.489	58.619	67.985
38	20.691	22.304	24.884	27.343	30.537	32.992	37.335	42.045	45.076	49.513	53.384	57.969	61.162	70.703
40	22.164	23.838	26.509	29.051	32.345	34.872	39.335	44.165	47.269	51.805	55.759	60.436	63.691	73.402
42	23.650	25.383	28.144	30.765	34.147	36.755	41.335	46.282	49.456	54.090	58.124	62.892	66.206	76.084
44	25.148	26.939	29.787	32.487	35.974	38.641	43.335	48.396	51.639	56.369	60.481	65.337	68.710	78.750
46	26.657	28.504	31.439	34.215	37.795	40.529	45.335	50.507	53.818	58.641	62.830	67.771	71.201	81.400
48	28.177	30.080	33.098	35.949	39.621	42.420	47.335	52.616	55.993	60.907	65.171	70.197	73.683	84.037
50	29.707	31.664	34.764	37.689	41.449	44.313	49.335	54.723	58.164	63.167	67.505	72.613	76.154	86.661
52	31.246	33.256	36.437	39.433	43.281	46.209	51.335	56.827	60.332	65.422	69.832	75.021	78.616	89.272
54	32.793	34.856	38.116	41.183	45.117	48.106	53.335	58.930	62.496	67.673	72.153	77.422	81.069	91.872
56	34.350	36.464	39.801	42.937	46.955	50.005	55.335	61.031	64.658	69.919	74.468	79.815	83.513	94.461
58	35.913	38.078	41.492	44.696	48.797	51.906	57.335	63.129	66.816	72.160	76.778	82.201	85.950	97.039
60	37.485	39.699	43.188	46.459	50.641	53.809	59.335	65.227	68.972	74.397	79.082	84.580	88.379	99.607
62	39.063	41.327	44.889	48.226	52.487	55.714	61.335	67.322	71.125	76.630	81.381	86.953	90.802	102.166
64	40.649	42.960	46.595	49.996	54.336	57.620	63.335	69.416	73.276	78.860	83.675	89.320	93.217	104.716
66	42.240	44.599	48.305	51.770	56.188	59.527	65.335	71.508	75.424	81.085	85.965	91.681	95.626	107.258
68	43.838	46.244	50.020	53.548	58.042	61.436	67.335	73.600	77.571	83.308	88.250	94.037	98.028	109.791
70	45.442	47.893	51.739	55.329	59.898	63.346	69.335	75.689	79.715	85.527	90.531	96.388	100.425	112.317

Note. For larger values of df, the expression $\sqrt{(X^2)^2} - \sqrt{2df} - 1$ may be used as a normal deviate with unit variance, remembering that the probability for X^2 corresponds with that of a single tail of the normal curve.

TABLE A.5

The *F*-Distribution for Given Probability Levels (.05 Level)

$df_1 df_2$	1	2	3	4	5	6	7	8	9	10	12	15	20	24	30	40	60	120	∞
1	161.4	199.5	215.7	224.6	230.2	234.0	236.8	238.9	240.5	241.9	243.9	245.9	248.0	249.1	250.1	251.1	252.2	253.3	254.3
2	18.51	19.00	19.16	19.25	19.30	19.33	19.35	19.37	19.38	19.49	19.41	19.43	19.45	19.45	19.46	19.47	19.48	19.49	19.50
3	10.13	9.55	9.28	9.12	9.01	8.94	8.89	8.85	8.81	8.79	8.74	8.70	8.66	8.64	8.62	8.59	8.57	8.55	8.53
4	7.71	6.94	6.59	6.39	6.26	6.15	6.09	6.04	6.00	5.96	5.91	5.86	5.80	5.77	5.75	5.72	5.69	5.66	5.63
5	6.61	5.79	5.41	5.19	5.05	4.95	4.88	4.82	4.77	4.74	4.68	4.62	4.56	4.53	4.50	4.46	4.43	4.40	4.36
6	5.99	5.14	4.76	4.53	4.39	4.28	4.21	4.15	4.10	4.06	4.00	3.94	3.87	3.84	3.81	3.77	3.74	3.70	3.67
7	5.59	4.74	4.35	4.12	3.97	3.87	3.79	3.73	3.68	3.64	3.57	3.51	3.44	3.41	3.38	3.34	3.30	3.27	3.23
8	5.32	4.46	4.07	3.84	3.69	3.58	3.50	3.44	3.39	3.35	3.28	3.22	3.15	3.12	3.08	3.04	3.01	2.97	2.93
9	5.12	4.26	3.86	3.63	3.48	3.37	3.29	3.23	3.18	3.14	3.07	3.01	2.94	2.90	2.86	2.83	2.79	2.75	2.71
10	4.96	4.10	3.71	3.48	3.33	3.22	3.14	3.07	3.02	2.98	2.91	2.85	2.77	2.74	2.70	2.66	2.62	2.58	2.54
11	4.84	3.98	3.59	3.36	3.20	3.09	3.01	2.95	2.90	2.85	2.79	2.72	2.65	2.61	2.57	2.53	2.49	2.45	2.40
12	4.75	3.89	3.49	3.26	3.11	3.00	2.91	2.85	2.80	2.75	2.69	2.62	2.54	2.51	2.47	2.43	2.38	2.34	2.30
13	4.67	3.81	3.41	3.18	3.03	2.92	2.83	2.77	2.71	2.67	2.60	2.53	2.46	2.42	2.38	2.34	2.30	2.25	2.21
14	4.60	3.74	3.34	3.11	2.96	2.85	2.76	2.70	2.65	2.60	2.53	2.46	2.39	2.35	2.31	2.27	2.22	2.18	2.13
15	4.54	3.68	3.29	3.06	2.90	2.79	2.71	2.64	2.59	2.54	2.48	2.40	2.33	2.29	2.25	2.20	2.16	2.11	2.07
16	4.49	3.63	3.24	3.01	2.85	2.74	2.66	2.59	2.54	2.49	2.42	2.35	2.28	2.24	2.19	2.1	2.11	2.06	2.01
17	4.45	3.59	3.20	2.96	2.81	2.70	2.61	2.55	2.49	2.45	2.38	2.31	2.23	2.19	2.15	2.10	2.06	2.01	1.96
18	4.41	3.55	3.16	2.93	2.77	2.66	2.58	2.51	2.46	2.41	2.34	2.27	2.19	2.15	2.11	2.06	2.02	1.97	1.92
19	4.38	3.52	3.13	2.90	2.74	2.63	2.54	2.48	2.42	2.38	2.31	2.23	2.16	2.11	2.07	2.03	1.98	1.93	1.88

(continued)

TABLE A.5 (CONTINUED)

The *F*-Distribution for Given Probability Levels (.05 Level)

df$_1$df$_2$	1	2	3	4	5	6	7	8	9	10	12	15	20	24	30	40	60	120	∞
20	4.35	3.49	3.10	2.87	2.71	2.60	2.51	2.45	2.39	2.35	2.28	2.20	2.12	2.08	2.04	1.99	1.95	1.90	1.84
21	4.32	3.47	3.07	2.84	2.68	2.57	2.49	2.42	2.37	2.32	2.25	2.18	2.10	2.05	2.01	1.96	1.92	1.87	1.81
22	4.30	3.44	3.05	2.82	2.66	2.55	2.46	2.40	2.34	2.30	2.23	2.15	2.07	2.03	1.98	1.94	1.89	1.84	1.78
23	4.28	3.42	3.03	2.80	2.64	2.53	2.44	2.37	2.32	2.27	2.20	2.13	2.05	2.01	1.96	1.91	1.86	1.81	1.76
24	4.26	3.40	3.01	2.78	2.62	2.51	2.42	2.36	2.30	2.25	2.18	2.11	2.03	1.98	1.94	1.89	1.84	1.79	1.73
25	4.24	3.39	2.99	2.76	2.60	2.49	2.40	2.34	2.28	2.24	2.16	2.09	2.01	1.96	1.92	1.87	1.82	1.77	1.71
26	4.23	3.37	2.98	2.74	2.59	2.47	2.39	2.32	2.27	2.22	2.15	2.07	1.99	1.95	1.90	1.85	1.80	1.75	1.69
27	4.21	3.35	2.96	2.73	2.57	2.46	2.37	2.31	2.25	2.20	2.13	2.06	1.97	1.93	1.88	1.84	1.79	1.73	1.67
28	4.20	3.34	2.95	2.71	2.56	2.45	2.36	2.29	2.24	2.19	2.12	2.04	1.96	1.91	1.87	1.82	1.77	1.71	1.65
29	4.18	3.33	2.93	2.70	2.55	2.43	2.35	2.28	2.22	2.18	2.10	2.03	1.94	1.90	1.85	1.81	1.75	1.70	1.64
30	4.17	3.32	2.92	2.69	2.53	2.42	2.33	2.27	2.21	2.16	2.09	2.01	1.93	1.89	1.84	1.79	1.74	1.68	1.62
40	4.08	3.23	2.84	2.61	2.45	2.34	2.25	2.18	2.12	2.08	2.00	1.92	1.84	1.79	1.74	1.69	1.64	1.58	1.51
60	4.00	3.15	2.76	2.53	2.37	2.25	2.17	2.10	2.04	1.99	1.92	1.84	1.75	1.70	1.65	1.59	1.53	1.47	1.39
120	3.92	3.07	2.68	2.45	2.29	2.17	2.09	2.02	1.96	1.91	1.83	1.75	1.66	1.61	1.55	1.50	1.43	1.35	1.25
∞	3.84	3.00	2.60	2.37	2.21	2.10	2.01	1.94	1.88	1.83	1.75	1.67	1.57	1.52	1.46	1.39	1.32	1.22	1.00

TABLE A.6

The F Distribution for Given Probability Levels (.01 Level)

df₂ \ df₁	1	2	3	4	5	6	7	8	9	10	12	15	20	24	30	40	60	120	∞
1	4052	4999.5	5403	5625	5764	5859	5928	5982	6022	6056	6106	6157	6209	6235	6261	6287	6313	6339	6366
2	98.5	99.00	99.17	99.25	99.30	99.33	99.36	99.37	99.39	99.40	99.42	99.43	99.45	99.46	99.47	99.47	99.48	99.49	99.50
3	34.12	30.82	29.46	28.71	28.24	27.91	27.67	27.49	27.25	27.23	27.05	26.87	26.69	26.60	26.50	26.41	26.32	26.22	26.13
4	21.20	18.00	16.69	15.98	15.52	15.21	14.98	14.80	14.66	14.55	14.37	14.20	14.02	13.93	13.84	13.75	13.65	13.56	13.46
5	16.26	13.27	12.06	11.39	10.97	10.67	10.46	10.29	10.16	10.05	9.89	9.72	9.55	9.47	9.38	9.29	9.20	9.11	9.02
6	13.75	10.92	9.78	9.15	8.75	8.47	8.26	8.10	7.98	7.87	7.72	7.56	7.40	7.31	7.23	7.14	7.06	6.97	6.88
7	12.25	9.55	8.45	7.85	7.46	7.19	6.99	6.84	6.72	6.62	6.47	6.31	6.16	6.07	5.99	5.91	5.82	5.74	5.65
8	11.26	8.65	7.59	7.01	6.63	6.37	6.18	6.03	5.91	5.81	5.67	5.52	5.36	5.28	5.20	5.12	5.03	4.95	4.86
9	10.56	8.02	6.99	6.42	6.06	5.80	5.61	5.47	5.35	5.26	5.11	4.96	4.81	4.73	4.65	4.57	4.48	4.40	4.31
10	10.04	7.56	6.55	5.99	5.64	5.39	5.20	5.06	4.94	4.85	4.71	4.56	4.41	4.33	4.25	4.17	4.08	4.00	3.91
11	9.65	7.21	6.22	5.67	5.32	5.07	4.89	4.74	4.63	4.54	4.40	4.25	4.10	4.02	3.94	3.86	3.78	3.69	3.60
12	9.33	6.93	5.95	5.41	5.06	4.82	4.64	4.50	4.39	4.30	4.16	4.01	3.86	3.78	3.70	3.62	3.54	3.45	3.36
13	9.07	6.70	5.74	5.21	4.86	4.62	4.44	4.30	4.19	4.10	3.96	3.82	3.66	3.59	3.51	3.43	3.34	3.25	3.17
14	8.86	6.51	5.56	5.04	4.69	4.46	4.28	4.14	4.03	3.94	3.80	3.66	3.51	3.43	3.35	3.27	3.18	3.09	3.00
15	8.68	6.36	5.42	4.89	4.56	4.32	4.14	4.00	3.89	3.80	3.67	3.52	3.37	3.29	3.21	3.13	3.05	2.96	2.87
16	8.53	6.23	5.29	4.77	4.44	4.20	4.03	3.89	3.78	3.69	3.55	3.41	3.26	3.18	3.10	3.02	2.93	2.84	2.75
17	8.40	6.11	5.18	4.67	4.34	4.10	3.93	3.79	3.68	3.59	3.46	3.31	3.16	3.08	3.00	2.92	2.83	2.75	2.65
18	8.29	6.01	5.09	4.58	4.25	4.01	3.84	3.71	3.60	3.51	3.37	3.23	3.08	3.00	2.92	2.84	2.75	2.66	2.57
19	8.18	5.93	5.01	4.50	4.17	3.94	3.77	3.63	3.52	3.43	3.30	3.15	3.00	2.92	2.84	2.76	2.67	2.58	2.49

(continued)

TABLE A.6 (CONTINUED)

The F Distribution for Given Probability Levels (.01 Level)

df$_2$ \ df$_1$	1	2	3	4	5	6	7	8	9	10	12	15	20	24	30	40	60	120	∞
20	8.10	5.85	4.94	4.43	4.10	3.87	3.70	3.56	3.46	3.37	3.23	3.09	2.94	2.86	2.78	2.69	2.61	2.52	2.42
21	8.02	5.78	4.87	4.37	4.04	3.81	3.64	3.51	3.40	3.31	3.17	3.03	2.88	2.80	2.72	2.64	2.55	2.46	2.36
22	7.95	5.72	4.82	4.31	3.9	3.76	3.59	3.45	3.35	3.26	3.12	2.98	2.83	2.75	2.67	2.58	2.50	2.40	2.31
23	7.88	5.66	4.76	4.26	3.94	3.71	3.54	3.41	3.30	3.21	3.07	2.93	2.78	2.70	2.62	2.54	2.45	2.35	2.26
24	7.82	5.61	4.72	4.22	3.90	3.67	3.50	3.36	3.26	3.17	3.03	2.89	2.74	2.66	2.58	2.49	2.40	2.31	2.21
25	7.77	5.57	4.68	4.18	3.85	3.63	3.46	3.32	3.22	3.13	2.99	2.85	2.70	2.62	2.54	2.45	2.36	2.27	2.17
26	7.72	5.53	4.64	4.14	3.82	3.59	3.42	3.29	3.18	3.09	2.96	2.81	2.66	2.58	2.50	2.42	2.33	2.23	2.13
27	7.68	5.49	4.60	4.11	3.78	3.56	3.39	3.26	3.15	3.06	2.93	2.78	2.63	2.55	2.47	2.38	2.29	2.20	2.10
28	7.64	5.45	4.57	4.07	3.75	3.53	3.36	3.23	3.12	3.03	2.90	2.75	2.60	2.52	2.44	2.35	2.26	2.17	2.06
29	7.60	5.42	4.54	4.04	3.73	3.50	3.33	3.20	3.09	3.00	2.87	2.73	2.57	2.49	2.41	2.33	2.23	2.14	2.03
30	7.56	5.39	4.51	4.02	3.70	3.47	3.30	3.17	3.07	2.98	2.84	2.70	2.55	2.47	2.39	2.30	2.21	2.11	2.01
40	7.31	5.18	4.31	3.83	3.51	3.29	3.12	2.99	2.89	2.80	2.66	2.52	2.37	2.29	2.20	2.11	2.02	1.92	1.80
60	7.08	4.98	4.13	36.5	3.34	3.12	2.95	2.82	2.72	2.63	2.50	2.35	2.20	2.12	2.03	1.94	1.84	1.73	1.60
120	6.85	4.79	3.95	3.48	3.17	2.96	2.79	2.66	2.56	2.47	2.34	2.19	2.03	1.95	1.86	1.76	1.66	1.53	1.38
∞	6.63	4.61	3.78	3.32	3.02	2.80	2.64	2.51	2.41	2.32	2.18	2.04	1.88	1.79	1.70	1.59	1.47	1.32	1.00

Answers to Selected Exercises

Chapter 1

1. Define the following terms:
   a. Latent variable: an unobserved variable that is not directly measured, but is computed using multiple observed variables.
   b. Observed variable: a raw score obtained from a test or measurement instrument on a trait of interest.
   c. Dependent variable: a variable that is measured and related to outcomes, performance, or criterion.
   d. Independent variable: a variable that defines mutually exclusive categories (e.g., gender, region, or grade level), or as a continuous variable, and influences a dependent variable.

3. List the reasons why a researcher would conduct structural equation modeling:
   a. Researchers are becoming more aware of the need to use multiple observed variables to better understand their area of scientific inquiry.
   b. More recognition is given to the validity and reliability of observed scores from measurement instruments.
   c. Structural equation modeling has improved recently, especially the ability to analyze more advanced statistical models.
   d. SEM software programs have become increasingly user friendly.

Chapter 2

1. LISREL uses which command to import data sets?
   c. File, then Import Data
3. Mark each of the following statements true (T) or false (F).
   a. LISREL can deal with missing data.   F

b. PRELIS can deal with missing data. T

c. LISREL can compute descriptive statistics. T

d. PRELIS can compute descriptive statistics. T

Chapter 3

1. Partial and part correlations:

$$r_{12.3} = \frac{.6-(.7)(.4)}{\sqrt{[1-(.7)^2][1-(.4)^2]}} = .49$$

$$r_{1(2.3)} = \frac{.6-(.7)(.4)}{\sqrt{[1-(.4)^2]}} = .35.$$

3. A meaningful theoretical relationship should be plausible given that:

a. Variables logically precede each other in time.

b. Variables covary or correlate together as expected.

c. Other influences or "causes" are controlled.

d. Variables should be measured on at least an interval level.

e. Changes in a preceding variable should affect variables that follow, either directly or indirectly.

Chapter 4

1. *Model specification*: developing a theoretical model to test, based on all of the relevant theory, research, and information available.

3. *Model estimation*: obtaining estimates for each of the parameters specified in the model that produced the implied population covariance matrix Σ. The intent is to obtain parameter estimates that yield a matrix Σ as close as possible to S, our sample covariance matrix of the observed or indicator variables. When elements in the matrix S minus the elements in the matrix Σ equal zero ($S - \Sigma = 0$), then $\chi^2 = 0$ indicating a perfect model fit to the data, and all values in S are equal to values in Σ.

5. *Model modification*: changing the initial implied model and retesting the global fit and individual parameters in the new respecified model. To determine how to modify the model, there are a number of procedures available to guide the adding or dropping of paths in the model so that alternative models can be tested.

7. How many distinct values are in a variance–covariance matrix for the following variables {hint: $[p(p+1)/2]$?
   a. Five variables = 15 distinct values
   b. Ten variables = 55 distinct values

Chapter 5

1. Define confirmatory models, alternative models, and model-generating approaches.

   In *confirmatory models*, a researcher can hypothesize a specific theoretical model, gather data, and then test whether the data fit the model.

   In *alternative models*, a researcher specifies different models to see which model fits the sample data the best. A researcher usually conducts a chi-square difference test.

   In *model generating*, a researcher specifies an initial model, then uses modification indices to modify and retest the model to obtain a better fit to the sample data.

3. Calculate the following fit indices for the model analysis in Figure 5.1:

   $\text{GFI} = 1 - [\chi^2_{model}/\chi^2_{null}] = .97$

   $\text{NFI} = (\chi^2_{null} - \chi^2_{model})/\chi^2_{null} = .97$

   $\text{RFI} = 1 - [(\chi^2_{model}/df_{model})/(\chi^2_{null}/df_{null})] = .94$

   $\text{IFI} = (\chi^2_{null} - \chi^2_{model})/(\chi^2_{null} - df_{model}) = .98$

   $\text{TLI} = [(\chi^2_{null}/df_{null}) - (\chi^2_{model}/df_{model})]/[(\chi^2_{null}/df_{null}) - 1] = .96$

   $\text{CFI} = 1 - [(\chi^2_{model} - df_{model})/(\chi^2_{null} - df_{null})] = .98$

   $\text{Model AIC} = \chi^2_{model} + 2q = 50.41$

   $\text{Null AIC} = \chi^2_{null} + 2q = 747.80$

   $RMSEA = \sqrt{[\chi^2_{Model} - df_{Model}]/[(N-1)df_{Model}]} = 0.083$

5. What steps should a researcher take in examining parameter estimates in a model?

A researcher should examine the sign of the parameter estimate, whether the value of the parameter estimate is within a reasonable range of values, and test the parameter for significance.

7. How are structural equation models affected by sample size and power considerations?

Several factors affect determining the appropriate sample size and power, including model complexity, distribution of variables, missing data, reliability, and variance–covariance of variables. If variables are normally distributed with no missing data, samples sizes less than 500 should yield power = .80 and satisfy Hoelter's CN criterion. SAS, SPSS, G*Power 3, and other software programs can be used to determine power and sample size.

9. What new approaches are available to help researchers identify the best model?

The expected parameter change value has been added to LISREL output. Tabu and optimization algorithms have been proposed to identify the best model fit with the sample variance–covariance matrix.

11. Use G*Power 3 to calculate power for modified model with alpha = .05 and NCP = 6.3496 at df = 1, df = 2, and df = 3 levels of model complexity. What happens to power when degrees of freedom increases?

Power decreases as the degrees of freedom increases (power = .73, df = 1; power = .63, df = 2, and power = .56, df = 3).

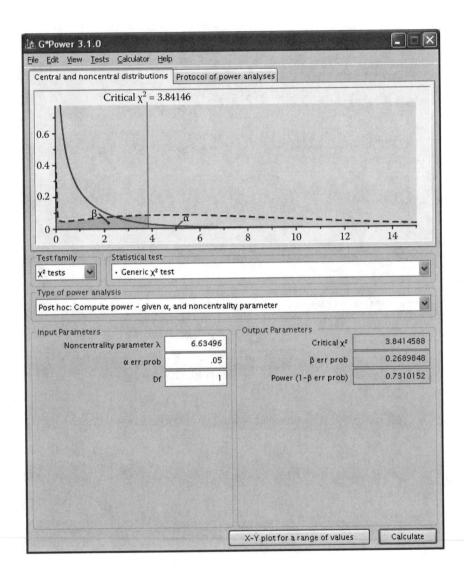

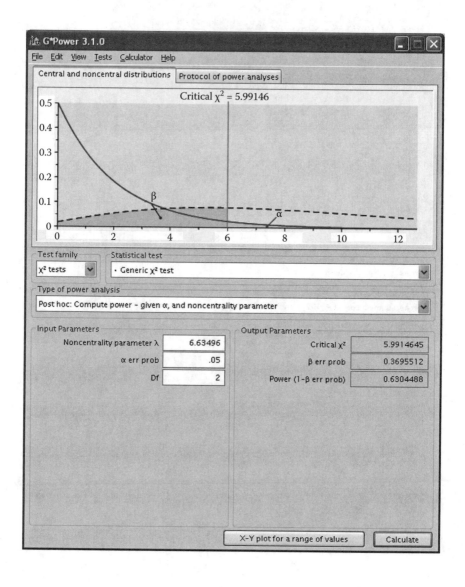

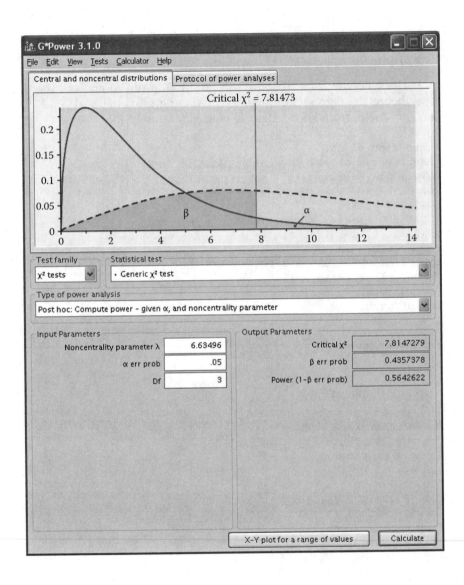

Chapter 6

1. The following LISREL–SIMPLIS program is run to analyze the theoretical regression model for predicting gross national product (GNP) from knowledge of labor, capital, and time:

```
Regression of GNP
Observed variables: GNP LABOR CAPITAL TIME
Covariance matrix:
 4256.530
 449.016 52.984
 1535.097 139.449 1114.447
 537.482 53.291 170.024 73.747
Sample size: 23
Equation: GNP = LABOR CAPITAL TIME
Number of decimals = 3
Path diagram
End of problem
```

Chapter 7

1. LISREL PROGRAM

```
Achievement path model
Observed variables: Ach Inc Abl Asp
Covariance matrix:
 25.500
 20.500 38.100
 22.480 24.200 42.750
 16.275 13.600 13.500 17.000
Sample size: 100
Relationships
Asp = Inc Abl
Ach = Inc Abl Asp
Print residuals
Options: ND = 3
Path diagram
End of problem
```

Partial LISREL Output

```
LISREL Estimates (Maximum Likelihood)

    Structural Equations
```

```
Ach = 0.645*Asp + 0.161*Inc + 0.231*Abl, Errorvar. = 6.507,
  R² = 0.745
       (0.0771)        (0.0557)        (0.0514)          (0.934)
        8.366           2.892           4.497            6.964

Asp = 0.244*Inc + 0.178*Abl, Errorvar. = 11.282, R² = 0.336
       (0.0690)   (0.0652)                (1.620)
        3.537      2.724                   6.964
```

```
Covariance Matrix of Independent Variables

                    Inc                 Abl
                 --------            --------
      Inc         38.100
                 (5.471)
                  6.964
      Abl         24.200              42.750
                 (4.778)             (6.139)
                  5.065               6.964
```

```
                Goodness-of-Fit Statistics

                 Degrees of Freedom = 0
         Minimum Fit Function Chi-Square = 0.00 (P = 1.000)
   Normal Theory Weighted Least Squares Chi-Square = 0.00 (P =
                           1.000)

       The model is saturated, the fit is perfect!
```

Chapter 8

1. The following LISREL–SIMPLIS program was written:

```
Confirmatory Factor Model Exercise Chapter 8
Observed Variables:
Academic Concept Aspire Degree Prestige Income
Correlation Matrix
1.000
0.487   1.000
0.236   0.206   1.000
0.242   0.179   0.253   1.000
0.163   0.090   0.125   0.481   1.000
0.064   0.040   0.025   0.106   0.136   1.000
Sample Size: 3094
Latent Variables: Motivate SES
```

```
Relationships:
  Academic - Aspire = Motivate
  Degree - Income = SES
Print Residuals
Number of Decimals = 3
Path diagram
End of problem
```

Results overall suggest a less than acceptable fit:

Normal Theory Weighted Least Squares Chi-Square = 114.115 (P = 0.0)

Degrees of Freedom = 8

Root Mean Square Error of Approximation (RMSEA) = 0.0655

Standardized RMR = 0.0377

Goodness-of-Fit Index (GFI) = 0.988

Consequently, the model modification indices were examined. The largest decrease in chi-square results from adding an error covariance between Concept and Academic (boldfaced), thus allowing us to maintain a hypothesized two-factor model.

```
The Modification Indices Suggest to Add the
Path to     from        Decrease in Chi-Square    New Estimate
Concept     SES                 21.9                 -0.14
Aspire      SES                 78.0                  0.21
Degree      Motivate            16.1                  0.31
Prestige    Motivate            18.1                 -0.22
```

```
The Modification Indices Suggest to Add an Error Covariance
Between     and         Decrease in Chi-Square    New Estimate
Concept     Academic            78.0                  0.63
Aspire      Academic            21.9                 -0.12
Degree      Aspire              75.3                  0.13
Prestige    Concept              8.9                 -0.04
Income      Degree              18.1                 -0.10
Income      Prestige            16.1                  0.07
```

The following error covariance command line was added.

Let the errors Concept and Academic correlate

The results indicated further model modifications. The largest decrease in chi-square was determined to occur by adding an error covariance between Income and Prestige (boldfaced in following text), thus maintaining our hypothesized two-factor confirmatory model.

```
The Modification Indices Suggest to Add the
Path to      from         Decrease in Chi-Square    New Estimate
Degree       Motivate            20.3                   0.71
Prestige     Motivate            18.4                  -0.39

The Modification Indices Suggest to Add an Error Covariance
Between      and          Decrease in Chi-Square    New Estimate
Degree       Aspire              10.0                   0.09
Prestige     Aspire               8.3                  -0.05
Income       Degree              18.4                  -0.10
Income       Prestige            20.3                   0.08
```

The following error covariance command line was added.

Let the errors Income and Prestige correlate

The final results indicated a more acceptable level of fit:

Normal Theory Weighted Least Squares Chi-Square = 14.519
(P = 0.0243)

Degrees of Freedom = 6

Root Mean Square Error of Approximation (RMSEA) = 0.0214

Standardized RMR = 0.0123

Goodness-of-Fit Index (GFI) = 0.998

The final LISREL–SIMPLIS program was:

```
Modified Confirmatory Factor Model - Exercise Chapter 8
Observed Variables:
Academic Concept Aspire Degree Prestige Income
Correlation Matrix
1.000
0.487    1.000
0.236    0.206    1.000
0.242    0.179    0.253    1.000
0.163    0.090    0.125    0.481    1.000
0.064    0.040    0.025    0.106    0.136    1.000
Sample Size: 3094
Latent Variables: Motivate SES
Relationships:
  Academic: Aspire = Motivate
  Degree: Income = SES
Let the errors concept and Academic correlate
Let the errors Income and Prestige correlate
Print residuals
Number of decimals = 3
Path diagram
End of problem
```

Chapter 9

1. Diagram two indicator variables *X1* and *X2* of a latent variable *LV*.

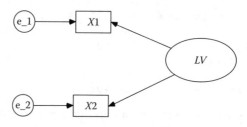

3. Diagram a latent independent variable *LIV* predicting a latent dependent variable *LDV*.

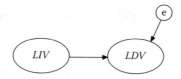

Chapter 10

1. The following LISREL–SIMPLIS program was written:

```
Chapter 10 Exercise
Observed variables: ACT CGPA ENTRY SALARY PROMO
Covariance matrix:
1.024
 .792     1.077
 .567     .537     .852
 .445     .424     .518     .670
 .434     .389     .475     .545     .716
Sample size: 500
Latent variables: ACAD JOB
Relationships:
 ACT = 1*ACAD
 CGPA = ACAD
 ENTRY = ACAD
 SALARY = 1*JOB
 PROMO = JOB
 JOB = ACAD
Path diagram
End of problem
```

The chi-square is statistically significant ($\chi^2 = 116.29$, $df = 4$, $p = .000$), so the modification indices are checked and it is suggested to add an error covariance between the measurement error variances of CGPA and ACT.

```
The Modification Indices Suggest Adding an Error Covariance
```

Between	and	Decrease in Chi-Square	New Estimate
ACT	SALARY	14.0	-0.06
CGPA	**ACT**	**113.5**	**0.43**
ENTRY	SALARY	40.8	0.10
ENTRY	ACT	24.9	-0.15
ENTRY	CGPA	23.9	-0.14

The following command line was added:

```
Let the error covariances between CGPA and ACT correlate
```

The modified model is acceptable ($\chi^2 = 3.04$, $df = 3$, $p = .39$; RMSEA = .005; GFI = 1.0). JOB is statistically significantly predicted, $R^2 = .70$, by the following structural equation:

```
Structural Equations
  JOB = 0.91*ACAD, Errorvar.= 0.18 , R² = 0.70
       (0.061)                    (0.027)
       15.01                       6.59
```

Chapter 11

1. SPSS and EXCEL matrix input.

SPSS Matrix Input Example

	rowtype_	varname_	academic	athletic	attract	gpa	height	weight	rating
1	n		209.00	209.00	209.00	209.00	209.00	209.00	209.00
2	corr	academic	1.00	.	.	.	.	.	.
3	corr	athletic	.43	1.00	.	.	.	.	.
4	corr	attract	.50	.48	1.00	.	.	.	.
5	corr	GPA	.49	.22	.32	1.00	.	.	.
6	corr	height	.10	-.04	-.03	.18	1.00	.	.
7	corr	weight	.04	.02	-.16	-.10	.34	1.00	.
8	corr	rating	.09	.14	.43	.15	-.16	-.27	1.00
9	stddev		.16	.07	.49	3.49	2.91	19.32	1.01
10	mean		.12	.05	.42	10.34	.00	94.13	2.65

Microsoft Excel Matrix Input Example

	A	B	C	D	E	F	G	H	I
1	rowtype_	varname_	academic	athletic	attract	GPA	height	weight	rating
2	n		209	209	209	209	209	209	209
3	corr	academic	1						
4	corr	athletic	0.43	1					
5	corr	attract	0.5	0.48	1				
6	corr	GPA	0.49	0.22	0.32	1			
7	corr	height	0.1	-0.04	-0.03	0.18	1		
8	corr	weight	0.04	0.02	-0.16	-0.1	0.34	1	
9	corr	rating	0.09	0.14	0.43	0.15	-0.16	-0.27	1
10	stddev		0.16	0.07	0.49	3.49	2.91	19.32	1.01
11	mean		0.12	0.05	0.42	10.34	0	94.13	2.65

Chapter 12

1. Multiple Samples

```
LISREL-SIMPLIS Program (EX11B.SPL)
Sample 1: Parental Socioeconomic Characteristics
Observed Variables: SOFED SOMED SOFOC FAFED MOMED FAFOC
Covariance Matrix
5.86
3.12 3.32
35.28 23.85 622.09
4.02 2.14 29.42 5.33
2.99 2.55 19.20 3.17 4.64
35.30 26.91 465.62 31.22 23.38 546.01
Sample Size: 80
Latent Variables: Fed Med Foc
SOFED = Fed
SOMED = Med
SOFOC = Foc
FAFED = 1*Fed
MOMED = 1*Med
FAFOC = 1*Foc
Set the Error Covariance between SOMED and SOFED free
```

Sample 2: Parental Socioeconomic Characteristics
Covariance Matrix
8.20
3.47 4.36
45.65 22.58 611.63
6.39 3.16 44.62 7.32
3.22 3.77 23.47 3.33 4.02
45.58 22.01 548.00 40.99 21.43 585.14
SOFED = Fed
SOMED = Med
SOFOC = Foc
Let the Error Variances of SOFED - SOFOC be free
Set the Error Covariance between SOMED and SOFED free

Sample 3: Parental Socioeconomic Characteristics
Covariance Matrix
5.74
1.35 2.49
39.24 12.73 535.30
4.94 1.65 37.36 5.39
1.67 2.32 15.71 1.85 3.06
40.11 12.94 496.86 38.09 14.91 538.76
SOFED = Fed
SOMED = Med
SOFOC = Foc
Let the Error Variances of SOFED - SOFOC be free
Set the Error Covariance between SOMED and SOFED equal to 0
Path diagram
End of problem
Global Goodness-of-Fit Statistics

Degrees of Freedom = 34
Minimum Fit Function Chi-Square = 52.73 (P = 0.021)

Root Mean Square Error of Approximation (RMSEA) = 0.077
90 Percent Confidence Interval for RMSEA = (0.019; 0.12)
P-Value for Test of Close Fit (RMSEA < 0.05) = 0.00038

Normed Fit Index (NFI) = 0.96
Comparative Fit Index (CFI) = 0.99
Critical N (CN) = 252.98

Chapter 13

1. Multiple Sample Model

The two semesters of data did not have means and standard deviations on the measures for the regression model, so no means and standard deviations would be included in the multiple sample LISREL–SIMPLIS program. (*Note:* Although two samples are used, we still use the GROUP command.) The LISREL–SIMPLIS program is:

```
Predicting Clinical Competence in Nursing
Group 1: Semester 1
Observed variables comp effort learn
Sample size: 250
Correlation matrix
1.0
.25 1.0
.28 .23 1.0
Equation
comp = effort learn

Group 2: Semester 2
Observed variables comp effort learn
Sample size: 205
Correlation matrix
1.0
.21 1.0
.16 .15 1.0
Path diagram
End of problem
```

Computer Output—Multiple Sample Model

The regression model output indicated a nonsignificant chi-square (chi-square = 1.55, $df = 3$, $p = .67$), which implies that the two semesters of sample data had similar regression coefficients. We find that the regression coefficient of *effort* predicting *comp* is .20 compared to .25 and .21, respectively, in the two samples. We also find that the regression coefficient of *learn* predicting *comp* is .19 compared to .28 and .16, respectively, in the two samples. The correlation between effort and learn is .23 in the common regression model, compared to .23 and .15, respectively, in the two samples of data. Finally, we see that the R-squared for the common regression model is .19 (1-R-squared = .91). The computer output (not shown) indicated R-squared = .09 and .085, respectively, for the two regression equations from the two samples of data.

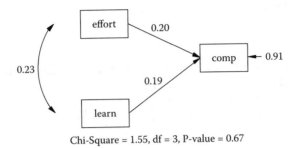

Chi-Square = 1.55, df = 3, P-value = 0.67

3. Structured Means Model

The two stacked LISREL–PRELIS programs are:

```
Group Low Motivation
Observed Variables: Prod1 Prod2 Prod3 Prod4 Prod5 Prod6
Correlation Matrix
1.00
 .64 1.00
 .78  .73  1.00
 .68  .63   .69  1.00
 .43  .55   .50   .59  1.00
 .65  .63   .67   .81   .60  1.00
Means 4.27 5.02  4.48 4.69  4.53  4.66
Sample Size: 300
Latent Variables: City1 City2
Relationships:
Prod1 = CONST + 1*City1
Prod2 = CONST + City1
Prod3 = CONST + City1
Prod4 = CONST + 1*City2
Prod5 = CONST + City2
Prod6 = CONST + City2
Group High Motivation:
Correlation Matrix
 1.00
 .72  1.00
 .76 .74  1.00
 .51 .46   .57  1.00
 .32 .33   .39   .40  1.00
 .54 .45   .60   .73   .45  1.00
Means 14.35 14.93 14.59 14.86 14.71 14.74
```

```
Sample size: 300
Relationships:
 City1 = CONST
 City2 = CONST
Path diagram
End of problem
```

The first thing you should check is the individual group and combined group model-fit statistics. They were:

Group Goodness-of-Fit Statistics: Low Motivation
   Contribution to Chi-Square = 52.92
   Root Mean Square Residual (RMR) = 0.11
   Goodness-of-Fit Index (GFI) = 0.94

Group Goodness-of-Fit Statistics: High Motivation
   Contribution to Chi-Square = 52.06
   Root Mean Square Residual (RMR) = 0.13
   Goodness-of-Fit Index (GFI) = 0.94

Global Goodness-of-Fit Statistics
   Degrees of Freedom = 24
   Minimum Fit Function Chi-Square = 104.98 (P = 0.00)
   Root Mean Square Error of Approximation (RMSEA) = 0.11
   90% Confidence Interval for RMSEA = (0.089; 0.13)
   P-Value for Test of Close Fit (RMSEA < 0.05) = 0.00
   Comparative Fit Index (CFI) = 0.97

These values are adequate, but modification indices were indicated and are suggested to yield a better model fit before proceeding with a test of latent variable mean differences.

The following command lines should be added to the LISREL–SIMPLIS program to allow observed variable error variance to be estimated, estimate latent variable variance, and allow the two latent variables to correlate:

```
Set the Error Variances of Prod1 - Prod6 free
Set the Variances of City1 - City2 free
Set the Covariance between City1 and City2 free
```

The final Structured Means Model with parameter estimates is:

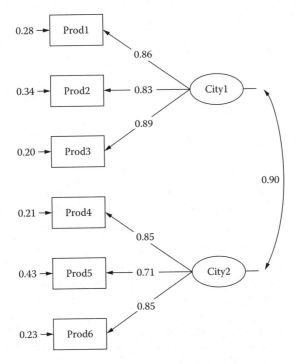

The Structured Means Model is testing the mean latent variable difference, which is indicated by the *Mean Vector of Independent Variables.* Results are interpreted based on the knowledge that the mean latent value on City1 (Los Angeles) and City2 (Chicago) are set to zero (0) in the first group (low motivation), so the values reported here are going to indicate that the second group (high motivation) was either greater than (positive) or less than (negative) the first group (low motivation) on the latent variables.

A latent variable mean difference value of 10.08 is indicated for the first latent variable (City1), which indicates a statistically significant mean difference (i.e., high motivation group) had mean production rates greater than the low motivation group in Los Angeles (City1).

A latent variable mean difference value of 10.18 is indicated for the second latent variable (City2), which indicates a statistically significant mean difference (i.e., high motivation group) had mean production rates greater than the low motivation group in Chicago (City2).

Overall, the high motivation groups outperformed the low motivation groups in both cities. City1 and City2 correlated .90, indicating similar mean difference production rates. The latent variable mean differences are divided by their standard error to yield a one-sample T value (i.e., 10.08/.08 = 122.17, within rounding error).

```
Mean Vector of Independent Variables

        City1              City2
      --------           --------
       10.08              10.18
      (0.08)             (0.08)
      122.17             128.16
```

Chapter 14

1. Second-Order Factor Analysis

The psychological research literature suggests that drug use and depression are leading indicators of suicide among teenagers. The following LISREL–SIMPLIS program was run to test a second-order factor model.

```
Second Order Factor Analysis Exercise
Observed Variables: drug1 drug2 drug3 drug4 depress1
depress2 depress3 depress4
Sample Size 200
Correlation Matrix
1.000
0.628  1.000
0.623  0.646  1.000
0.542  0.656  0.626  1.000
0.496  0.557  0.579  0.640  1.000
0.374  0.392  0.425  0.451  0.590  1.000
0.406  0.439  0.446  0.444  0.668   .488  1.000
0.489  0.510  0.522  0.467  0.643   .591   .612  1.000
Means   1.879  1.696  1.797  2.198  2.043  1.029  1.947 2.024
Standard Deviations  1.379  1.314  1.288  1.388  1.405 1.269
1.435 1.423
Latent Variables: drugs depress suicide
Relationships
drug1 - drug4 = drugs
depress1 - depress4 = depress
drugs = Suicide
depress = Suicide
Set variance of drugs - Suicide to 1.0
Path diagram
End of problem
```

The second-order factor model with standardized coefficients had an acceptable fit (Chi-square = 30.85, df = 19, p = .042) and is diagrammed as:

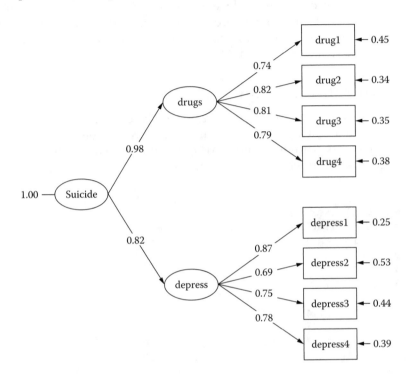

The structure coefficients indicate that the first factors are strong indicators of the second factor (suicide). Drug use (R-squared = .96) was the stronger indicator of suicide among teenagers.

Structural Equations

```
drugs = 0.98*Suicide, Errorvar. = 0.044, R² = 0.96
                                  (0.17)
                                   0.26
depress = 0.82*Suicide, Errorvar. = 0.33, R² = 0.67
          (0.12)                   (0.13)
           6.96                     2.51
```

NOTE: Missing t-values and standard errors in SIMPLIS output.

Second-Order Factor Analysis—Suicide example.

Since the ETA variables (drugs and depress) are indicators of the corresponding KSI variable (suicide), LISREL by default fixes the loading of the first indicator to one. Then, after convergence the value of 1 is rescaled using the estimated ETA1 variance. Although the corresponding standard error estimate can be computed using the Delta method, LISREL does not compute it. As a result, no standard error estimate and t value is written to the output file. The LISREL 8 syntax program with a raw data file should produce the standard errors and t-value.

3. MULTITRAIT–MULTIMETHOD MODELS

a. The LISREL–SIMPLIS program to analyze the three methods (student, teacher, and peer) and three traits (behavior, motivate, and attitude) as a MTMM model using start values and admissibility check off (increase iterations to achieve convergence) is:

```
MTMM Model Exercise
Observed Variables: X1 X2 X3 X4 X5 X6 X7 X8 X9
Correlation Matrix
1.0
 .40   1.0
 .31    .38   1.0
 .35    .23    .16   1.0
 .26    .22    .21    .62   1.0
 .15    .11    .15    .49    .62   1.0
 .43    .31    .24    .61    .48    .33   1.0
 .40    .35    .19    .49    .45    .32    .74   1.0
 .26    .20    .18    .43    .41    .33    .52    .47   1.0
Sample Size: 300
Latent Variables: behavior motivate attitude student
teacher peer
Relationships:
X1 = (.3)*behavior + (.5)*student
X2 = (.3)*motivate + (.5)*student
X3 = (.3)*attitude + (.5)*student
X4 = (.3)*behavior + (.5)*teacher
X5 = (.3)*motivate + (.5)*teacher
X6 = (.3)*attitude + (.5)*teacher
X7 = (.3)*behavior + (.5)*peer
X8 = (.3)*motivate + (.5)*peer
X9 = (.3)*attitude + (.5)*peer
Set variance of behavior - peer to 1.0
Set correlation of student and behavior to 0
Set correlation of student and motivate to 0
Set correlation of student and attitude to 0
Set correlation of teacher and behavior to 0
Set correlation of teacher and motivate to 0
```

```
Set correlation of teacher and attitude to 0
Set correlation of peer and behavior to 0
Set correlation of peer and motivate to 0
Set correlation of peer and attitude to 0
Options: AD = FF
Path diagram
End of problem
```

The MTMM model is displayed after dragging the three methods to the left side of the diagram in the LISREL graph. The MTMM model had acceptable fit indices (Chi-square = 10.85, df = 12, and p = .54).

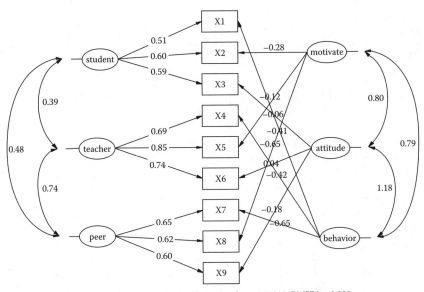

Chi-Square = 10.85, df = 12, P-value = 0.54203, RMSEA = 0.000

The MTMM model results are displayed in Table C.1 to help the interpretation of trait and method effects. The assessment of *Attitude* regardless of which method was used had the higher error variance; Student ratings (error = .64), Teacher ratings (error = .46), or Peer ratings (error = .61), thus *Attitude* was the most difficult trait to assess, based on the three methods used. The student and teacher rating methods were higher for motivate (factor loading = .60 and factor loading = .85, respectively). The *peer* rating method worked best with behavior, but was fairly similar across all traits.

TABLE C.1

MTMM Estimates of Three Methods on Three Traits (*N* = 300)

	Traits			Methods			
	Behavior	**Motivate**	**Attitude**	**Student**	**Teacher**	**Peer**	**Error**
Behavior	−.41			.51			.57
Motivate		−.28		.60			.56
Attitude			−.06	.59			.64
Behavior	−.41				.68		.35
Motivate		−.12			.85		.27
Attitude			.04		.74		.46
Behavior	−.65					.65	.15
Motivate		−.65				.62	.19
Attitude			−.18			.60	.61

b. The LISREL–SIMPLIS program to run a Correlated Traits–Correlated Uniqueness Model (CTCU) is:

```
Correlated Traits-Correlated Uniqueness Model Exercise
Observed Variables: X1 X2 X3 X4 X5 X6 X7 X8 X9
Correlation Matrix
1.0
 .40  1.0
 .31   .38  1.0
 .35   .23   .16  1.0
 .26   .22   .21   .62  1.0
 .15   .11   .15   .49   .62  1.0
 .43   .31   .24   .61   .48   .33  1.0
 .40   .35   .19   .49   .45   .32   .74  1.0
 .26   .20   .18   .43   .41   .33   .52   .47  1.0
Sample Size: 240
Latent Variables: behavior motivate attitude
Relationships:
X1 = behavior
X2 = motivate
X3 = attitude
X4 = behavior
X5 = motivate
X6 = attitude
X7 = behavior
X8 = motivate
X9 = attitude
Set variance of behavior - attitude to 1.0
Let error covariance of X1-X3 correlate
```

```
Let error covariance of X4-X6 correlate
Let error covariance of X7-X9 correlate
Path diagram
End of problem
```

The CTCU model is diagrammed as:

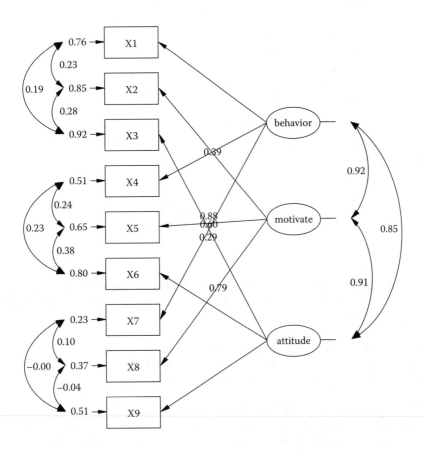

The results are presented in Table C.2. Findings indicated that all three traits were statistically significantly correlated. More importantly, the *peer* method was the best for assessing any of the three traits, as indicated by the higher trait factor loadings and lower correlated uniqueness error terms. Students are probably not rating themselves well and teachers seemed a little better at rating student behavior and motivation than attitude. The data also had an acceptable fit to the CTCU model ($\chi^2 = 13.43$, $p = .57$, $df = 15$; RMSEA = .000; n = 300).

TABLE C.2

Correlated Uniqueness Model with Correlated Traits and Errors

Method	Trait	Factor Loading	Uniqueness	R^2	Correlated Uniqueness of Error Terms		
Student	Behavior	.49	.76	.24	1.0		
	Motivate	.39	.85	.15	.23	1.0	
	Attitude	.29	.92	.08	.19	.28	1.0
Teacher	Behavior	.70	.51	.49	1.0		
	Motivate	.60	.65	.35	.24	1.0	
	Attitude	.45	.80	.20	.23	.38	1.0
Peer	Behavior	.88	.23	.77	1.0		
	Motivate	.79	.37	.63	.10	1.0	
	Attitude	.70	.51	.49	.00	−.04	1.0

Trait correlations

Behavior	1.0		
Motivate	.92	1.0	
Attitude	.85	.91	1.0

Note: $X^2 = 13.43$, p = .57, df = 15; RMSEA = .000; n = 300.

The LISREL Program was run again to estimate a correlated trait (CT) only model with no correlated error terms. To accomplish this, you simply delete the following command lines:

```
Let Error Covariance of Var1-Var3 Correlate
Let Error Covariance of Var4-Var6 Correlate
Let Error Covariance of Var7-Var9 Correlate
```

The results yielded a nonpositive definite matrix among the latent variables (i.e., correlations were greater than 1.0.) Also, the modification indices suggested adding the very error covariance you deleted. So, the CT Model is rejected in favor of the CTCU Model.

```
              behavior        motivate        attitude
behavior      1.00
motivate      1.07            1.00
attitude      0.95            1.10            1.00


W_A_R_N_I_N_G: is not positive definite
```

The Modification Indices Suggest to Add an Error Covariance

Between	and	Decrease in Chi-Square	New Estimate
X2	X1	19.8	0.22
X3	X1	12.6	0.17
X3	X2	25.0	0.26
X5	X4	22.3	0.18
X6	X4	17.3	0.16
X6	X5	64.2	0.34
X7	X5	32.9	-0.22
X7	X6	20.5	-0.16
X8	X4	23.6	-0.18
X8	X6	11.2	-0.14
X8	X7	49.7	0.27

Although the MTMM model achieved an acceptable model fit, the findings were mixed as to which method worked best with the three traits (behavior, motivate, and attitude). The CTCU model in contrast more clearly indicated that *peers* did a better job of rating the traits. Students tend to know other students more on these traits both in and outside the classroom, thus providing a theoretical argument for the findings.

Chapter 15

1. Multiple Indicator and Multiple Cause Model

The following LISREL–SIMPLIS program would be created and run to determine the parameter estimates and model fit.

```
MIMIC Model of Job Satisfaction
Observed Variables peer self income shift age
Sample Size 530
Correlation Matrix
1.00
 .42  1.00
 .24   .35  1.00
 .13   .37   .25  1.00
 .33   .51   .66   .20  1.00
Latent Variable satisfac
Relationships
peer = satisfac
self = satisfac
satisfac = income shift age
Path diagram
End of problem
```

Initial MIMIC Model Results

The MIMIC model results indicated an adequate fit with chi-square = 6.81, df = 2, and p = .033. The measurement equations indicated that job satisfaction (satisfac) was adequately defined with self ratings being a better indicator of job satisfaction than peer ratings.

Measurement Equations

peer = 0.48*satisfac, Errorvar. = 0.77, R^2 = 0.23
                                (0.053)
                                 14.49
self = 0.87*satisfac, Errorvar. = 0.25 , R^2 = 0.75
        (0.11)   (0.078)
         8.10   3.16

The structural equation indicated that 45% of job satisfaction was predicted by knowledge of income, what shift a person worked, and their age. However, the coefficient for income was not statistically significant (T = −.59). Consequently the model should be modified by dropping this variable and re-running the analysis.

Structural Equations

satisfac = − 0.032*income + 0.31*shift + 0.56*age, Errorvar.= 0.55, R^2 = 0.45
              (0.054)   (0.054)   (0.082)   (0.11)
              −0.59   5.71   6.77   5.14

MIMIC Modification

The MIMIC model modification resulted in little improvement with chi-square = 6.11, df = 1, and p = .01. The measurement equations were not very different. Other measures would help to define the latent variable, *job satisfaction*. The structural equation resulted in the same R-squared value, which indicates that income did not add to the prediction of *job satisfaction*. A parsimonious model was therefore achieved, but the 55% unexplained variance implies that other variables could be discovered to increase prediction.

Measurement Equations

peer = 0.49*satisfac, Errorvar. = 0.76, R^2 = 0.24
                                (0.053)
                                 14.48
self = 0.87*satisfac, Errorvar. = 0.25, R^2 = 0.75
        (0.11)   (0.078)
         8.12   3.21

Structural Equations

```
satisfac = 0.31*shift + 0.54*age, Errorvar.= 0.55 , R² = 0.45
          (0.053)       (0.073)                (0.11)
           5.72          7.39                    5.14
```

3. Multilevel Model

The multilevel analysis of data in the PRELIS system file, *income.psf,* was used with the pull down multilevel menu to create and run 3 different PRELIS programs. Results are summarized in a table with the intra-class correlation (hand computed) for comparative purposes.

Model 1 is the baseline model (constant), followed by the added effects of gender, and the added effects of marital status (marital). The 3 different PRELIS programs should look as follows:

```
Model 1 (intercept only)

OPTIONS OLS=YES CONVERGE=0.001000 MAXITER=10 OUTPUT=STANDARD ;
  TITLE=income decomposition;
  SY='C:\LISREL 8.8 Student Examples\MLEVELEX\INCOME.PSF';
  ID3=region;
  ID2=state;
  RESPONSE=income;
  FIXED=constant;
  RANDOM2=constant;
  RANDOM3=constant;

Model 2 (intercept + gender)

OPTIONS OLS=YES CONVERGE=0.001000 MAXITER=10 OUTPUT=STANDARD ;
  TITLE=income decomposition;
  SY='C:\LISREL 8.8 Student Examples\MLEVELEX\INCOME.PSF';
  ID3=region;
  ID2=state;
  RESPONSE=income;
  FIXED=constant gender;
  RANDOM2=constant;
  RANDOM3=constant;

Model 3 (intercept + gender + marital)

OPTIONS OLS=YES CONVERGE=0.001000 MAXITER=10 OUTPUT=STANDARD ;
  TITLE=income decomposition;
  SY='C:\LISREL 8.8 Student Examples\MLEVELEX\INCOME.PSF';
  ID3=region;
```

```
ID2=state;
RESPONSE=income;
FIXED=constant gender marital;
RANDOM2=constant;
RANDOM3=constant;
```

The PRELIS program results for the three analyses are summarized in Table C.1. The baseline model (intercept only) provides the initial breakdown of level 3 and level 2 error variance. The multilevel model for the added effect of *gender* is run next. The chi-square difference between Model 1 and Model 2 yields chi-square = 5.40, which is statistically significant at the .05 level of significance. *Gender*, therefore, does help explain variability in *income*. Finally, *marital* is added to the multilevel model, which yields a chi-square difference between Model 2 and Model 3 of chi-square = 1.18. The chi-square difference value is not statistically significant; therefore, marital status does not add any additional significant explanation of variability in *income*.

TABLE C.3

Summary Results for Multilevel Analysis of Income

Multilevel Model Fixed Factors	Model 1 Constant	Model 2 Constant + Gender	Model 3 Constant + Gender + Marital
Intercept Only(B_0)	10.096 (.099)	10.37 (.15)	10.24 (.19)
Gender (B_1)		−0.42 (.16)	−0.43 (.16)
Marital (B_2)			.19 (.17)
Level 2 error variance (e_{ij})	.37	.31	.30
Level 3 error variance (u_{ij})	.02	.05	.06
ICC	.051 (5%)	.138 (14%)	.166 (17%)
Deviance (−2LL)	11144.29	11138.89	11137.71
Df	3	4	5
χ^2 Difference (df = 1)		5.40	1.18

Note: $\chi2 = 3.84$, df = 1, p = .05.

Note: $ICC_1 = \dfrac{\Phi_3}{\Phi_3 + \Phi_2} = \dfrac{Tau - Hat(Level - 3)}{Tau - Hat(Level - 3) + Tau - Hat(Level - 2)} = \dfrac{.02}{.02 + .37} = .051$

Chapter 16

1. Interaction Model

An organizational psychologist was investigating whether *work tension* and *collegiality* were predictors of *job satisfaction*. However, research indicated that *work tension* and *collegiality* interact, so a SEM Interaction Model was hypothesized and tested. [*Note*: You need to use a raw data file so that values for latent variables can be added.]

First open the PRELIS system file, *jobs.psf*, to view the 9 observed variables.

Second, create the LISREL–SIMPLIS program to create and save the latent variables in the PRELIS system file, *jobs.psf*:

```
Computing Latent Variable Scores
Observed Variables v1-v9
Raw Data from File jobs.psf
Latent Variables : job work colleg
Relationships:
v1=1*job
v2-v3= job
v4=1*work
v5-v6=work
v7=1*colleg
```

```
v8-v9=colleg
PSFfile jobs.psf
End of problem
```

NOTE: Remember to close the PRELIS system file, *jobs.psf*, and then open it again to see that the latent variables have been added.

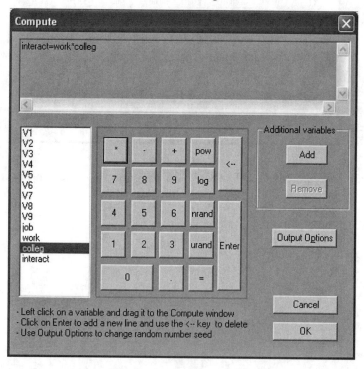

Third, create the latent interaction variable by using the *TRANSFORMATION*, then *COMPUTE* on the pull down menu. Select *ADD*, enter name for new variable (*interact*), then drag variable names to the *Compute* window (interact=work*colleg).

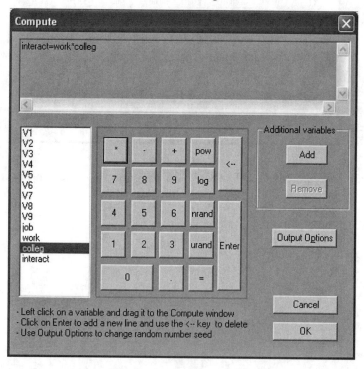

Click OK, and the latent interaction variable, *interact*, will automatically be added to the PRELIS system file, *jobs.psf.*

	v1	v2	v3	v4	v5	v6	v7	v8	v9	job	work	colleg	interact
1	3.00	2.00	3.00	4.00	4.00	4.00	2.00	0.00	4.00	0.92	1.47	0.69	1.00
2	2.00	1.00	2.00	3.00	2.00	3.00	0.00	0.00	1.00	-0.08	0.16	-0.73	-0.11
3	2.00	1.00	4.00	2.00	2.00	2.00	0.00	4.00	4.00	0.40	0.14	0.69	0.10
4	1.00	1.00	2.00	2.00	4.00	4.00	3.00	4.00	4.00	-0.08	1.13	1.47	1.66
5	2.00	0.00	1.00	2.00	3.00	2.00	1.00	4.00	4.00	-0.63	0.27	0.92	0.24
6	4.00	3.00	3.00	2.00	4.00	2.00	1.00	3.00	4.00	1.25	0.84	0.85	0.72
7	0.00	0.00	1.00	2.00	1.00	2.00	0.00	2.00	1.00	-1.17	-0.62	-0.55	0.34
8	4.00	2.00	2.00	2.00	2.00	2.00	0.00	4.00	4.00	0.55	0.16	0.70	0.11
9	3.00	3.00	2.00	2.00	3.00	4.00	2.00	4.00	4.00	0.84	0.98	1.24	1.21
10	0.00	3.00	3.00	3.00	1.00	3.00	1.00	4.00	4.00	0.39	0.26	0.90	0.24
11	0.00	0.00	0.00	0.00	0.00	0.00	0.00	0.00	0.00	-1.68	-1.84	-1.40	2.57

Finally, create and run a LISREL–SIMPLIS program to analyze the Interaction Model.

```
Latent Interaction Variable Model - No Intercept Term
Observed Variables: v1-v9 job work colleg interact
Raw Data from File jobs.psf
Sample Size = 200
Relationships:
job = work colleg interact
Path diagram
End of problem
```

The structural equation indicates that no interaction effect is present between *work tension* and *collegiality*. Rather, *work tension* and *collegiality* are predictors of job satisfaction as direct linear effects.

Structural Equations

job = 0.98*work – 0.18*colleg + 0.036*interact, Errorvar.= 0.22 , $R^2 = 0.80$
    (0.065)   (0.079)   (0.038)   (0.022)
     15.16   –2.29   0.96   9.90

The latent interaction variable should be dropped and the LISREL–SIMPLIS program run again. The R-squared value does not change indicating that the interaction effect did not contribute to the prediction of job satisfaction.

Structural Equations

job = 0.97*work – 0.17*colleg, Errorvar. = 0.22 , $R^2 = 0.80$
    (0.064)   (0.078)   (0.022)
     15.20   –2.17   9.92

3. MONTE CARLO Methods

The SPSS program would input the population matrix values as follows:

```
MATRIX.
compute popr =
{1,   .50,   .30,   .90;
.50,   1,   .70,   .50;
.30,   .70,   1,   .50;
.90,   .50,   .50,   1}.
Print popr.
compute pi = 3.14159.
compute rown = nrow(popr).
compute n = 10000.
compute corr = sqrt(–2*ln(uniform(n,rown)))&*cos((2*pi)*uniform(n,rown)).
compute corr=corr*chol(popr).
save corr /outfile = pop.sav.
END MATRIX.
```

The SPSS output would look like this:
Run MATRIX procedure:
POPR
```
 1.000000000 .500000000 .300000000 .900000000
 .500000000 1.000000000 .700000000 .500000000
 .300000000 .700000000 1.000000000 .500000000
 .900000000 .500000000 .500000000 1.000000000
------ END MATRIX -----
```

You would now open the *pop.sav* file which would look like the following (*Note:* Our *pop.sav* file was in c:\program files\spssinc\spss16 folder).

	COL1	COL2	COL3	COL4	var	var
1	1.34	-0.35	0.16	1.58		
2	-1.76	-0.36	0.11	-1.24		
3	2.29	1.55	0.98	1.27		
4	0.18	1.02	0.92	0.36		
5	0.60	-0.72	-0.28	0.11		
6	-1.73	-0.65	-1.09	-1.37		
7	0.78	0.14	-1.14	0.13		
8	1.45	0.19	0.57	2.24		

The SPSS correlation procedure was selected and ran:

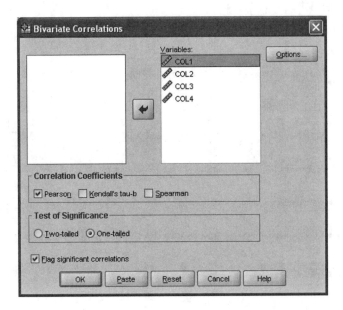

The output from the SPSS correlation procedure yielded population correlation values in Table C.4 similar to what we specified in the SPSS MATRIX program.

TABLE C.4

		Correlations			
		COL1	COL2	COL3	COL4
COL1	Pearson Correlation	1.000	.489**	.287**	.899**
	Sig. (1-tailed)		.000	.000	.000
	N	10000.000	10000	10000	10000
COL2	Pearson Correlation	.489**	1.000	.696**	.488**
	Sig. (1-tailed)	.000		.000	.000
	N	10000	10000.000	10000	10000
COL3	Pearson Correlation	.287**	.696**	1.000	.491**
	Sig. (1-tailed)	.000	.000		.000
	N	10000	10000	10000.000	10000
COL4	Pearson Correlation	.899**	.488**	.491**	1.000
	Sig. (1-tailed)	.000	.000	.000	
	N	10000	10000	10000	10000.000

** Correlation is significant at the 0.01 level (1-tailed).

Chapter 17

1. The diagrammed structural equation model is shown as Figure 17.4.

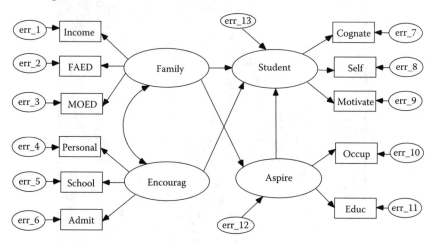

FIGURE 17.4
Student characteristic model.

The measurement equations are as follows:
For the *X* variables using variable names

family income = function of Family Background + error
father's education = function of Family Background + error
mother's education = function of Family Background + error
personal encouragement = function of Encouragement + error
institutional characteristics = function of Encouragement + error
admission status = function of Encouragement + error.

The measurement equations for the Xs are

$$X_1 = 1.0\ \xi_1 + \delta_1$$

$$X_2 = \lambda x_{21}\ \xi_1 + \delta_2$$

$$X_3 = \lambda x_{31}\ \xi_1 + \delta_3$$

$$X_4 = 1.0\ \xi_2 + \delta_4$$

$$X_5 = \lambda x_{52}\, \xi_2 + \delta_5$$

$$X_6 = \lambda x_{62}\, \xi_2 + \delta_6.$$

The matrix equations for the Xs are

$$
\begin{bmatrix} X_1 \\ X_2 \\ X_3 \\ X_4 \\ X_5 \\ X_6 \end{bmatrix}
=
\begin{bmatrix} 1 & 0 \\ \lambda x_{21} & 0 \\ \lambda x_{31} & 0 \\ 0 & 1 \\ 0 & \lambda x_{52} \\ 0 & \lambda x_{62} \end{bmatrix}
\begin{bmatrix} \xi_1 \\ \xi_1 \end{bmatrix}
+
\begin{bmatrix} \delta_1 \\ \delta_2 \\ \delta_3 \\ \delta_4 \\ \delta_5 \\ \delta_6 \end{bmatrix}
$$

For the Y variables using variable names:

```
cognitive abilities = function of Student Characteristics + error
interpersonal skills = function of Student Characteristics + error
motivation = function of Student Characteristics + error
occupational aspirations = function of Aspiration + error
educational aspirations = function of Aspiration + error.
```

The measurement equations for the Ys are

$$Y_1 = 1.0\, \eta_1 + \varepsilon_1$$

$$Y_2 = \lambda y_{21}\, \eta_1 + \varepsilon_2$$

$$Y_3 = \lambda y_{31}\, \eta_1 + \varepsilon_3$$

$$Y_4 = 1.0\, \eta_2 + \varepsilon_4$$

$$Y_5 = \lambda y_{52}\, \eta_2 + \varepsilon_5.$$

The matrix equations for the Ys are

$$
\begin{bmatrix} Y_1 \\ Y_2 \\ Y_3 \\ Y_4 \\ Y_5 \\ Y_6 \end{bmatrix}
=
\begin{bmatrix} 1 & 0 \\ \lambda y_{21} & 0 \\ \lambda y_{31} & 0 \\ 0 & 1 \\ 0 & \lambda y_{52} \\ 0 & \lambda y_{62} \end{bmatrix}
\begin{bmatrix} \eta_1 \\ \eta_1 \end{bmatrix}
+
\begin{bmatrix} \varepsilon_1 \\ \varepsilon_2 \\ \varepsilon_3 \\ \varepsilon_4 \\ \varepsilon_5 \\ \varepsilon_6 \end{bmatrix}
$$

The structural equations using variable names are

Students' Characteristics = Family Background + Encouragement + Aspirations + error
Aspirations = Family Background + Encouragement + error.

The structural equations are written as

$$\eta_1 = \beta_{12}\eta_2 + \gamma_{11}\xi_1 + \gamma_{12}\xi_2 + \zeta_1$$
$$\eta_2 = \gamma_{21}\xi_1 + \gamma_{22}\xi_2 + \zeta_2.$$

In matrix form the structural equations are

$$\begin{bmatrix} \eta_1 \\ \eta_2 \end{bmatrix} = \begin{bmatrix} 0 & \beta_{12} \\ 0 & 0 \end{bmatrix} \begin{bmatrix} \eta_1 \\ \eta_2 \end{bmatrix} + \begin{bmatrix} \gamma_{11} & \gamma_{12} \\ \gamma_{21} & \gamma_{22} \end{bmatrix} \begin{bmatrix} \xi_1 \\ \xi_2 \end{bmatrix} + \begin{bmatrix} \xi_1 \\ \xi_2 \end{bmatrix}$$

The matrix of the structural coefficients for the endogenous variables is

$$B = \begin{bmatrix} 0 & \beta_{12} \\ 0 & 0 \end{bmatrix}$$

The matrix of the structural coefficients for the exogenous variables is

$$\Gamma = \begin{bmatrix} \gamma_{11} & \gamma_{12} \\ \gamma_{21} & \gamma_{22} \end{bmatrix}$$

The matrix of the factor loadings for the endogenous variables is

$$\Lambda_y = \begin{bmatrix} 1 & 0 \\ \lambda y_{21} & 0 \\ \lambda y_{31} & 0 \\ 0 & 1 \\ 0 & \lambda y_{52} \end{bmatrix}$$

The matrix of the factor loadings for the exogenous variables is

$$\Lambda_x = \begin{bmatrix} 1 & 0 \\ \lambda x_{21} & 0 \\ \lambda x_{31} & 0 \\ 0 & 1 \\ 0 & \lambda x_{52} \\ 0 & \lambda x_{62} \end{bmatrix}$$

The covariance matrix for the exogenous latent variables is

$$\Phi = \begin{bmatrix} \phi_{11} & \\ \phi_{21} & \phi_{22} \end{bmatrix}$$

The covariance matrix for the equation errors is

$$\psi = \begin{bmatrix} \psi_{11} & \\ 0 & \psi_{22} \end{bmatrix}$$

The covariance matrix for the measurement errors of the indicators of the exogenous latent variables is

$$\Theta_\delta = \begin{bmatrix} \theta_{\delta11} & & & & & \\ 0 & \theta_{\delta22} & & & & \\ 0 & 0 & \theta_{\delta33} & & & \\ 0 & 0 & 0 & \theta_{\delta44} & & \\ 0 & 0 & 0 & 0 & \theta_{\delta55} & \\ 0 & 0 & 0 & 0 & 0 & \theta_{\delta66} \end{bmatrix}$$

The covariance matrix for the measurement errors of the indicators of the endogenous latent variables is

$$\Theta_\varepsilon = \begin{bmatrix} \theta_{\varepsilon11} & & & & \\ 0 & \theta_{\varepsilon22} & & & \\ 0 & 0 & \theta_{\varepsilon33} & & \\ 0 & 0 & 0 & \theta_{\varepsilon44} & \\ 0 & 0 & 0 & 0 & \theta_{\varepsilon55} \end{bmatrix}$$

The structural equation model can be interpreted from the direct and indirect effects to yield the total effects for the model. The direct effects for Aspirations are Family Background (γ_{21}) and Encouragement (γ_{22}). The direct effects for Students' Characteristics are Family Background (γ_{11}), Encouragement (γ_{12}), and Aspirations (β_{12}). The indirect effects for Students' Characteristics is Family Background through Aspirations ($\gamma_{21}\beta_{12}$). Thus, the total effects are as follows:

Family Background -> Aspirations = γ_{21}
Encouragement -> Aspirations = γ_{22}
Family Background -> Students' Characteristics = $\gamma_{11} + (\gamma_{21})(\beta_{12})$
Encouragement -> Students' Characteristics = γ_{12}
Aspirations -> Students' Characteristics = $\beta_{12.}$

Author Index

Subject Index